Contents

FOREWORD PAGE 5

1. Introduction

(or, Welcome to the Holiday of a Lifetime). Getting to grips with Orlando, what's in store, facts and figures, the attractions outlined, what's new and central Florida festivals.

PAGE 6

2. Planning and Practicalities

(or, How to *Almost* Do It All and Live to Tell the Tale). When to go, the main tourist areas, the principal holiday companies, holiday strategy, how to beat the crowds, clothing and health matters, travellers with disabilities, Disney special occasions, learning American-speak, weddings, safety advice.

PAGE 18

3. Driving and Car Hire

(or, The Secret of Getting Around on Interstate 4). Arriving in Orlando, the main roads and tourist roads, car hire guide, learning to drive on the wrong side of the road, Orlando for non-drivers.

PAGE 45

4. Accommodation

(or, Making Sense of American Hotels, Motels and Condos). Understanding American-style accommodation, Walt Disney World Resort hotels, Lake Buena Vista and Kissimmee, International Drive, suites, resorts and holiday homes, B & B; buying a home.

PAGE 56

5. Disney's Fab Four

(or, Spending the Day with Mickey Mouse and Co). Theme park tickets, ratings, tactics, plus full guides to the Magic Kingdom Park, Epcot, Disney-MGM Studios and Disney's Animal Kingdom Theme Park.

PAGE 85

6. Five More of the Best

(or, Expanding Orlando's Universe). Full guide, ratings, tickets and tactics to Universal Studios Florida, Islands of Adventure, SeaWorld Adventure Park and Discovery Cove, and Busch Gardens.

PAGE 135

7. The Other Attractions

(or, One Giant Leap for Tourist Kind). The Kennedy Space Center, US Astronaut Hall of Fame, Silver Springs, Historic Bok Sanctuary, Splendid China, Gatorland, Fantasy of Flight; International Drive Area: Ripley's Believe It Or Not, Titanic Exhibition, Hard Rock Vault, Skull Kingdom, Fun Spot, Magical Midway, WonderWorks, Trainland Inc; Downtown Orlando: Orlando Science Center, Orange County History Center, The Holy Land Experience; Water Parks: Disney's Typhoon Lagoon Water Park, Disney's Blizzard Beach Water Park, Wet 'n Wild, Water Mania.

PAGE 180

8. Off The Beaten Track

(or, When You're All Theme-Parked Out). A taste of the real Florida: Winter Park, Aquatic Wonders Boat Tours, Boggy Creek Airboats and Parasail, Cypress Glades Adventure Tours, Orange Blossom Balloons, Everglades and the Bahamas, Flying Tigers Warbird Restoration Museum and Warbird Adventures, Green Meadows Petting Farm, Disney and Cruising, Seminole County, Forever Florida, Disney's Wilderness Preserve; The Beaches: St Pete's/Clearwater, Cocoa Beach and Daytona; Sports, including golf, fishing, water sports, horse riding, spectator sports and Disney's Wide World of Sports Complex™, motor sport.

PAGE 208

9. Orlando by Night

(or, Burning the Candle at Both Ends). Downtown Disney, Pointe*Orlando, Universal's CityWalk, Downtown Orlando, Disney shows, Arabian Nights, Pirate's Dinner Adventure, Medieval Times, Sleuth's, SoulFire Dinner Theatre, Dolly Parton's Dixie Stampede, Gator Safari by Night, theatre, nightclubs, live music, discos, bars.

PAGE 236

10. Dining Out

(or, Man, These Portions Are *Huge!*). Full guide to local-style eating and drinking, rundown of the fast-food outlets, best family restaurants, American diners and speciality restaurants.

PAGE 255

11. Shopping

(or, How to Send Your Credit Card into Meltdown). Your duty-free allowances, full guide to the main tourist shopping complexes, discount outlets, flea markets, malls, supermarkets and speciality shops.

PAGE 276

12. Going Home

(or, Where Did the Last Two Weeks Go?). Avoiding last-minute snags, returning the car, full guide to Orlando International and Orlando Sanford Airports and their facilities for the journey home.

PAGE 288

13. Your Holiday Planner

Examples of how to plan for a 2-week holiday with a Disney 5-Day Hopper Park Ticket. Plus, the Theme Parks' Busy Day Guide.

PAGE 295

INDEX PAGE 298

COPYRIGHT NOTICES PAGE 303

ACKNOWLEDGEMENTS PAGE 304

A Brit's Guide

to

rlando

and

Walt Disney World

2004

★

Simon Veness

foulsham

The Publishing House, Bennetts Close, Cippenham, Berkshire, SL1 5AP, England

ISBN 0-572-02925-X

Text copyright © 2004 Simon Veness

Series, format, logo and layout design copyright © 2004 W. Foulsham & Co. Ltd

Other books in this series:
A Brit's Guide to Las Vegas 2004–2005, Karen Marchbank, 0-572-02926-8
Choosing A Cruise, 6th edition, Simon Veness, 0-572-02946-2
A Brit's Guide to Disneyland Resort Paris, Simon Veness, 0-572-02845-8
A Brit's Guide to New York 2004, Karen Marchbank, 0-572-02917-9

SPECIAL THANKS

Special thanks for this edition go to: Travel City Direct, The Walt Disney Company, Alamo Rent A Car, Thomas Cook Signature Holidays, Virgin Holidays, British Airways Holidays, Universal Orlando, Orlando Convention and Visitors Bureau, Kissimmee Convention and Visitors Bureau, Synergy and Anheuser-Busch Parks, Summerfield Suites Lake Buena Vista, the Celebration Hotel, the Gaylord Palms Resort, the Peabody Hotel, the Hyatt Regency Orlando Airport, The Renaissance Orlando Resort and Embassy Suites International Drive.

My sincere thanks also go to all the hard-working people at Foulsham who help to bring my work to life every year, plus editor Caroline Radula-Scott.

Printed in Malaysia

Foreword

Welcome to the start of a brand new adventure in the most exciting holiday destination on earth! This is where the fun really starts and you can begin preparing for a truly magical and memorable time. For those already familiar with the Brit's Guide *(and we know who you are!), welcome back; for those new to our style and our destination, get ready for a completely different experience in vacation anticipation.*

Orlando has developed in astonishing fashion since a certain Walter Elias Disney decided it suited his plans for creating a new style of theme park entertainment under the title Project X in 1966. And, although the master entertainer himself had some pretty detailed and creative ideas, even he might have been amazed at how this area of central Florida has flowered after his initial investment.

In simple enjoyment terms, this is Entertainment Central – a region dedicated and devoted to ensuring people have the most wonderful and enchanting holiday possible. Nowhere else is your choice of attractions so broad and detailed, and things continue to change and develop all the time. Of course, that also means it can be confusing, vexing and tiring (especially the latter), but you have definitely made the right start if you want the full inside track on how to get the most out of your holiday with the minimum of hassle.

This latest edition (the ninth) of Britain's best-selling guidebook continues to represent, I firmly believe, the most user-friendly and authoritative companion to all that lies in store for you in this holiday wonderland, especially if used in conjunction with our friends at the website www.wdwinfo.com, by far the best internet resource on all things Disney out there. I like to think this book is researched and written with a real tourist's eye for detail and value, including all the information you really need to know, not just what the brochures want you to believe. It aims to give you a good idea of what to expect and (most importantly) how to plan and budget for it.

The three principal areas that comprise this vast 'resort' (the counties of Orange, Osceola and Seminole) also remain vigorously engaged in making things newer, bigger and better almost by the day. Here at the Brit's Guide *we are also constantly looking at ways to add other useful features and information according to the vast amount of feedback we receive. To that end, this edition sees the addition of a section on buying a home in central Florida, as well as more for the repeat visitor, including a section on Disney special events and central Florida festivals. It is quite a challenge keeping up with it all, but I can't pretend it isn't also great fun (see pic!).*

Over the last 11 years (and around 50 visits), Orlando has become a real home away from home for me, and so, knowing all the fun and excitement that lies in store, it is with an unwavering enthusiasm that I ask you to read on and allow me to escort you through my second 'home'. There is just so much to do and see here, I hate the thought of people not getting the most out of their visit to central Florida. More significantly, you will get the inside track on how to have the best holiday you can, at the best price and with the least fuss. Prepare to be amazed (and exhausted!) by what's in store, but don't say I didn't tell you so. Now, excuse me while I put my feet up for a while … have a nice day now.

Simon Veness

(email me at simonveness@yahoo.co.uk or join me on the Discussion Forums at www.wdwinfo.com)

Introduction
(or, *Welcome to the Holiday of a Lifetime*)

Welcome to the most exciting **holiday experience in the world, bar none, guaranteed. This area of central Florida we call Orlando is a vast conglomeration of adventure rides, thrills, fun and fantasy the like of which exists nowhere else, and we are not talking just about the *Walt Disney World Resort in Florida* here.**

First off, you need to be aware of the bewilderingly extensive and complex nature of most of what lies in wait in this tourist wonderland. Disney remains the leading attraction in town, but there is a strong supporting cast, of which Universal Orlando and SeaWorld are outstanding examples.

There is something to suit all tastes and ages – young or old, families, couples or singles – but it exacts a high physical toll. You'll walk a lot, queue a lot and probably eat a lot. You will have a fabulous time, but you'll end up exhausted as well. It is not so much a holiday as an exercise in military planning.

Eight theme parks

In simple terms, there are now eight major theme parks that are generally reckoned to be essential holiday fare, and at least one of those will require 2 days to make you feel it has been well and truly done. Add on a day at one of the water parks, a trip to see some of the wildlife or other more 'natural' attractions, and the lure of the nearby Kennedy Space Center, and you're talking at least 12 days of pure adventure-mania. Then mix in the night-time attractions of *Downtown Disney*, Universal's CityWalk and a host of dinner shows, and you get an idea of the awesome scale of the entertainment on offer. Even with 2 weeks, something has to give – just make sure it isn't your patience/pocket/sanity!

So, how do we innocents abroad, many of us making our first visit to the good ol' USA, get full value from what is still, without doubt, a truly magical holiday?

There is no set answer of course, but there are some pretty solid guidelines to steer you in the right direction and help avoid some of the more obvious pitfalls. Central to most of them is **planning**. At the back of this guide there is a useful 'calendar' to use as a ready reference guide. Don't be inflexible, but be aware of the time demands of the main parks, and give yourself a few quiet days by the pool or at one of the smaller attractions to recover your strength. With so much on offer, it simply isn't possible to do it all, so try to ensure you get full value for what you do decide to do.

Also, be aware of the vast scale and complexity of this wonderland, and try to take in as much of the clever detail and breadth of imagination on offer, especially in the Disney parks.

Orlando

Orlando itself is a relatively small but bright young city which has been taken over to the immediate south-west by *Walt Disney World Resort in Florida*, to give it its full title, which opened with the *Magic Kingdom Park* in 1971 and has encouraged a massive tourist expansion ever since. New attractions are being added all the time and it is easy to get carried away by the artificial (and highly commercial) fantasy of it all. However, there is still a genuine concern for the environment, and there are only a few areas where the development looks as if it has got out of hand.

The tourist area generally known as Orlando actually consists of three counties. Orange County is the home of the city of Orlando, but much of Disney's fun and frolics are to be found in Osceola County, with Kissimmee its main town. Seminole County, home of Orlando Sanford Airport, is immediately to the north of Orange County.

The local population numbers slightly above 1.7 million, of which some 211,000 are actively employed in the tourist business, but in 2001 some 40 million people made Orlando their holiday choice, spending almost $20 billion in the area!

Britain accounts for more than 40% of all foreign visitors to Orlando, and in 2001 that was 1,073,000 of us. Those figures represent a near 100% increase in the last 10 years, with the international airport seeing its traffic boom from 8 million passengers in 1983 to a massive 30 million just 17 years later. In addition, the full Orlando area boasts more than 110,000 hotel rooms and 4,500 places to eat. And, for shopaholics, there are an amazing 250 shopping centres, including 30 malls. But let's

give you a quick taster of the main areas and attractions.

Walt Disney World Resort in Florida

This is where the 'Magic' really starts – and the effect is vividly real. This vast resort actually consists of four distinct, separate theme parks, 20 speciality hotel resorts, a camping ground, two water parks, a state-of-the-art spectator sports complex, five 18-hole golf courses, four mini-golf courses and a huge shopping and entertainment complex *(Downtown Disney)*. It covers 47 sq miles (122 sq km). The likes of Alton Towers and Thorpe Park would comfortably fit into its car park! Indeed, Alton Towers, Britain's biggest theme park, is 60 times smaller. Disney's most popular park, the *Magic Kingdom Park*, has a single-day record attendance in the region of 92,000 – most British parks peak at around 20,000. The Disney organisation does things with the most style, but the others have caught on fast and are creating new amenities almost as fast as they can think of them.

Intriguingly, less than half of Disney's massive site has been developed, leaving plenty of room for new accommodation and attractions, while even the existing parks have potential for an extra ride or two, and there are several major projects on the drawing board. Disney maintains an extremely high level of customer service and is always looking at ways to refresh the existing attractions. Everyone who works for Disney is officially a Cast Member, not just staff, and they take that ethic to heart.

Here's a quick rundown of what's on offer:

Magic Kingdom Park: this is the essential Disney, including the fantasy of their wonderful animated films, the adventures of the Wild

FLORIDA

How far from Orlando to . . .

Bradenton . . . . . . 130 miles/210 km	Miami . . . . 220 miles/354 km
Clearwater . . . . . . 110 miles/176 km	Naples . . . . .230 miles/370 km
Cocoa Beach . . . . . . 40 miles/64 km	Sarasota . . . . 140 miles/225 km
Daytona . . . . 60 miles/97 km	Silver Springs . . . .80 miles/129 km
Fort Lauderdale . . 205 miles/330 km	St Augustine . . . .120 miles/193 km
Fort Myers . . . . . . 190 miles/306 km	St Petersburg . . . . 105 miles169 km
Jacksonville . . . . . 155 miles/250 km	Tampa . . . . 75 miles/120 km
Key West . . . . . . .375 miles/604 km	Venice . . . . 160 miles/257 km

Jimmy Neutron at Universal

West and Africa, the excitement of thrill rides like Space Mountain (a huge indoor roller-coaster), the fear factor of the ExtraTERRORestrial Alien Encounter and the fabulous new 3-D film fun of Mickey's PhilharMagic.

Epcot: Disney's look at the world of tomorrow through the gates of Future World, plus a potted journey around our planet in World Showcase. It's more educational than adventurous, but still possesses some memorable rides, including Test Track and Universe of Energy – plus the amazing new Mission: SPACE – and some great places to eat.

Disney-MGM Studios: here you can ride the movies in style, meeting up with Star Wars™, the Muppets, Indiana Jones and drop into the fearsome Tower of Terror or the thrilling Rock 'n Roller Coaster and learn how films are really made.

Disney's Animal Kingdom Theme Park: billed as 'a new species of theme park', this delivers another contrasting and hugely entertaining scenario. With cleverly realistic animal habitats, including a 100-acre (40.5ha) safari savannah, captivating shows and several terrific rides, it

offers a change of pace from the other parks.

Disney's Typhoon Lagoon Water Park: bring your cossie and spend a lazy day splashing down water-slides and learning to surf in the world's biggest man-made lagoon.

Disney's Blizzard Beach Water Park: this is the big brother of all the water parks, with a massive spread of rides and slides in a 'snowy' environment.

Disney's Wide World of Sports Complex™: offers the chance to watch world-class events like baseball, basketball, athletics, volleyball and many others.

Downtown Disney area: incorporates *Pleasure Island*, Marketplace and the West Side with themed restaurants, a cinema multiplex, the *DisneyQuest* arcade of interactive games, Virgin Megastore and the world-famous Cirque du Soleil® company. New Year's Eve is the *Pleasure Island* theme, with eight nightclubs on offer. One last additional feature is the picture-perfect **Wedding Pavilion**, which appears in many brochures and offers marriage ceremonies in fairytale style.

The other parks

If you think Orlando is all about Disney, you will be in for a pleasant surprise when you encounter some of the other attractions on offer.

Universal Orlando is the other big resort development, with a

Minnie meets mini-Minnie!

© Disney

choice of two theme parks, water park, wonderful entertainment district and three speciality hotels. **Universal Studios:** here you Ride The Movies as you encounter Jaws, Earthquake, the Men In Black and Back to the Future rides and the brand new Shrek 4-D show and Jimmy Neutron ride, plus Woody Woodpecker's KidZone and the mind-boggling Terminator 2: 3-D Battle Across Time. **Islands of Adventure:** new in 1999, Universal's second park is a superb blend of thrill rides, family attractions, shows and awesome, eye-catching design, with some of the most technologically advanced hardware in the world.

Wet 'n Wild: although on International Drive (I-Drive), this water park is Universal-owned and offers plenty of fun rides and slides.

SeaWorld: don't be put off thinking it's just another dolphin show, this is *the* place for the creatures of the deep, with killer whales being the main attraction, a bright, refreshing atmosphere (check out their new Waterfront district) and a pleasingly serious ecological approach, plus the 5-star thrill rides Journey to Atlantis and Kraken. SeaWorld also has an exclusive neighbour, **Discovery Cove**, that offers the chance to swim with dolphins, among other things.

Busch Gardens: the sister park to SeaWorld, here it's creatures of the land, with the highlights being the Rhino Rally ride, Myombe Reserve, a close-up look at the endangered central African highland gorillas, the Edge of Africa safari experience, and the new Haunted Lighthouse 3-D film show. A real treat, plus a number of brain-numbing roller-coasters and other rides.

Kennedy Space Center: the dramatically upgraded home of space exploration.

Silver Springs: a close look at Florida's nature via jeep and boat safaris through real swampland, with several alligator displays.

Splendid China: a novel alternative attraction, a 5,000-mile (8,000-km) journey through China with miniaturised reproductions of features like the Great Wall and the Terracotta Warriors, plus live shows, great shopping and food.

Fantasy of Flight: this aviation museum experience has the world's largest private collection of vintage aircraft, plus fighter-plane simulators.

Disney tickets

Most people buy one of the multi-day passes which allow you to move between the various parks on the same day, while all grant unlimited access to the monorails, buses and ferries (always get your hand stamped if you leave one park but intend to return). Make no mistake, you can't walk between the parks (except for a fairly long haul between *Epcot* and *Disney-MGM Studios*), and trying to do more than one in a day is a recipe for disaster. The choice of tickets for Disney in particular is bewildering, so make sure you buy only what you need.

The main options at the ticket booths are: **1-day ticket**, giving access to one of the four main parks (you may NOT move from park to park with this ticket); **4-** or **5-Day Park Hopper**, providing 4/5 days at the main parks, with multiple parks on the same day; **5-, 6-, 7-Day Park**

> BRIT TIP: Buy Disney Park Hopper and Park Hopper Plus tickets in advance, NOT at the park gates. You will save time AND money as there is a built-in advance purchase discount.

GETTING AROUND ORLANDO

MOTORWAYS

A	INTERSTATE 4 (14)
B	CENTRAL FLORIDA GREENEWAY
C	ROUTE 528 (BEELINE EXPRESSWAY)
D	FLORIDA TURNPIKE
E	ROUTE 408 (E-W EXPRESSWAY)

SCALE   MILES
0   1   2   3

Hopper Plus, 5/6/7 days at the four parks, with multiple same-day visits, PLUS 2/3/4 visits to any of *Disney's Blizzard Beach* and *Typhoon Lagoon* water parks, *Pleasure Island* and *Disney's Wide World of Sports Complex*™ (excluding special events at WWoS). All multi-day passes offer savings against buying 1-day tickets, and unused days never expire, so can be saved for any time in the future. In the UK, you can buy the 5- and

BRIT TIP: Be wary of travel agent pressure to buy too many tickets. You may well find you can't fit everything in, plus, for some attractions, you can often buy cheaper in Orlando, even from the tour operators' reps.

KEY TO ORLANDO – MAIN ATTRACTIONS

A Magic Kingdom Park
B Epcot
C Disney-MGM Studios
D Universal Orlando
E SeaWorld Adventure Park
F Busch Gardens
G Kennedy Space Center
H US Astronaut Hall of Fame
I Splendid China
J Historic Bok Sanctuary
K Silver Springs
L Gatorland
M Disney's Typhoon Lagoon Water Park

N Disney's Blizzard Beach Water Park
O Festival Bay
P Water Mania
Q Wet 'n Wild
R Discovery Cove by SeaWorld
S Holy Land Experience
T Ripley's Believe It or Not
U Hard Rock Vault/Titanic Exhibition
V Orange County History Center
W Downtown Disney area
X Green Meadows Petting Farm
Y Fantasy of Flight
Z Disney's Animal Kingdom Park

Orlando City Hall

7-Day Park Hopper Plus through tour operators, ticket brokers and *Disney Stores*.

The **10-Day World Ticket** is available ONLY in the UK and gives 10 days' entry to the four main parks, water parks, *Pleasure Island*, *DisneyQuest Indoor Interactive Theme Park* and Disney's *Wide World of Sports Complex*™ (excluding special events), plus a FREE character breakfast. However, this pass expires 20 days after its first use (unlike the Hopper passes, which are valid until all the days are used up). In summer 2003, the World Ticket was possibly the best value at £199 for adults and £159 for children (3–9), as against its regular price of £259 and £208.

Guests at Disney hotels can buy an **Ultimate Park Hopper** ticket, giving entry to all the parks, *Pleasure Island, Disney's Wide World of Sports Complex*™ AND *DisneyQuest Indoor Interactive Theme Park* for the length of their stay, plus a few valuable extras like 'kids eat free' at the hotel. The price varies according to how long you stay. For stays of 2 weeks or more, it is worth considering the **Annual Pass** or **Premium Annual Pass** (check the Ticket Prices section on www.wdwinfo.com). You can also save money on many Disney tickets by booking online at www.disney.co.uk (go to Holidays and then Buy Tickets).

Other tickets

When it comes to Universal Orlando, SeaWorld and Busch Gardens, the choice is a little simpler. Again, you have a **1-Day Ticket** but, for Universal, it's cheaper to buy a **2-** or **3-Day Ticket**, giving access to Universal Studios, Islands of Adventure and the clubs of CityWalk. There is also a clubs-only pass ($8.95 plus tax) or a clubs-plus-film ticket ($12), as CityWalk has a 20-screen cinema. Even better value (and highly recommended) are the 2-week **Orlando FlexTickets**. The 4-Park Ticket gives admission to Universal Studios, Islands of Adventure, SeaWorld and Wet 'n Wild, while the 5-Park Ticket adds Busch Gardens, and both are valid for 14 days from first use. There is even a **Universal Bonus Pass** if you order online at www.universalorlando.com for 5 consecutive days at Universal Studios, Islands of Adventure and CityWalk for the price of a 2-day ticket. Finally, SeaWorld and Busch Gardens have a 2-park **Adventure Pass Ticket** (with a saving of almost $20 on two 1-Day Tickets), but most people prefer the extra value of the FlexTickets.

With price hikes every year, it is worth shopping around for tickets and buying as soon as possible. **Tour operators** tend to be ABOVE the gate price for the convenience of being able to pre-book and budget for your main costs at once. I recommend the **Keith Prowse**

Lake Eola

agency (02890 232425, www.keithprowsetickets.co.uk or see your travel agent) as one of the best for competitive prices AND pre-booking convenience, while they do several one-off tickets, excursions and 2-day trips especially for the UK market. They also supply the actual tickets as opposed to a voucher, which you have to exchange at the ticket booths, and are fully ABTA bonded for extra security. You could also try Theme Park Holidays (www.themeparkholidays.com, 0870 247 1000), or Attraction Tickets Direct (0845 130 3876, www.attraction-tickets-direct.co.uk).

A first word of warning: you don't want to try to do the main parks in one chunk. Apart from ending up with serious theme park indigestion, you'll probably also hit one of the parks on a busy day (check the Busy Day Guide on page 297). The *Magic Kingdom Park* and *Epcot* can be particularly exhausting (especially with children) and you'll need a quiet day afterwards.

The climate

The next question is when to go? Florida's weather does vary a fair bit, from bright but cool winter days in November, December and January, with the odd drizzly spell, to furiously hot and humid summers punctuated by tropical downpours.

The most pleasant option is to go in between the two extremes in

BRIT TIP: The humidity levels – up to 100% – and fierce daily rainstorms in summer take a lot of visitors by surprise, so take a lightweight, rainproof jacket or buy one of the cheap plastic ponchos available in local shops.

spring or autumn. You will also avoid the worst of the crowds. However, as most families are governed by school holidays, July to September remain the popular months for British visitors, and so this guide contains advice on how to get one jump ahead of the high-season crush.

And now to business: it's big, brash and fun, but above all it's American, and that means everything is exceedingly well organised, with a tendency towards the raucous rather than the reserved. It's clean, well maintained and very anxious to please: Floridians generally are an affable bunch, but they take affability to new heights in the theme parks, where staff are almost painfully keen to make sure you 'have a nice day'.

Tipping

Close to every American's heart is the custom of tipping. With the exception of petrol pump attendants and fast-food restaurant servers, just about everyone who offers you any sort of service in hotels, bars, restaurants, buses, taxis, airports and other public amenities will expect a tip. In bars, restaurants and taxis, 15% of the bill is the usual going rate while porters will expect $1 per bag. Brits are notoriously forgetful of this little habit but, as all service industry workers are automatically taxed on the assumption of receiving 15% in tips, you will be doing a major service to the local economy if you remember those few extra dollars each time.

It is also useful to know that dollar travellers' cheques can be used as cash, so it is not necessary (as well as not being advisable) to carry large amounts of cash around. Do NOT try to cash sterling travellers cheques anywhere other than major banks – most outlets will not accept them. Take note that all Orlando prices, both where indicated in this book and on every price tag you see, do not include the 6–7% Florida Sales Tax. There is also a 4–5% Resort Tax on hotel rooms.

Credit cards are accepted everywhere, are easy to carry and use and provide an extra degree of buying security. In some cases, like car hire, you can't operate without your one, so don't leave it at home!

BRIT TIP:
Tipping Guide

Bill	Suggested Tip
$15	$2.25
$20	$3.00
$25	$3.75
$30	$4.50
$40	$6.00
$50	$7.50

Visa requirements

Holiday visitors to America do not need a visa providing they hold a valid British passport showing they are a British citizen (and which does not expire before the end of the holiday). Instead, all you do is fill in a green visa waiver form (usually given out on your flight or when you check in) and hand it in with your passport to the US immigration official who checks you through after landing. However, British subjects do need a visa (£30), and should apply at least a month in advance to the US Embassy.

In England, Scotland and Wales write to the Visa Office, US Embassy, 5 Upper Grosvenor Street, London W1A 2JB (0891 200 290). In Northern Ireland, write to US Consulate General, 3 Queens House, 14 Queen Street, Belfast BT1 6EQ. Alternatively, call 0906 8200 290 (60p/minute) for more detailed visa advice, or visit www.usembassy.org.uk.

Central Florida festivals

As well as the full What's New guide to the area, here are some major – and unusual – annual events that are also worth keeping an eye out for in 2004 (and even planning your holiday round).

Blue Springs Manatee Festival, Jan 24–25 (www.dep.state.fl.us/parks/): this beautiful state park is home to the wonderful manatee, and special celebrations are staged around their seasonal migrations, with craft shows, park tours and interpretive programmes. In Orange City, well worth seeing at any time of year. (Off Exit 118 on Interstate 4 or I-4.)

Silver Spurs Rodeo, Feb 13–15, and Oct 8–10 (www.silverspurs rodeo.com): a twice-yearly celebration of an original American sport, this is held at the new Osceola Heritage Park in Kissimmee and features some top quality events, plus associated crafts and activities. (Just off the eastern end of Highway 192.)

Plant City Strawberry Festival, Feb 26–Mar 7 (www.flstrawberry festival.com): one of the most unusual and fun events – a fully grown country fair based on the local produce, but with concerts, shows, exhibitions and parades, plus lots of activities for kids. One of Florida's great social events. (Off Exit 19 on I-4.)

Daytona Beach Bike Week, Feb 27–Mar 7 (www.daytona chamber.com/bwhome.html): a celebration of all things two-wheeled and mechanical, with races at Daytona Speedway, concerts, parades and street festivals.

Sidewalk Arts Festival, Mar 19–21 (www.wpsaf.org): Winter Park is home to one of America's most prestigious fine arts festivals, with three days of art, food, music and children's events, from 9am–5pm.

Fun 'n Sun, Apr 14–20 (www.sun-n-fun.org): the annual aviation spectacular in Lakeland, with museums, vintage planes, aerobatics and more. One of the biggest in the USA. (Off Exit 27 on I-4.)

Zellwood Corn Festival, May 15–16 (www.zellwoodsweet cornfest.org): offbeat but fun offering, with the festival featuring corn-eating contests, carnival rides, live entertainment, games, arts and crafts. (25 miles/40km north-west of Orlando, Route 436 to Route 411.)

Independence Day, July 4: a huge national holiday throughout the country, but watch out for big annual special events at Lake Eola (downtown Orlando), Lakefront Park (Kissimmee), Mount Dora and Winter Park, as well as the main theme parks.

Aquamania, Nov 7–8: right at the end of the annual 8-week Anglers Challenge (a huge fishing festival on the local lakes that attracts devotees from all over the US) is this environmental celebration of family fun, races, live music and outdoor recreation exhibits, at Kissimmee's Lakefront Park South on Lake Toho.

Sanford Heritage Festival, Oct/Nov (www.visitseminole.com): a major 3-day waterfront party in downtown Sanford, with fireworks each night, musical events and fun for kids, too (2004 dates not known at time of writing).

A Disney character breakfast

STOP PRESS!

Here's what's new in this region of the Sunshine State.

Walt Disney World Resort in Florida has three of the latest and greatest in **Mission: SPACE** (an *Epcot* blockbuster that opened in September 2003) and **Mickey's PhilharMagic** (a hugely imaginative and family-friendly 3-D giant-screen film show, full of special effects, at the *Magic Kingdom Park*, which opened in October). At the same time, the *Magic Kingdom Park* unveiled a new nightly fireworks spectacular, **Wishes**, a breath-taking combination of sights, sounds and pyrotechnics. The first half of the fun **Pop Century Resort** was due to open in December.

Magic Kingdom's Alien Encounter has shut to make way late in 2004 for **Stitch's Great Escape**, a revamped version of this show in which the audience will get a real close-up encounter with the cheeky alien from *Lilo & Stitch*, featuring some of the most sophisticated and fun audio-animatronics.

From spring 2004, visitors will see the opening of **Disney's Saratoga Springs Resort & Spa** (opposite *Downtown Disney*), which is the latest development for the *Disney Vacation Club* (their version of timeshare). With a mixture of studios and villas,

Jungle Cruise at Silver Springs

it will offer a themed pool, dining, shopping and a full-service health spa.

Watch out for a new **Motor Stunt Show** at *Disney-MGM Studios* in early 2005, with the hugely acclaimed Moteurs…Action! attraction from *Disneyland Resort®️ Paris*. The park's Backlot area is also being extensively reworked to include Chicago and San Francisco scenes. *Epcot* will also have another blockbuster in 2005 with the amazing **Soarin' Over California**, a ground-breaking simulator ride at The Land pavilion. This combines cinematic artistry with a unique motion-base 'hang-glider' set inside a giant projection dome.

For spring 2006, Disney has announced its biggest-ever ride for *Disney's Animal Kingdom Park*. **Expedition Everest** will be a high-speed train adventure, backwards and forwards around the glaciers, canyons and caverns of a 200-ft (60-metre) 'Everest' in search of the mythical Yeti. It will cover a full acre just beyond Kali River Rapids and the first design drawings are mouth-watering.

Universal Orlando opened two major new attractions in 2003 (**Jimmy Neutron's Nicktoon Blast** and the **Shrek 4-D** film show) and follow up in spring 2004 with another, **The Mummy's Revenge**, which replaces Kongfrontation. This promises to be an absolute blockbuster (with an $80 million price tag!), an indoor coaster full of state-of-the-art animatronics, indoor pyrotechnics and thrilling special effects. The Wild, Wild, Wild West Stunt Show has closed and there is no news of anything to replace it.

SeaWorld continues to impress and the new **Waterfront** district is a fine addition there with a range of shops, diners and live entertainment, as well as the stunning **Odyssea** show at the Nautilus Theater. The **Sharks Deep Dive** programme is an excellent addition to their line-up of personal animal encounters. Sister park Busch Gardens added a 3-D film attraction in 2003 with **Haunted Lighthouse**, and a new coaster is rumoured for 2004, as well as a new show for the Moroccan Palace Theater.

The International Drive area continues to maintain its development of contrasting attractions, with the opening in June 2003 of **Dolly Parton's Dixie Stampede**, a welcome and spectacular addition to the dinner-show scene, plus the completion of the second phase of the impressive **Festival Bay** shopping and entertainment complex.

Finally, thrill-ride fans should head for Kissimmee's **Old Town**, where G-Force opened in October 2003 and is billed as the 'fastest ride on the planet'. It features twin racing dragsters that blast from 0–120mph in TWO SECONDS! It costs a whacking $27 (driver) or $10 (passenger) to ride.

As ever, there will be announcements that beat our deadline, so check the Discussion Boards of www.wdwinfo.com for all the latest.

Now plan your visit

The next few chapters will help you plan your days and tell you everything you need to know to make your holiday perfect. Draw up a rough itinerary and then fine tune it with the help of the UK Discussion Boards on www.wdwinfo.com. Enjoy!

Mural at Kissimmee

2 Planning and Practicalities
(or, How to Almost Do It All and Live to Tell the Tale)

There is one simple rule once you have decided Orlando is the place for you. Sit down (preferably with this book) and **PLAN** what you want to do very carefully. This is not the type of holiday you can take in a freewheeling, carefree 'make it up as you go along' manner. **Frustration and exhaustion lie in wait for all those who do not have at least a basic plan of campaign.**

First of all work out WHEN you want to go, then decide WHERE in the vast resort is the best place for you. Then consider WHAT sort of holiday you are looking for, WHO you want to entrust your holiday with and finally HOW much you want to try to do.

> BRIT TIP: Thanksgiving is always the fourth Thursday in November; George Washington's birthday, or President's Day, is the third Monday in February. Try to avoid those weeks!

When to go

If you are looking to avoid the worst of the crowds, the best periods to choose are October to December (but not the week of the Thanksgiving holiday in November or between Christmas and New Year), early January up until 2 weeks before Easter (avoiding President's Day in February) and April (after Easter) to the end of May. Orlando gets down to some serious tourist business from Memorial Day (the last Monday in May, the official start of the summer season) to Labor Day (the first Monday in September and the last holiday of summer), peaking on the Fourth of July, a huge national holiday. The Easter holidays are similarly uncomfortable (although the weather is better), but easily the busiest is Christmas time, starting the week before December 25 and lasting until January 2. It is not unknown for some of the parks to close as their massive car parks fill up by mid-morning.

The best combination of comfortable weather and smaller crowds is to be had in April (avoiding Easter) and October. However, few of the main attractions are affected by rain, although the roller-coasters and water rides will close if lightning threatens, and you will be one jump ahead if you have waterproofs, as the crowds noticeably thin out when it gets wet. In any event, all the parks sell cheap, plastic ponchos (cheaper at Wal-Mart or other supermarkets). In the colder months, take a few lightweight but warm layers for early morning queues then, when it warms up later, leave them in the lockers provided in all the parks. If it's too hot, take advantage of the air-conditioned attractions and restaurants.

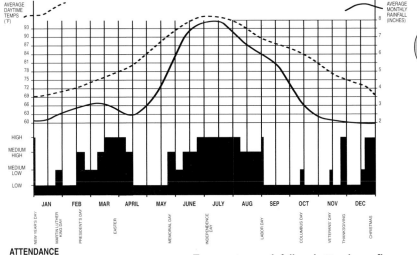

ATTENDANCE

Temperature, rainfall and attendance figures

Where to stay

The choice of where to stay is equally important, especially if you have a family that demands swimming pools and games rooms.

BRIT TIP: Having the use of a pool where you are staying is a major plus for relaxing at the end of a busy hot day.

Inevitably, there is a huge choice of accommodation areas and prices. As a guide, four main areas make up the greater Orlando tourist conglomeration:

Walt Disney World Resort in Florida: some of the most sophisticated, convenient and fun places to stay are to be found in Disney's great range of hotels. The same imagination that has gone into the creation of the theme parks has been at work on the likes of *Disney's Polynesian Resort* and *Disney's Animal Kingdom Lodge*. They all feature free, regular transport to all of the attractions, your own resort ID card

(so you can charge meals and souvenirs to your room, and have your purchases delivered to the hotel), free parking and the BIG bonus of the **Extra Magic Hour**. This latter allows Disney resort guests entry to one theme park each day a full HOUR before the official opening time, meaning you can do many of the main attractions before the majority have arrived. Many resorts also have great kids' clubs and baby-sitting services. The drawbacks here are, with the exception of *Disney's All-Star Resorts* and the new *Pop Century Resort*, Disney hotels are among the most expensive, especially to eat in, and are a fair drive from the likes of Universal Orlando and Kennedy Space Center. For a 1-week holiday it takes some beating, though.

Lake Buena Vista: a loosely defined area around the eastern fringes of *Walt Disney World Resort in Florida* and along Interstate 4 (I-4), this again features some upmarket hotels. It is also handy for all the Disney fun, with most hotels offering free transport to the parks, while there are excellent restaurants and shops. Still a bit pricey, but its proximity to I-4 makes it convenient for much of Orlando.

International Drive: this ribbon development lies midway between Disney and downtown Orlando and is therefore an excellent central location. Running parallel to I-4, it is about 15–20 minutes drive from the main theme parks, while it is also a well-developed tourist area in its own right, with some great shopping, restaurants and attractions like Wet 'n Wild, Ripley's Believe It Or Not, WonderWorks and Skull Kingdom. The down side is it does get congested and occasionally chaotic with tourist traffic in peak periods, so you have to make a slightly earlier start in the morning. But it does represent good value for money and is one of the few areas with extensive pavements, making it easy to explore on foot. A sub-district off I-Drive is the Universal area of Kirkman Road and Major Boulevard, where new hotels are regularly being added.

Kissimmee: budget holiday-makers can be found in their greatest numbers along the tourist sprawl of Highway 192 (the Irlo Bronson Memorial Highway), an almost unbroken 12-mile (19-km) strip of hotels, motels, restaurants and shops. It offers some of the best economy accommodation in the area and is handy for all Disney's attractions, although it is furthest away from Universal Orlando and downtown Orlando. A car is most advisable here, although the completion of the first phase of the BeautiVacation project, which has enhanced the heavily built-up stretch of 192 – from Route 535 as far west as Splendid China – with pavements, landscaping, bus shelters, benches and water fountains, making it a much better location for getting around on foot or by bus.

> **BRIT TIP:** Phase II of the Beautivacation of Highway 192 has now started, meaning serious roadworks from Route 535 to Hoagland Boulevard. Use (toll) Osceola Parkway to beat the traffic.

Split holidays

You can't go far wrong with whatever you're seeking, as long as you plan well. The Atlantic coast and some great beaches are only an hour's drive to the east, the magnificent Florida Everglades are some 3–4 hours to the south, and there are more wonderful beaches and pleasant coast roads to the west. Great shopping is to be found almost everywhere, while Orlando has some stunning golf courses, and there are plenty of opportunities to play or watch tennis, baseball and basketball, go fishing, boating or canoeing.

A common choice is to split the holiday by having a week or two in Orlando as well as a week elsewhere in Florida like the Gulf Coast or Florida Keys. The main tour companies offer a huge variety of packages, with cruise-and-stay options also popular.

If you can afford the time (and expense), the best option is to have 2 weeks in Orlando itself, then a week relaxing on one of Florida's many fabulous beaches. A 2-week, half-and-half split is a regular choice, but can make your time in

International Drive

2

© Disney

Disney's All-Star Sports Resort

Orlando rather hectic, unless your additional week is on the Atlantic coast at somewhere like Cocoa Beach. This resort, near to Cape Canaveral and the Kennedy Space Center, is only an hour from Orlando and gives you the chance to return to Disney for the day.

Several companies offer a highly worthwhile 10-day Orlando and 4-day coast split. Fly-drives obviously offer the greatest flexibility, but there is a lot to tempt you in just 2 weeks and you may find it better to book a 1-centre package that includes a car as well as your accommodation, so you can still travel around but avoid too much packing and unpacking.

Travel companies

There is serious competition for your hard-earned holiday money and the travel companies have been working hard to keep the cost of an Orlando holiday down, whether you fly-drive, book your own flights or take a package.

Shop around to get the best value for your holiday £, but make sure your package is booked with an ABTA agent for security should anything go wrong. At the last count, there were more than 70 tour operators offering holidays to

Florida, and here is a rundown of the biggest and best:

Travel City: the UK's largest independent direct-sell Florida specialist looks likely to be the No 1 operator in the near future, with some 130,000 customers a year. They offer a wide range of holidays at ultra-competitive prices, including fly-drives, 1- and 2-centre holidays, private pool villas and Caribbean cruises. New for 2004 is an increased range of apartments, suites and townhouses, which provide the catering comforts of home with the facilities of a resort. A sharp reservations team has excellent local knowledge and can advise you on where to stay, what to do and keep you up to date with what's new.

Most flights year-round are now with their own direct charter service (from Gatwick and Manchester, eight flights a week in summer months), using Boeing 747s and with one of the most generous seat pitches (31–32in/79–82cm of knee room) of any charter operator, plus free drinks, meals and headsets in all classes (unlike many nowadays). There is an economy cabin (the Sunshine Cabin), the Sunshine Upper Deck (no under-10s allowed, still economy-size seats but with enhanced in-flight service and meals, 30kg luggage allowance and priority check-in and disembarkation, for an extra £99) and Sunshine First (22 seats with a 54in/137cm pitch that recline almost flat, upgraded menus and in-flight entertainment, 40kg luggage allowance, priority boarding

The Disney Cruise Line at Castaway Cay

© Disney

and late check-in for £249 extra). You can also pre-book seats on most flights (for £20 return or £69 for a family of four). They have a double baggage allowance offer (£15/person, or £99 for a family of four if buying pre-bookable seats too) where you increase your limit from 20kg to 40kg (well worthwhile if you are planning to shop in Orlando!). Other flights depart from six regional airports, including Belfast and Cardiff.

Travel City has two dedicated arrivals centres and their own check-in for selected flights at Orlando Sanford Airport, as well as a user-friendly welcome centre at the Lake Buena Vista Factory Shops, open 7 days a week. Travel City can be found on Teletext page 298, for direct bookings on 01792 600177 or at www.travelcity.co.uk.

Airlines: EAL (European Aviation Ltd), plus British Airways, Continental Airlines, Virgin and select charters.

Airport: Orlando Sanford (EAL and charters), Orlando International (BA, Virgin and Continental).

Virgin Holidays: the other main operator to MCO (that means Orlando International in airport-speak), Virgin also has the biggest and most exhausting brochure. They offer the largest variety of combinations, including Miami, the Keys, New York, Washington, Boston, the Bahamas, Mexico, nine Caribbean islands (including Cuba) and some tempting cruises, as well as the Florida coasts.

A strong selling point is Virgin's non-stop scheduled service to Orlando (from Manchester and Gatwick, plus occasional flights with other scheduled services) with award-winning in-flight entertainment, free drinks, kids' packs, meals and games. They have a wide choice of accommodation in the different areas (including every Disney resort), and are popular for fly-drives, flying into Orlando and out from Miami.

Flight upgrades to their Premium Economy (extra leg room and bigger seats from £150–225), Club Orlando (from Manchester only, with extra luxurious seats for £160 on top of the Premium Economy supplement) or the unequalled Upper Class service (from £850–1,025, with seats that recline fully, plus personal attention and service, use of the wonderful Virgin Atlantic Clubhouse in UK airports and a double car upgrade in Florida) are all available and the service throughout is impeccable. You can pre-book seats free of charge (on 0871 222 0050) no more than 180 days before departure and even check in the evening before your flight at Gatwick.

Orlando is becoming increasingly popular as a wedding venue, and Virgin have their own wedding co-ordinators for ceremonies throughout Florida. Other bonuses include single-parent discounts, extra help for passengers with disabilities, 'kids eat free' deals at selected hotels and some excellent non-driver packages, using their own dedicated coach service, plus a chartered bus from Orlando to Miami or Fort Lauderdale. For more details call 0870 990 4215 or visit www.virginholidays.com for a brochure.

Airline: Virgin Atlantic.
Airport: Orlando International.
Thomson: another of the largest, mass-market operators, Thomson has an excellent reputation in Orlando, having a large team of reps and Service Centres on I-Drive, and offers six departure airports (including Birmingham, Newcastle and Glasgow). You can pre-book your flight seats (£17 per adult, £7 per child), while good in-flight entertainment and kids' packs are provided (with Britannia).

Thomson prices packages well for

the family market, with special children's fares and bonuses like 'kids eat free' and 'extra value' hotels, while offering a decent selection of cruises, coastal resorts for 2- or even 3-centre holidays (including Miami and Key West) and even pre-bookable golf packages. An increased range of private villas (sleeping up to 10) is available as are wedding packages (from £519) at Cypress Grove, the Wyndham Palace or Wyndham Orlando hotels.

Flight upgrades cost £60 (for extra leg room) and £140 for Premium service (with complimentary drinks, wider seats, choice of meals and priority boarding). Call 0870 550 2567 or book online at www.thomson.co.uk.

Airline: Britannia, and other charters.

Airport: Orlando Sanford.

Airtours: also in the leading group who take almost 100,000 British tourists to Orlando every year, Airtours flies from eight UK airports with good in-flight entertainment, children's fun packs and seat-back TVs. They offer an excellent Premiair Gold upgrade (extra leg room and baggage allowance, free bar, pre-selected menu, late UK check-in) for £149 or £179/person (see below).

Airtours has some novel 10- and 11-night packages (from Manchester and Gatwick only) for a more flexible choice and offer a 15-seater mini-van. There is an Airtours service desk at the huge McDonald's on I-Drive and Sand Lake Road (with special meal deals!) and Welcome Meetings are imaginatively held in Universal's CityWalk (with free parking), so you're well placed to hit the fun straight away.

Airtours offers some good 2-centre combos, including a week at a *Walt Disney World Resort in Florida* hotel and a week at a Universal resort, the Gulf Coast, Fort

Lauderdale and 7-night cruises to Mexico and the Caribbean. Private villa accommodation is now a feature, with good quality pool homes available in Kissimmee and the Gulf Coast. Airtours fly-drives also has a range of 'Drive and Stay' holidays.

Their flexible-price approach puts the onus on you to select the exact package for you, which means you can be more price-conscious as you select from: *Holiday Plus*, which includes pre-booked flight seating, 90-minute latest check-in, in-flight refreshment voucher, choice of meals, pre-departure pack, a reduced price Premiair Gold upgrade (£149) or extra leg-room seat (£50), 25kg luggage allowance (per person) and low deposit; *Standard Holidays*, with 2-hour check-in, 20kg luggage allowance, pre-bookable seating (£24), Premiair Gold upgrade option (£179) or extra leg-room seat (£70); *Sundeal Holidays*, the no-frills option, with accommodation assigned on arrival, a 2½-hour latest check-in, only 15kg luggage allowance and no optional upgrades or in-flight meal (it is £15 extra); and *Flight Only* (as Sundeal, but no accommodation and no in-flight meal unless you pre-book seating). For a brochure, call 0870 900 8639 or visit www.airtours.co.uk.

Airline: My Travel.

Airport: Orlando Sanford.

BRIT TIP: Beware the low baggage allowances, as there are some steep charges for any excess, especially on the return flight. An empty suitcase can weigh a good 5kg, and you will be tempted to buy a lot of souvenirs in Orlando!

First Choice: a comprehensive flight programme uses five UK airports (including Glasgow, Birmingham and Newcastle), plus a Classic Premium upgrade (extra leg room and in-flight services, plus special check-in facilities) for £159 and pre-bookable seats on their smart in-house Air 2000 airline (£17 per adult, £7 per child, at least 7 days in advance). They offer a choice of twin-centre Gulf Coast options (with coach transfers for non-drivers) and 4- and 7-night cruises. First Choice has a family-friendly touch offering hotels (mainly the 3- and 4-star variety) with themed kids' suites and 'kids eat free' deals, plus villas and apartments (with their own reps). A new service desk at the Holiday Inn Resort is staffed every day. Their more luxurious Premier Choice properties provide 50% discounts off VIP lounges in UK departure airports. You can also check in the day before departure (between noon and 10pm) at Gatwick, Birmingham and Manchester, but this costs £10 per booking (up to 6 people), £15 (7–10 people) or £20 (more than 11). Call 0870 757 2757.

Airlines: Air 2000, Britannia.

Airport: Orlando Sanford.

Four other First Choice brands also sell Florida – **First Choice Villas** (0870 750 0001), for a solely villa-based holiday, **Eclipse**, a direct-sell operator with a standard range of accommodation, including holiday homes, and some coast combinations (08705 010203 or www.eclipseholidays.com), and **Unijet** and **Sunstart** (see below). Look them up online at www.firstchoice.co.uk or request a brochure on 020 8880 8155.

Unijet: flying from five UK airports, Unijet favours more flexible options for more experienced and independent-minded travellers (although they still feature many family-friendly deals, including 'kids eat free' hotels). Holiday homes, which are great value for larger families or groups, are heavily featured, with a full range of hotels, from budget choices to top quality. Two-centre and tailor-made options include the Gulf Coast, south-east Florida and the Keys, while you can even take in the likes of New York, Las Vegas and Hawaii. Most flights offer pre-bookable seats (£17 per adult, £7 per child), kids' meals and fun packs, plus upgrades (from £159) to the Premium service for greater comfort and choice. You can also pre-book extra legroom seats for £45/person round trip. Call 08705 336 336 or visit www.unijet.co.uk.

Airlines: Air 2000 and Britannia, plus various scheduled airlines with tailor-made choices.

Airport: Orlando Sanford (Air 2000 and Britannia), Orlando International (others).

Sunstart: this is the budget operator in the First Choice range, featuring mainly a handful of 2- and 3-star hotel types. One brochure covers all their destinations (mainly Europe), and their flights operate from four UK airports – Gatwick, Birmingham, Manchester and Newcastle. There are optional airport-hotel transfers and a 'rep on demand' service, in addition to the usual airport meet-and-greet and welcome meetings.

Airlines: Air 2000, Britannia.

Airport: Orlando Sanford.

Kids have fun on Virgin flights

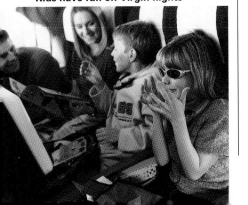

British Airways Holidays: another company to benefit from its own direct, scheduled air service, BA Holidays offers great flexibility with almost any duration and combination possible. Beach add-ons, twin centres – both coasts and the Florida Keys – and an extensive selection of quality but great-value private homes (including some with guaranteed lake views) are all on offer. BAH also flies to Miami and Tampa, opening up plenty of fly-drive and multi-centre possibilities (all children booked on Tampa flights receive 200 Disney Dollars to spend anywhere in *Walt Disney World Resort in Florida*).

However, you won't find them in most travel agents as they only do direct-sell, but their packages are all well tried and trusted. New in 2003 was a Disney tie-up, providing special in-flight entertainment and fun packs for the kids. BA flights also come with the option to upgrade to the luxurious Club World (with fully flat beds) or World Traveller Plus (larger seats with more leg room), plus special kids' meals and seat-back TVs. Call 0870 243 4224 or browse their online brochure at www.baholidays.com.

Airline: British Airways.
Airport: Orlando International.

Thomas Cook: there are two choices under the famous Cook banner here, a new mass-market *Thomas Cook* brochure and the more distinctive *Thomas Cook Signature* programme (see below). The straightforward Thomas Cook brand is a fairly standard choice, broken down into three value ranges – Extra, Standard and Economy – primarily using their own Thomas Cook charter airline (with optional upgrades available), which has replaced the old and unloved jmc brand. Extra legroom seats (for £30 each way), pre-bookable seating (at a small charge – call 0870 243 0416) and executive lounge facilities are all available at selected UK airports (for a charge). They also have one of the best punctuality records of all the charter airlines in recent years and their in-flight service is one of the best, from my observations. You can either book through their own High Street agencies, by phone (0870 0100 437), online at www.thomascook.co.uk or via their own satellite/cable TV channel, with excellent deals from time to time. They offer some good wedding packages (from £1,500/couple at a Disney location, to just £399 in Winter Park) and the standard range of twin-centre options and cruises.

Airline: Thomas Cook.
Airport: Orlando Sanford.

Thomas Cook Signature: now here's an operation to compete with the Virgins of this world – a more quality-conscious and selective offering using ONLY scheduled air services (although their prices are still pretty competitive). They tend to suit repeat visitors especially, and bonuses include free night offers (stay 6 and get another free), 'kids eat free' and free room upgrades at many hotels. Their ticketing info and material is first class and there is a strong tailor-made element to the range of choice. And, as with many nowadays, Disney's Ultimate Park Hopper ticket now comes with a 'kids eat breakfast free' offer at the Disney resort where you're staying. Their selection of holiday homes is

Fishing on Disney's Bay Lake

© Disney

particularly good (with some of the most upmarket properties in the area), and the twin-centre options include both coasts, Miami, the Keys and the Caribbean. Call 0870 442 3897 or visit www.tcsignature.com.

Airlines: Virgin Atlantic, British Airways and American Airlines.

Airports: Orlando International.

Kuoni: as with all their holidays, Kuoni offers the upmarket version of Orlando, with some of the best hotels, a strong Disney tie-up, a comprehensive wedding and honeymoon service and a Price Watch guarantee (money back if you find an identical holiday for less). They have a range of twin-centre options, including the Florida Keys, exclusive Boca Raton and Marco Island, the Caribbean and even New York and Las Vegas. The average price reflects the more exclusive nature of many of their packages (plus their flexible, tailor-made choice facility), but there are some big child reductions, 'kids eat free' hotels, and Kuoni use only scheduled airlines. Free airport-hotel transfers for non-drivers are provided, too. Call 0870 0745 8664 for a brochure or visit their website at www.kuoni.co.uk.

Airlines: Virgin Atlantic, United (via Washington), Continental (via New York), American (via Miami) and British Airways.

Airport: Orlando International.

Funway Holidays: this is the sister company of America's largest tour operator and a leading specialist in holidays to the US, hence they offer a tailor-made service to match Orlando with any other option, providing total flexibility of choice from no less than 17 UK airports. Their private homes are a big feature of the Florida programme, but they also serve up some terrific-value deals, especially with low children's prices, if you book early, making them consistently among the best prices for a family of four. They

also use only scheduled airlines (with an option to upgrade to Virgin's Premium Economy service for £175 each way).

A wide range of 2-centre choices include the Gulf Coast, Miami and the Keys, plus cruises to the Bahamas and Caribbean from Miami, Fort Lauderdale and Port Canaveral. Other extras include 'kids eat free' hotels, free kids' clubs, free hotel nights at certain times and free shuttles at selected hotels for non-drivers. Look them up at www.funwayholidays.co.uk or call 0870 220 0626 for a brochure.

Airlines: various scheduled, including Virgin Atlantic, British Airways and Continental.

Airport: Orlando International.

Style Holidays: one of the UK's top self-catering specialists (and a Thomas Cook-owned company), this company offers a huge selection of private-pool homes and hotel suites, with accommodation up to luxurious 5- and 6-bed varieties, as well as the usual range of hotel and *Walt Disney World Resort* options. All properties are in named, well-described situations and can be booked on an accommodation-only basis, leaving you free to book your flights. Their comprehensive brochure has an excellent range of Gulf Coast villas (all of which can be combined with Orlando), while they maintain a high standard of in-resort service. Transfers can be arranged for non-drivers (£15 per person each way). For a brochure, call 0870 444 4474 or e-mail brochures@style-holidays.co.uk. Or check out www.style-holidays.co.uk.

Airline: Various charters.

Airport: Orlando Sanford.

A number of other travel companies worth checking out include: **Jetsave** (Florida specialists with a highly flexible approach; call 0870 161 3402 or visit www.jetsave.co.uk); **Trailfinders** (the UK's largest independent travel company and highly recommended by several readers; 020 7937 5400 or www.trailfinders.com); **Travelplanners** (a division of USAirtours, and mainly villas; 0870 528 0002 or www.travelplanners.skynet.co.uk); **Travelbag** (0870 890 1456, www.travelbag.co.uk); **Transolar Holidays** (also great for attraction ticket offers on 0151 630 3737 or www.transolarholidays.com); **Premier Holidays** (0870 889 0850 or www.premierholidays.co.uk); and **Ebookers** (the travel agent arm of Flightbookers, 0870 010 7000, www.ebookers.com).

Flight Centre (0870 8908 099 or www.flightcentre.co.uk) and the excellent **Cheap Flights** (an internet-only service, www.cheapflights.co.uk) feature keen flight-only offers. A look at the pages of **Teletext** (page 222 on TV, or www.teletextholidays.co.uk) often reveals special deals, as do www.expedia.co.uk, www.lastminute.com and www.opodo.co.uk. A new internet company, **Vacation Florida** (www.vacation-florida.co.uk, and partner website www.cheapestflights.co.uk, 0800 015 8030), offers the full range of flights, packages and car hire.

> BRIT TIP: The important thing is to establish a plan of what you want to do on your holiday, then get a selection of brochures and compare the prices and attractions of each one, to help you decide on the best accommodation to suit your needs.

Finally, for those looking to book things themselves but wanting help with Disney accommodation, meal reservations, etc, the excellent **Dreams Unlimited Travel** service is a must. Visit their website at www.dreamsunlimitedtravel.com for the essential information on this *no-cost* service which can save time, money and hassle. Other Orlando hotels (with some serious discounts) feature on their DreamsRes online booking service plus a discount ticket agency, TicketRes.

What to see when

Once you arrive, the temptation is to head for the nearest theme park, then the next, and so on. Hold on! If there is such a thing as theme park indigestion, that's the best recipe for it. Some days at the parks are busier than others; it is simply not possible to cover more than one a day, and it may be inadvisable to attempt two of the main parks on successive days. So here's what you do.

With the aid of the Holiday Planner on pages 295–97, make a note of all the attractions you want to see over the length of your holiday.

The most sensible strategy is to plan around the eight 'must-see' parks – *Magic Kingdom Park*, *Epcot*, *Disney-MGM Studios*, *Disney's Animal Kingdom Theme Park*, Universal Studios, and the Islands of Adventure theme park, SeaWorld and Busch Gardens. If you have only a week, consider dropping Busch Gardens (it's furthest away from Orlando and doesn't have quite the same magical appeal as the others) and concentrate on the Disney parks and Universal Studios, with SeaWorld as an extra if it fits into your plan. Space travel fans will be hard-pressed not to include the Kennedy Space Center, but it will probably bore small children.

As a basic rule, the *Magic Kingdom Park* is the biggest hit with children, and families often find it requires 2 days. The same can be said of *Epcot*, but there are fewer rides to amuse

Liki Tiki Village

small children and the emphasis is as much on education as entertainment, although it all has Disney's slick, easily digestible coating. Only the most fleet of foot, given the benefit of a relatively crowd-free period, will be able to negotiate *Epcot* in a day. *Disney's Animal Kingdom Theme Park* is also a little short on attractions for the youngest kids (unless they really love their animals, as mine do), but it still requires nearly all of its 9am–6pm opening hours.

Disney-MGM Studios is usually possible to do in a day (not forgetting the early evening Fantasmic! show), while SeaWorld occasionally needs rather longer and Universal Studios can be a 2-day park when Orlando is at its busiest. Islands of Adventure will almost certainly keep everyone, except possibly under-5s, busy all day, too. Busch Gardens, extremely popular with British families, is another full-day affair, especially as it is a 75–90 minute drive away in Tampa to the south-west. However, an early start to the Kennedy Space Center (an hour's drive away on the east coast) will mean you can be back in your hotel swimming pool by teatime, confident you have fully enjoyed One Small Step For Man.

All the attractions are described in detail in Chapters 5–8, so it's best to try to get an idea of the time requirements of them all before you pick up your pencil.

Smaller attractions

Of the other, smaller-scale attractions, the nature park of Silver Springs is a full day out as it also involves a near 2-hour drive to get there, but everything else can be fitted around your Big Eight Itinerary. The water parks provide a good place to spend a relaxing afternoon, while Historic Bok Sanctuary is another quieter spot to while away half a day or so (NB: the wonderful park of Cypress Gardens closed in 2003, and there was no word on it re-opening as we went to press). There are also a number of smaller-scale attractions in Orlando which will probably keep the children amused for several hours (often after the major theme parks have closed).

Gatorland is a unique look at some of Florida's oldest inhabitants and is a good combination with a ride at Boggy Creek Airboats. Ripley's Believe It Or Not museum and WonderWorks interactive house of fun are both good family centres for several hours. Add in the terrific haunted house attraction, Skull Kingdom, the imaginative model railway set-up of Trainland Inc, and the more old-fashioned lure of go-karts and other fairground-type rides at Fun Spot or Magical Midway (all on the I-Drive corridor), and you have a full day of alternative fun and frolics. Aviation fans must not miss a trip to Fantasy of Flight (further down I-4) or the Flying Tigers Warbird Air Museum in Kissimmee for a novel experience.

DisneyQuest, another part of the *Downtown Disney* area, is a hugely imaginative interactive 'arcade' that guarantees up to half a day's fun (especially for older children). Each main tourist area is also well served with creatively designed mini-golf courses that will absorb any excess energy (if you are not already exhausted!) for an hour or two.

Evenings

Then, of course, there is the evening entertainment, with a similarly wide choice of extravagant fun-seeking. By far the best, and a must for at least one evening each, are *Downtown Disney, Pleasure Island*, Universal's CityWalk and the fast-developing Pointe*Orlando area. All will keep you fully entertained until the early hours. Another popular source of fun are the various dinner shows, 2-hour cabarets based on themes like medieval knights, pirates, Arabian Nights and murder mysteries that all include a hearty meal. Then there are the huge variety of nightclubs and bars, many offering live music.

What to do when

There are a couple of handy general guidelines for avoiding the worst of the tourist hordes, even in high season. The vast majority of fun-seekers in town are American, and they tend to arrive at the weekends, get settled in their hotels, and then head for the main theme parks first. That means Monday is generally a bad time to visit the *Magic Kingdom Park* and Tuesday is usually humming at *Epcot*.

The Extra Magic Hour, which allows Disney hotel guests early entry to one of the parks on a set day each week, also creates a greater build-up of crowds, which tends to mean the following parks are best avoided on these days: Sunday, *Magic Kingdom Park*; Monday, *Disney's Animal Kingdom Theme Park*; Tuesday, *Disney-MGM Studios*; Wednesday, *Epcot*; Thursday, *Magic Kingdom Park*; Friday, *Disney's Animal Kingdom Park*; Saturday, *Disney-MGM Studios. Disney's Animal Kingdom Theme Park* is also the hardest park to get round when it's crowded. The popular water parks of *Disney's Blizzard Beach* and

Typhoon Lagoon hit high tide at the weekend, and Thursday and Friday in summer.

At Universal Orlando, the picture is different as there are no early entry days and the weekends are usually busiest as the locals tend to visit then. This often means Monday is quietest in both parks, getting busier through the week, with the Universal Studios park slightly the more crowded of the two.

> **BRIT TIP:** If your hotel is not far from the park take a couple of hours out to return for a siesta or a swim. Have your hand stamped for re-entry when you leave (your car park ticket will also be valid all day) and then return to enjoy the evening entertainment, which is often the most spectacular part of the day.

If *Walt Disney World Resort in Florida* is humming in the early part of the week, that makes it a good time to visit SeaWorld, Busch Gardens, Silver Springs or the Kennedy Space Center. Wet 'n Wild and Water Mania are best avoided at the weekends when the locals come out to play (see Busy Day Guide on page 297). Making sure you get the most out of your days at the main theme parks is another art form, and there are a number of practical policies to pursue. The official opening times seldom vary from 9am but arriving early is highly advisable. Apart from the obvious advantage of being near the head of the queues (and you will encounter some SERIOUS queues, or lines as the Americans call them), the parks do sometimes open earlier than scheduled if the crowds build up quickly before the official hour. So, you can get a step ahead of the masses by arriving at least 30 minutes before the expected opening time, or an hour early during the main holiday periods. Apart from anything else, you will be better placed to park in the vast, wide open spaces of the public car parks and catch the tram to the main gates (anything up to half a mile away!).

Once you've put yourself in pole position, don't waste time on the shops, scenery and other frippery which will lure the unprepared first-timer. Instead, head straight for some of the main rides and get a few big-time thrills under your belt before the main hordes arrive. You will quickly work out where the most popular attractions are as the majority of the other early birds will be flocking to them. Use Chapters 5 and 6 to help you plan your individual park strategies.

You can also benefit from doing the opposite of what the masses do after the initial rush has subsided.

Pace yourself

A word of warning: Disney's parks, notably the *Magic Kingdom Park*, stay open late in the evening during the main holiday periods, occasionally until 11pm, and that can be a long day for young children. Therefore, it is important to pace yourself, especially if you have been one of the first through the gates.

There are plenty of opportunities to take time off and stop for a drink or bite to eat, and you can take

BRIT TIP: The water IS safe to drink in the US but it may not taste great as they tend to put a lot of fluoride in it.

advantage of the American propensity to take meal-times seriously by avoiding lunchtime (12 noon–2pm) and dinnertime (5.30–7pm). So, after you've had a couple of hours of real adventure-mania, it pays to take an early lunch (i.e. before midday), plunge back into it all for another 3 hours or so, have another snack-sized meal mid-afternoon and then return to the main rides, as the parks quieten down a little in late afternoon.

Finally, a word about shopping in Orlando – it's world class. Your battle plan should also include at least half a day to visit one of the spectacular shopping malls, as well as some of the discount outlets and speciality centres like Old Town in Kissimmee, the excellent Orlando Premium Outlets, and the likes of Pointe*Orlando and Festival Bay on I-Drive.

BRIT TIP: If you fear the onset of blisters, head to the nearest supermarket or chemist (drug store) and seek out some Moleskin footpads from the footcare counter. They work wonders on tender skin.

Clothing and comfort

The most important part of your holiday wardrobe is your footwear – you will spend a lot of time on your feet, even during the off-peak periods. The smallest of the parks covers 'only' 100 acres (40ha), but that is irrelevant to the amount of time you will spend queuing. This is not the time to break in those new sandals or trainers! Comfortable, well-worn shoes or trainers are essential.

Otherwise, you need dress only as the climate dictates. T-shirts and shorts are quite appropriate in all of the parks (swimwear is not acceptable away from pool areas) and most restaurants and other eating establishments will happily accept informal dress.

BRIT TIP: One of the best ways to keep cool in the Florida sun is to visit one of the supermarkets and buy a simple mist spray fan (about $7.99) which you carry with you and just refill with water from time to time.

If, after a long day, you feel the need for a change of clothes or a sweater for the evening, take advantage of the handy lockers (unlimited use all day, even if you change parks). All the parks are also well equipped with pushchairs (or strollers) for a small charge, and baby services are freely located at regular intervals.

It is absolutely *vital* to use high-factor sun creams at all times, even during the winter months when the sun may not feel that strong but can still burn. Nothing is guaranteed to ruin your holiday like severe sunburn. Orlando has a sub-tropical climate and requires higher factor sun creams than even the Mediterranean. Use sun blocks on sensitive areas like your nose and ears, and splash on the after-sun lotion liberally at the end of the day. Skincare products are widely available and usually inexpensive (especially at Wal-Mart or Kmart).

BRIT TIP: Don't be tempted to pack a lot of smart or formal clothing – you really won't need it in hot, informal Florida.

Don't forget a waterproof sun cream if you are swimming. Wear a hat if you are out in the hottest parts of the day, and try to avoid alcohol, coffee and fizzy drinks until the evening as they can dehydrate and make you susceptible to heatstroke. You will need to increase your fluid intake *significantly* during the summer months in Orlando, but stick to still soft drinks such as Gatorade, a squash-like energy drink, or water.

Medical aid

Should you require medical treatment, whether it be for sunburn or other first aid, consult your tour company's information about local hospitals and surgeries. In the event of a medical, or other, emergency, dial 911 as you would 999 in Britain.

BRIT TIP: The summer is mosquito time. Buy a spray-on insect repellent. Alternatively, try any of Avon's Skin So Soft skincare products, which work wonders at keeping bugs at bay.

It cannot be over-stressed that you should have comprehensive travel and health insurance for any trip to America as there is NO National Health Service and ANY form of medical treatment will need to be paid for – and is usually expensive. Keep all the receipts and reclaim on your return home.

Emergency out-patients departments can be found with Centra Care at Florida Hospital Medical Center in five locations and can provide in-room services (407 238 2000) and free transport (407 239 6463). Open from 8am–5, 6, 7, 8 or 9pm, **Centra Care** can be found at 12139 South Apopka-Vineland Road, and 12500 Apopka-Vineland Road, next to Eckerd Drugs in The Shoppes at Buena Vista, and next to Turner Drugs, near the Crossroads shopping centre, at Lake Buena Vista (the latter is open until midnight on weekdays – 407 239 7777 or 407 934 2273); 7848 West Irlo Bronson Memorial Highway (192), in Formosa Gardens Village near Splendid China (407 397 7032); 6001 Vineland Road, near Universal Studios (407 351 6682); and 4320 West Vine Street, near Medieval Times (407 390 1888). Sand Lake Hospital on 9400 Turkey Lake Road also has an **emergency out-patients** department.

The **East Coast Medical Network** (407 648 5252) and **House Med Inc** (407 239 1195) both make hotel 'house calls' 24 hours a day. House Med also operates **MediClinic**, a walk-in facility on 2901 Parkway Boulevard, Kissimmee (open daily 9am–9pm) and Orlando Regional Healthcare System (operator of Sand Lake Hospital) has **Walk-In Medical Care** centres on I-Drive (407 351 3035 and 239 6679) open 8am–8pm.

A 24-hour tourist-orientated **dentist** can be found at J Antonellis on W Colonial Drive (407 292 8767).

The two largest **chemists** ('drug stores' in America) are Eckerd Drugs and Walgreens, and their branches at 908 Lee Road and 6201 I-Drive are both open 24 hours.

If you are taking regular prescription drugs, check with your doctor or pharmacist to see if they have a different name in the US. Many do (adrenaline is known as epinephrine) and it is worth finding out and carrying the drug with both names in case of an emergency. (Many thanks to Valerie Mulcare-Tivey for this advice.) Another reader points out the American term for paracetamol is acetaminophen.

ORLANDO THEME PARK ATTENDANCES 2002
(As estimated by *Amusement Business* magazine)

1 Magic Kingdom, 14.7 million (down 5% on 2001)
2 Epcot, 8.3 million (down 7%)
3 Disney-MGM Studios, 8 million (down 4%)
4 Disney's Animal Kingdom, 7.3 million (down 6%)
5 Universal Studios, 6.9 million (down 6%)
6 Islands of Adventure, 6.1 million (up 10%)
7 SeaWorld, 5 million (down 2%)

Travel insurance

Having said you should not travel without good insurance, you should also not pay over the odds for it. Tour operators are notoriously expensive or may imply you need to buy their insurance policy when you don't. In all cases make sure your policy covers you in the USA for: **medical cover** of at least £2 million; **personal liability** up to £2 million (though this won't cover driving abroad; you would still need Supplementary Liability Insurance with your car-hire firm); **cancellation** or **curtailment** cover up to £3,000; **personal property** cover up to £1,500 (but check on expensive items, as most policies limit single articles to £250; **cash and document** cover, including your passport and tickets; and finally that the policy gives you a 24-hour **emergency helpline**. If you want to go bungee jumping or even horse riding, check your policy includes **dangerous sports cover**.

Shop around at reputable dealers like **American Express** (0800 700 737), AA (0191 235 6513), **Bradford & Bingley** (0800 435642), **Club Direct** (0800 0744 558), **Columbus** (0207 375 0011), **Direct Travel** (01903 812345), **GA Direct** (0800

121007), **Options** (0870 848 0870), **Premier Direct** (0990 133218), **Primary Direct** (0870 444 3434), **Thomas Cook** (0845 600 5454), **Travel Insurance Direct** (0990 168113), **Worldcover Direct** (0800 365121) and **Worldwide Travel Insurance** (01892 833338).

> BRIT TIP: Avoid making phone calls from your hotel room – it's very expensive. It's cheaper to buy a local phonecard and use a normal payphone (see page 42).

Florida with children

I am often asked what I think is the right age to take children to Orlando, and there is no set answer, I'm afraid. Some toddlers take to it instantly, while some 6- or even 7-year-olds are left rather bemused. Quite often, the best attractions for young children are the hotel swimming pool or the tram ride to a park's front gates! Some love the Disney characters at first sight, while others find them quite frightening. There is simply no predicting how they will react, but I do know my oldest boy at 4½ loved just about every second of his first experience (apart from the fireworks – see page 34) and still talks about it. Yes, a 3-year-old may not remember much, but they WILL have fun and provide you with some great memories, photos and video.

Here are some top tips for travelling with youngsters – with thanks to the folks at www.wdwinfo.com for chipping in! (Additional tips are given in the theme parks chapters.):

The flight: Try to look calm (even if you don't feel it) and relaxed. Small children soon pick up on any anxieties and make them worse! Pack a bag with plenty of little bits for them (comics, sweets, colouring books, small surprise toys, etc) and keep vital 'extras' like Calpol (in sachets, if possible), change of clothes, small first-aid kit (plasters, antiseptic cream, baby wipes), sunglasses, hat and sunscreen in your hand luggage.

Once you're there: take things slowly and let your children dictate what pace you go at, to a large extent. The heat, in particular, can result in grizzly children in no time, so take breaks for drinks, splash zones or attractions with air-conditioning. Remember to carry your small first-aid kit with you. Things like baby wipes always come in handy, and it is a good idea to take spare clothes, which you can leave in the lockers at all the main parks. Going back to the hotel for an afternoon snooze is a good idea – the late afternoon/early evening is usually the best time at the parks in terms of cooler temperatures, less crowds and pure fun.

In the sun: carry sun cream and sun block at all times and use it frequently, in queues, on buses, etc. A children's after-sun lotion is also advisable. And make sure they drink a lot of water or non-fizzy drinks. Tiredness and irritability are often a result of mild dehydration.

Dining out: look for the 'kids eat free' deals in many places, as they can apply to children up to 12, and take advantage of the many buffet options (see Chapter 10, Dining Out) to fill the family up or for picky eaters. 'Many restaurants do Meals

Stormalong Bay at Disney's Yacht and Beach Club Resort

© Disney

To Go if you want a quiet meal in your own accommodation without the worry of the kids playing up!' says Lisag on www.wdwinfo.com. Try to let your children get used to the (size of the) characters before you go to one of the many fab Disney character meals.

Having fun: let your children do some of the decision-making and be prepared to go with the flow if they find something unexpected they like (the many squirt fountains and splash zones in the main parks are an example – bring along swimsuits and/or a change of clothes!). The Orlando rule of 'You Can't Do It All' applies especially with children. And beware the evening fireworks at many of the parks – they are loud, and young children can get quite distressed (my eldest – then 4 – had to be taken out of *Epcot* in a hurry!). The resort hotels around the *Magic Kingdom Park* offer safer ways to view the fireworks – at a distance!

BRIT TIP: Pushchairs are essential, even if your children are a year or two out of them. The distances involved around the parks wear kids out quickly, and a pushchair can save a lot of discomfort (for dads especially!). You can take your own, hire them at the parks or even buy one there at a local supermarket for around £10.

All the parks have **Baby Centers** for nursing mothers and can provide baby food and nappies on request (check the park map for the locations). The centres can even provide spare children's underpants for those little 'accidents'! All of Disney's resort hotel gift shops stock baby food and nappies. Expectant mothers are strongly advised not to ride some of the more dynamic attractions and coasters, and there will be clear warnings of these on the maps and at the rides themselves. Basically, the rides to avoid are: *Magic Kingdom Park:* Space Mountain, Tomorrowland Indy Speedway, Splash Mountain; *Epcot:* Test Track, Body Wars, Maelstrom, Mission: SPACE; *Disney-MGM Studios:* Tower of Terror, Rock 'n Roller Coaster starring Aerosmith, Star Tours; *Disney's Animal Kingdom Park:* Dinosaur!, Primeval Whirl, Kali River Rapids, Kilimanjaro Safaris; *Universal Studios Florida:* Back To The Future – The Ride, Men In Black – Alien Attack, Earthquake, Jimmy Neutron ride; *Islands of Adventure:* Incredible Hulk Coaster, Dr Doom's Fearfall, Popeye and Bluto's Bilge Rat Barges, Dudley Do-Right's Ripsaw Falls, Jurassic Park River Adventure, Dueling Dragons; *SeaWorld:* Wild Arctic (avoid simulator ride), Journey to Atlantis, Kraken. *Busch Gardens:* Gwazi, Kumba, Montu, The Python, The Scorpion, Congo River Rapids, Stanley Falls Log Flume, Tanganyika Tidal Wave, The Phoenix, Sandstorm, Crazy Camel, Akbar's Adventure Tours.

Travellers with disabilities

The parks pay close attention to the needs of holiday-makers with disabilities. There are few rides that cannot cater for them, while wheelchair availability and access is almost always good. For hearing-impaired guests, there are assistive listening devices and reflective captioning at attractions where a commentary is part of the show, and guidebooks in Braille are available, too, plus rest areas for guide dogs. All Disney hotels have rooms accessible for guests with disabilities – call 407 939 7807 or visit www.disneyworld.com – and Disney publishes a *Guidebook for Disabled Guests* (as does Universal), available in all three main parks (and online). Life-jackets are always on hand at the water parks, and there are even special tape cassettes for blind visitors.

Disabled drivers should take their orange car badge with them as this is honoured in the US and there are designated parking areas at all theme parks. For local assistance, **Walker Medical & Mobility Products** specialises in 3-wheeled electric scooters and wheelchair rentals, with free delivery and pick-up even from holiday homes. Call 407 331 9500 for more info. **Rainbow Wheels** (www.rainbowwheels.com) is another specialist company that rents full-size or mini vans equipped for wheelchair users. Call them on 407 365 8813.

Reader Les Willans confirms: 'Orlando is superb when it comes to accessibility for wheelchair users like myself, but Americans often use quite offensive language, such as the term "handicapped", when referring to the disabled.'

Another helpful website is www.accessibleverything.com which aims to provide detailed info to plan holidays for wheelchair, pram or walking stick users.

Orlando for grown-ups

It may sound daft to include information specifically for adults, but it is an often overlooked aspect that you don't need to have kids in tow to enjoy Orlando. In fact, I've often felt the place is actually too good for kids! There is so much clever detail and imagination that it is usually the grown-ups who get the most out of the experience. In fact, just as many couples and singles visit the parks.

BRIT TIP: If you have a fridge in your accommodation, put drink cartons in the freezer overnight and they will be cool for much of the next day in your back-pack. Better still, buy a cheap cool bag, freeze it with some water bottles in, and leave it in the car – great after a day in the parks.

Certainly, when you look at some of the entertainment on offer at places like *Pleasure Island* and CityWalk, the downtown district and The Pointe*Orlando, the great range of bars and the proliferation of fine restaurants in recent years, with a good number of romantic offerings, it is easy to see the attraction for those 21 and over. As well as Florida being a key honeymoon destination, its friendly, social atmosphere provides an ideal place for singles, while couples without children can also take advantage of the late opening hours at the parks and clubs like Jellyrolls at *Disney's Boardwalk Resort*.

Orlando for Seniors

If it's true Orlando has just as much to offer grown-ups as kids, then the more mature traveller can also benefit from a healthy dose of the Sunshine State. And, if my parents (both in their 60s) are any guide, they will have just as much fun, within slightly different parameters. For the older person, staying on site in *Walt Disney World Resort Florida* is recommended as it removes the stress of driving. The extra cost is offset, my parents felt, by the beauty and convenience of their

Top 10 Romantic Restaurants

1 Tchoup Chop, Universal's Royal Pacific Resort
2 Park Plaza Gardens, Winter Park
3 California Grill, Disney's Contemporary Resort
4 Jiko, Disney's Animal Kingdom Lodge
5 The Boheme, Grand Bohemian Hotel
6 Manuel's on the 28th, Bank of America building, downtown Orlando
7 Old Hickory Steakhouse, Gaylord Palms Resort
8 Atlantis, Renaissance Orlando Resort
9 Arthur's 27, Wyndham Palace Resort
10 Moonfish, Sand Lake Road

surroundings. In the parks, they found there was still plenty for them to do, even if they weren't keen on most of the thrill rides (although just watching can be entertainment enough!). *Epcot* and *Disney's Animal Kingdom Theme Park* both have much to engage the older visitor,

The Disney Wedding Pavilion

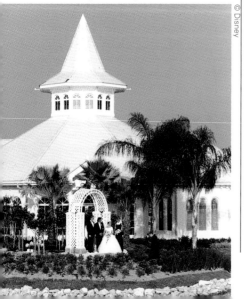

© Disney

while the shows of *Disney-MGM Studios* make that a popular choice, too, and the *Magic Kingdom Park*, while 'probably the noisiest of all the parks', still represents an essential experience.

The *Downtown Disney* area can feel a bit frenetic for the senior crowd, but *Disney's Boardwalk Resort* is popular and the whole of the *Epcot* resort area offers much in the way of fine dining and relaxation. In fact, this is often a prime area for seniors, notably the quieter *Disney's Yacht and Beach Club Resorts*, and the superb Swan-Dolphin complex. For my parents in particular, the highlights they recommend for their age group are: Jim Henson's Muppet Vision 3-D and Fantasmic! at *Disney-MGM Studios*; Kilimanjaro Safaris, the Maharajah Jungle Trek and Festival of the Lion King at *Disney's Animal Kingdom Theme Park*; Spaceship Earth, Universe of Energy, Test Track and IllumiNations at *Epcot* (plus the wonderful gardens and architecture); The Haunted Mansion, Jungle Cruise, Pirates Of The Caribbean and the monorail ride to the *Magic Kingdom Park*; watching the children at the many parades and character greetings; dinner at the California Grill in *Disney's Contemporary Resort*; shopping at Orlando Premium Outlets; most of Universal Studios, but less of Islands of Adventure (although they were wowed – as most are – by the Amazing Adventures of Spider-Man).

Weatherwise, March was just about ideal for them, but they wouldn't be keen to visit in the summer. Seniors can also take advantage of many discounts and special deals for their age group at the attractions as well as at many restaurants and hotels. The Official Visitor Center on I-Drive (see map on page 76) publishes a brochure of all the deals (www.orlandoinfo.com).

Repeat visitors

Repeat visitors create a large part of the Orlando market and are always on the lookout for something new after they have done all the main parks. To that end, our Off The Beaten Track chapter (see pages 208–35) is largely designed with them in mind. However, it is useful here to list 10 things which are worth doing once you have Been There and Done That:

1) Behind the scenes tours at the Disney parks.
2) Pony rides at *Disney's Fort Wilderness Resort* and carriage rides at both Fort Wilderness and *Disney's Port Orleans Resort*.
3) A weekend visit to *Disney's Wilderness Preserve* in Poinciana, Kissimmee.
4) The scenic boat ride at Winter Park.
5) Historic Bok Sanctuary in Lake Wales.
6) Lunch or dinner (and a visit to the soup cannery!) at the eclectic Chalet Suzanne – also Lake Wales.
7) Breakfast at East Lake Fish Camp, followed by an airboat ride.
8) Sunset celebration at Key West area inside Gaylord Palms Resort.
9) Jazz evenings in Bosendorfer Lounge at The Grand Bohemian Hotel downtown.
10) Friday night rodeo at Kissimmee Sports Arena.

Measurements

American clothes sizes are smaller than ours, hence a US size 12 dress is a UK size 14, or an American jacket sized 42 is really a 44. Shoes are the opposite: a US 10 should fit a British size 9 foot. Their measuring system is also still imperial and NOT metric.

American-speak

Another thing to watch out for are words or phrases that have a different meaning across the Atlantic. For instance, when Americans say the first floor, they mean the ground floor, the second floor is really the first, and so on. (NB: NEVER ask for a packet of fags. Fag is a crude, slang term for homosexual.) See table on page 38.

Wedding bells

Florida is increasingly sought after by couples looking to tie the knot (some 20,000 couples a year at the last count), and Orlando offers a terrific range of wedding services, from ceremony co-ordinators, photography and flowers to a wonderfully scenic range of venues like Cypress Grove Park, Winter Park and Leu Gardens, plus more unusual ones, such as in a balloon, the pit-lane of the Richard Petty Driving Experience at *Walt Disney World Resort in Florida* or even at 145mph (233 kph) around the speedway itself!

Walt Disney World's Wedding Pavilion offers true fairytale romance, with the backdrop of Cinderella Castle and Seven Seas Lagoon. You can opt for traditional elegance in this Victorian setting with up to 260 guests or the full Disney experience, arriving in Cinderella's glass coach with Mickey and Minnie among the guests.

The Gaylord Palms Wedding Pavilion

American	English	American	English
Check or Tab	Bill	Lines	Queues, so 'Stand in line' not 'Queue up'
Restroom	Public toilet		
Bathroom	Private toilet		
Eggs 'over easy'	Eggs fried both sides but soft	Elevator	Lift
		Underpass	Subway
Eggs 'over hard'	Eggs fried both sides but hard!	Subway	Underground
		Mailbox	Postbox
Eggs 'sunny side up'	Eggs fried on just one side (soft)	Faucet	Tap
		Collect call	Reverse charge phone call
French fries	Chips		
Chips	Crisps	Gas	Petrol
Cookie	Biscuit	Gas pedal	Accelerator
Grits	Porridge-like breakfast dish made out of ground, boiled corn	Trunk	Car boot
		Hood	Car bonnet
		Fender	Car bumper
		Antenna	Aerial
		Windshield	Windscreen
Biscuit	Savoury scone	Stickshift	Manual transmission
Hash browns	Grated, fried potato (delicious!)	Trailer	Caravan
Jelly	Jam	Freeway	Motorway
Silverware or place-setting	Cutlery	Divided highway	Dual carriageway
		Denver boot	Wheel clamp
Liquor	Spirits	Turn-out	Lay-by
Seltzer	Soda water	No standing	No parking OR stopping
Shot	Measure		
Liquor store	Off-licence	Parking lot	Car park
Broiled	Grilled	Semi	Articulated truck
Grilled	Flame-grilled	Ramp	Slip-road
Sub	Torpedo roll	Intersection	Junction
Shrimp	King prawn	Construction	Roadworks
Sherbet	Sorbet	Yield	Give way
Eggplant	Aubergine	Purse	Handbag
Appetiser	Starter	Fanny pack	Bumbag
Entree	Main course	Pants	Trousers
To go	Take-away (as in food)	Undershirt	Vest
		Vest	Waistcoat
Candy	Sweets	Pantyhose	Tights
Drug store	Chemist	Sneakers	Trainers
Bandaid	Plaster	Shorts	Underpants
Movie theater	Cinema	Facecloth/ washcloth	Flannel
Sidewalk	Pavement		
Pavement	Roadway	Quarter	25 cents
Bill	Note (as in $5 note)	Dime	10 cents
		Nickel	5 cents
Crib	Cot	Downtown	The city or town centre (not the rundown part!)
Cot or rollaway	Fold-up bed		
Diaper	Nappy		
Stroller	Pushchair	A/C	Air-conditioning

Disney's wedding organisers can tailor-make the occasion for individual requirements (407 828 3400). Universal provides a wedding service based at their beautiful Portofino Bay Hotel. Call 407 503 1120 for their wedding specialist.

All the main tour operators feature wedding options and co-ordinated services, and offer a variety of ceremonies including ones aboard a hot air balloon or helicopter, on the beach or a luxury yacht. Prices vary from £595 per couple (Cypress Grove Park in Orlando – Thomson) to £1,980 (Disney's Premium Intimate Wedding package – Virgin).

You can also **do it yourself** by calling at the Osceola County Administrative Building, 17 South Vernon Street, Room 231-A, Kissimmee between 8.30am–4.30pm, Mon–Fri (407 847 1424). In Orange County, apply to the Orange County Courthouse on 425 N Orange Avenue (407 836 2067) 8am–5pm, Mon–Fri. Both parties must be present to apply for the marriage licence, which costs $88.50 (in cash) and is valid for 60 days, while the ceremony (equivalent to a British register office) can be performed at the same time by the clerk for an extra $20 (8–11am or 2–4pm, Mon–Fri). Passports and birth certificates are required and, after acquiring a marriage licence, a couple can get married anywhere in Florida. Witnesses are not required, neither are blood tests.

BRIT TIP: If you shop at any Wal-Mart store in America, you can return faulty or wrong-size goods to your local Asda for a refund, provided you keep your receipts.

The County's Marriage Department can also supply names of public notaries to conduct the ceremony if you want to marry elsewhere, like at one of the more picturesque resort hotels. Call the Orlando/Orange County Convention & Visitors' Bureau for an info pack (407 363 5872), visit www.orlandoweddinglocations.com or call 407 876 6433.

Those looking for a church or other place of worship can visit the **Center of Light Church & Spiritual Center** on East Robinson Street (407 228 0101), the **First Baptist Church** on John Young Parkway (407 425 2555), **St Nicholas Catholic Church** on Sand Lake Road (407 351 0133) or **Trinity Lutheran Church** on East Livingston Street downtown (407 422 5704, www.trinitydowntown.org).

Disney Special Occasions

Birthday badges: free badges can be found at City Hall in the *Magic Kingdom Park* and Guest Services at *Epcot, Disney-MGM Studios* and *Disney's Animal Kingdom Park*. Cast Members like to make a fuss over children (and even adults!) wearing a birthday badge.

Birthday cakes: contact room service at your resort, or Guest Services at one of the parks. All Disney restaurants can offer cakes (starting at $7.99). Be sure to tell the Cast Member at check-in (or when you make your hotel reservation) as well as hostesses and/or servers in restaurants, if someone in your party has a birthday. While it is not guaranteed, Disney staff often go out of their way to make the day special. If characters know it's a birthday when they sign a child's autograph book, they may add a special birthday wish to their signature.

Birthday cruise: the IllumiNations cruises (to the *Epcot* park) and the motorboat *Breathless* (from *Disney's Yacht and Beach Club Resorts*) both host birthday celebrations, with cake and refreshments provided, and the boat can be decorated (by Disney). Small boat holds 8 guests for $150 (plus tax), large pontoon boat holds 12 guests at $220 (plus tax).

Birthday parties: *Disney's Yacht and Beach Club Resorts* arrange birthday parties for ages 4 and up. A 3-hour party for up to 12 guests is $300. Decorations, birthday cake, use of the games at the Sandcastle Club, arcade games (free), video games, Disney movies on TV and access to Stormalong Bay are included. Parties can be booked at either 11am or 12 noon. Menu is pizza, hot dogs, hamburgers, chips, and soda. Call 407 934 3750.

The *Winter Summerland Miniature Golf* hosts 2-hour birthday parties for 10 or more, including pizza, sodas, cake, party favours and a round of mini golf. Cost is $16.95 a head, plus tax. Call 407 WDW-PLAY, and you need to book at least one week ahead.

Sunset over Clearwater

DisneyQuest has Birthday Tickets at $33 for adults, $27 per child (3–9), which includes admission, one meal coupon, one $5 Prize Play card and 20% off merchandise at the Emporium (good only for the day of the event).

Anniversaries: a *Re-hitching Ceremony* is free at the Garden Grill in the Land Pavilion in *Epcot*. You must request it when you book. Sometimes, the Cast Member may not be familiar with it, but insist they include it in your notes. Once you arrive, be sure it has been noted when you check in. A Cast Member will act as the 'preacher', and sometimes characters take the part of 'witnesses'. The quick ceremony includes a cake for 6–8 (from $7.99), and a certificate and ends with a timed kiss! Great fun.

Ice Cream Social: for a birthday or anniversary event (Re-hitching Ceremony available), or for no occasion at all, at just $6.75, the same Garden Grill serves up a huge ice cream creation with Mickey, Pluto and Chip 'n Dale. Offered twice daily at 3 and 3.30pm, the Social can easily replace a meal and provides good character interaction at a price far below a typical character meal. Booking is advisable, though, on 407 WDW-DINE.

Safety first

While crime is not a serious issue in central Florida, this is still big-city America and, as with all big cities, you need to keep your wits about you. You don't leave your common sense at home.

The area has its own Tourist Oriented Policing Service (or TOPS), centred on I-Drive, with more than 70 officers patrolling purely the main tourist areas, arranging crime prevention seminars with local hotels and generally ensuring Orlando takes good care of its visitors. You will often see the local police in these areas out on mountain bikes, and they are a polite, helpful bunch should you need their assistance or to ask them directions. Tourism is such a vital part of the local economy the authorities cannot afford not to be seen to be taking an active role against crime, hence the area has a highly safety-conscious attitude.

However, it would be foolish not to stick to the usual safety guidelines when travelling abroad.

For example, just as it would be inadvisable to walk around the darker corners of London late at night, so it would be the same in parts of Florida.

Emergencies

General: in an emergency of any kind, for police, fire department or ambulance, dial 911 (9-911 from your hotel room). It is a good idea to make sure your children are aware of this number, while for smaller-scale crises (mislaid tickets or passports, rescheduled flights, etc) your holiday company should have an emergency contact number in the hotel reception. If you are travelling independently and run into passport or other problems that require the assistance of the British Consulate in Orlando, their office is located in Sun Bank Towers, 200 South Orange Avenue, with walk-in visitors' hours 9.30am–noon and 2–4pm, or phone 9.30am–4pm on 407 426 7855.

> BRIT TIP: A handy idea for your journey over is to use a business address rather than your home address on all your luggage. It is less conspicuous and safer should any item be stolen or misplaced.

Great shopping at Lake Buena Vista

Phone and 2-way radio rentals

Mobile phones and 2-way radios are among the most useful gadgets at the best of times, but they take on a popular new role in Orlando, in terms of both safety and convenience. Many families now hire a phone or radio to keep in touch around the parks and it is common to see them in use. And, when it comes to either one, a *Brit's Guide* partner provides an excellent service in this field. **Action Radio & Cell** at 7611 South Orange Blossom Trail rents both mobile phones (or cellphones, as they are known in the US) and radios at $10/day, $30/week or $75/month, with minute usage at $1/minute, and calls back to the UK at an additional $1.75/minute (substantially cheaper than any hotel rate). For the more advanced Nextel phone/radio, it is $15/day or $50/week with the same per minute call charges. Action Radio & Cell can be found just north of the Florida Mall, and they can also deliver to your hotel. For more details, call 407 354 4890 outside the US or freephone 1-800 717 3717 in Florida, or check out their website at www.radiogirlz.com.

Phonecards which you need to make a call from a local payphone – and is a much cheaper option than phoning from your hotel room – are available from most 7-Eleven stores or your tour representative.

Hotel security

While in your hotel, motel or guesthouse, you should always use door peepholes and security chains whenever someone knocks at the door. DON'T open the door to strangers without asking for identification, and check with the hotel desk if you are still not sure.

It is stating the obvious, but keep doors and windows locked at all times and always use deadlocks and security chains. It is still surprising how many people forget basic precautions when they are on holiday (the local police never cease to be amazed at how many people leave their common sense at home!). Always take your cash, credit cards, valuables and car keys when you go out (or use room safes, which are often provided), and don't leave the door open at any time, even if you are just popping down the corridor to the ice machine. And make a point of asking hotels about their safety precautions when you make a reservation. Do their rooms have electronic card-locks (which can't be duplicated) and do they have security staff?

Don't be afraid to ask reception staff for safety pointers in the surrounding areas or if you are travelling somewhere you are not sure about. Safety is a major issue for the Central Florida Hotel/Motel Association and hotel staff are usually well briefed to be helpful. Using a bumbag (the Americans call them fanny packs!) is a better bet than a shoulder bag or handbag.

Nothing is guaranteed to get the local police shaking their heads in disbelief than the tourist who goes round looking like an obvious tourist. The map over the steering wheel is a giveaway, but other no-nos are wearing large amounts of jewellery, carrying masses of photographic equipment or flashing wads of cash around. The biggest giveaway is leaving your camera or camcorder on view in the car (which is also inadvisable, as the heat build-up in a car in summer can ruin some equipment).

Finally, and this is VERY strong police advice, in the unlikely event of being confronted by an assailant, DO NOT resist or 'have a go', as it can often result in making the situation more serious.

Money and valuables

It is unnecessary to carry large amounts of cash around with you. US travellers' cheques are accepted almost everywhere as cash and can be readily replaced if lost or stolen, as can credit cards, which are another widespread form of currency. Visa, Mastercard and American Express are all widely accepted. The Sun Bank in *Disney's Magic Kingdom Park* and *Epcot* is open 7 days a week should you need extra help with any financial transactions. It is worth separating the larger notes from the smaller ones in your wallet to avoid flashing all your money in view. Losing £200 of travellers' cheques shouldn't ruin your holiday – but losing $300 in cash might.

Most hotels will offer the use of safes and deposit boxes for your valuables, and many rooms now have mini-safes in which it is a good idea

> **BRIT TIP:** If your room has already been cleaned before you go out for the day, hang the 'Do Not Disturb' sign on the door.

to leave your passports, return tickets, cameras etc, when you don't need them. Always keep your valuables out of sight, whether in the hotel room or the car. Shut your jacket or camera in the boot.

Car safety

Car crime is one of the biggest forms of criminal activity in America and has led to some of the most lurid headlines, especially in the Miami area in the mid-1990s. Once again, it pays to make a number of basic safety checks before you set off anywhere. The first thing is to familiarise yourself with the car's controls BEFORE you leave the hire company's depot. Which button is the air-conditioning, which side of the steering wheel are the indicators and where the windscreen wipers are.

Also, make sure you know your route in advance, even if it is only a case of memorising the road numbers. Most hire firms now give good directions to all the hotels from their depot, so read them before you set off – trying to drive with the map over the steering wheel is just asking for an accident.

BRIT TIP: If you want to be extra safety conscious, you can hire mobile phones, pagers and even 2-way radios from as little as $50 a week from Action Radio & Cell (see page 41).

Check that the petrol tank is full and never let it get near empty. Running out of 'gas' in an unfamiliar area holds obvious hazards. If you stray off your pre-determined route, stick to well-lit areas and stop to ask directions only from official businesses like hotels and petrol stations or better still, a police patrol. Always try to park close to your destination where there are plenty of lights and DO NOT get out if there are any suspicious characters lurking around. Always keep your windows closed (you've got air-conditioning, remember?), and don't hesitate to lock the doors from the inside if you feel threatened (larger cars have doors that lock automatically as you drive off). And don't forget to lock the doors when you leave the car. Not many rental cars have central locking, so it's wise to double check.

BRIT TIP: Be forewarned all American banknotes are EXACTLY the same green colour and size. It is only the picture of the president and the denomination in each corner that change.

Miami crooks developed the habit of trying to get cars to stop by trying to look official or deliberately bumping into hire cars from behind. The easily identified hire car plates have now been phased out, but still NEVER stop for a non-official request. Go instead to the nearest petrol station or police station, and always insist on ID before unlocking your car and getting out of it for an official.

It is comforting to know that a unique aspect of driving in Orlando is none of the main tourist areas have any no-go areas. The nearest is the portion of the Orange Blossom Trail south of downtown Orlando. This houses a selection of strip clubs and 'adult bars' that can be downright seedy at night.

For more information on safety, contact the Community Affairs office of Orange County Police on 407 836 3720 or the TOPS office on 407 351 9368.

Know before you go

You can contact these organisations for advance tourist information. Florida Tourism (www.flausa.com) have an info line on 0900 1600 555 (60p/minute) that lists all Florida destinations and gives other consumer lines in the UK, while they have a free information pack if you call 01737 644882 (plus some more great ideas on www.culturallyflausa.com). The Orlando Tourism Bureau in London has a 24-hour information line on 0800 018 6799, on which you can request their free *Destination Imagination* info pack or visit www.orlandoinfo.com/uk. The Orlando/Kissimmee information line is 09001 600 220 (calls 60p per min). You can also visit the Kissimmee Convention & Visitors Bureau at www.floridakiss.com.

When you arrive in the area, it is also worth checking out Orlando's ONLY official **Visitor Center** at 8723 International Drive (407 363 5872) for discounted attraction tickets, free brochures and accommodation advice and free information pamphlets and maps. The Kissimmee Visitor Center is at the eastern end of the Highway 192 tourist drag (407 847 5000 or 1-800 327 9159 in the States) and they have a toll-free accommodation line in the US on 1-800 333 KISS.

Of course, THE website for all things Orlando and Disney is the fun and info-packed **www.wdwinfo.com**, to which I also contribute. The creation and maintenance of this independent site is a mind-boggling feat. It provides up-to-the-minute advice and assistance including the complete range of theme park info (right down to rides under refurbishment, park hours and ride height requirements), news, weather, facts, figures and tips, plus discounts throughout Orlando, discussion boards and a chat forum. I also rate www.wdwig.com very highly (especially for its restaurant info).

The official sites are pretty good, too, with Disney's the pick of the bunch: www.disneyworld.co.uk (check opening hours, parades and book online). Then there is www.universalorlando.com, plus www.seaworld.com and www.buschgardens.com. The local newspaper has a Calendar 'what's on' section, (www.orlandosentinel.com) and the free Orlando Weekly (www.orlandoweekly.com) is full of helpful info.

Among the many unofficial websites (not approved by Disney) are www.wdwmagic.com (great for Disney trivia and rumours), the well-designed www.wdisneyw.co.uk (with more pages for UK visitors) and www.orlandorocks.com (for all theme park addicts).

Now, on to the real thing…

International Drive by night

Driving and Car Hire
(or, The Secret of Getting Around on Interstate 4)

For the vast majority, introduction to Orlando proper comes immediately after clearing the airport via the potentially bewildering local road systems in a newly acquired, left-hand drive hire car. Yet driving here is a lot more simple and, on the whole, enjoyable than driving in the UK. In fact, anyone used to the M25 should find Orlando's motorways far less stressful.

Before you get to your hire car, however, a quick note about Orlando International Airport and Orlando Sanford Airport, which you need to be aware of on arrival (see also Chapter 12).

Orlando International – in the process of completing a major refurbishment project – is one of the most modern and enjoyable airports you will encounter, but it does have a bewildering double baggage collection system. You disembark at one of four satellite terminals and collect your luggage straight after going through Immigration, then put it on another baggage carousel that takes it to the main terminal while you ride the shuttle.

Once in the main terminal you will be on Level 3 and need to descend to Level 2 for baggage reclaim. Porters will help you down to Level 1 for car pick-up (remember the $1/bag tip), while the trolleys need $1 in change to operate, or a credit card. Taxis and limos are also on Level 1. Several tour operators have help desks here, too. The public bus system, Lynx (see next page), operates from the A side of Level 1, in spaces A32–34.

If you are arriving in the evening, consider checking straight into the **Hyatt Regency** hotel (see page 79) inside Orlando International Airport rather than driving off tired, then you'll feel refreshed ready to drive the next day.

> BRIT TIP: Make sure you follow the correct instructions to collect your hire car. There are several desks for each of the companies and if you do not check in at the right one, you will waste a lot of time.

The main hire companies with check-in desks at the airport are Dollar, National, Budget, Avis, and of course *Brit's Guide* partners Alamo, and all offer a comprehensive service (Alamo used to work out of a depot but are now on site in the airport, boosting their all-round efficiency). However, there is also a phone desk at Level 1 that connects to another 14 companies at off-airport depots, which can sometimes work out better value.

The off-airport rental firms will have a regular free shuttle outside on Level 1 to take you to their nearby depots, which will give you a

The I-Ride trolley

BRIT TIP: If you are hiring a car from one of the Big Five, save time by going to their desk to complete forms BEFORE collecting your luggage again.

preview of the roads before you take to them. Hertz and Avis are the biggest companies in the US, but Dollar and Alamo are tops for tourist business. Dollar is included in typical packages by Thomson, Airtours, Virgin, Style Holidays, Travel City and First Choice, while Alamo are the main clients for Unijet, Funway, Jetlife, Jetsave, Kuoni, British Airways Holidays and Thomas Cook, among others.

Orlando without a car

Although being mobile is advisable, it is possible to survive without a car. However, few of the attractions are within walking distance of hotels and taxis can be expensive, and you also need to plan your campaign with much greater precision to allow for extra travelling time between attractions (and, with children, taking buses can be tiring). If you decide not to drive, your best base is either *Walt Disney World Resort in Florida* (free transport throughout, but harder to get to the rest of Orlando) or International Drive (I-Drive) for its location, good pavements and the great I-Ride Trolley.

Many hotels have free shuttles to some of the main parks or a cheap regular mini-bus service.

There are basically three different transport routes. The reliable, cheap, but slightly plodding **Lynx bus system** covers much of Metro Orlando. For information visit www.golynx.com, or call 407 841 8240. Ask for a copy of their excellent System Map, which shows

all their routes (or 'Links') and the main attractions. Worth noting are **Link 42** from Orlando International Airport to I-Drive; **Links 56** and **304**, respectively from Kissimmee and the I-Drive area to *Walt Disney World Resort in Florida*; **Link 18** from Kissimmee to downtown Orlando; **Link 55**, which covers a large part of Highway 192 in Kissimmee from Osceola Square Mall all the way west past Splendid China to Secret Lake Drive; **Link 38**, I-Drive to downtown Orlando; and **Links 50** and **300**, which both operate from Disney to downtown Orlando. It costs $1 a ride (plus 10 cents for transfers) or $10 for a weekly pass (children 6 and under go free with a full-fare passenger). The service is every 30 minutes in the main areas, every 15 minutes from 6–9am and 3.30–6.30pm, but remember to have the right change. Lynx bus stops are marked by pink paw-print signs and all the buses are wheelchair accessible. There can be a considerable queue for the Lynx buses back from Disney at closing time, and it may be more worthwhile getting Disney transport to *Downtown Disney*, spending some time there, then getting a cab back to your hotel (about $25 to I-Drive).

The I-Drive area also has the great-value **I-Ride trolley**, which operates two routes along a 14-mile (23-km) stretch of this tourist corridor. The *Main Line* runs from the Universal Orlando resort area of Windhover Drive and Major Boulevard in the north, via Belz shopping centre at the top of I-Drive, to SeaWorld via Westwood Boulevard and Sea Harbor Drive, and on to Orlando Premium Outlets in the south. The *Green Line* basically covers Universal Boulevard, from the Orange County Convention Center up to the junction of I-Drive and Kirkman Road (407 354 5656, www.iridetrolley.com). Running

BRIT TIP: Don't want to drive? Consider a multi-centre stay within Orlando itself, staying first at, say, International Drive or Universal Orlando and then a Disney resort, to get the best out of the free/cheap transport options.

every day, 7am–10.30pm at roughly 15-minute intervals (30 minutes on the Green Line), it costs 75cents per trip (25 cents for seniors) – please have the right change – or you can buy Unlimited Ride passes for 1, 3, 5, 7 or 14 days at $2, $3, $5, $7 or $14. You can buy your 14-day pass at the official Visitor Center on I-Drive by Austrian Court and save $2 (see map on page 76). If you need to transfer between routes, ask for a transfer coupon when you board (transfers are free with Unlimited Ride passes). Kids 12 and under go free with an adult, and all trolleys have hydraulic lifts for wheelchairs. Passes are sold at 75 locations along the I-Drive area, including most hotel service desks and visitor centres.

One other regular service worth noting is from SeaWorld to Busch Gardens in Tampa, with six departure points daily from 8.15–9.30am. Called the **Busch Shuttle Express**, it costs $5 a person but is free if you have bought Busch tickets in advance (included in the 5-Park Orlando FlexTicket). For more details, see page 171.

As an alternative to public transport, there is a raft of well-organised firms who offer **shuttle services** to the attractions for a set fee and excursions to places like Kennedy Space Center and Busch Gardens that pick up at the hotels.

The main firms are Mears (407 423 5566 or visit www.mearstransportation.com) and Coach USA (407 826 9999, www.coachusa.com). Mears offers the most comprehensive service, from limousines to coaches, and typical round-trip shuttle fares would be: Airport–Walt Disney World, $28/person ($20/child, ages 4–11; or $16 and $12 one-way); Airport–I-Drive, $24/person ($17/child; $14 and $10 one way); Airport–Highway 192 in Kissimmee $28–40/person ($20–31/child); *Walt Disney World*–Universal Orlando, $13/person round trip; I-Drive–*Walt Disney World*, $13/person; I-Drive or *Walt Disney World*–Kennedy Space Center, $20/person. Mears also offers a SuperPass service of 3, 4, 5, 6, 7 days of unlimited service to and from the main area attractions (including airport transfers) from I-Drive or *Walt Disney World* for $59, $70, $81, $92, $103 ($53, $63, $74, $85, $96 per child 3–11). You can book a Mears shuttle on arrival at one of their desks in the luggage halls, but it can be a long journey to your hotel if they have a full van. **Coach USA** offers a full-day's excursion to the Kennedy Space Center (including entry) for $66 ($54 children 3–9; $30 transport only), or $30 for a day trip to Cocoa Beach. Coach USA also provides shuttle services from Orlando Sanford Airport at $40 round trip per person to most of the main tourist areas ($21/person one way).

Quick Transportation comes well recommended for its excellent luxury van, town car and limousine service. They offer a highly personal and efficient alternative to taxis and shuttles for airport transfers and can be more economical for larger groups. Town cars will cope with a family of four, while there are spacious vans for larger parties (plus the limos). The driver meets you in the baggage hall and takes you directly to the hotel with no stops. Look up their useful website

> **BRIT TIP:** The boot size of American cars tends to be smaller than the British equivalent. And you will not get 7 people PLUS their luggage in a 7-seater people carrier!

(www.quicktransportation.com) for an insight into arriving at Orlando International. Luxury van rates (for up to 7) one way from the airport range from $41.50 to the I-Drive area up to $66.50 for the farthest parts of *Walt Disney World*. Up to 12 can be accommodated in a van for a small additional fee per person. Town car rates are $68.50 one way from the airport to anywhere in Greater Orlando and $136 round trip, while stretch limos are $106 and $208.75. Larger parties may need a luggage trailer for $17.50 extra each way. They offer a personalised service to all the theme parks and attractions, plus round-trip transportation from Orlando to Port Canaveral for any cruise connections. Every Tuesday they organise a shuttle to Kennedy Space Center for $25/person round trip. Look up their website or call 1-888 784 2522 (in the USA) or 407 354 2456 (outside the US).
You can also try **Florida Tours** (1-800 790 6290, www.fltours.com), who operate town cars, luxury vans – for up to 10 people – and limousines, or Tiffany Town Car (www.tiffany towncar.com), but Quick Transportation get the official *Brit's Guide* seal of approval.

Downtown Orlando

Excursion services are offered by the likes of Coach USA, Gray Line (303 433 9800, www.grayline.com), International Divers (407 352 5151, www.swimdolphins.com), and Keith Prowse (see page 13).
Several of the big shopping malls have their own shuttle or pick-up service. **Lake Buena Vista Factory Stores** collects guests free on a daily basis from more than 40 hotels in the Orlando and Kissimmee areas (check with your hotel for details, or call 407 363 1093). **Orlando Premium Outlets** offers a shuttle service with Maingate Transportation at $6 round-trip from hotels in the Lake Buena Vista area and $9 from Kissimmee hotels (call 407 390 0000). The **Florida Mall** has a free shuttle service twice daily from hotels in the I-Drive and Lake Buena Vista area (check with your hotel concierge or call the Mall at 407 851 6255 or visit www.florida-mall-fl.com).

Taxis

For groups of four or five, **taxis** can be a more cost-effective option than the shuttles. Orlando International to I-Drive would cost around $35, plus tip (about $8 each for five), $12 from I-Drive to Universal Orlando and $25 from I-Drive to *Downtown Disney*. You will find plenty of taxis waiting in ranks at the parks, hotels and shopping centres, but they don't cruise around looking for fares, so it is usually best to book one in advance. You also need to ensure you choose a reliable, fully insured company (Orlando has what is known as 'Gypsy' cab drivers, who appear to be with reputable firms but often do not have full passenger insurance). Look to see that the name and phone number of the cab company is clearly displayed on the side, that the driver's ID and insurance is visible and their rates are shown on the window or inside the car. 'Gypsy' drivers look for fares in the airport baggage hall, which is strictly illegal – all legitimate taxis should be in the rank on Level 1. The Mears group (407 699 9999) has three firms who work (via computer system) through them, Checker Cabs, Yellow Cabs and City Cabs, all of which are reliable. Most taxis are metered but it is also acceptable to ask what the fare will be in advance. Other reputable firms include Central Florida Taxi (407 851 7523 or freephone 1-800 441 3276 in Florida), Star Taxis (407 857 9999), Diamond Cab Co (407 523 3333) and Town & Country (407 828 3035; they tend not to run their meters, but they will happily do so if you ask, or just ask what the fare will be in advance). Several hotels have Town Cars (a smarter, more upmarket taxi) at their ranks, and these will not have meters, so you can either ask what the fare will be or call one of the companies listed above yourself.

The car

Ultimately, having a car is the key to being in charge of your holiday and, on a weekly basis, it tends to work out quite reasonable.

Weekly rental rates can be as low as $100 for the smallest size of car, an **Economy** (or Sub-compact), usually a Corsa-sized hatchback; next up is the **Compact**, a small family saloon like a Vauxhall Astra; the **Midsize** (or Intermediate) is a more spacious 4-door, 5-seater like a Vectra; and the **Fullsize** would be a large-style executive car like an Omega, and you can go up the scale still, with **Premium**, **Luxury** and **Convertible**, plus the **Minivan**, a Renault Espace or VW Sharan type.

But beware these low starting rates. There are a number of essential insurances, taxes and surcharges, and these can easily take the final weekly rate to $280 or more. However, all the big rental companies now offer all-inclusive rates, which can work out significantly cheaper if booked in advance in the UK. Rates can be as low as £150 a week, and you also benefit from easier processing at the Orlando end, making the whole business quicker. To book, call **Alamo** (see inside the front cover for our special readers' offer) or **Dollar** on 0800 252897. Or you could try **Avis** (0990 900 500); **Budget** (0880 181181); **Thrifty** (0990 168 238); **Hertz** (0990 906090); **National** (0345 222525); or **Suncars** (0990 005566).

The scale of the car-hire operation is huge, with as many as 400 visitors arriving at a time. Most British holiday companies offer 'free car hire', but that does not mean it won't cost you anything. It is only the *rental* cost that is free and you must still pay the insurance, taxes and other extras BEFORE you drive away (which makes the all-inclusive packages even more attractive).

Having a credit card is essential, and there are two main kinds of insurance, the most important being the Loss or Collision Damage Waiver, LDW or CDW. This costs around $20 a day and covers you for any damage to your hire car. You can manage without it, but the hire company will insist on a huge deposit in the order of $1,500 on your credit card (and you are also liable for ANY damage).

You will also be offered Supplemental Liability Insurance

BRIT TIP: Double-check that you have your driving licence BEFORE you leave home. Without it you will simply NOT be given a hire car.

(SLI) or Extended Protection at around $13 a day. This covers you against being sued for astronomical amounts by any court-happy American you may happen to bump into (not essential, but good for your peace of mind). Relatively new and again optional is the Underinsured Motorists Protection (in case somebody with only minimal cover runs into you) at around $6 a day. Drivers under 25 have to pay an extra $15–20 a day, while all drivers must be at least 21. Other rental costs include local and Florida state taxes, which

> BRIT TIP: Be firm with the hire company check-in clerk, some can push you into extras, like car upgrades that you don't need.

add $7 a day to your final bill, and Airport Handling Tax and Access Fee at $6–7 a day. Then there's petrol, although this is still appreciably cheaper than in the UK (about $10–15 to fill up). Ask to return the tank full yourself, as this will save a few dollars on their fill-up option.

For those on a tight budget, you can cut costs by arranging travel insurance before you go through specialists like Extrasure (020 7480 6871), whose Americasure policy offers both LDW and SLI at around £5 a day. You may still need to leave a credit card imprint with the hire firm, but they should accept these policies (but do still check in advance).

You may feel the effects of jet-lag for a day or two after arrival, but this can be reduced by avoiding alcohol and coffee on the plane and drinking plenty of water.

Most people soon find driving in America is a pleasure rather than a pain, mainly because nearly all hire cars are automatics and rarely more than a year old. And, because speed limits are lower (and rigidly enforced), you won't often be rushed into taking the wrong turn. Keep your foot on the brake when you are stationary as automatics tend to creep forward, and always put the automatic gear lever in 'P' (for Park) after switching off.

Controls

All cars are fitted with air-conditioning, which is essential for most of the year. Turn the fan on before the A/C button or it may not work! Don't be alarmed by a small pool of liquid under your car in summer – it's condensation off the A/C unit.

Power steering is common on many hire cars and larger cars have cruise control, which lets you set the desired speed and take your foot off the accelerator. There will be two buttons on the steering wheel, one to switch the cruise control on, the other to set the desired speed. To take the car off cruise control either press the first button again or simply touch the brake. The handbrake may also be different. Some cars have an extra foot pedal to the left of the brake, and you need to push this to engage the handbrake. To release it, you pull the tab just above it, if there isn't one, you give a second push on the pedal. The car probably won't start unless the gear lever is in 'P'. To put the car in 'D' for Drive, you also have to depress the main brake pedal. D1 and D2 are extra gears for steep hills (none in Florida!). Few cars have central locking, so make sure you lock ALL the doors.

> BRIT TIP: With an automatic, you probably won't be able to take the keys out of the ignition unless you put the car in 'Park' first.

Getting around

Your car-hire company should provide you with a basic map of Orlando, plus directions to your hotel. Insist they give you these, as all the hire companies make a big point of this in their literature. Try to familiarise yourself with the main roads of the area in advance and learn to navigate by the road numbers (as those are mainly given on the signposts) and the exit numbers of the main roads.

When you drive out of **Orlando International Airport** (or the hire company's off-airport depot) don't look for signs to 'Orlando' – the airport's new signage should be a big help here. The main tourist areas are all south and west of the city proper, so follow the appropriate signs for your hotel. For the International Drive area (or I-Drive), you want the Beeline Expressway (usually listed as Route 528) all the way west until it crosses I-Drive just north of SeaWorld. The main hotel area of I-Drive is to the north, so keep right at the exit.

For western Kissimmee and *Walt Disney World Resort in Florida* go south out of the airport and take the Central Florida Greeneway (Highway 417) all the way west until it intersects with State Route (SR) 536 at Exit 6 (for *Animal Kingdom* resorts, stay on until Exit 3 and take Osceola Parkway). Then you can follow SR536 straight across into *Walt Disney World Resort in Florida* or take the Interstate 4 (I-4) west for one junction until it hits the main Kissimmee routeway, Highway 192 (aka the Irlo Bronson Memorial Highway).

For eastern Kissimmee, come off Highway 417 at Exit 11 with the Orange Blossom Trail (Highway 441), where going south brings you on to Highway 192 at the other end of the main tourist drag.

Leaving **Orlando Sanford**

> BRIT TIP: The Beeline Expressway (528) and Greeneway (417) are both toll roads, so keep some change in the car. Toll booths are reluctant to change a note over $20.

Airport is also a straightforward affair, boosted by the airport's simple design. Dollar and Alamo have made a big impression here with their British-dedicated operations. There is no off-airport shuttle to your car to slow you down, just a quick walk from the airport's baggage reclaim hall to the car-hire office.

It may be further to the north and involve more driving (and taxis and shuttles are a lot more expensive), but you usually save time overall. Leave the airport on East Lake Mary Boulevard and quickly hit the junction with the Central Florida Greeneway (Highway 417) on which you head south. The slip-road on to this toll motorway is just under the fly-over on your LEFT, and you will need about $4.50 to reach Kissimmee or *Walt Disney World Resort in Florida* or $3.75 to reach I-Drive (via the Beeline Expressway, Route 528).

You can avoid the tolls by staying on Lake Mary Boulevard for 4 miles (6km) until you hit I-4, but you may encounter the 4–6pm snarl-up through the city centre. The Greeneway is an excellent, easy-driving introduction to Orlando roads, even if it does cost a few dollars.

For radio traffic news and reports, tune in to 1680AM.

Signs and road names

The system of signposting and road-naming can be confusing. For instance, you cannot fail to find the main attractions, but retracing your

3

steps back to the hotel afterwards can prove tricky because they often take you out of the parks a different way. (Disney is notoriously poor at sign-posting to help find your way out. A good tip is to get a copy of their Transportation Guide/Map from Guest Services at any park to help navigation.) It is vital to learn the main road numbers (and directions, either east-west or north-south) around the attractions so you know where you are heading, and whether you want I-4 east or west or 192 as you exit *Epcot* or *Disney-MGM Studios*.

> **BRIT TIP:** On the Greeneway (417) heading south, just after Exit 34, it appears to split into two where it meets Highway 408. Stay in the RIGHT lane to stay southbound.

Exits off the I-4 and other main roads can be on EITHER side of the carriageway, not just on the right. This potential worry is offset by the fact you can overtake in ANY lane on multi-lane highways, not just the outside ones. Therefore, you can sit in the middle lane until you see your exit. However, you don't get much advance notice of turn-offs.

Orlando has yet to come up with a comprehensive tourist map of its streets and the maps supplied by the car-rental companies tend to be simplified. It helps that none of the main attractions are off the beaten track, but the support of a front-seat navigator can be useful.

The Orlando airport shuttle

> **BRIT TIP:** The Osceola Parkway toll road which runs parallel to Highway 192 is a much easier route into *Walt Disney World Resort in Florida* from much of Kissimmee and costs only $1.50. Use Sherberth Road for Disney access from west 192.

Around town, road names are displayed at every junction, hung underneath the traffic lights suspended ABOVE the road. This road name is NOT the road you are on, but the one you are CROSSING. Once again there is no advance notice of each junction and the road names can be difficult to read as you approach them, especially at night, so keep your speed down if you think you are close to your turn-off so you can get in the correct lane. If you do miss a turning, nearly all the roads are arranged in a simple grid system so it is usually easy to work your way back.

Occasionally, you will meet a crossroads where no right of way is obvious. This is a **4-way stop**, and the priority goes in order of arrival, so when it's your turn you just indicate and pull out slowly (America doesn't have many roundabouts, so this is the closest you will get to one).

Tolls and traffic lights

For the toll roads, have some change handy in amounts from 25 cents to $1. They all give change (in the GREEN lanes), but you will get through much quicker if you have the correct money (in the BLUE lanes). On minor exits of Osceola Parkway and the Greeneway, there are auto-toll machines *only*, so try to keep some loose change in your car.

BRIT TIP: Be organised – get your directions in advance off the internet at excellent map sites like www.mapquest.com.

As well as the obvious difference of driving on the 'wrong' side of the road, there are also several differences in procedure. The most frequent British errors occur at traffic lights (which are hung above the road, not on posts). At a red light it is still possible to turn RIGHT, providing there is no traffic coming from the left and no pedestrians crossing, unless otherwise specified (signs will occasionally indicate 'No turn on red'). Turning left at the lights, you have the right of way with a green ARROW, but you have to give way to traffic from the other direction on a SOLID green.

The majority of accidents involving overseas visitors take place on left turns, so take extra care here. There is also no amber light from red to green, but there IS an amber light from green to red. A flashing amber light at a junction means proceed but watch for traffic joining the carriageway, while a flashing red light indicates it is okay to turn if the carriageway is clear.

Restrictions

Speed limits are always well marked with black numbering on white signs and the police are pretty hot on speeding with steep on-the-spot fines. Limits vary from 55–70mph (88–113kph) on the Interstates and can change frequently – where there is also a 40mph (64kph) *minimum* speed – to just 15 or 20mph (24 or 32kph) in some built-up areas.

Flashing orange lights suspended over the road indicate a school zone and school buses must not be overtaken in either direction when they are unloading and have their hazard lights on. U-turns are forbidden in built-up areas and where a solid line runs down the middle of the road.

It is illegal to park within 10ft (3 metres) of a fire hydrant or a lowered kerb, and never park in front of a yellow-painted kerb – they are stopping points for emergency vehicles and you will be towed away. Never park on a kerb, either.

Seat belts are compulsory for all front-seat passengers, while child seats must be used for under 4s and can be hired from the car companies at around $5 a day (better still, bring your own). Children aged 4 or 5 must either use a seat belt, whether sitting in the front or back, or have a child seat fitted for them.

You must put your lights on in the rain, and park bonnet first. Reverse parking is frowned upon because number plates are often found only on the rear of cars and police then can't see them. If you park parallel to the kerb you must be facing in the direction of the traffic. You must pull to the side of the road to allow any emergency vehicles to pass you when they have lights and/or sirens going.

Disabled drivers should note their orange disabled badge IS recognised in Florida for parking in the well-provided disabled parking spaces.

Finally, don't drink and drive. Florida has strict laws, with penalties of up to 6 months in prison for first-time offenders. The legal blood-alcohol limit is lower than in Britain,

International Drive

BRIT TIP: The Kissimmee-St Cloud tourist information office on east Highway 192 has the best free map, clearly indicating main routes and attractions.

so it is safer not to drink at all if you are driving. It is also illegal to carry open containers of alcohol in the car.

Bonus for AA members: Your membership is recognised by the equivalent AAA in the States and you also benefit from several special deals, including area maps and ticket and hotel discounts. The Florida AAA centre is in Heathrow, north of Orlando, just off Exit 98 of I-4 (turn left on Lake Mary Boulevard, then first right on to International Parkway and the AAA is half a mile down on the left). For details call the info number on the back of your AA card and ask for their USA pack. It is even worth joining the AA (about £40) for the discounts, which could add up to several hundred dollars. Call the AA on 0870 544 4444.

Accidents

In the unlikely event of having an accident, no matter how minor, you must contact the police before the cars can be moved (except on the busy I-4). Car-hire firms will insist on a full police report for the insurance. If you break down, there should be an emergency number for the hire company in their literature or, if you are on a major highway, raise the bonnet and wait for one of the frequent police patrol cars to stop (or dial *FHP on your mobile). Always carry your driving licence and hire agreement forms in case you are stopped by the police. Should you be pulled over, remain in

your car with your hands on the wheel and always be polite. Once they learn you are British, you *may* just get away with a ticking-off!

Key routes

The main route through Orlando is **Interstate 4** (or I-4), a 4-, 6- or 8-lane motorway linking the two coasts. Interstates are always indicated on blue shield-shaped signs. For most of its length, I-4 travels east-west but, around Orlando, it swings north-south, although directions are still given east (for north) or west (for south). All main motorways are prefixed I, the even numbers generally going east-west and the odd numbers north-south. Federal Highways are the next grade down and are all numbered with black numerals on white shields, while state roads are known as Routeways and prefixed SR (black numbers on white circular or oblong signs). All the attractions of *Walt Disney World Resort in Florida*, plus those of SeaWorld and Universal Orlando are well signposted from I-4. Historic Bok Sanctuary is a 45-minute drive from central Orlando (south) west on I-4 and Highway 27, while Busch Gardens is 75–90 minutes down I-4 to Tampa. The Kennedy Space Center is a good hour's drive along the Beeline Expressway (Route 528), which intersects I-4 at Junction 72.

International Drive (or I-Drive) is the second key local roadway, linking a 16-mile (26-km) ribbon of hotels, shops, restaurants and

BRIT TIP: All the Interstate exits have been renumbered, so repeat visitors must be aware that I-4 exit numbers are now different.

attractions like Wet 'n Wild, The Mercado centre and Belz Factory Outlet. (I-Drive south, from Highway 192 north to Route 535, is NOT the main stretch, although they will eventually link up.) From I-4, take Exits 71, 72, 74A or 75A going (north) east, or 75B, 74A or 72 going (south) west. To the north, I-Drive runs into Oakridge Road and then the South Orange Blossom Trail, which leads into downtown Orlando (Junctions 82C–84 off I-4). I-Drive is also bisected by Sand Lake Road and runs into Epcot Drive, via Route 536, to the south, which is also convenient for Disney's attractions.

I-Drive is a major tourist centre and makes an excellent base, especially to the south of Sand Lake Road, near The Mercado, where you have the benefit of proper pavement. It's a 20-minute drive to Disney and 10 minutes from Universal. However, it can be congested at peak times, especially around Sand Lake Road in the evening, so try to use Universal Boulevard instead.

The other main tourist area is the town of **Kissimmee**, south of Orlando and south-east of Disney and it's an attraction in its own right. Its features are grouped along a 19-mile (31-km) stretch of the Irlo Bronson Memorial Highway (192), which intersects I-4 at Junction 64B, and is only 10 minutes from *Walt Disney World Resort in Florida*, 20 from SeaWorld and 25 from Universal. The downtown area of Kissimmee is off Main Street, Broadway and Emmett Street and is ideal for walking.

A handy visual along **Highway 192** are the markers from Splendid China (Number 4) to just past Medieval Times (Number 15). These highly visible signs are good locators of many hotels, restaurants and attractions.

Fuel

At American gas stations, you will often have a choice of attendant or self-service. You do not tip the attendant but you do pay slightly more. Most gas stations will also require you to pay in advance at night, and will require the exact amount in cash or your credit card. Some pumps also allow you to pay by credit card without having to go into the cashier's office. The American gallon is smaller (by about a fifth) than the British version. Always use unleaded fuel and, to activate the petrol pump, first lift the lever underneath the pump nozzle. RaceTrac petrol stations are usually the cheapest (even for soft drinks and cigarettes), although they don't take credit cards.

Local maps

The best and most up-to-date free maps are the bright orange Welcome Guide-Map (also full of discount coupons), available in the main tourist areas, and the pull-out map inside the Kissimmee-St Cloud Visitors' Guide (from the official Visitor Center on east Highway 192, call 407 847 5000). AA members are well catered for (see page 54), but the best paid-for maps are the Trakker series, with four products covering Orlando: the Pocket Map ($4.95) is almost as detailed as the AAA ones, while the City Slicker (a laminated fold-out of the main areas, $5.95) is useful in the car. They also do a full Orlando Street Atlas ($19.95). You can contact them (and order maps) via www.trakkermaps.com or call 407 447 6485 in Orlando.

Now, let's go on to your holiday accommodation...

4 Accommodation
(or, Making Sense of American Hotels, Motels and Condos)

To list all the accommodation in the Orlando area would fill a book. Metropolitan Orlando has the second highest concentration of hotels in the world and more are being built all the time – with some 110,000 rooms and still counting. Therefore what follows is a general guide to the bigger, better or budget types.

Hotels

American hotels, particularly in the tourist areas, tend towards the motel type. The facilities and service are still great, but you won't necessarily be located in one main building. Your room may be in one of several blocks arranged around the other facilities, such as the swimming pool, restaurant, etc. This also means it is more important to be security-conscious (see page 42). The room size rarely alters, even between 2- and 4-star accommodation; extra amenities and services tend to give a hotel extra star rating. A standard room usually has two double beds and will comfortably accommodate a family of four. Most hotels offer non-smoking rooms.

Disney's Caribbean Beach Resort

The other surprising feature of motel-type accommodation is the lack of a restaurant in some cases. This is because the American hotel scene operates almost exclusively on a room-only basis – meals are usually extra – so you may have to drive to the nearest restaurant (of which there are many – see Chapter 10) just for breakfast. Check the dining facilities on offer before you book.

> **BRIT TIP:** Few hotels provide hair-dryers, although they can often be ordered from the front desk. For your own, you will need a US plug adaptor (with two flat pins). Their voltage is 110–120 AC as opposed to our 220, so your appliances will work sluggishly.

Most Orlando hotels are big, clean, efficient and great value. You'll find plenty of soft-drink and ice machines, with ice buckets in all the rooms (although drinks from the machine may be more expensive).

All accommodation will be fully air-conditioned and, when it is really hot, you have to live with the drone of the A/C unit at night. DON'T turn it off when you go out, even when it is cool in the morning or, by the time you return, your room will have turned into an oven.

Note that the most expensive place from which to make a telephone call is your hotel room! Nearly every hotel adds a 45–70%

surcharge (Disney resorts add a $15 'connection fee') to every call (you can also be charged for a call even if no one answers, if it rings five or more times). Buy a phonecard instead (see page 42).

Remember, too, that hotel prices (both in this book and in Orlando) are always *per room*. They will be cheaper out of the main holiday periods, but they can still vary from month to month, with special deals offered at times. Always ask for rates if you book independently and check if any special rates apply during your visit (don't be afraid to ask for their 'best rate' at off-peak times which can be lower than any published rate). There may be an additional charge ($5–15 per person) for more than two adults sharing the same room.

If you've just arrived and are still looking for accommodation, head for one of the two official Visitor Centers: one on International Drive (I-Drive) just south of The Mercado (on the corner of Austrian Court, open daily 8am–7pm); and the other on the eastern stretch of Highway 192 in Kissimmee (open 8am–5pm), where they keep brochures and the latest deals on all the hotels. If you are comfortable with auction-type websites like www.priceline.com, you may pick up a bargain.

The full-service tourist centres of **Know Before You Go** (407 396 5400 or 1-800 749 1993, www.knowbeforeugo.com) and **Vacation Works** (407 396 1844 or 1-800 396 1883, www.vacationworks.com) also deal in discounted accommodation as well as attraction tickets. Another new booking service to try is Hotel Anywhere on 01444 410555 or www.hotelanywhere.co.uk.

We have placed hotels, motels and holiday homes in four price bands to give you a rough and ready reckoner, although bear in mind no price is set in stone. These bands are:

> **BRIT TIP:** Buy your soft drinks at the supermarket, and a neat polystyrene cooler for about $4 that you can fill with ice from your hotel ice machine to keep your drinks cold.

$	=	up to $50 per night
$$	=	$51–$99
$$$	=	$100–$160
$$$$	=	$161–plus

Also, as there is no widely accepted star rating system for American hotels and bearing in mind there is little difference in the size of rooms (usually quite generous, with two double beds, TV and full en-suite) we have our own C grades, based on the number of facilities and extra comforts. Hence, a CCCCC grading will include the highest level of facilities and service, while a CC or C will be a more basic motel-type.

Resort hotels

Our review of Orlando's hotels starts with *Walt Disney World Resort in Florida*. Conveniently sited almost on the doorstep of the main attractions – and linked by an excellent free transport system of monorail, buses and boats – Disney's hotels, holiday homes and campsites

The Hard Rock Hotel

are all magnificently appointed and maintained. They range from the futuristic *Disney's Contemporary Resort* to the more basic but still oversized fun of the new *Pop Century Resorts* – and their imagination and attention to detail are as good as the theme parks! In all, there are more than 28,000 rooms, while the 780-acre *Disney's Fort Wilderness Resort & Campground* has 1,190 sites.

Grand accommodation comes at a price. A standard room at *Disney's Grand Floridian Resort & Spa* can cost $500 a night in high season (the suites can top $2,000!) and even the more modest *Disney's Caribbean Beach Resort* can be more than $150 a night. Dining at the hotels in the resorts is not cheap either, and you'll find very few fast-food outlets on site.

However, there is also a budget choice in the shape of *Disney's All-Star Sports, Music and Movies Resorts* and the new *Pop Century Resort* so you can stay right in the heart of the 'magic', great in high season when the surrounding roads are packed.

Staying with the Mouse is one of the great thrills, for the style, service and extras. The 21 resorts offer a superb array of facilities, and children especially love being a part of Disney full time. The benefits are: **Resort ID card:** every guest receives a card with which to charge almost all your food, gifts and services while on site to your room account. **Package delivery:** in conjunction with your ID card, you can have any purchases shipped straight back to your hotel room. **Free parking:** with your ID card, there is no charge for your car at any

---

BRIT TIP: It is usual in American hotels to tip the housemaid by leaving $1 per adult each day before your room is made up.

BRIT TIP: Disney resort restaurants CAN (and should!) be visited even if you are not staying there. You can book in advance at any of the parks, from any Disney phone (dial *88) or on 407-WDW-DINE.

---

of the parks. **Free transport:** forget the car and use the monorail-bus-boat network. **Refillable mugs:** all Disney resorts sell their own plastic drinking mugs, which are worth buying (about $13.99 each) as you simply help yourself to drinks at their self-service cafés thereafter. **Dining priority:** guests can make Priority Seating bookings up to 90 days in advance (two years in the case of dinner shows). Call 407 939 3463. Note: a Priority Seating (or PS) is not strictly a reservation but a guarantee of the first available table when you turn up. **Priority golf:** the best tee times are reserved for Disney resort guests and can be booked 90 days in advance on 407 939 4653. **Children's services:** all resorts have in-room or group baby-sitting (subject to availability; you can book in advance on 407 827 5444) and the eight Deluxe resorts have supervised activity centres and dinner clubs (around $7/child per hour), usually open until midnight. **E Nights:** periodically, resort guests get the chance to buy a $12 ticket for an extra 3 hours' access to the main rides at one of the parks after official closing time (great value). **Mickey on call:** okay it's a bit twee, but what better way to wake up than with an alarm call from the Mouse himself? **Extra Magic Hour:** this is the big bonus, the chance to get in to one of the parks an hour early each day (see page 29) and do several of the main rides before the crowds arrive.

Magic Kingdom Resorts

Around the *Magic Kingdom Park* are four of the grandest properties, plus the campground style of *Fort Wilderness*. The 15-storey **Disney's Contemporary Resort** has 1,030 rooms, a cavernous foyer, shops, restaurants, lounges, a real sandy beach, a marina, two swimming pools (with water-slide), six tennis courts, a video games centre and a health club – and magnificent views, especially from the superb, hotel-top California Grill restaurant (try to arrange a Priority Seating to coincide with the park's fireworks). Don't miss **Chef Mickey's** for a breakfast or dinner buffet with all your favourite characters. There is the Mouseketeer Club for 4–12s, while the monorail runs *through* this hotel – an endless source of fascination for kids. As with all resort accommodation, rooms are large, scrupulously clean and well furnished. $$$$+, CCCCC.

Disney's Polynesian Resort is a South Seas tropical fantasy brought to life with modern sophistication and comfort. Beautiful sandy beaches, lush vegetation and architecture are home to 853 rooms built in film-set wooden longhouse style, and all with balconies and wonderful views. It also boasts a stunning 3-storey atrium lobby, with 75 varieties of tropical plants, parrots and a waterfall.

> BRIT TIP: Watch the fireworks over the *Magic Kingdom Park* from the beach area of the Resort.

There are excellent eating opportunities: **'Ohana** is an entertaining dinner venue, which also offers lively character breakfasts – plus there are canoe rentals, a beautiful pool area complete with water slide, a games room, shops and children's playground. **The Neverland Club** caters for 4–12s (4pm–midnight). $$$$+, CCCCC. **The Poly** is also home to the nightly *Spirit of Aloha* dinner show (see page 244), which is open to non-resort guests and makes a fabulous evening among the torch-lit paths and gardens.

> BRIT TIP: Dine in wonderful South Seas style at the 'Ohana restaurant, but don't ask for the salt – unless you want to spark an amazing reaction!

Disney's Wilderness Lodge is one of the most picturesque places to stay. It is an imposing and detailed re-creation of a National Park lodge, down to the stream running through the massive wooden balcony-lined atrium and into the gardens, past the swimming pool (with hot and cold spas) to the resort's own geyser, which erupts faithfully each hour!

Offering authentic backwoods charm with true luxury, the resort is connected to the *Magic Kingdom Park* by boat and bus only. It also has two full-service restaurants: the outstanding **Artist's Point** (for lunch and dinner) and the **Whispering Canyon Café** (for a lively breakfast and huge all-you-can-eat buffets), a snack bar and a pool bar. The Cubs Den is for 4–12s (4.30pm–midnight). $$$$, CCCCC. This is one of my favourite resorts and a great romantic destination.

The Villas at Wilderness Lodge are a recent development of 136 studios and 1- and 2-bedroom villas. Facilities include fully equipped kitchens, living areas, private balconies and whirlpool baths. There is a quiet pool area, spa and health club.

BRIT TIP: From all the *Magic Kingdom* resorts, watch out for the free nightly **Electrical Water Pageant** out on Bay Lake, (see page 245).

Disney's Grand Floridian Resort & Spa,

a hugely elaborate mock Victorian mansion with 867 rooms, an impressive domed and towered foyer and staff in Edwardian dress, completes the quartet of Magic Kingdom resort hotels. The rooms are luxurious, hence the mega prices, and it is worth a look even if you are staying elsewhere. It also has six restaurants, including *Walt Disney World Resort* in Florida's top-of-the-range **Victoria and Albert's** (where their set, 6-course dinner with wine will set you back more than $110 a head) and the chic seafood-orientated **Narcoossee's** (one of my favourites), with its excellent view over Seven Seas Lagoon and the nightly Electrical Water Pageant, plus four bars and impressive sporting and relaxation facilities. A wonderful second pool area, complete with zero-depth entry and

Disney's Pop Century Resort

© Disney

water-slide, has recently been added. The Mouseketeer Club caters for 4–12s (4.30pm–midnight) and the **1900 Park Fare** restaurant is one of the most popular for character meals. $$$$+, CCCCC.

Camping Disney Style

Disney's Fort Wilderness Resort & Campground, on Bay Lake, opposite the *Magic Kingdom Park*, offers an impressive array of camping facilities and chalet-style homes that can house up to 6 in a 750-acre (304-ha) spread of Florida countryside. Two 'trading posts' supply fresh groceries, there are two bars and cafés and a range of on-site activities, including the thrice-nightly Hoop-Dee-Doo Musical Revue, campfire programme, films, sports, games and a prime position from which to view the nightly Electrical Water Pageant. You can rent bikes and take horse-rides around some of the country trails, or go boating on Bay Lake, while the Tri-Circle D ranch offers a small petting zoo. Buses and boats link the resort with other areas (and the short boat ride to the *Magic Kingdom Park* is a great way to start the day). $–$$$$, CCC.

Epcot Resorts

The *Epcot* area features six hotels, including arguably the best-value properties. The unmistakable **Walt Disney World Swan** and **Dolphin** hotels are within walking distance of *Epcot* and *Disney-MGM Studios*, *Disney's Boardwalk Resort* entertainment district and the Fantasia Gardens Miniature Golf Courses. The 'entertainment architecture' style is extensive and fun, they have the full range of resort benefits, facilities and style, yet are privately run and so are a little cheaper than Disney's other

4

BRIT TIP: *Disney's Grand Floridian, Contemporary* and *Polynesian Resorts* are situated on the monorail, the best way to get into the *Magic Kingdom Park* and *Epcot*, although you are close enough to walk in from the *Contemporary*.

deluxe hotels. The Swan features a 45-ft (14-metre) statue atop the hotel and has 758 large rooms (including 55 suites), while the Dolphin (1,509 rooms, with 136 suites) is crowned by two even bigger statues of dolphins. The duo make up one mega-resort, and both have been extensively refurbished in 2002/03, including the signature 'heavenly beds' (with duvets – a rarity in the US) of the Westin hotel group, high-speed Internet access and 27-in (69-cm) TVs. Together, this extensive resort boasts 17 restaurants, four tennis courts, three pools (one, an amazing grotto pool with hidden alcoves and a water-slide), a kids' pool and a white-sand beach, two health clubs, bike and paddle boat rentals, a great range of shops, video arcade and the Camp Dolphin centre for kids aged 4–12 (1–4.30pm, 6–11pm, \$12 per hour). Even for non-guests, the Italian restaurant **Palio's** (Swan) and **Shula's Steak House** (Dolphin) are worth seeking out. The **Coral Café** (Dolphin) and **Garden Grove** (Swan) feature Disney character breakfasts, with some immensely thoughtful little touches for children. Tubbi's buffeteria in the Dolphin is also open 24 hours a day. And, at night, the resort looks magnificent. Visit www.swandolphin.com or call 407 934 3000 for details on these perfectly situated gems. Transport is by boat (to *Epcot* and *Disney-MGM Studios*) and bus. \$\$\$\$, CCCCC.

The 45-acre (18-ha) **Disney's BoardWalk Inn and Villas Resort** is the most extravagant on-site property, featuring a 372-room inn, 520 villas, four themed restaurants, a TV sports club and two nightclubs, plus an impressive array of unique shops, sports facilities and a huge, free-form swimming pool with a 200-ft (60-metre) water-slide, all on a re-created semi-circular boardwalk around Crescent Lake. The overall effect is stunningly pretty, and the attention to detail in the rooms is excellent. Outstanding features are the summer-cottage style villas, Mediterranean restaurant **Spoodles** (tapas-style in the evening) and the **Big River Grille Brewing Company** for a great range of beers. Top of the range is the expensive but excellent seafood restaurant, the **Flying Fish**. Even if you are not staying here, it is a delightful resort to visit for a meal, the nightlife (especially **Jellyrolls** piano bar and the **ESPN Club**) or just to wander along the boardwalk. The Harbor Club caters for 4–12s (4pm–midnight). \$\$\$\$+, CCCCC.

Disney's Caribbean Beach Resort has 2,112 rooms spread over five Caribbean islands (own bus service) and with the accent on moderate prices and good value. The rooms tend to be a little plainer (although they still comfortably house a family of four), but the food court, main restaurant, **Shutters**, and outdoor activities (including a lakeside recreation area with themed

Disney's Wilderness Lodge

© Disney

waterfalls, slides and games arcade) are still a big hit with children. The six counter-service outlets in the food court at **Old Port Royale Town Center** (the hub of this pretty resort, and extensively refurbished in 2002/03) can get busy in the morning, and the Trinidad South and Barbados 'islands' are a fair walk from the centre (hence the bus). However, it is an action-packed resort with some imaginative touches, like Parrot Cay Island Playground with its tropical birds and play area. Transport to the parks is purely by bus. $$$, CCCC.

Going upmarket again, the refined, almost intimate, **Disney's Yacht Club Resort** has 630 rooms designed with nautical themes, all set around an ornamental lake. For dinner, the **Yachtsman Steakhouse** offers fine dining options and underlines the resort's polished yet friendly elegance. Sister hotel **Disney's Beach Club Resort** completes the *Epcot* line-up. With 583 spacious rooms set along a man-made white-sand beach, it's like a tropical island paradise. **Cape May Café** is the lovely character breakfast opportunity and also offers a nightly New England-style clambake buffet. You can go boating or catch a water-shuttle to Epcot, while other transport is provided by bus. Water fun is 'on tap' for both Yacht and Beach Club resorts at the shared Stormalong Bay, a magnificent 2½-acre (1-ha) recreation area with water-slides and a sandy lagoon. The Sand Castle Club caters for 4–12s (4.30pm–midnight). Both $$$$+, CCCCC.

Disney's Animal Kingdom Resorts

Disney's All-Star Resorts were Disney's first serious venture into the budget hotel market in 1997. Here, for just $77–109 a night year-

round, you can stay in one of the five sports-themed blocks (Surfing, Basketball, Tennis, Baseball and American Football) centred around a massive food court, two swimming pools, a games arcade and shops; the music-themed version (Jazz, Rock, Broadway, Calypso and Country); or the movies complex (*Mighty Ducks*, *101 Dalmatians*, *Fantasia*, *Love Bug* and *Toy Story*). The latter is possibly the most imaginative, with its Fantasia pool and kids' play areas, and the most popular blocks are *Toy Story* and *101 Dalmatians* (both of which are non-smoking). All three centres, which total 5,760 rooms, have pool bars, shops, laundry facilities, video games rooms and a pizza delivery service. Bright and compact, they are well designed for budget-conscious families who still want to enjoy all the Disney conveniences. Transport to the parks is provided by an efficient bus schedule. $$–$$$, CCC.

Disney's Coronado Springs Resort is possibly the best value of the moderate resorts (Caribbean Beach and Port Orleans) as it's the newest and has slightly more facilities for its 1,921 rooms spread over 125 acres (50ha): four pools, including the massive, beautiful Lost City of Cibola feature pool, two games arcades, a boating marina, bike rentals, restaurant, food court and convenience store, lounge bar, gift shop, beauty salon and health club, business centre and two guest launderettes. Constructed in a scenic Mexican/Spanish architectural theme in three 'villages' (Casitas,

> BRIT TIP: To make a reservation at any *Walt Disney World* resort, call 407 934 7639. For information, don't forget www.disneyworld.co.uk.

Ranchos and Cabanas), Coronado is an often-overlooked treasure. Check out the **Maya Grill** and its New Latino cuisine style for a memorable meal. Coronado is 5 minutes from *Disney's Animal Kingdom Theme Park* and is well served by Disney's bus network. $$$, CCCC.

Disney's Animal Kingdom Lodge opened in 2001 and is a stunning example of architectural artistry. It is a private game lodge on the edge of a 33-acre (13-ha) animal-filled savannah, which many of the rooms overlook. The African theme – from decor to shopping, cuisine, restaurant styling and even the musky smells – is almost overwhelming, and the effect of opening your curtains to a vista of giraffes and zebras is immense. This wonderful creativity comes before you consider the amenities of this 1,293-room deluxe resort: two restaurants, café, bar, elaborately themed 'watering-hole' main pool (with water-slide) and kids' pool, massage and fitness centre, large gift shop, children's play area and an awesome 4-storey atrium. The main restaurant, **Jiko**, is spectacular, but there is also the buffet-style **Boma**, a 'marketplace' restaurant featuring African dishes from a wood-burning grill and rotisserie for both breakfast and dinner.

BRIT TIP: Jiko at *Disney's Animal Kingdom Lodge* offers an imaginative, African-tinged menu, wonderfully attentive service and authentic ambience.

The lavishness and detail of the design are unmatched anywhere I have seen, plus there's 200 animals on the savannahs. Guides are on hand to tell guests about the animals and their habitats, while children can listen to African folklore stories around the outdoor firepit or become junior safari researchers while Mum and Dad do some wine-tasting (the hotel boasts the largest collection of South African wines in America). Rooms range from standard doubles (with the same slightly dated layout of the moderate resorts) to 1- and 2-bedroom suites, some with bunk beds for the kids. Simba's Cubhouse is for the 4–12s (4.30pm–midnight), and Disney transport is by bus. $$$$, CCCCC.

Disney's Pop Century Resort (the first half of its 5,760-room spread) is in a similar vein to *Disney's All-Star Resorts*. Its theme is the decades of the 20th century, hence there are 10 blocks with giant icons – like yo-yos, Rubik's cubes and juke-boxes – and a riot of period words, sayings and visual gags! The Classic Years of the 1950s–90s feature a gigantic 10-pin bowling lane incorporating one of the three pools (the others are shaped like a flower and a computer), a huge table football set-up and open-air Twister mats. The five blocks are grouped around a main building housing a spacious check-in area (with large-screen TV showing Disney films), a large food court, a lounge (with quick-breakfast facility), a Disney store and games arcade. The 177-acre (72-ha) complex also features a central lake, while the Legendary Years section, the 1900s–40s, will have identical facilities and should be in operation later in 2004. It adds significantly to Disney's budget-orientated offerings and, like *Disney's All-Star Resort*, has a well-organised bus service to the parks. $$–$$$, CCC.

Downtown Disney Resorts

The other main accommodation centre within *Walt Disney World in Florida* is the *Downtown Disney* area. Here you will find: **Disney's Port**

Orleans Resort, a 2-part complex (formerly the two distinct resorts of Port Orleans and Dixie Landings) split into the 2,048-room Riverside area – with a steamboat as a reception area, a great cotton mill-style food court, a full-service Cajun-themed restaurant and an old-fashioned general store (gift shop) – and the 1,008-room French Quarter, which has the **Sassagoula Floatworks and Food Factory** court, two bars, a games room and shopping arcade (the French Quarter is closed for refurbishment for much of 2004).

The Riverside includes **Ol' Man Island**, a magnificent 3½-acre (1.5-ha) playground with swimming pool, kids' area and a fishing hole, while the French Quarter has Doubloon Lagoon. Kids will especially enjoy the Mardi Gras dragon slide and alligator fountains, plus the play area. The eye-catching landscaping and architecture vary from rustic Bayou backwoods to turn-of-the-century New Orleans. Transport for both sections is by bus or boat to *Downtown Disney*. $$$–$$$$, CCCC.

Disney's Old Key West Resort is partly a holiday ownership scheme of 5-star proportions, but the 1-, 2- or grand 3-bed studios in a great Key West setting can also be rented on a nightly basis ($$$$+, CCCC) when not in use by club members. Facilities include swimming pools, tennis courts, games room, shops and fitness centre plus **Olivia's** restaurant (for superb Key Lime Pie!).

Disney's Coronado Springs Resort

© Disney

Disney Hotel Plaza

In addition to the official *Walt Disney World* hotels, there are another seven 'guest' hotels inside *Walt Disney World Resort in Florida* itself at the **Disney Hotel Plaza** on the doorstep of the *Downtown Disney* area. There's a free bus service to the attractions and guaranteed admission to the theme parks, and you can make reservations for shows and restaurants before the public, but they are almost all more expensive than similar hotels outside Disney property (although being able to walk to *Downtown Disney* and Crossroads shopping plaza is worth a lot).

Top of the list (for service, mod cons and price) is the 10-storey, 814-room **Hilton** (407 827 4000) $$$$+, CCCC. With two excellent pools, seven restaurants and lounges and a health club, it fully deserves its four-star, four-diamond rating. It is also the only 'outside' hotel to enjoy Disney's Extra Magic Hour feature at the theme parks. The **Benihana** restaurant is a standout feature, offering sushi, sashimi, chicken and great steaks.

Also fairly expensive are the **Grosvenor Resort** (626 excellent rooms, exceptional service and colonial decor, plus a great windmill-shaped pool area and a health spa, a daily Disney character breakfast at Baskerville's, a sports bar and a 24-hour café, Crumpets; 407 828 4444. $$$–$$$$, CCCC) and the **Wyndham Palace Resort & Spa** (a bustling, 27-storey cluster offering 1,014 rooms, many with a grandstand view of *Epcot*'s Spaceship Earth, a European-style spa, three heated pools, tennis courts, a marina with boat rentals and the superb **Arthur's 27** restaurant, with stunning views; 407 827 2727. $$$$, CCCC).

Then there is the contemporary **Doubletree Guest Suites** (229 spacious family suites offering every

Disney's All-Star Music Resort

in-room convenience – from in-room safe to cookies! – and great kids' facilities, with their own check-in area, pool, cinema, games room and video arcade; 407 934 1000. $$$$, CCCC).

The more modestly priced and tropically themed **Best Western Lake Buena Vista** (refurbished in 2002) has 325 rooms with good views over the Marketplace, in-room coffee-makers and hair-dryers. The top-floor suites are huge and magnificent. Garden-themed **Traders** restaurant is a pleasant choice for breakfast or dinner, while there is also a quick-service deli, **Parakeets**, a lounge, bar and Toppers nightclub on the 18th floor (worth visiting during Disney firework shows!), plus a large pool, video arcade and even a small gym (www.orlandoresorthotel.com, or call 407 828 2424). The convenience of this area marks the Best Western out as a real bargain. Like all the hotels in the Boulevard, it is well positioned for a stroll to *Downtown Disney* and features free bus transport and guaranteed access to the parks, plus preferred tee times at Disney golf courses. $$$, CCC.

The well-priced **Courtyard by Marriott** has 323 extra-large rooms in a 14-storey tower and 6-storey annex featuring glass-walled lifts, three heated swimming pools – including one for kids – small gym, games room, Courtyard Café & Grill, snack bar and lounge/bar, plus

wonderful gardens, 407 828 8888, $$$, CCC).

Finally, the lovely **Hotel Royal Plaza** has a pleasant aspect, boasting 372 spacious and well-equipped rooms and 22 suites, along with a full-service diner-restaurant and lounge bar, landscaped pool area, four tennis courts, a health club and Disney gift shop (407 828 2828). $$$, CCCC. For more details on all these properties, check out www.downtowndisneyhotels.com.

4

> BRIT TIP: To save time from the Hotel Plaza properties, walk to *Downtown Disney* Marketplace to catch the free bus service to the theme parks.

Lake Buena Vista

As you move further away from *Walt Disney World Resort in Florida* the prices tend to moderate.

You can still spend a small fortune, however, at the **Hyatt Regency Grand Cypress**. This 1,500-acre (608-ha) resort offers three nine-hole and one 18-hole golf course (designed by Jack Nicklaus), a swimming pool with waterfalls and slide, 21-acre (9-ha) boating lake, tennis complex, health club and equestrian centre. Rates START around $200, but the 750 rooms and

Disney's Port Orleans Resort

suites are magnificently appointed and the resort is lovely (it also has five restaurants, three lounges and a poolside bar), 407 239 1234. $$$$+, CCCCC.

Nearby is **Orlando World Center Marriott**, another personal favourite and an impressive landmark on Disney's outskirts, set in 200 landscaped acres (810ha) and surrounded by another golf course. An elaborate lobby, Chinese antiques and its sheer size (2,003 rooms, including 110 suites, seven restaurants, four pools, tennis courts and a health club) put it in the expensive range, but it is conveniently situated and has one of the most picturesque pool areas, plus the whizziest glass-fronted lifts! It does get busy, especially with convention business. 'Try their Christmas Day Buffet,' says Roy Carlisle. 'Pricey but brilliant.' (www.orlando.com/owcm or call 407 239 4200). $$$$, CCCCC.

The **Holiday Inn Sunspree Resort** at Lake Buena Vista (507 rooms) is excellent for children's facilities, featuring a highly rated supervised childcare programme and a good range of other facilities. All rooms have mini-kitchenettes. It also features the trademark 'Kidsuites' – a private playhouse/bedroom built into the hotel room, with its own TV, cassette player, video game player, clock, fun phone, table and chairs. They offer a fun alternative to normal hotel accommodation, down to the separate kids' check-in. Sunspree, perfectly situated for Disney and with free transport, also has a 2,100sq ft (195sq metre) Cyber Arcade, with access to the Internet and other high-tech elements, while it has 50 two-room suites for more family comfort. Kids 12 and under eat free. (www.kidsuites.com or call 407 239 4500). $$$, CCCC.

A novel choice is the African-themed **Sheraton Safari Hotel**, which sports the Python water-slide, a heated pool and kids' pool, with free transport to Disney parks and kids eat free with parents at **Casablanca's** restaurant (its breakfast buffet is highly recommended). Rooms are well equipped, with hair-dryers, coffee-makers and ironing boards, and all within walking distance of the Crossroads shopping centre, a good selection of shops and restaurants, and close to *Downtown Disney* Marketplace. It has 489 rooms, including 96 huge suites, all with a safari theme. With its great location and expansive style, the Sheraton Safari is an ideal mid-range family choice. Look up www.sheratonsafari.com or call 407 239 0444. $$$, CCC.

Some of the big hotel chains also have one or two of their smartest properties in this area, notably the **Radisson Inn Lake Buena Vista**, which has 200 rooms (407 239 8400; $$$, CCC) and the recently refurbished **Doubletree Club Hotel** with 246 rooms (407 239 4646; $$$, CCC ½).

Kissimmee

Moving out along Highway 192 (the Irlo Bronson Memorial Highway) into Kissimmee, you will find the biggest choice of budget accommodation in the area. Facilities vary little and what you see is what you get. All the big hotel chains can be found along this tourist sprawl, and rates can be as low as $29 per room off-peak, or $35 for a room with a kitchenette (what the Americans call an 'efficiency'). Be prepared to shop around for a good rate (off-peak discounts may be available), especially along Highway 192, where many hotels advertise their rates on neon signs. As a rule, prices drop the further you go from Disney. Don't be afraid to ask to see inside rooms before you settle on your holiday base (some of the motels can be pretty ordinary).

Chains

Among the leading chain hotels are **Best Western** (all with pools, family-orientated but large, in the $$–$$$ range); **Days Inn** (rather characterless and some without restaurants, but the newer properties are good value, mainly $$, and convenient, with some rooms with kitchenettes); **EconoLodge** (akin to Best Western), **Howard Johnson** (a bit dearer, but with more spacious rooms and some with free continental breakfast); **Quality Inn** (sound, popular chain in $–$$ range), **Ramada** (rates can vary more widely between hotels in the $$–$$$ range, some offer free continental breakfast); and **TraveLodge** (another identikit, budget group, $–$$). The **Fairfield Inns** are the budget version of the impressive Marriott chain ($$ range).

Doubletree hotels and suites are another upmarket chain with excellent facilities, as are the **Radisson** group (both $$$). The Marriott chain has three other family-friendly brands: the **Residence Inn by Marriott, SpringHill Suites** and **Courtyard by Marriott** (both $$$). Their smart new Lake Buena Vista complex at the junction of I-4 and Route 535 features a Fairfield Inn, Courtyard and Springhill Suites (www.marriott-village.com), with 24-hour gated security, free *Walt Disney World* transport and some great facilities.

The **Renaissance World Gate Hotel** (577 rooms; 407 496 1400; $$$, CCCC) scores highly in value-for-money terms with its oversized rooms, excellent facilities and good service. In budget territory, the motel-type **Inns of America, Knights Inn, Motel 6, Comfort Inn** and **Super 8 Motel** brands all deliver a basic $ service, but the **Hampton Inn** and **Red Roof** groups manage a more quality-conscious approach in the same price band. The **La Quinta Inn and Suites** series ($$–$$$) has six well-equipped new properties in the area, two on I-Drive.

Independent organisations

There are dozens of smaller, independent outfits that offer special rates from time to time to compete with the big boys. Look out in particular for useful 'kids eat free' offers. Of the non-chain operators, the **Casa Rosa Hotel** offers simple, relatively peaceful Mediterranean-style hospitality (on west Highway 192; 407 396 1060; $–$$$, CC). The **Park Inn International** (same place; 407 396 1376) also has one of the better lake-front locations to go with its budget rates ($–$$, CCC) and some rooms have kitchenettes.

The budget-priced **Magic Castle Inn and Suites Maingate** take some beating with their range of amenities: free continental breakfast, free Disney transport to the parks, fridges in all rooms, kids' playground, guest laundry and picnic area (107 rooms and 15 suites; 407 396 2212 or 1-800 446 5669; $–$$, CC½).

> **BRIT TIP:** Hotels designated Maingate East or Maingate West should be close to Disney's main entrance on Highway 192, although it is wise to check.

A firm personal choice is the **Holiday Inn Hotel and Suites Maingate East**, which also boasts Kidsuites rooms and Camp Holiday children's programmes, making it an outstanding family resort. Good attention to detail (hair-dryers, coffee-makers, microwaves and fridges even in standard rooms), free

Disney transport and its proximity next door to Old Town make for great flexibility and value for money (614 rooms and 110 suites; 407 396 4488; $$–$$$, CCC½). There's a children's check-in area, and under-13s eat free, as they do at the smart **Holiday Inn Maingate West**, with its tropical courtyard, free-form heated pool and kids' pool (287 rooms; 407 396 1100; $$, CCC).

The **Holiday Inn Nikki Bird Resort**, just west of Disney's Highway 192 entrance, is another good family location with its 23-acre tropical setting, three pools, basketball and volleyball courts and children's entertainment (529 rooms; 407 396 7300; $$, CCC). **Angel's Diner**, the hotel's outstanding restaurant, offers some fabulous breakfast and dinner buffets.

The **La Quinta Inn Lakeside** (formerly the Four Points by Sheraton Lakeside) on west Highway 192, is another consistent choice, providing excellent value with its three pools, tennis courts, kids' playgrounds, mini-golf, paddleboats and two restaurants and there is free Disney transport (651 rooms; 407 396 2222; $$–$$$, CCC½).

Equally, the **Radisson Resort Parkway** has above-average facilities and service after recent renovations. Just 1½ miles (2.4km) from Disney, with free transport, the resort boasts an elaborate free-form pool with waterfall, lovely rooms, and kids stay and eat free with their parents (718 rooms; 407 396 7000; $$$, CCCC).

Slightly off the beaten track, although well situated for all the parks and with extra charm, is the **Celebration Hotel** in the Disney-inspired town of Celebration. Just off Highway 192, the Central Florida Greeneway and I-4, this unique hotel offers a refreshing small-town America style. You are greeted by an elegant lounge and two reception desks, and you are a long way from the usual tourist hurly-burly. With 115 rooms in its 1920s' wood-frame design, the Celebration has a classy ambience and a wealth of high-quality touches, notably in the ultra-comfy rooms. These come in a choice of an attic-like Retreat, Traditional (with either 1 king or 2 queen-size beds), Studio or a 2-room Suite and are all beautifully furnished. Lovely artwork, unhurried, courteous staff and a good array of facilities – pool, jacuzzi and fitness centre, plus the superb **Plantation Restaurant** (excellent buffet breakfasts and a range of superb 'new Florida' dishes) – mark this out as a real gem. It is also within a short stroll of the town's shops, restaurants and peaceful walks. There's an inexpensive shuttle service to the parks. For a quieter or more romantic retreat, this member of the Grand Theme Hotels group (the Sheraton Safari, Doubletree Castle, Sheraton Studio City and Westin Grand Bohemian), is ideal (407 566 6000, www.celebrationhotel.com) $$$$, CCC).

One of the newest – and possibly most dramatic – properties is the 1,406-room **Gaylord Palms Resort** on the junction of I-Drive South and Osceola Parkway (very convenient for Disney). A cross between a convention centre and a vast turn-of-the-century Florida mansion, it

Orlando Airport Hyatt atrium

KEY TO
WALT DISNEY WORLD
AND LAKE BUENA VISTA
ACCOMMODATION

1 Disney's Contemporary Resort
2 Disney's Polynesian Resort
3 Disney's Wilderness Lodge
4 Disney's Grand Floridian Resort & Spa
5 Walt Disney World Swan Hotel
6 Walt Disney World Dolphin Hotel
7 Disney's Caribbean Beach Resort
8 Disney's Yacht Club Resort
9 Disney's Beach Club Resort
10 Disney's Boardwalk Resort
11 Disney's All-Star Resorts
12 Disney's Port Orleans Resort (French Quarter)
13 Disney's Port Orleans Resort (Riverside)
14 Disney's Coronado Springs Resort
15 Disney's Saratoga Springs Resort and Spa (2004)
16 Disney's Old Key West Resort
17 Disney's Fort Wilderness Resort and
   Campground
18 Disney's Animal Kingdom Lodge
19 Disney's Pop Century Resort (Dec 2003)
20 Hilton At Walt Disney World
21 The Grosvenor
22 Wyndham Palace Resort and Spa
23 Doubletree Guest Suites Resort
24 Best Western At Walt Disney World
25 Hotel Royal Plaza
26 Courtyard By Marriott
27 Hyatt Regency Grand Cypress
28 Marriott's Orlando World Center
29 Embassy Suites Resort Lake Buena Vista
30 Sierra Suites Hotel
31 Radisson Inn Lake Buena Vista
32 Buena Vista Suites
33 Summerfield Suites At Lake Buena Vista
34 Vistana Resort
35 Sheraton Safari Resort
36 Holiday Inn Sunspree Resort
37 Marriott Village
38 Holiday Inn Family Suites
39 Gaylord Palms Resort

4

features 4½ acres (2ha) of indoor gardens, fountains and landscaped waters under a glass dome. Three intricately themed areas bear witness to a Disney-like creativity, and the resort offers just about every creature comfort, with an array of restaurants and bars, an adults-only pool, family activity pool and beach (with octopus water-slide), full-service spa, children's day care centre and a range of shops.

Standard rooms are some of the smartest and most spacious in the area, while the suites are enormous, and there is even a hotel-within-a-hotel, as the central Emerald Tower offers an even more upmarket room choice and concièrge facilities.

One area is landscaped like the Everglades, complete with native plants, trees and atmospheric effects (watch out for the gators!), another copies the old world charm of St Augustine – with replica Spanish Fort – while the third reproduces the style and eclecticism of Key West, with a mock-up marina and sailboat (and a fun-themed daily Sunset Celebration, with live entertainment) and the rooms are themed after each area. To walk into the resort, with its marbled lobby and cavernous interior, at night is like entering some future world.

The elaborate settings add to the resort's signature fine dining, with the choice of **Old Hickory Steakhouse** (naturally aged Black Angus beef a speciality, along with an artisanal cheese course), **Sunset Sam's** (for fine seafood) and the wonderful Spanish buffet-style **Villa de Flora** (with six show kitchens). The Canyon Ranch SpaClub is one of the largest in central Florida and features a state-of-the-art spa, fitness facilities and a full-service beauty salon. There are 13 stores sprinkled through the resort, the **Planet Java** coffee shop, Auggie's Jammin' Piano Bar, the Gaylord Yacht Bar and the St Augustine Piazza. (407 586 0315, www.gaylordpalms.com). $$$$, CCCCC.

International Drive

I-Drive is further from *Walt Disney World Resort in Florida*, but handy for Universal Orlando, SeaWorld and closer to downtown Orlando. For location and value for money, it is hard to beat. It is more thoughtfully laid out, some attractions are within walking distance, and a good base for non-drivers.

Top of the range for quality is the **Peabody Orlando**, a luxurious, 891-room tower block, including an Olympic-size pool, health club, four tennis courts and some of the best restaurants in Orlando, notably the gourmet cuisine of **Dux** (jacket advisable) and the classy Italian **Capriccio**, plus the amazing **B-Line Diner** (see Dining Out, Chapter 10), all of which get high marks from the locals. Service is superb and the style is a cut above normal tourist fare – just check out the Royal Duck Palace! Larger-than-average rooms and some huge suites add to the all-round quality, but rates are impressive and the convention business can make it hectic (407 352 4000, www.peabodyorlando.com). $$$$+, CCCCC.

The **Wyndham Orlando Resort** (1,052 rooms) is similarly extravagant but with less of the price tag. It

BRIT TIP: For an attraction with a difference, don't miss Peabody's twice-daily Duck March, when their trademark ducks take up residence 11am–4pm in the huge lobby fountain. A great place for afternoon tea, just watching the red carpet roll out for the mallards!

boasts a formidable line-up of facilities – three swimming pools, a full-service restaurant and bar, a deli and an ice cream shop, two pool bars, a pool restaurant, tennis courts, a kids' club and game arcade, and even a health club – in its beautifully landscaped grounds and is well situated at the junction of I-Drive and Sand Lake Road (and has a 'back door' on to Universal Boulevard when I-Drive is busy). The resort covers 42 acres (17ha), which takes some getting around, but it represents one of the best all-round hotels for the money (407 351 2420, www.wyndham.com). $$$, CCCC.

Going upscale again, the magnificent **Renaissance Orlando Resort** (on Sea Harbor Drive, 778 rooms) is a personal favourite. It claims the world's largest atrium – a full 10 storeys – and boasts some equally enormous rooms and suites, an Olympic-size pool, tennis courts, fitness centre including sauna and steam room, and kids' play areas and activities. The Renaissance is also home to one of the most romantic restaurants in town, the seafood-themed **Atlantis**, plus a regular breakfast, lunch and dinner offering, **Tradewinds**, as well as a coffee shop, pool bar/grill and a stupendous Sunday buffet (see Chapter 10). There is a choice of bars and shops, and all the rooms have recently been renovated to a high standard. There is a 24-hour health club and a self-serve laundry. As the closest hotel to SeaWorld (a two-minute walk across the car park), the Renaissance also offers some great packages in conjunction with the SeaWorld and Discovery Cove. Well worth checking out (407 351 5555, www.renaissance hotels.com). $$$, CCCCC.

Nearby, the recently remodelled **Sheraton World Resort** offers things on a slightly more modest budget, but is still a great holiday base, just off the main I-Drive scene. Set in 28 acres

(11ha) and with 1,102 rooms and extra-large suites, the resort offers three pools, two kiddie pools, a playground and mini-golf and extremely well furnished rooms. The dining options are fairly standard, but the tropically styled grounds give it a more upmarket feel (407 352 1100, www.sheratonworld.com). $$$, CCCC.

The remodelled 21-storey **Sheraton Studio City Hotel** (formerly Universal Tower) is an I-Drive landmark at the entrance to Universal Orlando and features a full art deco film-theme design, from the shower curtains to the large-scale landscaping. Facilities include a heated outdoor pool and paddling pool, games room, fitness room, **Starlight Grille** restaurant and free shuttle service to Universal, Wet 'n Wild (within walking distance) and SeaWorld. The clever 1950s' film styling is startling, and even the staff add to the theme, which makes you feel like you are 'on set'. Check out www.sheratonstudiocity.com. All rooms have hair-dryers, coffee-makers and Nintendo games (302 rooms; tel 497 321 2100). $$$, CCCC.

Next door, the new **Red Horse Inn** (formerly the nondescript Universal Inn) is a fun budget choice, with a striking Southwestern design theme and 159 large, comfy rooms, all of which have been refurbished. There is a Cantina lobby bar (with free continental breakfast featuring Starbucks coffee) and a neat oasis-themed pool area that represents a nice haven on busy I-Drive. There is no restaurant but the neighbouring Sheraton Studio City is only a short walk and a 24-hour Denny's diner is next door (407 351 4100, www.redhorseorlando.com). $$, CC.

The **Quality Inn International** (728 rooms, in the heart of I-Drive, kids under 12 eat free, 407 996 1600; $$, CCC) and **Quality Inn Plaza** (a massive 1,020 rooms in multiple blocks with multiple pools and another kids-eat-free restaurant, 407 345 8585; $–$$, CCC) are both firmly in budget territory but make excellent bases in this area.

Another I-Drive landmark (next door to The Mercado) is the **Doubletree Castle Hotel**, a 9-storey fantasy modelled on Cinderella's castle at the *Magic Kingdom Park*. It features tower and turret rooms, a grand outdoor heated pool, hot tub, pool bar and grill, fitness centre, gift shop and a kids' play area. Rooms are immaculately furnished and there is a free shuttle to *Walt Disney World*, SeaWorld and Universal (216 rooms; 407 345 1511). $$$–$$$$, CCCC.

The other eye-catching property on I-Drive is the **Rosen Center Hotel**, the third largest hotel in Orlando, next to the Beeline Expressway. It caters primarily for the convention trade (it is next door to the massive Convention Center), but also offers excellent tourist facilities with 1,334 rooms and 80 suites. It has a huge swimming grotto, exercise centre, tennis courts, two top-quality restaurants (including the seafood-based **Everglades**) and two bars (407 354 9840). $$$, CCCC.

The new (in June 2002) **Crowne Plaza Hotel** also offers a touch of elegance to the I-Drive scene, with 304 rooms and 94 suites in two distinct, stylish blocks and a spectacular circular atrium. Two restaurants, a cocktail lounge, fitness centre, guest laundry and baby-sitting facilities, plus a huge outdoor heated pool, add up to excellent quality and value on Universal Boulevard's junction with Sand Lake Road (407 355 0550, www.crowneplazauniversal.com) $$$$, CCCC.

Universal Orlando

With the expansion of Universal as a major resort destination has come the development of the surrounding locale on Kirkman Road and Major Boulevard, highlighted by Universal's own resort hotels, which are some of the best in the area. *They also come with a rare theme park privilege – Universal Express, front-of-line access to all the main attractions.*

The **Portofino Bay Hotel** is the jewel in the crown, a splendid re-creation of the famous Italian port and a stunning resort with every possible facility and a bit more. The elaborate porticos, the genuine *trompe l'oeil* painting, the lovely harbourside piazza and the faithful ornamentation of the waterfront make it one of the most memorable hotel settings in Florida, and the 750 rooms are impeccably appointed, with lashings of Italian style. The standard rooms are truly deluxe, with huge beds (and proper duvets), spacious bathrooms, mini-bar and coffee facilities, ironing board and hair-dryer, while the exclusive Villa rooms feature butler service, CD and video players, fax facility and separate showers, plus their own private pool area. There are also 18 elaborate Kidsuites for extra fun, with separate themed rooms that include TV, CD player, Sony Playstation and play area.

The resort facilities are equally breathtaking – a Roman aqueduct-

The Plantation Restaurant at the Celebration Hotel

KEY TO HIGHWAY 192 ACCOMMODATION

1 Orlando World Center Marriott
2 Buena Vista Suites
3 Caribe Royale Resort Suites
4 Radisson Resort Parkway
5 Renaissance World Gate Hotel
6 Casa Rosa Hotel
7 Park Inn International
8 Magic Castle Inn & Suites Maingate
9 Holiday Inn Hotel & Suites Maingate East
10 Holiday Inn Maingate West
11 Holiday Inn Nikki Bird Resort
12 La Quinta Inn Lakeside
13 Celebration Hotel
14 Gaylord Palms Resort
15 Comfort Suites Maingate
16 Tropical Palms Funsuites
17 Holiday Inn Family Suites
18 Orange Lake Resort
19 Villages at Mango Key
20 Liki Tiki Village
21 Wonderland Inn
22 Comfort Suites Resort Maingate East
23 Hampton Inn Maingate West
24 Buenaventura Lakes

style pool with water-slide, a completely enclosed kids' play area and wading pool, a separate quiet pool, jacuzzis, a full (if expensive) health spa, business centre, gift shops (check out Galleria Portofino for some magnificent artwork and jewellery) and video games room. There is also the Campo Portofino activity centre for kids 4–14, from 5–11.30pm every day ($45 for the first child and $35 for each additional child).

For wining and dining, the Portofino boasts eight restaurants and lounges, including the 5-star (and very romantic) **Delfino Riviera**, the boisterous **Trattoria del Porto**, **Mama Della's**, an authentic Italian family dining experience (watch out for Mama herself!), an aromatic deli, a pizzeria and gelateria. $$$$+, CCCCC.

New in 2001 was the **Hard Rock Hotel**, possibly the coolest hotel in Orlando. This home of rock chic is themed as a former rock star's home converted into a hotel! It has 650 rooms and suites in the style of a Californian mission, with public areas decorated with the Hard Rock group's collection of rock 'n roll memorabilia. High ceilings, wooden beams, marble floors and eclectic artwork give an eye-catching and elegant style, with a rock-star theme to most of the public areas, from the black-suited foyer staff to the music that plays fairly constantly.

The 14-acre (6-ha) site includes three bars (the ultra-cool Velvet Bar, Lobby Lounge and Beach Club poolside bar and grill), two restaurants (the full-service **Sunset Grill** and the 5-star, dinner-only **Palm Restaurant**), a fitness centre, Hard Rock gift shop (with live TV links to other HR Cafes around the world), Camp Lil' Rock (for the 4–14s, like Campo Portofino) and games room. The pool area which is the hotel's focus is terrific, with a large, free-form pool and 240-ft (73-

metre) water-slide, two jacuzzis, a sand beach and volleyball court, shuffleboard, and life-size chess and draughts. There is even an underwater sound system in the pool! The rooms (including 14 Kidsuites) are big, modish, beautifully furnished in the hotel's trademark chic style and wonderfully comfortable. $$$$, CCCC.

The 53-acre (21-ha), 1,000-room **Royal Pacific Resort** opened in June 2002, adding an exotic South Seas touch to the Universal portfolio, and bags more style. The theme transports you back to a 1930s luxury hotel in the tropics (with all mod cons), and you really do feel as if you have stepped into another world as you cross the bamboo bridge, over the rice terraces, into the elegant lobby, which is faced by the splendidly colourful Orchid Garden courtyard. The extensive use of rich, dark woods, cool stone floors and masses of greenery (some 58,000 plants and 2,500 trees – including 1,200 palms) around the resort give the place an opulent, colonial feel, while the rooms and facilities are equally impressive. The spacious standard rooms all feature hand-carved Balinese wood furniture, among many refined touches, and there is also a Club level of accommodation, with separate lounge and extended facilities, and some superlative suites.

Islands Dining Room offers breakfast, lunch and dinner in a setting of oriental simplicity (children also have their own buffet area with TV screen), while fine dining is taken to a new dimension by a magnificent restaurant by top American chef Emeril Lagasse called **Tchoup Chop** (see Chapter 10). Then there is a pool snack bar, lobby lounge and Luau garden party area (with barbecue buffet for the Saturday night **Wantilan Luau**, featuring a Polynesian feast and dinner show; from 6–9pm, $49.50

for adults, $29 for under 12s, and open to non residents; book on 407 503 3463). The huge freeform pool is ideal for kids, with zero-depth entry at one end and a boat-shaped interactive water play area of squirting fountains, water jets and canons, paddling pool, sandcastle pit and a 'lifeboat' that fills with water and tips up at regular intervals. Add a health club (including jacuzzi, sauna and gym), kids' club (with computer games, TVs and organised activities), video games room and two shops. $$$$, CCCC.

Finally, all Universal resort guests benefit from a number of exclusive privileges: **resort ID card** (for buying food, merchandise and other items throughout Universal Orlando); **free water taxi** transport; **priority seating** at most restaurants (just show your room key card); **package delivery** to your room; the chance to buy a special **Length of Stay pass** (for unlimited access to the parks while you are at the resort); and, most importantly, **Universal Express** no-wait access to all the rides all day (just by showing your room key card). For all Universal hotels, call 407 224 7117 or visit www.universalorlando.com.

Mid-range hotels

The choice around Universal is also growing. There are recent examples of the budget **Days Inn**, **Hampton Inn**, **TraveLodge** and **Country Inn** chains, plus the **Extended Stay America** group (good, clean efficiency studios, but few other amenities), but there are also two excellent mid-range properties.

The **Radisson Hotel Universal Orlando** is a twin-tower, 742-room complex which has a smart resort feel, with spacious, tropical-themed rooms, a large pool, kids' playground and jacuzzi, pool bar, video games room, hair salon, gym

and sauna, plus a sports bar, full-service restaurant and food court. It also offers a free shuttle to Universal (across the road), SeaWorld and Wet 'n Wild (407 351 1000; www.radissonuniversal.com, $$, CCC). The **Holiday Inn Hotel & Suites** is similar, with 256 rooms and 134 1- and 2-bedroom suites, a large heated outdoor pool and on-site TGI Friday's restaurant (407 351 3333), $$–$$$, CCC.

Best of the rest

A recent trend to provide more deluxe accommodation has also added a touch of class to the downtown scene with the **Westin Grand Bohemian**. Part of the Grand Theme Hotels group, it features an early 20th-century Austrian theme, with the accent on fine art, fine dining and fine service. Its 14 storeys make it a major landmark, and it also boasts the sensational **The Boheme** restaurant, one of the most stylish bars I have been to (the Bosendorfer Lounge, with great live jazz most evenings), and a 14th-floor concierge suite, plus an in-hotel **Starbucks** coffee lounge, a heated pool, spa and fitness centre. The rooms are superbly appointed with high-speed Internet access, mini-bars, radio/CD players and huge interactive TVs, while there are 36 sumptuous suites. All rooms feature the ultra-comfy Westin Heavenly Bed. The art collection, classic and modern, liberally sprinkled through the public rooms, makes it more like an art gallery than a hotel (407 313 9000, www.grandbohemianhotel.com). $$$$, CCCC.

This quality element took a turn for the even more luxurious in July 2003 with the opening of the 500-acre (200-ha) **Grande Lakes Orlando**, a combination of a 584-

KEY TO INTERNATIONAL DRIVE ACCOMMODATION

1 Peabody Orlando
2 Wyndham Orlando Resort
3 Renaissance Orlando Resort
4 Sheraton Studio City
5 Red Horse Inn
6 Days Inn Lakeside
7 Holiday Inn Express
8 Quality Inn International
9 Quality Inn Plaza
10 Embassy Suites Jamaica Court
11 Howard Johnson Plaza
12 Howard Johnson Inn
13 Rosen Plaza Hotel
14 Crowne Plaza Hotel
15 Enclave Suites
16 Quality Suites At Parc Corniche
17 Wynfield Inn
18 Summerfield Suites Hotel

19 Comfort Suites
20 The Doubletree Castle
21 Rosen Center Hotel
22 Hawthorn Suites
23 Holiday Inn & Suites At Universal
24 Best Western Plaza
25 Embassy Suites I-Drive/Conv. Center
26 Radisson Hotel Universal Orlando
27 Portofino Bay Hotel
28 Hard Rock Hotel
29 Amerisuites Convention Center
30 Sheraton World Resort
31 Sierra Suites
32 Homewood Suites
33 Country Inn & Suites
34 Royal Pacific Resort
35 Grande Lakes Orlando
36 Holiday Inn Convention Center

Summerfield Suites

room, 5-star Ritz-Carlton Hotel, a 1,000-room JW Marriott Hotel, a 40,000sq ft (3,700sq metre) health spa, an 18-hole Greg Norman-designed golf course, tennis centre and a rich spread of shops and 11 restaurants, including the outstanding **Norman's**, featuring the 'new world' cuisine of celebrity chef Norman Van Aken. It is all bordered along one side by a natural forestry preserve, making it feel secluded and remote – quite a feat in this area. It is slightly off the beaten tourist track – at the junction of John Young Parkway and Central Florida Parkway – yet is only 2 miles (3km) from SeaWorld, 7 (11km) from Universal Orlando and 10 (16km) from Disney and Orlando International Airport.

It is the first **Ritz-Carlton** property in central Florida, and the scale and detail are wonderful. Lush gardens, abundant lakes and streams, Venetian-inspired architecture and a wealth of genuine antiques put this hotel on a different level to anything else around. The Ritz has a large, sloped-entry pool, kids' pool, three floodlit tennis courts, a signature shop and five restaurants. There is a separate children's check-in and the excellent Ritz Kids Club (for 5–12s; $25/child half day, $40 full day, including lunch) to ensure family-friendly attributes, and all the restaurants offer child menus. The rooms are gorgeous – beautifully furnished, with high-quality products

in the marbled bathrooms – and feature large plasma-screen TVs, radio/CD, mini-bar, hair-dryer, slippers and robe, and all have balconies. There are 66 spacious suites and 92 Club rooms on the top two floors, which add concièrge and butler service, food and beverage presentations in the Club Lounge, and Bvlgari amenities.

> **BRIT TIP:** Head for the Ritz-Carlton's lobby lounge for afternoon tea in style with a magnificent view, especially at sunset.

The **JW Marriott** is the new flagship hotel for the Marriott group, with Spanish-Moorish design, a formal Italian restaurant, French brasserie, Starbucks coffee lounge and a pool bar and grill. There is also a unique 'lazy river' mini water-park (making for the largest pool deck in Florida), plus an additional children's zero-depth-entry pool, a splash fountain and a separate kids' check-in. And, while the Marriott is more convention orientated, it is still well geared for families with all the facilities, a variety of shops and the option to use the Ritz Kids activity programme and all the dining options in the sister hotel. The rooms are plush and ultra-comfortable, 70 per cent have balconies and there are 64 spacious suites.

The **golf** course here is immaculate, and every foursome receives a free caddie (virtually unknown for a public course in Florida). The beautiful citrus-tinged

Portofino Bay Hotel

health spa is the best in the region, with a huge fitness centre and aerobics studio, lap pool (all free to guests at both hotels), spa cuisine restaurant and a huge array of massages, treatments and beauty therapies, with a *sanitas per aqua* (health through water) philosophy that guarantees a revitalising experience. The pricing is upscale, but there may be some deals early on (407 206 2400/2300, www.grandelakes.com). $$$$–$$$$$, CCCCC.

One final hotel worth considering is the **Hyatt Regency** at Orlando International Airport, especially if you arrive late and would benefit from a first-night rest. It boasts two excellent restaurants – including the elegant, upscale Hemisphere, with monthly wine-tasting evenings and a magnificent runway view – and a smart pool deck, plus a fitness room, lounge and business centre. The 446 rooms are superbly spacious, especially their 'corner' rooms, and many feature internal balconies overlooking the 6-storey airport atrium. The most surprising feature is how quiet it is. There is no noticeable aircraft noise and none of the bustle you would associate with an airport hotel. There is valet and self-parking, with the added advantage of going to collect your hire car in the morning rather than at the end of a long flight (407 825 1234, http://orlandoairport.hyatt.com). $$$, CCC½.

Suites and holiday homes

A fast-growing area of accommodation in Orlando, suites hotels and holiday homes are a valuable way of larger family groups or friends staying together and cutting costs by self-catering. The homes, whether individual houses, collections of houses, resorts or condominiums (apartment blocks),

usually have access to excellent facilities, such as pools and recreation areas, and are equipped with microwaves, TVs and washer-dryers. For these, a hire car is just about essential, but the savings for larger groups are obvious.

Suite things

Suites hotels are virtually unknown in the UK but provide a combination of hotel and apartment, with extra value for larger families or groups. Typically, a suites room gives you a living room and mini-kitchen, including microwave, coffee-maker, fridge, cutlery and crockery, while many offer a complimentary continental breakfast (or better). All have swimming pools and grocery stores or snack bars. They vary only in the number of bedrooms and can sleep 6 to 10 people.

They include the **Comfort Suites** on west Highway 192 near Splendid China (407 390 9888), on Turkey Lake Road (407 351 5050), adjacent to I-4 and I-Drive, plus their smart new 198-room development behind Old Town in Kissimmee, which even offers a fitness centre (407 397 7848; $$–$$$, CCC); the **Tropical Palms Funsuites**, on Holiday Trail, next to Old Town (407 396 4595; $$–$$$, CCC½) with well-equipped studio and 2-bedroom suites; the 2-bedroom, two-bath studios of **Enclave Suites** (on Carrier Drive, off Kirkman Road, $$–$$$, CCC½) where kids eat free with their parents; or the **AmeriSuites** group (on I-Drive, in Lake Buena Vista and by the airport, tel 1-800 833 1516; $$–$$$, CCC), which have a pool, fitness centre and a free breakfast.

The **Country Inn & Suites** offer four new properties in the I-Drive area, Lake Buena Vista, Kissimmee and by the International Airport. Good value, with large, clean rooms, free continental breakfast, local phone calls, Disney transport, pool and fitness centre. The property on Universal Boulevard is possibly the best, with 170 standard rooms with in-room safe, coffee-maker, hair-dryer and iron/ironing board; while the 48 king suites include microwave and fridge. It is about 1 mile (1.6km) from Universal Orlando and half that from Wet 'n Wild, yet much quieter than many I-Drive hotels (407 313 4200, www.jaytelhotels.com). $$–$$$, CCC.

One of the most remarkable properties is the **Holiday Inn Family Suites Resort** at Lake Buena Vista (almost opposite Orlando World Center Marriott, on I-Drive South). From the lobby, themed as a turn-of-the-century railway station, through the amazing range of facilities (food court, general store, Club Car casual dining, lounge bar, toddlers' play area, video games room, fitness centre, mini-golf, swimming pool and elaborate kiddie pool), to the choice of six different 1- and 2-bedroom suites, here is a dazzling family choice, especially with their Camp Holiday activity programme and separate check-in for kids. The Kidsuites feature a semi-private bedroom with bunk beds (additional fold-out child's sleeper available), TV, video and CD/cassette player, video game system, activity table and chairs, plus the private adult king bedroom. The **Club Car Restaurant** has an excellent free buffet breakfast, and there is free transport to all the Disney parks. The zero-depth-entry water playground, with its array of squirty fountains, will keep the young 'uns happy! (407 387 5437, www.hifamilysuites.com.) $$$, CCCC.

Other one-off suites properties worthy of note include the well-appointed **Buena Vista Suites** (407 239 8588, $$$, CCC) and the eye-catching **Caribe Royale Resort Suites** (407 238 8000, $$$$,

CCCC½), both at the lower end of I-Drive, with their choice of 1-bedroom suites and 2-bedroom villas, super pool area with water-slide and one of the best free breakfast buffets in town. Equally, the **Hawthorn Suites** (three properties in Orlando), **Homewood Suites** (two in Lake Buena Vista and one on I-Drive) and the **Sierra Suites** (Lake Buena Vista and I-Drive) offer a more upmarket feel with mid-range pricing ($$–$$$, facilities vary).

Highly recommended

The two **Summerfield Suites by Wyndham** (on I-Drive, 407 352 2400, and Lake Buena Vista, 407 238 0777, www.summerfield-orlando.com) are another fine example, with suites sleeping up to 8, appetising free breakfast, convenience store and fresh, inviting ambience ($$$, CCC). The LBV site features a deli, while the I-Drive property also offers a lobby bar. The 1-bedroom suite is wonderfully spacious for a family of four, the standard 2-bed adds a second bathroom, and the 2-bed trio suite is ideal for eight. Both properties have relaxing pool decks, with kids' pool and whirlpool, are perfectly situated for the attractions and represent a relaxing retreat at the end the day.

The Embassy Suites group boasts eight properties throughout Orlando, but arguably the best is the **Embassy Suites International Drive/Convention Center** (407 352 1400, $$$, CCCC). It is the most prominent and consistently gets good reader feedback. 'I would strongly recommend the Embassy Suites,' says Gary Baldwin. 'It includes an "all you can eat" buffet breakfast, which is great when you're planning a day at a theme park. Also, there are free drinks and snacks from 5.30–7.30 every evening.' It is

4

wonderfully smart, with excellent service, and rooms (either standard 2-room suites sleeping four or double-doubles, sleeping six) that are spacious, providing two TVs, coffee-maker, fridge and microwave. The outdoor pool deck is comfortable and there is also a kids' splash pool and an indoor pool, plus a sauna, steam room and gym. The Southwestern-style Sedona Café and Hurricane's Lounge give them a real edge in dining options, irrespective of their great I-Drive location. They also offer a free Disney shuttle service and transport to the other attractions from $4–8/person. One to look out for.

Holiday resorts

Another accommodation type, which combines the best of hotels, suites and private villas, is the handful of genuine resort-style, purpose-built complexes, some of which double as timeshare resorts. A kind of cross between condominiums and motels, they have the advantage of great in-resort facilities. The best include the **Orange Lake Resort** (4½ miles/ 7km west of Maingate on Highway 192, 407 239 0000; $$$–$$$$, CCCC), with a mixture of 2-bedroom, 2-bath villas and suites, golf, watersports and even a cinema, and the **Villages at Mango Key** (on Lindfields Boulevard, 4 miles (6.4km) west of Maingate, 407 239 7100; $$$, CCC), a collection of smart, new 2- and 3-bedroom townhouses, with pool, jacuzzi, tennis and volleyball.

Grande Lakes Resort

Liki Tiki Village on the western fringe of Highway 192 is a timeshare set-up that often has good-value apartments to rent on a weekly basis. Their newest blocks offer huge 2-bedroom flats, with well-equipped kitchens (down to coffee-makers and ice-makers), while the 64-acre (26-ha) complex boasts two pools plus the Liki Tiki Lagoon mini water park, tennis courts, paddle boats, bikes, poolside bar and grill and a free continental breakfast Mon–Fri (when timeshare presentations are held). You don't have to attend any timeshare hard-sell, just enjoy the great facilities (407 239 5000, www.islandone.com). $$$, CCCC.

Top of the range in this category is the **Vistana Resort**, just off the lower end of I-Drive in Lake Buena Vista, where facilities include fitness centres with steam and sauna rooms, five pools and 13 tennis courts, to back up their luxurious 2-bedroom villas that sleep up to 8 (407 239 3100). $$$–$$$$, CCCCC.

Holiday homes

Vacation homes have become big business in this area and now account for a huge slice of the British market as they are ideal for repeat visitors, large family groups and those who just like their own privacy and facilities. They tend to be grouped in newly built estates and several are 'gated' communities for added security. Nearly all offer a private pool and can sleep up to 16. Some are also classed as executive homes, and this usually means the range of facilities will be much greater (DVD players, games consoles, outdoor barbecue grills, etc) rather than any increase in size. There are now dozens of companies offering private homes in central Florida, and if you are booking independently, there are several key questions to ask before you make your choice.

First, what are the arrangements for picking up the keys – do you need to go to an office that may be some way from the house or do they have a lock-box at the house which you access via a combination? Is there a local contact if anything is wrong with your booking (many homes are rented by private owners who may not live in Florida), or is the property maintained by a management company (who should be able to provide on-the-spot service)? Do they offer a security bonding for your cash booking, and are they members of a reputable organisation like the Better Business Bureau of Central Florida? If it's winter, is the pool heated, and how much do they charge for heating? Finally, are they really as close to Disney as they say – some homes can be down in Polk County, 20–45 minutes' drive away. One final warning – once you have sampled pool home life, you may never go back to a hotel!

The bottom line is you need to do your homework and shop around as you would for any significant purchase, checking with organisations like the Central Florida Property Managers' Association (www.cfpma.com). The following all pass the *Brit's Guide* credibility test. **Welcome Homes USA** have condos, villas and private homes in the Kissimmee area, with some smart properties at a broad range of prices. Their full-size houses (3–5 bedrooms) come with communal or private pools. Homes are only 10–15 minutes' drive from *Walt Disney World*, in residential areas, and feature everything from dishwashers to teaspoons (but not hair-dryers). $$–$$$$, CC. Call 407 933 2233 for their holiday homes and 407 933 2889 for their well-equipped condo complex, or visit www.welcome-homes.com.

For similar great value and excellent properties **Alexander**

Holiday Homes, also in Kissimmee, manage some 260 properties, from standard condo villas to ultra-luxury large executive homes sleeping up to 10, all with pools and immaculately furnished, within 15 minutes of *Walt Disney World Resort*, with private pools. This company was the first of its kind in Orlando, and still offers a friendly, efficient service. They were also only the third management company in Florida to earn a prestigious AAA rating (the American Automobile Association). Visit www.floridasunshine.com (407 932 3683). $$–$$$, CC.

Premier Vacation Homes offers a great range of spacious properties with 2 to 6 bedrooms, sleeping up to 14, in secure residential communities within a 15-minute drive of *Walt Disney World Resort*. The homes are privately owned and have been purchased and furnished as 'vacation' homes, with screened pools, two TVs, fully equipped kitchens (including dishwasher, washer-dryer, microwave and coffee-maker), at least one king or queen bed, and free local phone calls. Maid service can be provided for an additional fee. The **Luxury homes** (2 to 4 bedrooms) are their standard accommodation, while the **Executive homes** (3 to 6 bedrooms)

The atrium at the Embassy Suites

4

are bigger, with an extra TV, VCR and gas barbecue grill (407 396 2401, or 0500 892634 in the UK, or visit www.premier-vacation-homes.com). $$$, CC.

A company I have got to know well and can highly recommend is **Florida Leisure**, British-owned and with great attention to detail. With some 90 homes – from 2 to 7 bedrooms – in the Kissimmee area (most of them barely two years old), they pride themselves on a personal touch. Many properties are in the Executive range, which means the fullest range of amenities in addition to their large, private, screened pools, and often in a secure, gated community. You can see all their homes on their website plus lots of local info, especially for restaurants and golf. Call Nigel or Marion on 407 870 1600 or look up www.floridaleisure.com. $$–$$$$, CCC.

An alternative, UK-based company is **Sun Villas Florida Direct**, launched in September 2001 by a former managing director of Lunn Poly to provide a bespoke holiday that can offer villa accommodation, flights, attraction tickets and car hire. They have a variety of properties, from Orlando down to Sarasota and Naples, and maintain consistently high standards. Contact Sun Villas Florida Direct on 01926 336611 or look up www.SVFDirect.com.

A final offering here is **Florida Choice Vacation Homes**, which offers townhomes (3–4 bed properties, with communal pools and other recreation facilities), standard and executive homes (3–7 bed private properties), some with heated pools and with free local phone calls. There is optional maid service and cot and high-chair rentals. Call 407 847 0284 or visit www.floridachoice.com. $$$–$$$$, CCC.

Bed and breakfast

Bed and breakfast in Orlando is in a more upscale, almost boutique style. Principle among them is the **Wonderland Inn** in Kissimmee, an 11-room, restored Historic Registry property off the beaten track but only 10 minutes from the Highway 192 area. Each room has a delightful, individual touch, and several are designed for singles as well as doubles, plus one honeymoon suite. The attentiveness of the staff is wonderful and even the lovely gardens have an old-fashioned charm light years from the hectic tourist whirl elsewhere. They also offer a four-course Romantic Candlelight Dinner served in the gazebo (weather permitting) and a Romantic Getaway Package that includes 3-hour limo service, dinner, breakfast in bed, massage or two, champagne and chocolates (tel: 1-877 847 2477, www.wonderlandinn.com). $$$, CC.

The pretty Lake Eola district downtown also has two fine properties. **The Veranda** has 12 intimate, cottage-style rooms, ranging from Queen Studio and King Suites to a lovely honeymoon suite, set in landscaped gardens with a private courtyard, swimming pool and spa area. Breakfast features fresh pastries, seasonal fruits, juices, tea and coffee, and the quiet setting is another bonus, although there are some good restaurants and shops within easy walking distance (407 849 0321). $$$–$$$$, CCC.

The nearby **Eo Inn** is another little gem, a genuine boutique hotel and spa (with a huge range of treatments, from massage to pedicures), featuring 17 deluxe rooms. The lush grounds, rooftop terrace and lake vistas provide a refreshing alternative to the usual hotel experience. (407 481 8485, www.eoinn.com). $$$–$$$$, CC.

Babysitting

For folks who want an evening off from parenthood to take advantage of Orlando's nightlife, babysitting is a ready option. The two most relied-upon, fully trained and licensed companies are KinderCare (also contracted to *Walt Disney World Resort in Florida* and Airtours, 407 846 2027) and Anny's Nannies (407 826 8949). Both will visit hotels, motels, condos and homes, while KinderCare also organises group events and activities.

Buying a holiday home

The quality of life, a favourable exchange rate and the fabulous Florida weather are all compelling reasons to look into the idea of acquiring your own vacation home either to provide a guaranteed holiday home in future, a source of investment, a winter retreat or even a future retirement home. But, apart from the fact that it is easy to be starry-eyed after a wonderful holiday, there are companies willing to exploit the naivety of tourists. Therefore, you need to do your homework, especially when it comes to understanding the terminology of American property buying.

So where do you start? Well, if like me you have looked in the window of a Realtor's (the American equivalent of an estate agent), you will have seen the tempting price differential compared with the UK. In the third quarter of 2002, the average price of a single-family home in Florida rose by 8% (to $141,300) on the same period in 2001, making the idea even more alluring. At a time of low interest rates, investing in property in such an obvious growth area represents good business sense.

The other key element is that new homes can often be cheaper than a comparable older property because of modern construction techniques and the number being built in central Florida, but this also means there is a lot of variety in terms of the build quality so you need a trustworthy builder for both quality and after-sales service.

That means you need help from someone who has built up an unimpeachable reputation in this field. In this instance, **Greater Homes of Orlando** gets the *Brit's Guide* seal of approval. It is a family-run company which has been building here since 1965 and has sold more than 2,000 homes to British owners. Not only is it a reliable and quality-conscious firm, its website carries essential info for anyone thinking of home ownership here. Look up www.greaterhomes.com (notably for their pages on mortgage terminologies) or call 407 869 0300. You will also find useful info on websites for **Alexander Holiday Homes** (www.floridasunshine.com) and **Florida Leisure** (www.floridaleisure.com, click on the Real Estate links). Florida Leisure is also a registered Realtor and publishes its own Home Buying Guide, available free from their web site. Other builders worth considering are Beazer Homes and KB Homes, both of which are also rated well above average for build quality.

Owning a piece of the Magic is tempting, but you must get all the facts first. If you are still tempted, you'd be well advised to look for a company which specialises in selling to British buyers. There are a dozen or so firms that primarily offer vacation-style properties, and several that deal mainly in the British buying market. You might then like to consider investigating one of the firms that allows you to fund your mortgage in sterling, through a UK bank, rather than opt for the dollar equivalent. If you live in the UK and are paid in sterling, a US dollar mortgage can be costly, inconvenient and potentially fraught. For instance, it is common practice for US mortgage companies to 'sell' their newly arranged mortgages to another bank or lender shortly after closing a loan, making it hard to track. Repayment of a US dollar mortgage with sterling is also subject to changing exchange rates, so UK borrowers can't be sure how much is needed to repay a dollar monthly mortgage. Two publications to note are *International Homes* and *Homes Overseas*, both of which have extensive Florida sections.

However, one company I have got to know well through my contacts with the British-American Chamber of Commerce, and that I am happy to recommend, is **British Homes Florida Group**. This is a well-established, specialist Orlando-based firm and (just as importantly) a certified Realtor, which deals almost exclusively in finding investment property, whether it be a short-term rental 'own to let' holiday home in the Disney area or an exclusive private coastal retreat. Through subsidiaries British Homes Florida-Sales, Inc, and British Home Florida-Loans, Inc, they have the one-stop-shop package. The Home Loans division works with various low-cost sterling mortgages, including UK 'Flexible Trackers,' fixed-rate and 'Interest only' options. Through *British Mortgages Abroad*, a GE Consumer Finance company, you can ensure your mortgage is arranged via a British

Bob's Buying Tips

1) ask for references from other UK owners; 2) check the management company for references – and look up the Better Business Bureau for Central Florida; 3) ensure the product has a warranty; 4) walk through the community where you're thinking of buying and talk to people there; 5) ensure the documentation allows you to let it on a short-term basis; 6) make sure you have all the proper fees, registrations and taxes in the US. (With thanks to Bob Mandell, Chairman of Greater Homes.)

currency loan at British rates.

British Homes Florida is also *independent* of any builder or seller in the UK or US. It has both UK and US real estate and mortgage professionals, who I can confirm are expert in all British and American procedures. It is a member of both the Florida Association of Mortgage Brokers and British-American Chamber of Commerce.

To contact British Homes (in Florida) call 407 396 9914, or (in the UK) 0800 096 5989 (24 hours) or email bhlflorida@earthlink.net. You can also look up their website, www.britishhomeloansflorida.com, or visit their offices if you are in Orlando at 2960 Vineland Road, Kissimmee (above the Edwin Watts golf shop at the T-Junction of routes 535 and 192).

Whoever you go with, ensure they can refer you to other experts in UK and US taxation, immigration, hazard insurance, structural warranties and other areas *essential* to hassle-free home-ownership in Florida. Property in Orlando has increased in value at a steady 10–12 per cent over the last 10 years, but there is never any guarantee, and rates *can* fluctuate.

Holiday Inn Family Suites

5

The Theme Parks – Disney's Fab Four

(or, Spending the Day with Mickey Mouse and Co.)

By now you should be prepared to deal with the main business of any visit to Orlando: *Walt Disney World Resort in Florida* and the other main theme parks of Universal Orlando, SeaWorld and Busch Gardens.

If you have only a week in the area this is where you should concentrate your attention but even then you may decide Busch Gardens is a bridge too far. If you have less than a week, you should focus on seeing as much of *Walt Disney World Resort* as possible. There is SO much packed into every park and the main tourist areas, even 2 weeks is scarcely enough to give first-timers more than an outline of central Florida.

Firstly, you can save money off many attractions if you shop around. Disney tickets are available at *The Disney Stores* in the UK, and through Keith Prowse, Theme Park Holidays (see page 13) and most of the tour operators. Buying your Disney tickets in advance is also advisable, but work out your requirements first – you wouldn't get full use out of, say, a 7-Day Park Hopper Plus AND a 5-Park Orlando FlexTicket in just a 2-week holiday. You will also find **discount coupons** in tourist publications distributed in Orlando for many of the smaller attractions (or from the Guest Services desk at your hotel – it's worth asking), while the **tour operators'** welcome meetings usually have special offers and tickets for the latest excursions.

The **Official Visitor Center** at 8723 International Drive (in the Gala Center on the corner of Austrian Row; 407 363 5871,

SpectroMagic Parade

© Disney

www.orlandoinfo.com; see map on page 76) is also worth checking out for discounts. Equally, the **Universal Attractions** booths at several shopping malls (notably Orlando Premium Outlets) have some great deals (3 days for the price of 2, 2-for-1 drinks, etc) on a huge range of attractions. It is possible to pick up free tickets for attending timeshare presentations but they can take up half a day of your precious holiday. Other sites worth visiting for discounts are www.ticketmania.com, www.discountorlandovacation.com, both of which are Florida based but ship to Britain, and the new UK-based Attraction Tickets Direct (www.attraction-tickets-direct.co.uk). Then there is the Orlando Sentinel info-based www.go2orlando.com. Try www.orlandosavings.com and www.orlando.floridacouponsavings.com for free coupons.

Ratings

All the rides and shows are judged on a unique rating system that splits them into the **thrill rides** and **scenic rides**. Thrill rides earn T ratings out of five (hence a TTTTT is as exciting as they get) and scenic rides get A ratings out of five (an AA ride is likely to be over-cute and missable). Obviously, it is a matter of opinion to a certain extent, but you can be sure a T or A ride is not worth your time, a TT or AA is

> **BRIT TIP:** Offers of 'Free' Disney tickets usually means timeshare firms, who also have several 'Official' visitor centres. I-Drive has the only genuinely Official Visitor Center (see page 85).

> **BRIT TIP:** If you DO want to check out timeshare options, look first at Disney Vacation Club for the guaranteed way to secure memorable holidays. Call 407 566 3300 or visit http://disney.go.com.

worth seeing only if there is no queue, a TTT or AAA should be seen if you have time, but you won't miss much if you don't, a TTTT or AAAA ride is a big-time attraction that should be high on your list of things to do, and finally a TTTTT or AAAAA attraction should not be missed! The latter will have the longest queues and so you should plan your visit around them. Some rides are restricted to children over a certain height and are not advisable for people with back, neck or heart problems, or for expectant mothers. Where this is the case I have just noted 'Restrictions: 3ft 6in/106cm', and so on. Height restrictions (strictly enforced) are based on the average 5-year-old being 3ft 6in/106cm tall, 6s being 3ft 9in/114cm and 9s being 4ft 4in/132cm.

Baby swap

Where families have small children, but Mum and Dad both want to try a ride, you DON'T have to queue twice. When you get to the front of the queue, tell the operator you want to do a 'baby swap'. This means Mum can ride while Dad looks after junior and, on her return, Dad can have his go.

Many children also get a big thrill from collecting autographs from the various Disney characters they meet, and most shops sell some neat **autograph books** for that purpose.

Magic Kingdom Park

The starting point for any visit has to be the *Magic Kingdom*, the park that best embodies the spirit of delight that Disney bestows on its visitors. It's the original development that sparked the tourist boom in Orlando back in 1971. In comparative terms, the *Magic Kingdom Park* is similar to the *Disneyland Park* at *Disneyland® Resort Paris* and *Disneyland Park* in Los Angeles. Outside those, it has no equal as an enchanting and exciting day out for all the family. All Disney employees are known as Cast Members and they are almost unfailingly cheerful and keen to help. It is also worth pointing out that while, superficially, some rides are the same as those in Paris or LA, there are key differences, notably on Pirates of the Caribbean, Big Thunder Mountain Railroad and the Haunted Mansion. And Space

5

The Magic Kingdom Park at a glance

Location	Off World Drive, Walt Disney World
Size	107 acres (43ha) in 7 'lands'
Hours	9am–7pm off peak; 9am–10pm Washington's birthday (see page 18), spring school holidays; 9am–11pm high season (Easter, summer holidays, Thanksgiving and Christmas)
Admission	Under 3 free; 3–9 $42 (1-day ticket), $167 (4-Day Park Hopper), $216 (5-Day Park Hopper Plus); adult (10+) $52, $208, $269. Prices do not include tax.
Parking	$7
Lockers	Yes; under Main Street Railroad Station; $7 ($2 refund)
Pushchairs	$8 and $15 (Stroller Shop to right of main entrance, $1 deposit refunded)
Wheelchairs	$8 ($1 deposit refunded) or $40 ($10 deposit refunded) (Main Ticket Centre or Stroller Shop)
Top Attractions	Splash Mountain, Space Mountain, Mickey's PhilharMagic, The ExtraTERRORestrial Alien Encounter, most rides in Fantasyland
Don't Miss	Share A Dream Come True Parade, SpectroMagic Parade (high season and weekends) and fireworks shows

Hidden Costs	**Meals**	Burger, chips and coke $7.48 3-course dinner $35 (Cinderella's Table)
	Kids' meal	$3.49
	T-shirts	$19–32
	Souvenirs	$1–895
	Sundries	Spray Fan (handy when it's hot) $16.04

ADVENTURELAND
1 Swiss Family Treehouse
2 Jungle Cruise
3 Pirates Of The Caribbean
4 The Enchanted Tiki Room (under new management)
5 Magic Carpets of Aladdin

FRONTIERLAND
6 Splash Mountain
7 Big Thunder Mountain Railroad
8 Country Bear Jamboree
9 Raft To Tom Sawyer Island

LIBERTY SQUARE
10 Goofy's Country Dancin' Jamboree
11 Liberty Square Riverboat
12 The Haunted Mansion
13 The Hall of Presidents

FANTASYLAND
14 'It's a Small World'
15 Dumbo The Flying Elephant
16 Mad Tea Party
17 The Many Adventures Of Winnie The Pooh
18 Snow White's Scary Adventures
19 Cinderella's Golden Carousel
20 Mickey's PhilharMagic
21 Peter Pan's Flight
22 Castle Forecourt Stage
23 Fantasyland Character Festival
24 Ariel's Grotto
25 Fairytale Garden

MICKEY'S TOONTOWN FAIR
26 Mickey's Country House
27 Minnie's Country House
28 Toontown Hall of Fame
29 The Barnstormer at Goofy's Wiseacre Farm
30 Donald's Boat

TOMORROWLAND
31 Space Mountain
32 Tomorrowland Indy Speedway
33 Astro Orbiter
34 Walt Disney's Carousel of Progress
35 Tomorrowland Transit Authority
36 The ExtraTERRORestrial Alien Encounter
37 Buzz Lightyear's Space Ranger Spin
38 The Timekeeper
39 Galaxy Palace Theater

TRANSPORT
40 Walt Disney World Railroad
41 Boat Dock
42 Monorail Station
43 Bus Station

MAGIC
KINGDOM
PARK

MAIN STREET USA

MAIN ENTRANCE

Cinderella's castle

Mountain here is a completely different ride.

I will now attempt to steer you through a typical day at the parks, with a guide to the main rides, shows and places to eat, how to park, how to avoid the worst of the crowds and how much you should expect to pay.

This essential park takes up just 107 acres (43ha) of Disney's near

BRIT TIP: For the smoothest entry to *Walt Disney World Resort in Florida* from west Highway 192, take Seralago Boulevard opposite the Holiday Inn Hotel & Suites next to Old Town, turn left on to a non-toll stretch of Osceola Parkway and follow the signs to your chosen park. On east 192, turn off on Sherberth Road, go north to the first traffic lights and turn right, then pick up the Disney signs.

31,000 acres (12,555ha) but attracts almost as many visitors as the rest put together! It has seven separate 'lands', like slices of a large cake, centred on Florida's most famous landmark, Cinderella Castle. More than 40 attractions are packed in, not to mention numerous shops and

BRIT TIP: Reader Roy Williams says: 'We bought a bright, 3-in plastic ball that we fixed to our car aerial in the car park, enabling us to find it easily on our return.' You could also leave a familiar, non-valuable item in the window for extra help.

restaurants (although the eating opportunities are less impressive than *Epcot* and *Disney-MGM Studios*).

It's easy to get overwhelmed by it all, especially as it does get so busy (even the fast-food restaurants have serious queues in high season), so study the notes and plan your visit around what most takes your fancy.

Disney's FASTPASS Service

Another essential aid to queuing here is *Disney's FASTPASS Service*. A number of the main attractions at the parks now have this wonderful service that allows you to roam while you wait for your allotted time to ride. How it works: insert your main

Beauty and the Beast

BRIT TIP: If you have pre-paid vouchers for park entrance rather than the actual tickets, you have to exchange them at a ticket booth. Go to the Guest Relations window and you will avoid the queues.

park entrance ticket into the FASTPASS (FP) turnstile (to the side of the attraction's entrance) and you get another ticket giving you a period in which to return for your ride with only a minimal wait (NB: you need one FP ticket for every person who wants to ride, not just one per party). You can hold only one FP ticket per 2-hour period, although once you've used it you can get another. If you start by going to one of the FP rides, collecting your ticket and returning later, you can by-pass a lot of standing in line. You can also get another FP as soon as your 'window' opens: if your time slot for Space Mountain is 10–11am, you could get another FP for, say, Buzz Lightyear's Space Ranger Spin at 10.05am and then go and ride Space Mountain! Many people still miss this, but it is FREE (FASTPASS rides are indicated by FP in attraction descriptions).

Pal Mickey

If you want the ultimate theme park friend, to help you queue, offer tips, play games and help find the characters, just ask Mickey – Pal Mickey, that is. This is a new, high-tech 10½-in (27-cm) tall cuddly toy that talks to you (using wireless communication at strategic points around the main parks) as a kind of tour guide, with helpful hints (e.g. in *Disney-MGM Studios:* 'Fantasmic! will be starting in about an hour'),

insider info (on Main Street USA: 'See the names written on those second-storey windows? Those folks helped Walt build his Magic Kingdom!') and interactive games while you wait in a queue (and which still work when you get back home). Pal Mickey can be rented (at $8, plus tax, a day, with a $50 refundable deposit) or bought outright ($46.94 plus tax). I'm unsure if this is the ultimate gimmick or just a wonderful extra, but certainly the early signs were that those who tried him just loved their cuddly Pal.

Cast members

Disney Cast Members (or CMs) are renowned for their helpful and cheerful style, and are always willing to help, offer advice or just stop and chat. Interaction with CMs often provides some of the best memories of visiting the parks and resorts. So, if you've had exceptional service or a CM has gone out of their way to help you out, let Disney know as they really value this feedback (and CMs get acknowledged for it, too). Call in at Guest Relations on your way out (or City Hall at the *Magic Kingdom Park*) and record your vote of thanks. Better still, write to: Walt Disney World Guest Communications, PO Box 10000, Lake Buena Vista, Florida, 32830-1000, USA, or email via www.disneyworld.com (go to the Guest Services link). You can even download a form to say thanks at www.whatwouldwaltdo.com.

Location

The *Magic Kingdom Park* is situated at the innermost end of the vacation kingdom, with its entrance toll plaza three-quarters of the way along World Drive, the main entrance road off Highway 192. World Drive runs north-south through *Walt Disney*

World Resort in Florida, while the Interstate 4 (I-4) entrance, Epcot Drive, runs basically east-west. Unless you are staying at one of *Walt Disney World Resort* hotels, you will have to pay your $7 parking fee at the toll plaza and that brings you to the car park (or 'parking lot' in American-speak) that can accommodate more than 10,000 cars.

The majority arrive between 9.30 and 11.30am, so the car parks can become pretty jammed then, which

> BRIT TIP: Staying at a Disney resort? You can sometimes get to ride up front on the monorail (and get a 'driver' certificate!) if you ask a Cast Member on the platform.

is another good reason to get here EARLY. If you can't make it by 9am during peak periods, you might want to wait until after 1pm, or even later when the park is open as late as 11pm (in high summer and Christmas). Remember to note on your parking ticket exactly what area you parked in and the row number, e.g. Mickey, Row 30. You will struggle to remember otherwise, and all hire cars look exactly the same!

A system of motorised trams carries you from the car park to the Transportation and Ticket Center at the heart of the operation. Unless you already have your ticket (which will save you valuable time), you will have to queue up at the ticket booths to go any further. From here, the monorail or a ferryboat will bring you to the doorstep of the *Magic Kingdom Park* itself. The monorail (dead ahead of you) is quicker, if there isn't a long queue, otherwise it is usually better to bear left and take a slower ferryboat. Of course, if you are staying at a Disney hotel, one of

the free resort buses will deliver you to the park's front door (or the monorail or boat will if you are at one of the *Magic Kingdom* resorts).

One final note, in all the main theme parks you may well find one or two attractions closed for refurbishment to mark the constant process of keeping everything fresh. However, you will never be short of things to do!

Main Street, USA

Right, we've finally reached the park itself... but not quite. Hopefully you've arrived early and are among the leading hordes aiming to swarm through the main entrance. The published opening times may say 9am, but the gates to the *Magic Kingdom Park* are likely to open up to 45 minutes before then.

You will find yourself in **Main Street, USA**, the first of the seven lands. If you are here at opening time, there is an informal Welcome parade, with costumed singers and dancers, and the Character Train then arrives at Main Street Station to bring a variety of characters for a friendly meet-and-greet in Town Square (get those autograph books ready!). A family is then chosen at random to sprinkle some 'pixie dust' on the Magic Kingdom to officially open the park for the day. Immediately on your right is **Exposition Hall**, a photographic centre featuring archive film material, a mini cinema showing Disney classics and a series of interactive games, plus some cartoon photo opportunities. On your left is **City Hall**, where you can pick up a park map and daily schedule (if you haven't been given one at the toll plaza) and make reservations for the main restaurants (highly advisable at peak periods). This is also the place to visit to find out where the characters will be appearing and when. Ahead of you is **Town Square**, where you can take a one-way ride down Main Street, USA on a horse-drawn bus or fire engine and visit the **Car Barn** mini museum. The Street itself houses some of the best shopping in the *Magic Kingdom Park* (check out the massive Emporium), plus the **Walt Disney World Railroad** (AAA), a Western-themed steam train that circles the park and is one of the better attractions when the queues are long elsewhere (although – be warned – Town Square station is the busiest).

> BRIT TIP: Save paying up to three times more for your drinks by bringing your own bottled water in a back-pack to all the parks and use the many drinking fountains for refills.

For dining, you have lunch and dinner at **Tony's Town Square Restaurant**, specialising in Italian meals, **The Plaza Restaurant** (lunch and dinner, sandwiches, salads and sundaes) and **The Crystal Palace** (breakfast, lunch and dinner, buffet-style food with Winnie the Pooh, Tigger and Co). Quick bites can be bought from **Casey's Corner** (hot dogs, chips and soft drinks), **Main Street Bakery** (coffee and pastries), **Main Street Cinema** and **Main Street Confectionary** (chocolate and sweets) and the **Plaza Ice Cream Parlor**. Disney characters also appear periodically outside Exposition Hall.

Barnstormer at Goofy's Wiseacre Farm

Main Street, USA

Look out for the **Guest Information Board** at the top of Main Street, USA (on the left) that gives waiting times for all the attractions through the day. The **Baby Center** (for nursing mothers) can also be found at the top of Main Street, to the left next to the Crystal Palace, along with the park's **First Aid** station.

Unless you are a late arrival, give Main Street no more than a passing glance for the moment and head for the end of the street where you will find the real entrance to the park. This is where you must await the official opening hour for the famous 'Rope drop', and you should adopt one of three tactics here, each aimed at doing one or two of the most popular rides before the queues become substantial (an hour or more for Splash Mountain is not unknown).

One: if you fancy heading straight for the 5-star, log-flume ride Splash Mountain, keep left in front of the Crystal Palace with the majority of the crowd who will be heading for the same place.

Two: if you have young children who can't wait to ride on Cinderella's Golden Carousel or the other Fantasyland rides, stay in the middle and head directly through the castle.

Three: if the thrills of the ExtraTERRORestrial Alien Encounter and the indoor roller-coaster Space Mountain appeal to you first, move to the right by The Plaza Restaurant and you'll get straight into Tomorrowland. Now you will be in pole position for the opening rush (and it will be a rush, believe me; take care if you're here with small children).

Adventureland

If you head to the left (effectively going clockwise around the park – always a good idea), you will enter Adventureland. If you're going to Splash Mountain first, you pass the Swiss Family Treehouse on your left and bear right through an archway (with restrooms on your right) into Frontierland, where you turn left and Splash Mountain is dead ahead. Stopping in Adventureland, however, these are the attractions:

Swiss Family Treehouse: this imitation Banyan tree is a clever replica of the treehouse from Disney's 1960 film *Swiss Family Robinson*. It's a walk-through attraction where the queues (rarely long) move steadily if not quickly, providing a fascinating glimpse of the ultimate treehouse, complete with kitchen, rope bridges and running water! AAA.

Jungle Cruise: it's not so much the scenic, geographically suspect boat ride (where the Nile suddenly becomes the Amazon) that is so amusing here as the patter of your boat's captain, who spins a non-stop yarn about your adventure that features wild animals, tropical plants, hidden temples and sudden waterfalls. Great detail but long queues, so visit either early morning or late afternoon (evening queues are shortest, but you'll miss some of the detail in the dark). AAAA (FP).

Pirates of the Caribbean: one of Disney's most impressive attractions that involves their pioneering work in audio-animatronics, life-size figures that move, talk and, in this instance, lay siege to a Caribbean island! Your underground boat ride takes you through a typical pirate adventure and the wizardry of the special effects is truly amazing. This is worth several rides, although it may be a bit spooky for very young children. Queues are rarely long and almost non-existent late in the day. AAAAA.

The Enchanted Tiki Room – Under New Management: this bird-laden, audio-animatronics venture features Iago (from *Aladdin*) and Zazu (*The Lion King*) at the head of a colourful, 16-minute revue that will appeal especially to younger children. Queues are rare here. AAA.

Magic Carpets of Aladdin: here, in an Agrabah-themed area styled after the animated film, the latest ride spins you up, down and around as you try to dodge the spitting

The Magic Carpets of Aladdin

© Disney

5

BRIT TIP: When you are faced by more than one queue for an attraction, head for the left-hand one. Almost invariably this will move slightly quicker than that on the right.

camel! Your 'flying carpet' tilts as well as levitates, but it is basically simple stuff geared towards younger children (and virtually identical to the Magic Carpets of Agrabah in the new Walt Disney Studios in *Disneyland® Resort Paris*). TT (TTTT for under 5s).

Shrunken Ned's Junior Jungle Boats: this costs an extra 50c for kids to try their hand at steering rather tame toy boats. T.

Disney characters also turn up outside Pirates of the Caribbean and the Magic Carpets of Aladdin, while the best of the shopping is in the **Pirates Bazaar** here. For food, you have Aloha Isle (yoghurt and ice cream) and **Sunshine Tree Terrace** (fruit, snacks, yoghurt, tea and coffee), plus the more substantial tacos, nachos and taco salads of **El Pirata Y el Perico Restaurante**.

Frontierland

Passing through Adventureland brings you to the target for many of the early birds. This Western-themed area is one of the busiest and is best avoided from late morning to late afternoon.

Splash Mountain: based on the 1946 classic Disney cartoon *Song of the South*, this is a watery journey into the world of Brer Rabbit, Brer Fox and Brer Bear. The first part is all jolly cartoon scenery and fun with the main characters and a couple of minor swoops in your 8-passenger log-boat. The conclusion, a 5-storey plummet at 45 degrees into a mist-

shrouded pool, will seem like you are falling off the edge of the world! A huge adrenalin rush, but busy almost all day (try it first thing or during one of the parades to avoid the longest queues). You will also get VERY wet! Restrictions: 3ft 4in/ 101cm. TTTTT (FP).

Big Thunder Mountain Railroad: when Disney does a roller-coaster you can be sure it will be one of the classiest, and here it is, a runaway mine train that swoops, tilts and plunges through a mock abandoned mine filled with clever scenery. You should ride at least twice to appreciate all the detail, but again queues are heavy, so go first thing (after Splash Mountain) or late in the day. Restrictions: 3ft 4in/ 101cm. TTTT (FP).

Country Bear Jamboree: now here's a novelty, a 16-minute musical revue presented by audio-animatronic bears! It's great family fun with plenty of novel touches (watch for the talking moose-head). Again, you'll need to beat the crowds by going early morning or early evening. It's possibly also the first theme park attraction to inspire a film, rather than vice versa, with the 2002 movie *The Country Bears*. AAAA.

Frontierland Shootin' Arcade: this is the only other attraction to cost extra (50 cents) as you shoot the animated targets. TT.

Tom Sawyer Island: take a raft over to this overgrown playground, with mysterious caves, grottos and mazes, rope bridges and Fort Sam Clemens, where you can fire air guns at passing boats. A good get-away in the early afternoon when the crowds are at their biggest, while **Aunt Polly's Dockside Inn** is a refuge within a refuge for snacks and soft drinks. TT.

Frontierland shops sell cowboy hats, guns and badges as well as Native American and Mexican handicrafts. For food, try **Pecos Bill**

Café (salads, sandwiches and burgers), **Frontierland Fries** (McDonald's fries and drinks) or the **Turkey Leg Cart** (massive, smoke-grilled turkey legs). For shopping here, try the nicely themed **Briar Patch** and the **Prairie Outpost**.

Liberty Square

Continuing the clockwise tour brings you next to a homage to post-Independence America. A lot of the historical content will go over the heads of British visitors, but it still has some great attractions.

Goofy's Country Dancin' Jamboree: at the old Diamond Horseshoe Saloon, this is a new character sing-along as Goofy and his pals (Chip 'n Dale, plus *Toy Story* trio Woody, Jessie and Bullseye) lead an 18-minute show designed purely for the young 'uns. The 'country music dance party' promises young guests the chance to learn classic dances like *Boot Scootin' Boogie* and *Electric Slide* while Mum and Dad take pictures from the second-floor gallery. AAA (under 8s only).

Liberty Square Riverboat: cruise America's 'rivers' on an authentic paddle steamer, be menaced by Indians and thrill to the stories of How the West Was Won. This is also a good ride to take at the busiest times of the day, especially early afternoon. AAA.

The Haunted Mansion: a clever delve into the world of ghost train rides that is neither too scary for kids nor too twee for adults. Not so much a thrill ride as a scenic adventure. Watch out for the neat touch at the end when your car picks up an extra 'passenger'. Longish queues during much of the day, however (so a good one for a FASTPASS). AAAA or TTTT for under 6s (FP).

The Hall of Presidents: this is the attraction that is likely to mean

least to us, a 2-part show that is first a film about the history of the Constitution and then an audio-animatronic parade of all 43 American presidents. Technically it's impressive, but dull for young children, although it is another air-conditioned haven. AAA.

Shopping here includes **Ye Olde Christmas Shoppe** and **The Yankee Trader**, while eating opportunities consist of the full-service **Liberty Tree Tavern** (serving hearty soups, steaks and traditional dishes like meatloaf and pot roast, plus dinner with Mickey and Co), **Columbia Harbour House** (for counter-service fried chicken or shrimp, fish and salads) and **Sleepy Hollow** (a picnic area serving snacks, fresh fruit and drinks).

Fantasyland

Leaving Liberty Square, you walk past Cinderella Castle and come into the park's spiritual heart, the area with which young children are most enchanted. The attractions are designed with kids in mind, but some of the shops are quite sophisticated.

'It's a Small World': this could almost be Disney's theme ride, a family boat trip through the different continents, each represented by hundreds of dancing, singing audio-animatronic dolls in delightful set-piece pageants. It sounds twee but it actually creates a surprisingly striking effect, accompanied by an annoyingly catchy theme song which young children adore. Crowds peak in early afternoon. AAAA.

Dumbo the Flying Elephant: parents hate it but kids love it and all want to do this 2-minute ride on the back of a flying elephant that swoops in best Dumbo style (even if the ears do not flap). Do this one early or

5

expect a long queue. TT (TTTT under 5s).

Mad Tea Party: again the kids will insist you take them in these spinning, oversized tea cups that have their own 'steering wheel' to add to the whirling effect. Actually, they're just a heavily disguised fairground ride. Again, go early or expect serious crowds. Characters from *Alice In Wonderland* also visit from time to time. TT (TTTT under 5s).

The Many Adventures of Winnie the Pooh: building on the timeless popularity of Pooh, Tigger and Co, this family ride offers a fairly predictable jaunt through Hundred Acre Wood with several notable special effects and another original soundtrack. AAA (AAAAA under 5s) (FP).

Snow White's Scary Adventures: this lively, fast-paced ride tells the cartoon story of Snow White with a few ghost train effects that may scare small children. Good fun, though, for parents and kids. Again, you will need to go early or late (or during the main afternoon parade) to beat the queues. TTT (TTTTT under 5s).

Cinderella's Golden Carousel: the centrepiece of Fantasyland shouldn't need any more explanation other than it is a vintage carousel ride which kids adore. Long queues

Buzz Lightyear's Space Ranger Spin

during the main part of the day. T (TTT under 5s).

Mickey's PhilharMagic: this dramatic and utterly fun 3-D film show (replacing *Legend of the Lion King*) has a host of in-theatre special effects as Donald tries to conduct the Enchanted Orchestra a la Sorcerer Mickey – to suitably comic effect. Set in the PhilharMagic Concert Hall, it features a massive 150ft- (46-metre) wide screen to immerse guests in the richly animated 3-D world of *Beauty & The Beast*, *The Little Mermaid*, *The Lion King*, *Peter Pan* and *Aladdin*, with the hapless Donald surviving a string of adventures with each before Mickey brings him back to earth. The lavishness of the theatre as it 'transports' you through the 10-minute film, the artistry of the all-new animation, the interweaving of the excellent special effects (you can even 'smell' the food on-screen!) and the sheer all-round family entertainment on offer add up to one of the most startling and enjoyable Disney attractions of them all. There is no scare factor at work here, either, while everyone will surely be enchanted as Tinkerbell

Mickey's PhilharMagic

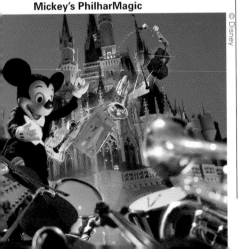

seems to fly right out of the screen to hover in front of you. AAAAA (expected) (FP).

Peter Pan's Flight: don't be fooled by the long queues, this is a rather tame ride, although it is still a big hit with kids. Its novel effect of flying up with Peter Pan quickly wears off, but there is still a lot of clever detail as your 'sailing ship' journeys over the heart of London to Neverland. AA (AAAAA under 6s) (FP).

In addition to the rides, there are different musical shows daily on the **Castle Forecourt Stage**, while the *Sword In The Stone* show is re-enacted several times a day near Cinderella's Golden Carousel.

Cinderella's Surprise Celebration: this show on the Castle Forecout Stage is superb for character interaction, a 20-minute fantasy featuring Cinderella, Mickey and the gang, and various Disney villains, with the action extending to the castle ramparts and featuring some clever special effects. Stay afterwards for a lovely character meet-and-greet. AAAA.

Fantasyland Character Festival behind Dumbo allows you to meet some more Disney characters, as does **Ariel's Grotto**, which draws quite a queue at peak periods. At the **Fairytale Garden**, on the corner of the Castle facing Tomorrowland, there's Storytime with Belle.

Eating opportunities are at **The Pinocchio Village Haus** (salads, burgers and hot dogs), the **Enchanted Grove** (ice drinks and juices), **Scuttle's Landing** and **Mrs Potts' Cupboard** (for ice creams and sundaes). **Cinderella's Royal Table** is a fine setting for a meal, be it lunch, dinner or the outstanding character breakfast (but you must book well in advance for the latter – 407 939 3463 – and give a credit card deposit). The majestic hall, waitresses in costume and well-presented food – salads, seafood,

roast beef, prime rib and chicken – make for a memorable experience. It's a touch pricey for dinner, though. Shop at **Tinkerbell's Treasures**, the excellent **Sir Mickey's** and **Pooh's Thotful Shop**.

Mickey's Toontown Fair

In the top corner of Fantasyland (just past the Mad Tea Party) is the shrub-lined entrance to **Mickey's Toontown Fair**. It is easy to miss, but it does have a station on the railroad. Its primary appeal is to young children, they can meet their favourite Disney characters. Exceptionally kid-friendly and well landscaped, it features a huge merchandising area, the **County Bounty** – wallets beware!

> **BRIT TIP:** Not many people think to watch the fireworks from Mickey's Toontown Fair, but you get a great view from there.

Mickey's Country House: here is a walk-through opportunity to see Mickey at home and have your picture taken with him in the Judge's Tent. AAAA (plus TTTTT for the photo opportunity.

Minnie's Country House: this is a chance to view Minnie's home and 'unique memorabilia', all designed in a Country and Western style. AAA.

Mickey's Toontown Fair Hall of Fame: three opportunities to meet a host of other Disney favourites in

Disney's Agrabah Bazaar

© Disney

5

the Villains Room, Mickey's Pals and Famous Faces. TTTTT (for kids!).

The Barnstormer at Goofy's Wiseacre Farm: a mini roller-coaster just for the young 'uns (although possibly a bit too much for the under 5s) and is another masterpiece of design as it swoops through the barn, even if it is a pretty short ride after all the queuing. TTT (TTTTT for 5–9s). Restrictions: 3ft/91cm.

Donald's Boat: parents beware, your youngsters could get seriously wet here. If you've seen the dancing fountains at *Epcot* between Future World and World Showcase (see page 107), prepare for more watery delights as this boat-themed fountain spouts off in all sorts of wonderful ways. Ideally, bring a change of clothes or swimsuit for your offspring. It's a great place to revitalise tired or irritable children. AAAA (under 10s). Check out the **Toontown Farmers Market** for fruit, snacks, and beverages.

Tomorrowland

Coming on round from Fantasyland finally brings you into the last of the seven lands. It has a cartoon-like space-age appearance, guaranteed to appeal to youngsters, and some of the park's more original shops.

Space Mountain: this is one of the three most popular attractions, and its reputation is deserved. It is a fast, tight-turning roller-coaster completely in the dark save for occasional flashes as you whiz through 'the galaxy'. Don't do this after eating! The only way to beat the crowds is to go either first thing, late in the day or during one of the parades (or, of course, get a FASTPASS). Restrictions: 3ft 8in/ 111cm. TTTTT (FP).

Tomorrowland Indy Speedway: despite the long queues, this is a rather tame ride on supposed race tracks that just putt-putts along on rails with little real steering required. Restrictions: children must be 4ft 4in/132cm to drive alone. T (TTTT under 6s).

Astro Orbiter: a jazzed-up version of the Dumbo in Fantasyland, this ride is just a bit faster, higher and on 'rockets'. Large, slow-moving queues are another reason to give this a miss unless you have children. TT (TTTT under 10s).

Walt Disney's Carousel of Progress: this one will surprise, entertain and amuse. It is a 100-year journey through modern technology with audio-animatronics and a revolving theatre that reveals different stages in that development. Its 22-minute duration is rarely threatened by crowds. AAA. (NB: only at peak periods in 2003)

Tomorrowland Transit Authority: a neat 'future transport system', the TTA gives an elevated view of the area, with a glimpse inside Space Mountain, in electro-magnetically powered cars. Queues are usually short, so give it a go. AAA (TTT for under 8s).

ExtraTERRORestrial Alien Encounter: (closing 2004; see page 16) this draws some HUGE queues (so go early) to its clever, high-tech preamble and scary show: a 'teleportation' demonstration that goes wrong and brings an alien to life in the middle of the audience. The fear factor will be too much for most under 9s and anyone scared of the dark! Restrictions: 3ft 8in/111cm. TTTT.

Buzz Lightyear's Space Ranger Spin: kids will not want to miss this chance to join the great *Toy Story* character in his battle against the evil Emperor Zurg. Ride into action against the robot army – and shoot them with laser cannons! A sure-fire family winner, especially as you get to keep score. Watch out for a new gift shop and ride photo opportunity as you exit. TTT (TTTTT for under 8s) (FP).

The Timekeeper: a combination of high-tech audio-animatronics and 360-degree film wizardry gives you an amusing plunge into time travel in the company of the zany robot Timekeeper (voiced by Robin Williams) and his camera-equipped assistant Nine-eye. AAAA (NB: liable to close off-peak).

The Galaxy Palace Theater hosts live musical productions, featuring Disney characters and talent shows, at various times of the day. For food, **Cosmic Ray's Starlight Café** has burgers, chicken and salads, **The Plaza Pavilion** does pizza, subs and salads, **Auntie Gravity's** (ouch!) **Galactic Goodies** serves ice cream and juices, the **Lunching Pad** (double ouch!) offers smoked turkey legs, snacks and drinks, and the **Cool Ship** provides various drinks.

Having come full circle you are now back at Main Street, USA and it's best to return here in early afternoon to avoid the crowds and look at the impressive array of shops.

The afternoon highlight, however, is the **Share A Dream Come True** parade. This 6-part extravaganza, along Main Street and through Frontierland, is designed as a flurry of classic Disney moments frozen inside giant snow globes full of special effects. All the favourite characters feature, along with a new musical score, plus some lighting tricks along the parade route. Watch out for the chance to be a part of the parade as it stops at intervals to allow characters to select people to dance and play act with. The globes themselves feature some outstanding effects, with Aladdin taking to the air on his flying carpet, the Wicked Queen turning into the evil old hag, and snow in the leading globes. It is a dazzling parade for all ages, but is especially popular with children. Don't miss it. AAAAA.

BRIT TIP: Try to sit on the left side of Main Street, USA (as you face the castle) to stay in the shade if it's hot. People start staking out the best spots here up to an hour in advance of the parade.

There's more

If you think the park looks good during the day, prepare to be amazed at how wonderful it appears at night – some of the lighting effects are astounding. When the park is open in the evenings (during the main holiday periods and weekends), you can see the **SpectroMagic parade** (when there are two a night, the second is less crowded), which is a mind-boggling light and sound festival full of glitter and razzamatazz, with the Disney characters at the centre of a multitude of sparkling lights and fibre-optic effects. It is difficult to do it justice in words, so make sure you see it. Another evening highlight is the fireworks. Up until November 2003, this was the **Fantasy in the Sky** show over the castle, but a new show, called **Wishes**, is due to take over from December, with several original pyrotechnic effects and a whole series of different launch points, including from the Castle itself.

BRIT TIP: After the fireworks crowd exits, you are often allowed to take the Resort Only monorail back to the Transportation & Ticket Center, rather than stand in the queues for the main monorail.

BRIT TIP: Main Street USA closes half an hour after the rest of the park, so you can avoid the mad rush for the car parks by lingering here and enjoying an ice cream or coffee.

At Easter and Christmas, the daily parade takes on extra seasonal charm with appearances by the Easter Bunny and Father Christmas.

Character meals

You can breakfast with Disney characters at Cinderella's Royal Table ($19 for adults, $9.99 for 3–11s; 8–10am and have dinner with them at the **Liberty Tree Tavern** ($21.99 and $9.99; 4pm–park close). Or visit the **Crystal Palace** for buffet breakfast ($16.99 and $8.99; 8–10.30am), lunch ($17.99 and $9.99; 11.30am–2.45pm) and dinner ($21.99 and $9.99; 4pm–park close) with Pooh, Tigger and Co. You can book a Disney character meal at the *Magic Kingdom Park* up to 90 days in advance on 407 939 3463. NB: Cinderella's breakfast is far and away the most popular character meal and requires a credit card to book.

If the crowds get too heavy, you CAN escape by leaving the park in the early afternoon (get a hand-stamp for re-admission and keep your car park ticket which is valid all day) and returning to your hotel for a few hours' rest or a dip in the pool.

Halloween and Christmas

Two additional annual events in the *Magic Kingdom Park* are **Mickey's Not So Scary Halloween Party** (on selected dates in October) and **Mickey's Very Merry Christmas Party** (late November and December) which provide a separate, party-style ticketed event from 7pm–midnight t, with most of the rides open and extra themed fun and games (and snow on Main Street with the Christmas party, plus free hot chocolate and cookies, which all makes for an utterly enchanting atmosphere), as well as a parade and more fireworks. Halloween party tickets cost $32.95 for adults and $27.95 per child on the day (or $29.95 and $24.95 in advance), while the Christmas party is $41.95 and $31.95 (or $35.95 and $25.95 in advance), which includes a souvenir family photo. Book in advance on 407 934 7639.

Finally, one of the park's little-known 'secrets' is the **Keys to the Kingdom**, a 4–5-hour guided tour of many backstage areas, including

Mickey opens the SpectroMagic parade

© Disney

the service tunnel under the park, and entertainment production buildings. It costs an extra $58 (including lunch; not available for under 16s). Call 407 939 8687 for more information. **Disney's Family Magic Tour** is a 2-hour guided adventure that takes you on a search for clues throughout the park at $25 ($20 for children) or you can experience **Disney's The Magic Behind Our Steam Trains** tour ($30/person; no under 10s) as you join the crew who prepare the park's trains each day.

MAGIC KINGDOM PARK with children

Here is a rough guide to the rides which appeal to different age groups. Obviously, children vary enormously in their likes and dislikes but, as a general rule, you can be fairly sure the following will have most appeal to the ages concerned (height restrictions have been taken into account):

Under 5s

Walt Disney World Railroad, Main Street Vehicles, Jungle Cruise, The Enchanted Tiki Room – Under New Management, Country Bear Jamboree, Liberty Square Riverboat, 'It's a Small World', Peter Pan's Flight, Mickey's PhilharMagic, Cinderella's Carousel, Dumbo The Flying Elephant, Many Adventures of Winnie The Pooh, Mickey's Country House, Donald's Boat, Tomorrowland Indy Speedway (with a parent), Buzz Lightyear's Space Ranger Spin, Tomorrowland Transit Authority.

5–8s

Walt Disney World Railroad, Pirates of the Caribbean, Jungle Cruise, Swiss Family Treehouse, The Timekeeper, Magic Carpets of Aladdin, The Enchanted Tiki Room – Under New Management, Country Bear Jamboree, Goofy's Country Dancin' Jamboree, Liberty Square Riverboat, Tom Sawyer Island, Big Thunder Mountain Railroad, Splash Mountain, Haunted Mansion, Mickey's PhilharMagic, Snow White's Scary Adventures, Mad Tea Party, Many Adventures of Winnie The Pooh, Mickey's Country House, Donald's Boat, The Barnstormer at Goofy's Wiseacre Farm, Tomorrowland Indy Speedway (with parent), Tomorrowland Transit Authority, Buzz Lightyear's Space Ranger Spin, Walt Disney's Carousel of Progress, Astro Orbiter, Space Mountain (with parental discretion).

9–12s

Pirates of the Caribbean, Big Thunder Mountain Railroad, Splash Mountain, Country Bear Jamboree, Goofy's Country Dancin' Jamboree, The Haunted Mansion, Mad Tea Party, Mickey's PhilharMagic, The Barnstormer at Goofy's Wiseacre Farm, Tomorrowland Indy Speedway (without parent), Buzz Lightyear's Space Ranger Spin, ExtraTERRORestrial Alien Encounter, The Timekeeper, Astro Orbiter, Space Mountain.

Over 12s

Pirates of the Caribbean, Big Thunder Mountain Railroad, Splash Mountain, Mickey's PhilharMagic, Haunted Mansion, Buzz Lightyear's Space Ranger Spin, The Timekeeper, ExtraTERRORestrial Alien Encounter, Mad Tea Party, Astro Orbiter, Space Mountain.

Epcot

Amaze and annoy your friends by revealing *Epcot* stands for 'Experimental Prototype Community Of Tomorrow' (or the visitor's version: Every Person Comes Out Tired!), once you have marvelled at the magnificent entertainment value of this 300-acre (122-ha) playground. Actually, it is not so much a vision of the future as a look at the world of today, with a strong educational and environmental message which children in particular are quick to pick up on.

At more than twice the size of the *Magic Kingdom Park*, it is more likely to require a 2-day visit (although under 5s might find it less entertaining) and your feet in particular will notice the difference!

Location

Epcot is located on Epcot Drive and the parking fee is again $7 as you drive into its main entrance (there is a separate entrance for guests at the *Epcot* resort hotels, called International Gateway). It opened in October 1982 and its giant car park is big enough for 9,000 vehicles, so a tram takes you from your car to the main entrance (although if you are staying at a Disney hotel you can catch the monorail, boat or bus service to its gates). And don't forget to note where you are parked (e.g. Create, row 78). Once you have your ticket, you wait by the turnstiles for the opening moment (often accompanied by a Disney character or two) and are then admitted to the central plaza, between the two Innoventions centres.

Epcot is divided into two distinct parts arranged in a figure of eight and there are two tactics to avoid the worst of the early morning crowds (which are likely to be considerable

after the new Mission: SPACE attraction is open, from September 2003). The first or lower half of the '8' consists of **Future World**, with seven different pavilions arranged around Spaceship Earth (the giant 'golfball' that dominates the *Epcot* skyline) and Innoventions. The second part, or the top of the '8', is **World Showcase**, a potted journey around the world via 11 internationally presented pavilions that feature a taste of each country's culture, history, shopping, entertainment and cuisine.

Once you are through the gates, start by heading for the Future World pavilions to your left (Universe of Energy, Wonders of Life, Test Track and Mission: SPACE) and then continue up into World Showcase. This way you will visit some of the best rides in *Epcot* ahead of the main crowds. Alternatively, if the rides don't appeal quite so much as a visit to such diverse cultures as Japan and Morocco, spend your first couple of hours in the Innoventions centres (busy from mid-morning), then head into World Showcase as soon as it opens at 11am and you will be ahead of the crowds for several hours. If you time your journey around the Showcase (which is a 1½-mile/2km walk) to arrive back in Future World by late afternoon, you will find the worst of the milling throng will have passed through (except for Test Track and Mission: SPACE).

The other thing you should do early on is book lunch or dinner at one of the many fine restaurants around World Showcase (Mexico, Morocco, Canada and Japan are all highly recommended). The best reservations go fast, but check in at Guest Relations (immediately on the left as you enter the Innoventions plaza) and they will be able to give you advice and make a Priority Seating (never just a reservation at Disney, remember – see page 58).

Epcot at a glance

Location	Off Epcot Drive, *Walt Disney World*
Size	300 acres (122ha) in Future World and World Showcase
Hours	9am–6pm Future World (except Test Track, Innoventions, Spaceship Earth, Honey I Shrunk the Audience, 9am–9pm), 11am–9pm (World Showcase)
Admission	Under 3 free; 3–9, $42 (1-day ticket), $167 (4-Day Park Hopper), $216 (5-Day Park Hopper Plus); adult (10+) $52, $208, $269. Prices do not include tax.
Parking	$7
Lockers	Yes; to left underneath Spaceship Earth and International Gateway; $7 ($2 refund)
Pushchairs	$8 and $15 ($1 deposit refunded); to the right underneath Spaceship Earth and International Gateway
Wheelchairs	$7 ($1 deposit refunded) or $40 ($10 deposit refunded) (same location as pushchairs)
Top Attractions	Mission SPACE, Test Track, Spaceship Earth, 'Honey, I Shrunk the Audience', Maelstrom, Universe of Energy, American Adventure
Don't Miss	IllumiNations, Disney character bus (around World Showcase), live entertainment (including Off Kilter in Canada, and dinner at any of the World Showcase pavilions.

Hidden Costs	**Meals**	Burger, chips and coke $7.58 3-course dinner $33 (Le Cellier, Canada)
	Kids' meal	$3.49
	T-shirts	$19–32
	Souvenirs	$1–1,100
	Sundries	Disney character imposed photo $12.95

Future World

Here is what you will find in the first part of your *Epcot* adventure:

Universe of Energy: there is just the one attraction here but it is a stunner. **Ellen's Energy Adventure** is a 45-minute show-and-ride with comedienne Ellen DeGeneres and Bill Nye the Science Guy exploring the creation of fuels from the age of dinosaurs to their modern-day usages. The film elements convince you that you are in a conventional theatre, but then your seats rearrange themselves into 96-person solar-powered cars and you are off on a journey through the sights, sounds and even smells of the prehistoric era, with some realistic dinosaurs! Queues are steady but not overwhelming throughout the day from mid-morning. AAAAA.

Wonders of Life: this used to be one of Future World's most popular pavilions, but is now often quiet in

FUTURE WORLD

1 Universe Of Energy
2 Wonders Of Life
3 Mission: SPACE
4 Test Track
5 Odyssey Center
6 Imagination! (Including Honey, I Shrunk The Audience)
7 The Land
8 The Living Seas
9 Spaceship Earth
10 Innoventions West
11 Innoventions East

WORLD SHOWCASE

12 Mexico
13 Norway
14 China
15 Germany
16 Italy
17 The American Adventure
18 Japan
19 Morocco
20 France
21 International Gateway (To Epcot Resort Hotels)
22 United Kingdom
23 Canada

EPCOT

MAIN ENTRANCE

the afternoon as the crowds flock to the other attractions nearby. Body Wars is a terrific simulator ride through the human body as in the film *Fantastic Voyage*. It is quite a violent adventure, too, hence it is not recommended for people who suffer from motion sickness, anyone with neck or back injuries, or pregnant women. Restrictions: 3ft 4in/101cm. TTTT.

Cranium Command is a hilarious theatre show set in the brain of a 12-year-old boy, showing how he negotiates a typical day. It is both audio-animatronic and film-based. See how many famous TV and film stars you can name in the 'cast'. AAAA. **The Making of Me** is a sensitive film on the creation of human life and will therefore require parental discretion for children as it has its explicit moments, although not without humour. AAA.

> BRIT TIP: The Wonders of Life pavilion is a good place in which to spend time if you need to cool down, or if it's raining.

The Fitness Fairground, with hands-on exhibits like exercise bikes, gives you the chance to see just how far all the holiday fun has taken its toll on your body!

The **Pure and Simple** restaurant serves breakfast until 11am and then a range of snacks thereafter.

Mission: SPACE: this is the new cutting edge of Disney's attraction technology, a journey 30 years into the future to join the International Space Training Center. The space-age building alone prepares you for a major adventure and you enter through Planetary Plaza, which has giant replica planets (have a look at the model showing all the Moon landings).

At the main entrance you have a choice of four queues – FASTPASS Collection, Stand-by (the main queue), Single riders and FASTPASS return, and the clever organisation here should keep lines to a minimum (it is the first ride purpose-built with FASTPASS in mind, but substantial queues are still likely for much of the day). As you enter the 'training facility' (and you WILL believe!), there are some superb models and graphics (like the revolving 35-ft/ 11-metre Gravity Wheel) to keep your attention while you wait in line, passing the Training Operations Room (the cleverly disguised ride controllers) and the story of 75 Years of Space Flight (this is now 2036, remember) to reach Team Despatch. Here the four 'ready rooms' form you up into teams of four for the ride itself, and you will be either the Navigator, Engineer, Pilot or Commander – and you each have different functions to perform, so pay attention!

Once briefed (by actor Gary Sinise), you enter the Preparation Room to learn your mission – a flight to Mars. And then it is quickly into the ride vehicle – capsules that close down tightly with outer doors, shoulder restraints and screens that move forward to just 18in (46cm) from your face (this is NOT the ride for you if you suffer from claustrophobia). The sense of realism, with the control consoles, individual speakers and the countdown is magnificent, and the blast off feels VERY real as you experience some of the genuine

Mission: SPACE at Epcot

© Disney

G-forces of a rocket launch (it is part ride and part simulator).

Each member of the team has to perform their duties on cue (Sinise will 'prompt' you if you forget) and you then experience a cleverly simulated flight around the Moon and on to Mars, where the 'landing' becomes an adventure in itself. From my sneak preview, the set-up looks quite superb, but you do need to be aware of the advice to keep your head still and look straight into the screen as it is a physically dynamic ride.

It strikes me as being too intense for younger children, and there is no backing out once you blast off (parents could try riding it themselves first to see if their children will enjoy it or not), while it is definitely not a ride for expectant mothers. Restrictions, 3ft 8in/ 112cm. TTTTT+ (expected; FP).

BRIT TIP: If Mission: SPACE and Test Track appeal to you most, head here FIRST when you arrive, grab a FASTPASS for one and then ride the other. When you have done your FP ride, consider grabbing another FP to re-ride your favourite!

As you exit the ride, there is an elaborate four-part post-show with even more activities. *Space Base* is an excellent play area for those children who can't ride (and those who just like to explore, climb, slide and crawl – enter through the gift shop if you just want to play here); *Space Race* is a game for two teams of 60 players, working in pairs, to propel their rocket to Mars first with a series of on-screen challenges; *Expedition Mars* is a computer game to rescue stranded astronauts; and *Portraits from Space* gives you the chance to

send someone a video email of yourself in one of eight space 'scenes.' There is then the inevitable (and well-stocked) gift shop to negotiate on the way out. All in all, it is a mind-boggling experience, and a real taste of space 'exploration' without leaving the building!

Test Track: this is another big production, a 5½-minute whirl along Disney's longest and fastest track to date. It starts with a pre-show into the world of General Motors' quality and safety techniques to prepare riders for a taste of vehicle testing. The way the cars whiz around the outside of the building (at up to 60mph/97kph) provides a glimpse of what's in store. The reality is pretty good, too, as you are taken on a tour of a GM proving ground, including a hill climb test, suspension test (hold on to those fillings!), brake test, environment chamber, barrier test (beware the crash test dummies!) and the steeply banked, high-speed finale.

For those who manage to regain their breath, there is a post-show area with a multimedia film, an animated presentation featuring future GM products and technological innovations, with a hint of virtual reality driving, and the chance to view the latest GM models. Along with a smart gift store and photo opportunity, it all adds up to an extremely involved exhibit (although a bit technical for youngsters).

The down side is the HUGE queues it attracts, topping 2 hours at times, while the available FP service often runs out. Head straight here after opening or return in the evening to keep your queuing to bearable levels. If you are on your own, you can save time by using the Singles Queue here. Restrictions: 3ft 4in/101cm. TTTT (TTT for teens) (FP).

The **Odyssey Center** next door offers baby-care and first-aid facilities, telephones and restrooms.

Imagination!: The 2-part attraction here starts with **Journey Into Imagination with Figment**, a recently revamped ride into experiments with imagination, in the company of Eric Idle (as Dr Nigel Channing of the Imagination Institute) and the cartoon dragon, Figment. The sight laboratory sees Figment having fun with a vision chart, the sound lab is a symphony of imaginative melodies and Figment's house is a truly topsy-turvy world (and watch out for the skunk in the smell lab!). It is gentle fun and rarely draws much of a crowd. AAA. (For fans of the original Dreamfinder ride here, Figment is highly prominent once again, while the ride's theme song, *One Little Spark*, makes a welcome return).

You exit into **Image Works – The Kodak 'What If' Labs**, an interactive playground of unusual sights and sounds, which will probably amuse children more than adults (although you may be tempted here to part with more money on various cartoon images and select-your-own CDs).

Come out of the building and turn right for the fabulous 3-D experience of **'Honey, I Shrunk The Audience'**, as Rick Moranis reprises his hapless inventor character Wayne Szalinski. A neat 8-minute pre-show is the perfect prelude to the fun and games in store. If you have seen Jim Henson's Muppet*Vision 3-D at *Disney-MGM Studios* you might have an idea of what to expect. Special effects and moving seats add to the feeling that you have shrunk in size. And beware the sneezing dog! AAAAA (FP).

Outside, kids are always fascinated by the **Jellyfish** and **Serpentine Fountains** that send water squirting from pond to pond, and there is always one who tries to stand in the way and 'catch' one of the streams of water. Have your cameras and camcorders ready!

The Land: this pavilion features four elements that combine to make a highly entertaining but educational experience on food production and nutrition. **Living with the Land** is an informative 14-minute boat ride that is worth the usually long queue. A journey through various types of food production may sound a dull idea, and it may not appeal to younger children, but adults and school-age kids will sit up and take notice of the three ecological communities, especially the greenhouse finale. AAAA (FP).

Having ridden the ride you can also walk the walk on the **Behind The Seeds** guided tour through the greenhouse complex and learn even more about Disney's horticultural projects. It takes an hour ($6 for adults, $4 for 3–9s), but you have to book in person at the desk near the Green Thumb Emporium. The old but funny Food Rocks show, just as you exit the Living With The Land ride, has now been closed to make way for the entrance plaza to The Land's newest attraction, **Soarin' Over California**, which is due to open in 2005 (see page 17).

The Circle of Life is a 15-minute live-action/ animated story, featuring characters from the film *The Lion King*, that explains environmental concerns and is easily digestible for kids. Queues not a problem here, either. AAA.

The **Sunshine Season Food Fair** offers the chance to eat some of Disney's home-grown produce, and there are healthy alternatives to the usual fast-food fare, while the **Garden Grill** restaurant is a slowly revolving platform that offers more traditional food, including pasta, seafood and delicious rotisserie chicken. Mickey and friends stage character meals here at lunch (11.30am–4.20pm; $19.99 for adults, $9.99 for children) and dinner (4.30pm–8pm; $21.99 and $9.99),

5

but book early. There is also the **Ice Cream Social**, an afternoon tea party with wonderful ice cream concoctions in the company of Mickey, Goofy and Co (at 3 and 3.30pm, $6.75/person).

The Living Seas: this pavilion does for the sea what The Land Pavilion does for the land. A 7-minute pre-show film leads on to a short journey to Sea Base Alpha by 'Hydrolator' (imagine an undersea lift simulator) and an elaborate marine research facility centred around a 5.7 million-gallon (25.9 million-litre) aquarium, with sharks, stingrays and other impressively large denizens of the deep. This 2-level development takes you through six modules that present stories of undersea exploration and marine life, including a research centre that provides a close-up encounter with the endangered manatee. Plenty of interactive elements and educational touch-screens are on offer, plus additional fish tanks displaying Caribbean reef fish, jellyfish and the curious cuttlefish, while there is also an excellent real-life demonstration of a diving chamber. Crowds build up steadily through the day, but queues rarely get too long. AAA.

The pavilion also includes the highly recommended **Coral Reef Restaurant** that serves magnificent seafood, as well as providing diners with a grandstand view of the massive aquarium. Dinner for two will cost around $70, which isn't cheap, but the food is first class.

Spaceship Earth: spiralling up the 18 storeys in the 'golfball', this ride tells the story of communication from early cave drawings to modern satellite technology. It is one of the most popular rides in the park, largely because of its visibility and location, hence you need to do it either first thing or late afternoon when the crowds have moved on from Future World into World Showcase. The highlight is the depiction of Michelangelo's painting of the Sistine Chapel, which will be lost on small kids, but it's an entertaining 15-minute journey all along. AAAA.

As you leave, you enter the **Global Activity Center**, with a host of interactive educational communications exhibits.

Innoventions West and East: these two centres of hands-on exhibits and computer games – subtitled **The Road to Tomorrow** – were revamped for the Millennium celebrations. They include a glimpse of Disney's latest investigations into virtual reality entertainment and other demonstrations of current and future technologies, especially the internet and computers, by companies like IBM, Xerox, Compaq, Motorola and General Motors. Both sides are routed like a journey into the future and will reward the enquiring mind in areas like People At Play and Mouse House Jnr.

In Innoventions West, the kids will gravitate to the free **Video Games of Tomorrow** selection presented by Disney Interactive and they may take a bit of moving along! Also worth waiting for are the 20-minute **Ultimate Home Theater Experience**, presented by Lutron, and the **Thinkplace** presented by IBM, featuring a demonstration of IBM's voice recognition technology.

In Innoventions East, you can send a video e-mail to friends in the **Internet Zone**, check out The **Underwriters Lab**, which offers an interactive area with various testing

Spaceship Earth at Epcot

© Disney

Epcot

stations and Video D-Mail, and take the 15-minute walk through the **House of Innoventions**, full of smart gadgets and new technologies. You must also take a look at the latest form of transport here – the mind-boggling two-wheeled Segway Human Transporter.

Musical entertainment is provided periodically in the Innoventions plaza, along with other innovative live acts (look out for the unique **JAMMitors** percussion group, **Kristos** dance troupe and the amazing new **Francis the Conversational Companion** robot), while the majestic fountains are choreographed to an hourly music performance. Food outlets include the self-service **Electric Umbrella Restaurant** for lunch and dinner (sandwiches, pizza, burgers and salads) and the **Fountain View Espresso and Bakery** for tea, coffee and pastries. At **Ice Station Cool**, presented by Coca-Cola™, you'll be given some free product samples and the chance to encounter real snow! You'll also find the huge gift shop **Mouse Gear** in Innoventions East, featuring stacks of quality *Epcot* and Disney souvenirs (and some wonderfully wacky ceiling architecture!).

World Showcase

If you found Future World a huge experience, prepare to be amazed also by the more down-to-earth but equally imaginative pavilions around the World Showcase Lagoon. Each features a glimpse of a different country in dramatic settings. Several have either amusing rides or films that show off the tourist features of their country, while in nearly every case the restaurants offering national fare are some of the best in Orlando.

Mexico: starting at the bottom left of the circular tour of the lagoon and moving clockwise, your first encounter is the spectacular pyramid that houses Mexico. Here you will find the amusing boat ride along **El Rio del Tiempo**, the River of Time, which gives you a potted 9-minute journey through the people and history of the country. Queues here tend to be surprisingly long from mid-morning to late afternoon. AAA. The rest of the pavilion is given over to a range of shops in the **Plaza de los Amigos**, which vary from pretty tacky to sophisticated, and the **San Angel Inn**, a dimly lit and romantic full-service diner offering traditional and tempting Mexican fare. Outside, on the lagoon, is the **Cantina de San Angel**, a fast-food counter for tacos, chilli and burgers. As in all the World Showcase pavilions, there is live entertainment and music.

Norway: next up is Norway, which probably has the best ride in World Showcase, the Viking-themed **Maelstrom**. This 10-minute longboat journey through the history and scenery of the Scandinavian country features a short waterfall drop and a North Sea storm. It attracts longish queues during the day, so the best tactic is to go soon after World Showcase's 11am opening. TTT (FP). There are periodical Norwegian-themed exhibits in the reconstructed **Stave Church** and twice-daily guided tours (sign up at the Tourism desk), while kids can play on the Viking boat. The pavilion also contains a clever reproduction of Oslo's Akershus Fortress. The popular

Test Track at Epcot

© Disney

5

Restaurant Akershus offers lunch and dinner buffets and the **Kringla Bakeri Og Kafé** serves open sandwiches, pastries and drinks. Brand new here is the Princess Storybook Breakfast (8.30–10.30am), which features various Disney princesses and friends. Can't get a seat at Cinderella's in the *Magic Kingdom Park?* Try here instead, although Cinderella does NOT appear here. However, you can book up to 90 days in advance ($19.99 adults, $9.99 3–11s. A credit card is needed to hold a reservation. Book on 407-WDW-DINE).

China: the spectacular architecture of China is well served by the pavilion's main attraction, the stunning **Reflections of China**, a brand new (in May 2003) 20-minute,

---

BRIT TIP: The Cantina in 'Mexico' is a great spot from which to watch the nightly IllumiNations fireworks and laser show, but you need to arrive at least an hour early.

360-degree film in the circular Temple of Heaven. Here you are surrounded by the sights and sounds of one of the world's most mysterious countries in a special cinematic production, the technology of which alone will leave you breathless. Queues build up to half an hour during the main part of the day. AAAA.

Land of Many Faces is an exhibit introducing China's ethnic peoples. Two restaurants, the **Nine Dragons** (table service, decent if unremarkable food) and the **Lotus Blossom Café** (self-service, fairly predictable spring rolls and stir-fries), offer tastes of the Orient, while the **Yong Feng Shangdian Department Store** is a virtual

warehouse of Chinese gifts and artefacts. Don't miss the periodic shows of Oriental music and acrobatic acts (including the stunning Dragon Legend Acrobats) on the plaza in front of the temple.

The **Outpost** between China and Germany features hut-style shops and snacks, with entertainment from Africa and the Caribbean.

Germany: this provides more in the way of shopping and eating than entertainment, although you still find strolling players and a magnificent recreation of a Bavarian **Biergarten**, with lively Oktoberfest shows featuring the resident brass band at regular intervals. It also offers hearty portions of German sausage, sauerkraut and rotisserie chicken. The **Sommerfest** is fast food German-style (bratwurst and strudel). This pavilion has more shops than any of the others in *Epcot* and includes chocolates, wines, porcelain, crystal, toys and cuckoo clocks. An elaborate outdoor model railway is popular with children.

Italy: similarly, Italy has pretty, authentic architecture (including a superb reproduction of St Mark's Square in Venice), lively music and amusing Italian folk stories, three tempting gift shops (including wine, Perugina chocolates, Armani collectables, fine crystal, porcelain and Venetian masks), and a restaurant, **L'Originale Alfredo di Roma Ristorante**. It's a touch expensive, but the atmosphere, decor and singing waiters (!) add extra zest to the meals, which include fettucine, chicken, veal and seafood. Expect a 3-course meal to cost about $38.

BRIT TIP: The lunch and dinner menus at the Nine Dragons restaurant are very similar, so choose the lunch version – it's cheaper!

America: at the top of the lagoon and dominating World Showcase is **The American Adventure**, not so much a pavilion as a celebration of the country's history and constitution. A colonial fife and drum band and wonderful *a cappella* group (Voices Of Liberty) add authentic sounds to the 18th-century setting, overlooked by a faithful reproduction of Philadelphia's Liberty Hall. Inside you have the spectacular American Adventure show, a magnificent film and audio-animatronic production lasting half an hour, which details the country's struggles and triumphs, its presidents, statesmen and heroes. It's a glossy, patriotic performance, featuring outstanding audio-animatronic effects and, while some of it will leave foreign visitors fairly cold, it is difficult not to be impressed by the sense of pride and achievement inherent in so much American history. Avoid at midday for the queues. ÁAAA.

Outside, handcarts provide touches of American nostalgia and antiques, along with the **Heritage Manor Gifts** store, while the **Liberty Inn** offers fast-food fare for lunch and dinner. **The America Gardens Theater**, facing the lagoon, presents musical performances from worldwide artists and Disney characters.

Japan: next up on the clockwise tour, you will be introduced to typical Japanese gardens and architecture, including the breathtaking Chi Nien Tien, a round half-scale reproduction of a

temple, some magnificent art exhibits (notably the Bijutsu-kan Gallery), musical shows and dazzling live entertainment (especially child-friendly **Miyuki**, a lovely lady who spins amazing candy creations out of toffee sugar). For one of the most entertaining meals in *Epcot*, the **Teppanyaki Dining** rooms and **Tempura Kiku** both offer a full, table-service introduction to Japanese cuisine while **Yakitori House** is the fast-food equivalent and the **Matsu No Ma Lounge** features sushi and cocktails. The restaurants are run by Mitsukoshi, as is the superb department store here. Periodic live music features the Matsuriza traditional drummers.

Morocco: as you would expect, this is a real shopping experience, with bazaars, alleyways and stalls selling a well-priced array of carpets, leather goods, clothing, brass ornaments, pottery and antiques (seek out that Magic Lamp!). All of the building materials were faithfully imported for the pavilion, which was hand-built to give Morocco a great degree of authenticity, even by the World Showcase's high standards. You'll be unable to keep your eyes off the clever detail around the winding alleyways and gardens, which can be enjoyed on daily (free) 45-minute walking tours. The **Gallery of Arts and History** offers more historical and cultural insight into the country, while the **Fez House** depicts the style of a typical Moroccan home.

Restaurant Marrakesh provides a full Moroccan dining experience, complete with traditional musicians and a belly dancer. It's slightly pricey ($59 for the Moroccan feast for two) but the atmosphere is lively and entertaining. **Tangierine Café** offers Mediterranean-style foods (hummus, tabouleh, couscous, roast lamb, lentil salad and Moroccan breads) at more down-to-earth prices, and with several vegetarian

5

> **BRIT TIP:** Kids, to get the best autographs from your Disney favourites, use a thick pen or pencil, as some characters have trouble writing otherwise!

options ($6.95–10.95). Watch out, too, for characters from Disney's film *Aladdin*.

France: France is predictably overlooked by a replica Eiffel Tower, but the smart streets, buildings and the sheer cleanliness of France is a long way from modern-day Paris! This is pre-World War One France, with official buskers and comedy street theatre acts adding to the rather dreamy atmosphere. Don't miss **Impressions de France**, another stunning big-film production that serves up all the grandest sights of the country to the accompaniment of the music of Offenbach, Debussy, Saint-Saëns and Satie. Crowds get quite heavy from late morning but it is a stunning performance (although kids might feel left out). AAAA.

This is also the pavilion for a gastronomic experience, with three restaurants, of which **Chefs de France** and **Bistro de Paris** are major discoveries. The former is an award-winning, full-service, and therefore expensive, establishment featuring top quality cuisine created by French chefs on a daily basis, while the latter, upstairs, offers more intimate bistro dining, still with an individual touch (and, if anything, slightly more expensive) and plenty of style (starters from $9–$16, main courses $29–35). The Bistro books only 30 days in advance. Alternatively, the **Boulangerie Patisserie** is a sidewalk café offering more modest fare (and some wonderful pastries, as you'd expect) at a more modest price. Shopping is also suitably chic, with a Guerlain perfumery, wine shop and patisserie.

United Kingdom: the least inspired of all 11 international pavilions, and certainly with little to entertain those who have been inside a traditional pub before or shopped for Royal Doulton or Burberry goods. It is partly offset by some good street entertainers and the excellent Beatles tribute band, the **British Invasion**, but that really is the sum total here. The **Rose and Crown Pub** is antiseptically authentic, but you can get far better elsewhere for these prices (ploughman's $10.79, cottage pie $12.99, fish and chips $14.79, and a pint of Bass, Harp Lager or Guinness for a whopping $6.75). There is also a takeaway **Harry Ramsden's** fish and chippie. Other shops are the Tea Caddy, the Magic of Wales, the Queen's Table, Crown And Crest (perfumes, heraldry) and the Toy Soldier (traditional games and Disney toys). It's all terribly twee, though.

Canada: completing the World Showcase circle, the main features here are **Victoria Gardens**, based on the world-famous Butchart Gardens on Vancouver Island, some spectacular Rocky Mountain scenery, a replica French gothic mansion, the Hôtel du Canada, and another stunning 360-degree film, **O Canada!** As with China and France, this showcases the country's sights and scenery in a terrific, 17-minute advert for the Canadian Tourist Board. It gets busiest from late morning to late afternoon. AAA. Resident band **Off Kilter** is also one of the most entertaining acts I've seen anywhere. Want to hear rock 'n roll bagpipes? This is the group for you! **Le Cellier Steakhouse** is a modestly priced dining room offering steaks, prime rib, seafood, chicken and several vegetarian dishes for lunch and dinner.

Around World Showcase are 11 **Kidcot Fun Stop** activity centres, at which children can play games and

Coral Reef Restaurant at Epcot

© Disney

collect a special Epcot Passport to get stamped at each pavilion.

Disney characters put on a show several times a day at **Showcase Plaza**, just across the bridge from Future World to World Showcase, and you can take their sight-seeing bus on tour to several locations in World Showcase, so have those autograph books handy!

Planning your visit

If you plan a 2-day visit, it makes sense to spend the first day in World Showcase, arriving early and heading there while most of the rest of the morning crowds go to Future World, booking your evening meal around 5.30pm, and then lingering around the lagoon for the evening entertainment.

For your second visit, try arriving in mid-afternoon and then doing Future World in a more leisurely fashion than it would be earlier. Queues at most of the pavilions are almost non-existent for rides like Universe of Energy, Body Wars and The Land, although Test Track stays busy all day (as Mission: SPACE is sure to do, too).

You CAN do *Epcot* in a day – if you arrive early, put in some speedy legwork and give some of the detail a miss. But, of all the parks, it is a shame to hurry this one. In the shops (almost 70 in all), try to save your browsing for when most people are on the rides. The Innoventions

> BRIT TIP: The Rose & Crown dining room is actually a great place from which to see the nightly IllumiNations fireworks spectacular, especially if you can manage to get a table on the Terrace.

centres are also busiest from mid-morning to mid-afternoon, and crowd-free in the evening.

IllumiNations: Reflections of Earth

The day's big finale is an absolute show-stopper. **IllumiNations: Reflections of Earth** is a firework and special-effect extravaganza, awesome even by Disney standards. British composer Gavin Greenaway provides original music for a 15-minute performance of vivid brilliance. Some 2,800 firework shells are launched as a celestial backdrop to a series of fire-and-water effects on the World Showcase lagoon. The central icon is a 28-ft (9-metre) video globe of Earth that opens in a spectacular climax of choreographed pyrotechnics. Magnificent. However, people do start staking out the best lagoon-side spots up to TWO HOURS in advance.

The ultimate way to view IllumiNations is by private boat on one of three **speciality cruises** from *Disney's Boardwalk* or Yacht/Beach Club resorts (for non-residents, too). They vary from $120–350 per boat (holding 4–12 guests) and can be used for special celebrations. The basic cruise costs $120 and the pontoon boat holds up to 12. The level-1 cruise adds soda, sandwiches, water and snacks and costs $200 for up to 4 guests and $20 for each additional person. The level-2 cruise adds fruit, cheese and dessert, costing $275 for 4 and $35 for each additional guest. A level-3 cruise adds alcohol and boat decoration, costing $350 for up to 4 people, plus $50 per additional person. Call 407 939 7529 up to 90 days in advance to book. Be aware that cruises launch regardless of whether fireworks are taking place.

5

Behind the scenes

Epcot also has some special behind-the-scenes tours (but not for under-16s). **Dolphins In Depth** ($150, including souvenir photo, T-shirt and refreshments) is a 3½-hour delve into the backstage and research areas of the Living Seas pavilion, including a chance to meet the resident dolphins (ages 13–17 must be accompanied by an adult). **Gardens of the World** ($59) is a 3-hour botanical tour of the gardens in *Epcot*, and includes tips for your own garden. **Hidden Treasures** is a 3-hour tour ($59) of the 11 countries of World Showcase. **Undiscovered Future World** is a 4½-hour journey into the creation of *Epcot*, Walt's vision for the resort and backstage areas like IllumiNations ($49). **Dive Quest** ($140/person, ages 10 and up) is a 2½-hour experience, with a 30-minute dive into the Living Seas aquarium, plus a behind-the-scenes look at the facility and training involved at either 4.30 or 5.30pm every day, and you need to have scuba certification (T-shirt and certificate for all participants; theme park admission not required). The new **Aqua Seas Tour** ($100/person, ages 8 and up; under 18s must be accompanied by an adult; inclusive of T-shirt and group photo; again, theme park admission not required) is similar to Dive Quest but without the scuba element (daily at 12.30pm).

The most comprehensive tour, **Backstage Magic** ($199; ages 16 and up), goes behind the scenes of *Epcot*, *Magic Kingdom Park* and *Disney-MGM Studios* on a 7-hour foray into little-seen aspects, like animators at work in *Disney-MGM Studios* and tunnels below the *Magic Kingdom Park*. These tours must be booked on 407 939 8687.

Annual Festivals

Two other *Epcot* specialities are the wonderful free **International Flower and Garden Festival** (which puts the whole park in full bloom with an amazing series of set-pieces, seminars and mini-exhibitions from mid-April to June), and the **Food and Wine Festival** (late October to November), which showcases national and regional cuisines, wines and beers, with the chance to attend grand Winemakers Dinners and Tasting Events, or just sample the inexpensive offerings of more than 20 food booths around World Showcase.

EPCOT with children

Here is our rough guide to the attractions which appeal to different age groups in this park:
Under 5s
Spaceship Earth, Universe of Energy, Journey Into Your Imagination, The Living Seas, Living with the Land, Circle of Life, El Rio del Tiempo.
5–8s
All the above, plus Body Wars, Cranium Command, Test Track, Innoventions, 'Honey, I Shrunk The Audience' (with parental discretion), Image Works, Food Rocks, Maelstrom, The American Adventure.
9–12s
All the above, plus Behind The Seeds tour, Mission: SPACE, Treasures of Morocco tour, Impressions de France, Wonders of China, O Canada!
Over 12s
All the above, plus Land of Many Faces (China), Bijutsu-kan Gallery, Norway guided tours, Off Kilter, British Invasion.

Disney-MGM Studios

Welcome to Hollywood! Well, the *Walt Disney World Resort in Florida* version of it. When it opened in May 1989, Michael Eisner, chairman of the Walt Disney Company, insisted it was 'the Hollywood that never was and always will be'. Sounds double Dutch? Don't worry, all will be revealed in your day-long tour of this real-life combination of theme park and working TV and film studio. The most common question about *Disney-MGM Studios* is 'Are they really working studios?', and yes, there are film and TV productions going on even while you're riding around the park peering into the backstage areas.

In 2002, *Disney-MGM Studios* was also the focus of the *100 Years of*

Disney-MGM Studios at a glance

Location	Off Buena Vista Drive or World Drive, Walt Disney World
Size	154 acres (62ha)
Hours	9am–7pm off peak; 9am–10pm high season (Easter, summer holidays, Thanksgiving and Christmas)
Admission	Under 3 free; 3–9 $42 (1-day ticket), $167 (4-Day Park Hopper), $216 (5-Day Park Hopper Plus); adult (10+) $52, $208, $269. Prices do not include tax.
Parking	$7
Lockers	Yes; next to Oscar's Super Service, to right of main entrance; $7 ($2 refundable)
Pushchairs	$8 and $15 ($1 deposit refunded) from Oscar's Super Service
Wheelchairs	$8 ($1 deposit refunded) or $40 ($10 deposit refunded); same location as pushchairs
Top Attractions	Twilight Zone™ Tower of Terror, Rock 'n Roller Coaster Starring Aerosmith, Star Tours, The Great Movie Ride, Who Wants To Be A Millionaire – Play It!, Voyage of the Little Mermaid, Jim Henson's Muppet*Vision 3-D
Don't Miss	Disney Stars and Motor Cars Parade, Indiana Jones™ Epic Stunt Spectacular!, Fantasmic!

Hidden Costs	**Meals**	Burger, chips and coke $7.48 3-course lunch $23 (Prime Time Café)
	Kids' meal	$3.49 and $4.99
	T-shirts	$19–34
	Souvenirs	$1.25–385
	Sundries	Rock 'n Roller Coaster Starring Aerosmith ride photo $16.95

5

DISNEY-MGM STUDIOS

1   Parade Route ... Disney Stars And Motor Cars Parade
2   Sorcerer Mickey
3   The Great Movie Ride
4   ABC Sound Studio 'Sounds Dangerous' Starring Drew Carey
5   Indiana Jones™ Epic Stunt Spectacular!
6   Star Tours
7   Jim Henson's Muppet*Vision 3-D
8   Honey, I Shrunk The Kids Movie Set Adventure
9   Catastrophe Canyon On Disney-MGM Studios Backlot Tour
10   Disney-MGM Studios Backlot Tour
11   Meet Mickey Mouse
12   Who Wants To Be A Millionaire – Play It!
13   Walt Disney: One Man's Dream
14   Voyage Of The Little Mermaid
15   The Magic Of Disney Animation
16   Playhouse Disney – Live On Stage!
17   Rock 'n Roller Coaster Starring Aerosmith
18   The Twilight Zone™ Tower Of Terror
19   Beauty and the Beast – Live On Stage
20   Fantasmic!
21   Guest Information Board
22   Toy Story Pizza Planet
23   Site of new Stunt Show (2005)

DISNEY-MGM STUDIOS

Magic celebration, when the awesome grand icon – a 12-storey **Sorcerer Mickey** hat – was added at the centre of the park, a gigantic, shimmering symbol of the Disney magic.

Rather bigger than the *Magic Kingdom Park* at 154 acres (62ha) but substantially smaller than *Epcot*, *Disney-MGM Studios* is a different experience yet again with its combination of rides, spectacular shows (including the unmissable Fantasmic!), street entertainment, film sets and smart gift shops. Like the *Magic Kingdom Park*, the food on offer may not win awards, but some of the restaurants (notably the **Sci-Fi Dine-in Theater** and **50s Prime Time Café**) have imaginative settings to keep everyone amused.

Disney-MGM Studios also has rather more to occupy smaller children than *Epcot*, but you can still easily see all of it in a day unless the crowds are heavy.

Location

The entrance arrangements will be fairly familiar if you have already visited any of the other parks. *Disney-MGM Studios* is located on Buena Vista Drive (which runs between World Drive and Epcot Drive) and the parking fee is $7. Remember to make a note of where you park before you catch your tram to the main gates, where you must wait for the official opening hour. If the queues build up quickly, the gates will open early, so be ready for a running start.

Once through the gates, you are into Hollywood Boulevard, a street of mainly gift shops, and you have to decide which of the main attractions to head for first, as these are the ones where the queues will be heaviest nearly all day. Try to ignore the lure of the shops as it is better to browse in the early afternoon when the queues build up at the rides. Incidentally, if you thought Disney had elevated queuing to an art form in their other two parks, wait until you see the clever ways they are arranged here. Just when you think you have got to the ride itself, there is another twist to the queue you hadn't seen or an extra element to the ride which holds you up. The latter are 'holding pens' which are an ingenious way of making it seem like you are being entertained instead of queuing. Look out for them in particular at the Great Movie Ride, Twilight Zone™ Tower of Terror and Jim Henson's Muppet*Vision 3-D.

An up-to-the-minute check on queue times at all the main attractions is kept on a **Guest Information Board** on Hollywood Boulevard, just past its junction with Sunset Boulevard, where you can also book for the restaurants. The **Baby Center** here is located just inside the main gates on the left, next to Guest Relations, along with the **First Aid** facility.

Disney-MGM Studios is laid out in a rather more confusing fashion than its counterparts, which have neatly packaged 'lands', so you need to

Disney-MGM Studios – Fantasmic!

© Disney

5

consult your map frequently to ensure you're going in the right direction.

The main attractions

The opening-gate crowds will all surge in one of four directions, which will give you a pretty good idea of where you want to go. By far the 'biggest' attraction in *Disney-MGM Studios* is the **Twilight Zone™ Tower of Terror**, a magnificent haunted hotel ride that culminates in a 13-storey drop in a lift, where queues build to 2 hours at peak periods. So, if the Tower appeals to you, do it first! Head up Hollywood Boulevard then turn right into Sunset Boulevard and it is at the end of the street, looming ominously over the park. **Rock 'n Roller Coaster Starring Aerosmith**, at the end of Sunset Boulevard on the left, is another huge draw but is also a FASTPASS (FP) ride (see page 89) like Tower of Terror, so you can get a pass for one and ride the other if you head here first.

Star Tours, the great Star Wars™ simulator ride, and **Voyage of the Little Mermaid** are also serious queue-builders and FP attractions. If you are not up for the really big thrills, grab a Pass for Mermaid (straight up Hollywood Boulevard, past Sunset, turn right into Animation Courtyard) then head for Star Tours (back across the main square past the Indiana Jones™ show). Finally, the new **Who Wants To Be A Millionaire – Play It!** attraction is a major success, but has only 10 shows (accommodating 1,600 people a time) a day, hence FPs can run out quickly. So, if this appeals to you, head here first (past the Little Mermaid and along Mickey Avenue).

Here's a full rundown of the attractions, in a clockwise direction:

The Great Movie Ride: this faces you (behind the hat icon) as you walk in along Hollywood Boulevard and is a good place to start if the crowds are not too serious. An all-star audio-animatronics cast recreates a number of box office smashes, including Jimmy Cagney's *Public Enemy*, Julie Andrews in *Mary Poppins*, Gene Kelly in *Singing in the Rain* and many more masterful set pieces as you ride through on your conducted tour. Small children may find the menace of *The Alien* too strong, but otherwise the ride has fairly universal appeal and features some clever live twists that I won't reveal (there are two slight variations on this ride, a cowboy and a gangster version – ask a Cast Member if you especially want to do either one). AAAA.

ABC Sound Studio 'Sounds Dangerous' Starring Drew Carey: this sound FX special features American comedian Drew Carey in an instalment of a spoof undercover police show *Sounds Dangerous*. Most of the 12-minute show is in the dark – which upsets some children – and is centred on your special headphones as Carey's stakeout goes wrong. Clever and amusing – if a bit tame for older children – you exit into the Sound Works Studio to try out some well-known sound effects. AAA.

Indiana Jones™ Epic Stunt Spectacular!: consult your park map for the various times for when this rip-roaring stunt cavalcade hits the stage. A specially made movie set creates three different backdrops for Indiana Jones™ stunt people to put on a dazzling array of clever stunts, scenes and special effects from the Harrison Ford film epics. Audience participation is an element and there are some amusing sub-plots. Queues for the 30-minute show begin to form up to half an hour beforehand, but the auditorium holds more than 2,000 so everyone usually gets in. TTTT (FP).

Star Tours: anyone remotely amused by the *Star Wars*™ films will enjoy just queuing for one of my own favourites, a breathtaking 7-minute spin in a Star Speeder. The elaborate walk-in area is full of *Star Wars*™ gadgets and gizmos that will make the long wait (often up to an hour) pass quickly. From arguing robots C-3PO and R-2D2 to your robotic 'pilot', everything has a brilliant sense of space travel, and the ride won't disappoint! Restrictions: 3ft 4in/101cm, no children under 3. TTTT (plus AAAAA) (FP).

Jim Henson's Muppet*Vision 3-D: the 3-D is crossed out here and 4-D substituted in its place, so be warned that strange things will be happening! A wonderful 10-minute holding-pen pre-show takes you into the Muppet Theater for a 20-minute experience with all of the Muppets, 3-D special effects and more – when Fozzie Bear points his squirty flower at you, prepare to get wet! It's a gem, and children in particular love it. Queues build up through the main parts of the day, but Disney's queuing expertise makes them seem shorter than they actually are. AAAAA (FP).

Honey, I Shrunk the Kids Movie Set Adventure: this adventure playground gives youngsters the chance to tackle gigantic blades of grass that turn out to be slides, crawl through caves, investigate giant mushrooms and more. However, some may turn round and say 'Yeah. A giant ant. So what?' and head back for the rides. There can be long queues here, too, so arrive early if the kids demand it (and bring plenty of film). TT (TTTT under 9s).

The Disney-MGM Studios Backlot Tour: this 35-minute walk-and ride tour starts with some special effects (involving an amusing water tank with a mock Pearl Harbor attack!) before you board the special trams for a look at the off-limits part of the studios. You are introduced to the production backlot, famous film and TV 'houses' and props and then a visit to **Catastrophe Canyon** for a demonstration of special effects that try both to drown you and blow you up! AAA (plus TTTT). You exit into the **American Film Institute Showcase** of costumes and props from recent films. Nearby, **Goofy's Prop Stop** is a neat photo opportunity with various Disney images ($12.95 and $16.95).

Who Wants To Be A Millionaire – Play It!: Disney's live version of the hit TV show is based on the US programme, but is still effectively the same show. The great twist is EVERYONE gets to play – all 1,600 members of the audience. Whoever is fastest with the put-them-in-order question starts in the hot seat and, as you play along, you build up a score, with the top 10 shown on screen at various stages. Then, when a contestant loses out, the person with the highest score in the audience is next up. The hosts do a terrific job of maintaining the TV 'illusion' and there are the usual rules and lifelines, which add to the sense of reality here (although you play for Disney points, not money, which add up to some great souvenirs). One difference is there can be no Phone A Friend lifeline. Instead, you have Phone A Complete Stranger, when a passer-by is grabbed off the street outside! It is addictive fun, and the only drawback is it has become so popular the FASTPASS tickets run out quickly, so try to get here early in the day. AAAAA (FP). As you come out, look for the **Meet Mickey Mouse** character greet nearby.

Walt Disney: One Man's Dream: as part of the *100 Years Of Magic* celebration, Disney's Imagineers came up with this interactive show-and-tell chronicle

Playhouse Disney – Live on Stage!

of Walt himself and his accomplishments. From archive school records to a model of the submarine Nautilus from *20,000 Leagues Under The Sea*, the story of the man behind the Mouse comes to vivid life with a number of hands-on

> BRIT TIP: Try to sit at least half-way back in the Mermaid Theatre, especially with young children, as the stage front is a bit high for little 'uns.

elements. The homage to the creator of the magic concludes with a preview of Disney's future developments, plus a 10-minute film encapsulating everything Walt achieved and dreamed about. AAAA.

Voyage of the Little Mermaid: this 17-minute live performance is primarily for children who have seen the Disney cartoon. It brings together a creative mix of live actors, animation and puppetry to recreate the highlights of the film. Parents will still enjoy the clever special effects, but queues tend to be long, so go early or late. Those in the first few rows may also get a little wet. AAA (AAAAA under 9s) (FP).

The Magic of Disney Animation: an amusing and entertaining 35-minute tour through the making of cartoons. It's up to you how you pace it, but don't miss Robin Williams in a special cartoon, *Back to Neverland*, with Walter Cronkite, and the fascinating view of some of Disney's animators at work. It concludes with a film of some of the highlights of Disney's many animated classics, and you will be amazed at how much you have learned by the end (although small children might be a bit lost by it all). Queues are rarely serious here, so it's a good one for the afternoon. AAAA.

Playhouse Disney – Live On Stage!: straight out of several popular kids' TV series comes this 20-minute live show with such pre-school favourites as *Bear in the Big Blue House* and *Rolie Polie Olie*, plus others like the *Book of Pooh* and *Stanley*. Much of this can be seen only on cable or satellite TV in the UK, so it is doubtful how much it will mean to the kids it is aimed at, but it is still colourful and entertaining. AAA (AAAAA under 5s).

Rock 'n Roller Coaster Starring Aerosmith: Disney's first big-thrill inverted coaster is a sure-fire draw for the high-energy ride addicts, with a magnificent indoor setting and nerve-jangling ride. It features a clever 3-D film show starring rock group Aerosmith in their recording studio. That preamble leads to the real fun, set to specially recorded tracks from the band itself and with outrageous speaker systems, as riders climb aboard Cadillac 'cars' for this memorable whiz through a mock Los Angeles setting (watch out for a close encounter with the 'Hollywood' sign!). The high-speed launch and inversions ensure an up-to-the-minute coaster experience. Go first thing or expect serious queues. Restrictions: 4ft 1in/124cm TTTTT (FP).

The Tower of Terror

The Twilight Zone™ Tower of Terror: the tallest landmark in *Walt Disney World Resort in Florida* (at 199ft/60 metres) invites you to experience another dimension in this mysterious Hollywood Tower Hotel that time forgot. The exterior is intriguing, the interior is fascinating, the ride is scintillating and the queues are mind-blowing! The only unfortunate aspect of this thrilling attraction, which is so much more than just the advertised 13-storey free-fall, is the fact that much of the queuing is outside in the sun, and, when it is hot, you are almost melting by the time you reach the air-conditioned, spooky hotel. Typically, just when you think you are through to the ride itself, there is another queue, but the inner detail is so clever you can spend the time inspecting how realistic it all is. The ride was also revamped in 2003 to add a new, random, element to the

> **BRIT TIP:** I always recommend the Sci-Fi Dine-In Theater Restaurant or '50s Prime Time Café for a main meal with a difference.

> **BRIT TIP:** Beat the crowds by booking a Fantasmic! dinner package when you enter the park (or in advance on 407 939 3463). Just make an early-evening Priority Seating for the Hollywood Brown Derby or Mama Melrose's, and you get no-wait VIP seating later for the show.

drop sequence, with other special effects, and most of the big lap bars have been replaced with seat-belts for a more hair-rising experience. You have been warned! Restrictions: 3ft 4in/101cm. TTTTT (FP).

Beauty and the Beast – Live on Stage: an enchanting live performance of the highlights of this Disney classic will entertain the whole family for 20 minutes in the nearby Theater of the Stars. Check the schedule for showtimes. AAA.

Fantasmic!: this epic special-effects spectacular is simply not to be missed. Staged every night in a 6,900-seat amphitheatre behind the Tower of Terror™, it features the 'dreams' of Mr M Mouse, portrayed as the Sorcerer's Apprentice, through films such as *Pocahontas, The Lion King* and *Snow White*, but hijacked by various Disney villains, leading to a tumultuous battle, with Our Hero emerging triumphant. Dancing waters, shooting comets, animated fountains, swirling stars, balls of fire and more combine in a truly breathtaking presentation – just beware of the giant, fire-

The Wicked Witch in Fantasmic!

breathing dragon! The 25-minute show begins seating up to 90 minutes in advance and it is advisable to head there at least half an hour beforehand (watch out for the splash zones!). AAAAA.

Daily parade

In keeping with the park's movie-star style, the daily parade (another designed for the *100 Years of Magic* celebration) is **Disney Stars and Motor Cars**, and is one of the highlights. The theme is a film premiere in 1930s' and 1940s' Hollywood, with a series of genuine vintage cars and clever replicas being used to mount a riotous cavalcade of Disney showbiz favourites. It kicks off with motorcycle police outriders and continues with some 15 crazily customised cars – including a 1929 Cadillac – that provide the likes of A*laddin*, *Mary Poppins*, *Mulan*, the *Muppets* and new films like *Atlantis* and *Monsters Inc* with a chance to show off in larger-than-life fashion. Watch out for the *Star Wars*™ 'Land Speeder' with a radio-controlled R-2D2 in the largest parade ever staged in *Disney-MGM Studios*. The lead car also features any special guests at the Studios that day – or a visiting family instead. AAAA

Disney characters are out and about along Mickey Avenue (including Sorcerer•Mickey) as are performing 'actors and actresses' in Hollywood Boulevard.

Places to eat

While the choice of food may not be wide, there is plenty of it and at reasonable prices. **The Hollywood Brown Derby** offers a full-service restaurant in fine Hollywood style (reservations necessary – special Early Evening Value meals 4–6pm), while **Mama Melrose's Ristorante Italiano** is a wonderful table-service Italian option (one of my favourites).

The **Sci-Fi Dine-In Theater Restaurant** is a big hit with kids as you dine in a mock drive-in cinema, with cars as 'tables', waitresses on roller skates and a big film screen showing corny old black-and-white science fiction clips. The **'50s Prime Time Café** is another hilarious experience as you sit in mock stage sets from American 1950s' TV sitcoms and eat meals 'just like Mom used to make'. (The waiters all claim to be your brother and warn you to take your elbows off the table, etc. Hilarious!) Priority Seatings are necessary.

The fast-food eateries consist of the **ABC Commissary** (breakfast to 10.30am, then burger, fish and chips, chicken yakitori and vegetable wraps), **Backlot Express** (excellent burgers and hot dogs), **Rosie's All-American Café** (chicken, burgers, salads) and the **Toy Story Pizza Planet** (pizza, salads and drinks). A good buffet lunch (high season only) and dinner is also available at **Hollywood & Vine Cafeteria of the Stars** ($19.99 adults, $9.99 3–11s).

Lunch special

Want to know how Disney's animators really work? Book up for the Animators Lunch, held at the Brown Derby on Mondays, Tuesdays and Wednesdays (not holiday periods) and you can hear first-hand from some of the people who bring the magic to life on screen. It starts at 11.30am and lasts 1½ hours, although it does cost a formidable $60.99 for adults and $34.99 for 3–11s. It can be booked up to 30 days in advance and includes an autographed decorative plate to take home.

Shopping

There are 21 gift and speciality shops around the Studios – six of them along Hollywood Boulevard – which are worth checking out in early afternoon. Sid Caheunga's **One-of-a-Kind** (just to the left of the main gates as you enter) stocks rare movie and TV items, including many celebrity autographs. Try the **Legends of Hollywood** (on Sunset Boulevard) for a rather different range of souvenirs and **It's a Wonderful Shop** (in the Backlot) for Christmas gifts and collectables. **Keystone Clothiers** (at the top of Hollywood Boulevard) offers some of the best Disney apparel.

Studios at Christmas

At Christmas (in fact, from late November to January 1), one of the most amazing spectacles anywhere is the **Osborne Family Lights**, which are switched on every evening in the park's Backlot Tour area.
If you have ever wondered what 5 million twinkling, themed fairy lights would look like, then take a walk through this fantasy wonderland. It draws a huge crowd twice a night (try to go during a Fantasmic! performance to avoid the worst of the throngs) and is simply the most stunning visual light display you are ever likely to see. NB: the Osborne Lights will not be shown in 2003 as the Backlot area is prepared for a new Auto Stunt Show in 2005.

Star Wars too

Star Wars™ film fans will want to make a beeline for the Studios during weekends in the latter half of May when the park becomes a playground for characters, film stars, photo-opportunities, competitions and other movie memorabilia based on anything to do with Luke Skywalker and Co. There is no additional fee to rub shoulders with (and get autographs from) various *Star Wars*™ personalities, and the Studios really takes on an extra (Space) dimension each weekend.

DISNEY-MGM STUDIOS with children

Here is our general guide to the rides which appeal to the different age groups in this park (and it is, possibly, the best spread of all):

Under 5s
Playhouse Disney – Live On Stage!, Voyage of the Little Mermaid, Beauty and the Beast – Live on Stage, Disney Stars and Motor Cars parade, Fantasmic!.

5–8s
Voyage of the Little Mermaid, Beauty and the Beast – Live On Stage, Honey I Shrunk the Kids Movie Set Adventure, Sounds Dangerous Starring Drew Carey, Jim Henson's Muppet*Vision 3-D, *Disney-MGM Studios* Backlot Tour, Disney Stars and Motor Cars parade, Star Tours (with parental discretion), Fantasmic!

9–12s
Sounds Dangerous Starring Drew Carey, Indiana Jones™ Epic Stunt Spectacular!, The Great Movie Ride, Star Tours, Jim Henson's Muppet*Vision 3-D, *Disney-MGM Studios* Backlot Tour, The Magic of Disney Animation, Beauty and the Beast – Live on Stage, Rock 'n Roller Coaster Starring Aerosmith, Twilight Zone™ Tower of Terror, Fantasmic!

Over 12s
Indiana Jones™ Epic Stunt Spectacular, Star Tours, The Great Movie Ride, Jim Henson's Muppet*Vision 3-D, Disney-MGM Studios Backlot Tour, Who Wants To Be A Millionaire – Play It!, The Magic of Disney Animation, Rock 'n Roller Coaster Starring Aerosmith, Twilight Zone™ Tower of Terror, Fantasmic!

Disney's Animal Kingdom Theme Park

The newest, smartest and most radical theme park at *Walt Disney World Resort in Florida* opened in 1998 and represents a completely different experience. With an emphasis on nature and conservation, it largely eschews the non-stop thrills and attractions which mark out the other parks, and instead offers a change of pace, a more relaxing motif, as well as Disney's usual seamless entertainment style – plus two excellent thrill rides (three when the under-construction blockbuster Expedition Everest opens in 2006).

The attractions are relatively few, just five out-and-out rides, plus two scenic journeys, two nature trails, five shows (including the hilarious 3-D film *It's Tough to Be a Bug!* and the full-blown theatre of *Festival of The Lion King*), an elaborate adventure playground, conservation station and petting zoo, and a Disney character greeting area. It's a far cry from the hustle-bustle of the *Magic Kingdom Park*, and it carries a strong environmental message that aims to create a greater understanding of the world's ecological problems. School-age children should find it quite educational, though under 5s may be a little left out. It is outrageously scenic, notably with the 145-ft (44-metre) Tree of Life and the Kilimanjaro Safaris, but it won't overwhelm you with Disney's usual sense of grand fantasy. Rather, it is a chance to experience a part of the world that is both threatened and threatening in a safe, secure manner. It is obviously not the Real Thing but it provides a genuine glimpse of some of the world's most majestic areas in a manner that allows ecology and the commercial world to co-exist happily and meaningfully.

The most conclusive word on Disney's first full-blown animal adventure goes to Professor David Bellamy, who told me: 'This park has been designed and looked after by the best animal welfare people you can think of. Bad zoos are bad news and should be closed down, but good zoos are good news and the only hope for keeping about 500 species of animal alive in the future.' The park does get horribly crowded, however, and the walkways can be very congested. There are also fewer areas to cool down in. It is definitely a good idea to be here on time and use FASTPASS (FP) to minimise queuing.

Disney's Animal Kingdom

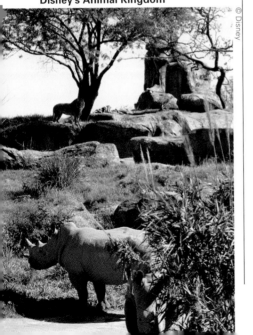

© Disney

Getting there

If you are staying in the Kissimmee area, *Disney's Animal Kingdom Theme Park* is the easiest to find. Just get on the (toll) Osceola Parkway and follow it all the way to the toll booths, where parking costs $7. Alternatively, coming down I-4, take

THE OASIS
1 The Oasis Tropical Garden

DISCOVERY ISLAND
2 The Tree Of Life
3 It's Tough to Be a Bug!
4 Discovery Island Trails

CAMP MINNIE-MICKEY
5 Character Greeting Trails
6 Pocahontas And Her Forest Friends
7 Festival Of The Lion King

DINOLAND USA
8 DINOSAUR!
9 The Boneyard
10 Tarzan™ Rocks!
11 Chester & Hester's Dino-Rama!
12 TriceraTOP Spin
13 Primeval Whirl

AFRICA
14 Harambe
15 Kilimanjaro Safaris
16 Pangani Forest Exploration Trail
17 Rafiki's Planet Watch

ASIA
18 Flights Of Wonder
19 Kali River Rapids
20 Maharajah Jungle Trek

21 Rainforest Café
22 Site of Expedition Everest (2006)

DISNEY'S ANIMAL KINGDOM

Take the Wildlife Express to explore Rafiki's Planet Watch

Disney's Animal Kingdom Theme Park at a glance

Location	Directly off Osceola Parkway, also via World Drive and Buena Vista Drive	
Size	500 acres (203ha) divided into 6 'lands'	
Hours	9am to 5 or 6pm	
Admission	Under 3 free; 3–9 $42 (1-day ticket), $168 (4-Day Park Hopper), $216 (5-Day Park Hopper Plus); adult (10+) $52, $208, $269. Prices do not include tax.	
Parking	$7	
Lockers	Yes; either side of Entrance Plaza; $7 ($2 refundable)	
Pushchairs	$8 and $15 ($1 refundable) at Garden Gate Gifts, through entrance on right	
Wheelchairs	$8 ($1 refund) and $40 ($10 refund); with pushchairs	
Top Attractions	DINOSAUR!, Kilimanjaro Safaris, It's Tough to Be a Bug!, Kali River Rapids, Festival of The Lion King	
Don't Miss	Pangani Forest Exploration Trail, Maharajah Jungle Trek, Rafiki's Planet Watch, Tarzan Rocks!, Mickey's Jamming Jungle Parade, dining at Rainforest Café	
Hidden Costs	**Meals**	Burger, chips and coke $7.48
	Kids' meal	$3.79
	T-shirts	$19–32
	Souvenirs	$1.99–275
	Sundries	Caricature drawings $15–28

the new Exit 65 which puts you on Osceola Parkway. From west Highway 192, come in on Sherberth Road (turn right at the first traffic lights).

If you arrive early (which is advisable), you can walk up to the Entrance Plaza. Otherwise, the usual tram system will take you in, so make a note of the area in which you park (e.g. Unicorn, row 67). The Plaza is overlooked by the mountainous **Rainforest Café**, with its 65-ft (20-metre) waterfall, which is a must for an early lunch or dinner (rarely busy). With Orlando so hot through the summer months, you need to be here as early as possible

to see the animals before they disappear into the shade.

For the early birds, here is your best plan of campaign. Once through the gates, animal lovers should head first for Kilimanjaro Safaris, through the Oasis, Discovery Island and into Africa. After the Safari, go straight to Pangani Forest Exploration Trail and you will have experienced two of the park's best animal encounters. Alternatively, thrill-seekers should turn right in Discovery Island for DinoLand USA, where the DINOSAUR! ride is the big attraction. With that one safely under your belt before the serious crowds arrive, head back through the Island to Asia and Kali River Rapids raft ride, followed by the scenic Maharajah Jungle Trek. The best combination for the first arrivals is to get a FASTPASS (FP) for DINOSAUR! then head straight for Kilimanjaro Safaris, and, once you have done that (and depending on your FP time), either do your DINOSAUR! ride (followed by a Kali River Rapids FP) or go straight to the Rapids. Check your show schedule for the *Festival of The Lion King* and try to catch one of the first two performances as the later ones draw sizeable queues. The 'wait time' board at the entrance to Discovery Island is also helpful.

Right, those are your main tactics, here is the full rundown.

The Oasis

The Oasis Tropical Garden is a gentle, walk-through introduction to the park, a rocky, tree-covered area featuring several animal habitats, studded with streams, waterfalls and lush plant life. Here you will meet miniature deer, macaws, parrots, iguanas, sloths and tree kangaroos in a wonderfully understated environment that leads you across a stone bridge to the main open park area. AAA.

Discovery Island

This hugely colourful 'village' is the hub of the park. Its theme is a tropical artists' colony, with animal-

BRIT TIP: The early start is especially advised for Kilimanjaro Safaris. You will see far more animals in the first few hours of the day than during the afternoon.

inspired artwork everywhere, four main shops and two eateries.

The Tree of Life: this 145-ft (44-metre) high arboreal edifice is the park centrepiece, an awesome creation that seems to give off a different perspective from wherever you view it. The 'trunk' and 'roots' are covered in 325 animal carvings representing the Circle of Life, from the dolphin to the lion. Trails lead round the tree, interspersed with more natural animal habitats that showcase flamingos, otters, ring-tailed lemurs, macaws, axis deer, cranes, storks, ducks and tortoises. For statistics lovers, the tree canopy spreads 160ft (49 metres), the trunk is 50ft (15 metres) wide and the roots spread out 170ft (52 metres) in diameter. There are 103,000 leaves (all attached by hand) on more than 8,000 branches! AAAA.

It's Tough to Be a Bug!: winding down among the Tree's roots brings you 'underground' to a 430-seat theatre and another example of Disney's artistry in 3-D films and special effects. This hysterically funny 10-minute show, in the company of Flick from the Disney/Pixar hit film *A Bug's Life*, is

BRIT TIP: The dark, special effects and creepy-crawlies often scare young ones in this show.

a homage to 80% of the animal world, featuring grasshoppers, beetles, spiders, stink bugs and termites (beware the 'acid' spray!) as well as a number of tricks I couldn't possibly reveal. Sit towards the back in the middle of a row (allow a good number of people in first as the rows are filled up from the far side) to get the best of the 3-D effects. Queues build up from midday onwards, but they do move quite steadily. Don't miss the 'forthcoming attractions' posters in the foyer for some

5

excruciating bug puns on well-known films. AAAAA (FP).

Shopping is at its best here, with a huge range of merchandise, souvenirs and gifts (notably in **Disney Outfitters** and **Island Mercantile**), while the two counter-service restaurants, **Pizzafari** and **Flame Tree Barbecue**, are both good choices. Indeed, provided it is not too hot, the Flame Tree is a relaxing and picturesque option, set among some pretty gardens, pools and fountains on the edge of Discovery River.

Camp Minnie-Mickey

A woodland retreat featuring gently winding paths and more of Disney's clever scenery – the benches, lighting and the gurgling stream, with Donald Duck and his nephews hiking down the side, that develops into a series of kid-friendly squirt fountains.

Character Greeting Trails: here, four trails lead to a series of jungle encounters with Disney characters like Mickey and Minnie (naturally), Winnie the Pooh and Tigger, Chip 'n Dale, Baloo and King Louie, Timon and Rafiki. AAAAA (for kids).

Pocahontas and Her Forest Friends: based on characters from the Disney film *Pocahontas*, this 15-minute show sees various animals – racoons, rabbits, cranes, a skunk, armadillo and porcupine –

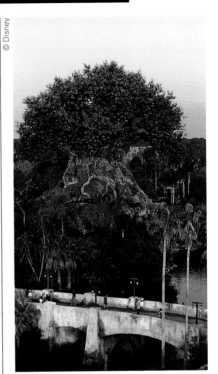

The Tree of Life

interacting with the central actress and Mother Willow in the question of 'Who can save the forest?' It doesn't seem to do much for small children, there is not much shade in summer and it is standing room only once the 350 seats have been filled. AAA.

Festival of The Lion King: not to be missed, this high-powered 40-minute production brings the hit film to life in spectacular fashion with giant moving stages, huge animated figures, singers, dancers, acrobats and stilt-walkers. All the well-known songs are given an airing in a coruscation of colour and sound, and it serves to underline the quality Disney brings to live shows. This is matched only by its popularity – people begin queuing 30 minutes in advance for the 1,000-seater theatre, so try to take in one of the earlier shows of the day. AAAAA.

The amazing Festival of The Lion King

© Disney

Chester and Hester's Dino-Rama!

DinoLand USA

Rather at odds with the natural theming of the rest of the park, DinoLand USA is a full-scale palaeontology exercise, with this mock 'town' taken over by a university fossil dig. Energetically tongue-in-cheek (the 'students' who work in the area have the motto 'Been there, dug that', while you enter under a mock brachiosaurus skeleton, the 'Oldengate Bridge' – groan!), it still features some glimpses into dinosaur research and artefacts.

DINOSAUR!: renamed after Disney's big animated film, its original fast, jerky ride has been toned down a little for a more family-friendly experience (although the dinosaur menace is still too scary for many children). It is a wonderfully realistic journey back to the end of the Cretaceous period and the giant meteor that put paid to dinosaur life. You enter the high-tech Dino Institute, 'a discovery center and research lab dedicated to uncovering the mysteries of the past', for a multimedia show of dino history that leads to a briefing room for your 'mission' 65 million years in the past to view Cretaceous life.

However, one of the Institute's scientists 'hijacks' your journey for his own project, to capture a dinosaur before the fateful meteor's arrival, and you go careering back to a prehistoric jungle in your 12-passenger Time Rover. The threat of a carnivorous carnotaurus and the impending doom of the meteor add up to a breathtaking whiz through a stunning environment. You will need to ride it at least twice to appreciate all the clever detail, but queues build up quickly, so go either first thing or late in the day. Restrictions: 3ft 4in/101cm. TTTT plus AAAA (FP).

BRIT TIP: Try to ride at the front left of your Time Rover car for maximum effect of the twists and turns and the dinosaur menace.

The Boneyard: a hugely imaginative adventure playground, it offers kids the chance to slip, slide and climb through the 'fossilised' remains of triceratops and brontosaurs, explore caves, dig for bones and splash through a mini-waterfall. The amusing signage will go over the heads of most kids, but it is ideal for parents to let their young 'uns loose for up to an hour (although not just after the neighbouring Tarzan show has finished). TTTT (kids only).

Tarzan™ Rocks!: and he really does. This amazing show is basically a 30-minute rock concert showcasing the songs from the animated film, with special effects

Primeval Whirl

© Disney

5

provided by dancers, acrobats and roller bladers, all in wonderful costumes and superbly choreographed. Tarzan and Jane make only a brief appearance, and then mainly as acrobats (ladies – no staring at that loincloth!). Its loud, high-energy style may not be everyone's cup of tea (especially for sensitive young ears) but it is visually stunning and the quality of the performers leaves you gasping. AAAA.

Chester & Hester's Dino-Rama!: this new mini-land of rides, fairground games and stalls adds a rather garish element to DinoLand USA. It's main icon is a towering Concretosaurus (!), and it is designed to have a quirky, tongue-in-cheek style reminiscent of 1950s' American roadside attractions. The top rides are:

TriceraTOP Spin: another version of the Dumbo/Aladdin rides in the *Magic Kingdom Park*, a flying, twirling, spinning top bounces you around, up and down (watch for the surprise dino appearance at the top!). AA (or TTTT for under 5s).

Primeval Whirl: coaster fans will definitely get a laugh out of this wacky offering that sends its riders through a maze of curves, hills and (quite sharp) drops that make it seem much faster than it actually is. It is basically a fairground lampoon of the DINOSAUR! ride, a mock journey 'way back in time', with plenty of cartoon frippery. The extra fun is provided by the cars free-spinning, which means an extra, unpredictable element to each 3-minute ride (plunging through the jaws of a skeleton dino at one point!). The queuing area alone is a riot of visual gags, but the ride itself is not recommended for anyone with back or neck problems (especially neck problems). Height restriction 4ft/121cm. TTTT (FP).

There are then six fairground-type games (each costing a rather

hefty $2 extra) to tempt you into trying to win a large cuddly dinosaur, all with the larger-than-life Dino-Rama trademark. Dining options include the **Restaurantosaurus**, counter-service burgers and hot dogs (presented by McDonald's, so you get McDonald's fries, Chicken McNuggets and Happy Meals but no Big Macs) and a snack bar, while shopping is centred on the huge **Chester and Hester's Dino-Rama! – Dinosaur Treasures**, the 'Fossiliferous Gift Store' with groan-inducing slogans like Merchandise of Extinction, Prehistoric Prices and Last Stop for 65 Million Years!

BRIT TIP: The Restaurantosaurus features Donald's Prehistoric Breakfastosaurus 8–10am with Mickey Mouse, Donald Duck and other character favourites. It costs $16.99 for adults and $8.99 for 3–11s.

Africa

The largest land in the park, it re-creates magnificently the forests, grasslands and rocky homelands of equatorial Africa's most fascinating residents in a richly landscaped setting that is part rundown port town and part endless savannah. In here, the outside world seems thousands of miles away and there is hardly a glimpse of it anywhere.

Harambe: a reconstruction Kenyan port village, complete with white coral walls and thatched roofs, is the starting point of your adventure. The Arab-influenced Swahili culture is depicted in the native tribal costumes and architecture. Here you will find two more shops, including the **Mombasa Marketplace/Ziwani Traders**, where you can suit up safari-style, and the counter-service **Tusker House Restaurant** for rotisserie chicken, fresh fish, salads, vegetarian sandwiches and a special African dish (a slightly healthier offering than most, but a touch expensive, I find), as well as four snack and drink bars. The splendid **Karuka Acrobats** also perform here on select days.

Kilimanjaro Safaris: the queuing area alone earns high marks for authenticity, preparing you for the sights and sounds of the 110-acre (45ha) savannah beyond. You board a 32-passenger truck, with your driver/guide relaying information about the flora and fauna on view and a bush pilot overhead relaying facts and figures on the wildlife, including the dangers threatening them in the real world. Hundreds of animals are carefully spread out in various habitats, with no fences in sight – the ditches and barriers are all well concealed – as you splash through fords and cross rickety bridges, and you are likely to get a close-up of rhinos, elephants, giraffes, zebras, lions, baboons, antelope, ostriches and hippos.

Halfway round, your journey becomes a race to stop elephant poachers, though the outcome is fairly obvious. Once again, the authentic nature of all you see (okay, some of the tyre 'ruts' and termite mounds are concrete and the baobab

BRIT TIP: The best (i.e. the most jolting) ride with the Kilimanjaro Safaris is at the back of the truck, although there's nothing much to see from midday to late afternoon when many animals take a siesta.

trees are fake) is quite awesome with the spread of the vegetation and the landscaping, and the only drawback is the lack of photo stops along the way (and the ride can be pretty bumpy). The animals can also roam over a wide area and disappear from view. Not recommended for expectant mothers or anyone with back or neck problems. AAAAA (FP).

Pangani Forest Exploration Trail: as you leave the Safari you turn into an overgrown nature trail that showcases gorillas, hippos, meerkats and rare tropical birds. You wander the trail at your own pace and visit several research stations to learn more about the animals on display, including the underwater view of the hippos (check out the size of a hippo skull and those teeth!) and the savannah overlook, where giraffe and antelope graze and the amusing meerkats frolic. The walk-through aviary gives you the chance to meet the carmine bee-eater, pygmy goose, African green pigeon, ibis and brimstone canary, among others, but the real centrepiece is the silverback gorilla habitat, in fact, two of them. The family group is often just inches away from the plate-glass window, while the bachelor group further along can prove more elusive. Again, the natural aspect of the trail is breathtaking and it provides a host of photo opportunities. It is best to visit early on to see the animals at their most active (and because it quickly becomes quite crowded). AAAAA.

Rafiki's Planet Watch: the little train journey here, with its peek into some of the backstage areas, is just the preamble to the park's interactive and educational exhibits. The 3-part journey starts with **Habitat Habit!**, where you can see cotton-top tamarins and learn how conservation begins in your own back garden. **Conservation Station** is next up, a series of exhibits, shows and hands-on information stations about the environment and its ecological dangers, aimed primarily at children.

Look out for *Song of the Rain Forest*, the story of endangered species at the **Mermaid Tales Theater** and the Eco-Heroes trying to redress the balance (who can be quizzed on screen), then take a self-guided tour of the park's backstage areas such as the veterinary treatment centre, the hatchery and neo-natal care. You can easily spend an hour absorbing the environmental message here, along with that of Disney's Wildlife Conservation Fund. Plus, youngsters can also meet Rafiki and some of his animal chums at various times. The **Affection Section**, a petting zoo of lambs, goats, donkeys, sheep and guinea pigs, completes the Planet Watch line-up.

Kilimanjaro Safaris

Asia

The final land of the park is elaborately themed as the gateway to the imaginary south-east Asian city of Anandapur, with temples, ruined forts, landscape and wildlife.

Flights of Wonder: another wildlife show, this portrays the talents and traits of a host of birds, built into a production of mythical proportions, as a treasure-seeking student encounters Phoenix, the birds' guardian, in a crumbling, fortified town. Vultures, eagles, toucans, macaws and many other feathered friends take a bow as Phoenix reveals the treasures of the avian world. Unfortunately, the Caravan Stage is not air-conditioned and is fiendishly hot in summer, so be warned. AAA.

Kali River Rapids: part thrill-ride, part scenic journey, this bouncy, raft-ride journey will get you pretty wet (not great for early morning in winter unless you bring a change of clothes). It starts out in tropical forest territory before launching into a scene of logging devastation, warning of the dangers of clear-cut burning. Your raft then plunges down a waterfall (and one unlucky soul – usually the rider with

Kali River Rapids

The cast at Disney's Animal Kingdom

their back to the drop – gets seriously damp) before you finish the journey more sedately, albeit with a few more watery encounters. Queues can be quite long through the main part of the day, so make good use of the FASTPASS here, and you will probably want to ride at least twice to appreciate all the clever detail. Restrictions: 3ft 6in/106cm (although a few rafts have adult-and-child seats allowing smaller children to ride). TTT (plus AAAA) (FP).

Maharajah Jungle Trek: Asia's version of the Pangani Forest Trail, this is another picturesque walk-through journey past decaying temple ruins and various animal encounters. Playful gibbons, tapirs, Komodo dragons and a bat enclosure (including the flying fox-bat, the world's largest variety) lead up to the main viewing area, the 5-acre (2ha) Tiger Range, which includes a pool and fountains and is a popular playground early in the day for these magnificent big cats. An antelope enclosure and walk-through aviary complete this breathtaking trek (which rarely draws heavy crowds) in fine style. AAAAA.

Finally, returning to the front entrance gives you the chance to sample or just visit (and shop at) the **Rainforest Café**, the second on Disney property. If you haven't seen the one at *Downtown Disney*

Marketplace, you should definitely call in to witness the amazing jungle interior with its audio-animatronic animals, waterfalls, thunderstorms and aquariums. A 3-course meal will set you back about $28 (kids' meals at $6.99), but the setting alone is definitely worth it and the food is above average.

Jammin' Jungle Parade

Following on from the park's *100 Years of Magic* offerings is the new daily (about 4pm) parade, a tour de force called **Mickey's Jammin' Jungle Parade**. Here, the Imagineers have created a series of fanciful, individually designed 'Expedition Rovers' that give various Disney characters the chance to celebrate all the animals who live here. The parade is enhanced by stilt-walkers, puppets, mobile sculptures, Disney characters and different 'party animals', plus live percussionists atop some of the sculptures, as it snakes down a narrow path from Harambe, around Discovery Island and back. Set to a memorable musical backing, it sounds truly delightful, while 25 park guests are chosen to take part each day, travelling on the back of amusingly designed rickshaws which follow each of the character jeeps.

Finally, for a behind-the-scenes look at the park, the **Backstage Safari** is a wonderful 3-hour journey into the handling and care of all the animals ($65, not for under 16s. Call 407 939 8687 to book).

Jammin' Jungle Parade

DISNEY'S ANIMAL KINGDOM PARK with children

Here is our general guide to the rides which appeal to the different children's ages in this park:

Under 5s
Character Greetings Trails, Festival of The Lion King, Discovery Island Trails, Kilimanjaro Safaris, Pangani Forest Exploration Trail, Affection Section, Maharajah Jungle Trek, TriceraTOP Spin, The Boneyard.

5–8s
All the above, plus Pocahontas and Her Forest Friends, Habitat Habit!, Conservation Station, Kali River Rapids, Flights of Wonder, It's Tough To Be a Bug! and DINOSAUR! (with parental discretion).

9–12s
All the above, plus Primeval Whirl and Tarzan™ Rocks!

Over 12s
Festival of The Lion King, It's Tough To Be a Bug!, Kilimanjaro Safaris, Pangani Forest Exploration Trail, Kali River Rapids, Maharajah Jungle Trek, Flights of Wonder, DINOSAUR!, Tarzan™ Rocks!, Primeval Whirl.

Walt Disney World Resort in Florida at Christmas

If you can visit prior to the seriously busy days from just before Christmas Day to New Year's Day, you get the benefit of all the added decorations and atmosphere and none of the overwhelming crowds. Each of the parks takes on a festive character, with the addition of artistic artificial snow, Christmas lights and a huge, magnificently decorated fir tree.

Disney-MGM Studios also features the eye-popping Osborne Family Lights while, at the **Magic Kingdom Park**, Main Street USA is transformed into a Christmas extravaganza, with a 60-ft (18-metre) tree dominating the scene. The unmissable **Mickey's Very Merry Xmas Parade** replaces the main 3pm parade in December and is a positive delight for its lively music and eye-catching costumes. Another seasonal extra is the lively *Twas the Night before Xmas* show at the Galaxy Palace Theater.

Epcot is the jewel in the Christmas crown, though, with two outstanding features. At 6pm, the daily Christmas tree lighting ceremony is quite breathtaking as the rest of the park lights go out and then the World Showcase bridge and the tree itself are illuminated in dramatic stages to some grand musical accompaniment. The nightly **Candlelight Processional** also draws a crowd, with a guest narrator telling the story of Christmas to the backdrop of a large choir and elaborate candle parade. It is tasteful, dramatic and eye-catching, but you should arrive early as people start queuing almost 3 HOURS in advance. However, you can get a reserved seat if you buy the *Candlelight Processional Dinner Package* (variously $26.99, $32.95 or $39.95, plus tax, depending on which World Showcase restaurant you select, and $10.95 for children 3–11), by calling well in advance on 407 939 3463 (credit card details required).

6 Five More of the Best

(or, Expanding Orlando's Universe)

It is time to leave the wonderful world of Disney and venture out into the rest of central Florida's great attractions. And, believe me, there is still a terrific amount in store.

For a start, they don't come much more ambitious than Universal Orlando. The area that used to consist of just the one theme park, Universal Studios Florida®, is fast developing into a fully fledged resort of similar scope to Disney's. A second dynamic theme park, Universal's Islands of Adventure, opened in 1999, hot on the heels of the 30-acre (12-ha) CityWalk entertainment district. The first resort hotel, the Portofino Bay, made its debut in 1999, followed by the Hard Rock Hotel in 2000, and the Royal Pacific Resort in 2002.

A waterway network connects the hotels to the CityWalk hub, while the multi-storey car parks, for more than 20,000 vehicles, have done away with the need for any other transport system, and it is quite convenient to move between parks.

The marketing tie-up with SeaWorld and Busch Gardens, plus their purchase of the Wet 'n Wild water park, has also proved a success, with the 14-day Orlando FlexTickets giving excellent value. The opening of Islands of Adventure has added 2- and 3-Day Tickets (which include a CityWalk Party Pass) allowing movement between both Universal parks. In summer 2003, both these tickets had special offers for extended visits – 7 consecutive days in the case of the 2-Day ticket, and an amazing 14 days in the case of the 3-Day, effectively 11 days free! They

have also introduced their excellent **Universal Express** system for most rides. Similar to Disney's FASTPASS, it allows all park guests to 'reserve' one ride at a time and then another once you have done that attraction, and so on. You just present your park entry ticket at the Distribution Center next to the Universal Express ride or show of your choice, then return at the allotted time for what should be no more than a 15-minute wait (instead of an hour or more at peak periods). NB: Universal hotel guests benefit from Express ride priority ALL DAY by producing their room key.

Additionally, many rides have **Single Rider** queues which can save time if you are the only one in your group who wants to do, say, Dr Doom's Fearfall, or if you don't mind being split up. Once again, any height restriction is noted and Universal Express attractions are indicated by UE.

BRIT TIP: Reader Tom Burton advises, 'If you buy an Orlando FlexTicket giving you 14 consecutive days at Universal, etc, try going to their parks a couple of times in the evenings only. There are virtually no queues this late in the day and I went on the Hulk Coaster (in Islands of Adventure) five times in an hour!'

PRODUCTION CENTRAL

1 Guest Services
2 Shrek 4-D
3 Nickelodeon Studios
4 Jimmy Neutron's Nicktoon Blast

NEW YORK

5 Twister
6 Revenge of the Mummy (spring 2004)
7 The Blues Brothers
8 Finnegan's Bar and Grill

SAN FRANCISCO/AMITY

9 Earthquake – The Big One
10 Jaws
11 All-New Beetlejuice Revue
12 The Wild, Wild, Wild West Stunt Show
13 Lombard's Seafood Grill

WORLD EXPO

14 Back To The Future… The Ride
15 Men In Black – Alien Attack

WOODY WOODPECKER'S KIDZONE

16 Animal Planet Live!
17 Fievel's Playland
18 A Day In The Park With Barney
19 ET Adventure
20 Woody Woodpecker's Nuthouse
     Coaster
21 Curious George Goes to Town

HOLLYWOOD

22 Universal's Horror Make-Up Show
23 Terminator 2: 3-D Battle Across Time
24 Lucy: A Tribute

UNIVERSAL
STUDIOS
FLORIDA

Universal Studios Florida®

Universal opened its Florida park in June 1990 (its original Los Angeles site has been open to the public since before World War Two) and quickly became a serious competitor to Disney. For the visitor, it means a consistently high standard and good value in everything on offer (although the choice is beginning to be utterly bewildering!). In addition, if you have been to the LA Universal Studios, this one is quite different.

The obvious question to ask here is if you need to do *Disney-MGM Studios* as well as Universal, and the answer is an emphatic YES! Universal is a very different kettle of fish to Disney, with a more in-your-face style of entertainment that goes down well with older kids and younger adults. Younger children are also well catered for in Woody Woodpecker's KidZone.

Universal can require more than a full day in high season. As with Disney's parks, the strategies for a successful visit are the same. Arrive EARLY (up to 30 minutes before the official opening time), do the big rides first, avoid main meal times, and step out for a few hours in the afternoon (try shopping or dining at CityWalk) if it gets too crowded.

Location

Universal Studios Florida® is sub-divided into six main areas, set around a huge, manmade lagoon, but there are no great distinguishing features, so keep the map handy to steer yourself around. The main entrance is found just off the new exit to Interstate 4 (I-4) or by the Universal Boulevard link from International Drive (I-Drive) by Wet 'n Wild. Parking costs $8 in their massive multi-storey car park and there is quite a walk (with some moving walkways) to the front gates.

Once through with the madding crowd, your best bet is to turn right on to Rodeo Drive, along Hollywood Boulevard and Sunset Boulevard and into World Expo for Back To The Future… The Ride and Men In Black: Alien Attack. From there, head across the bridge to Jaws, then go back along the Embarcadero for Earthquake and into New York for Twister. This will get most of the main rides under your belt before the crowds build up, and you can then take it a bit easier by putting your feet up for a while at one of the shows or taking advantage of Universal Express. Alternatively, try to be among the early birds

6

Shrek 4-D at Universal Studios

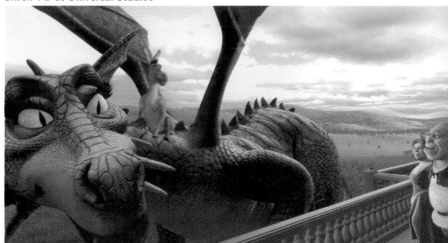

Universal Studios Florida® at a glance

Location	Off Exits 75A and 74B from I-4; Universal Boulevard and Kirkman Road
Size	110 acres (45ha) in 7 themed areas
Hours	9am–7pm off peak; 9am–10pm high season (Washington's birthday, Easter, summer holidays, Thanksgiving, Christmas)
Admission	Under 3 free; 3–9 $42.95 (1-Day Ticket), $83.95 (2-Day Ticket), $96.95 (3-Day Ticket), $133.95 (4-Park FlexTicket), $164.95 (5-Park FlexTicket); adult (10+) $52.95, $96.95, $111.95, $169.95, $201.95; Universal Bonus Pass (5 consecutive days, online sales only) $76.95 and $89.95.
Parking	$8
Lockers	Yes; immediately to left in Front Lot; $5 ($2 refundable)
Pushchairs	$9 and $15, next to locker hire
Wheelchairs	$8 and $40 (with photo ID as deposit), same location as pushchairs
Top Attractions	Men In Black, Jaws, Back to the Future, ET, Earthquake, Shrek 4-D, Terminator 2
Don't Miss	Curious George Playground (for kids), The Blues Brothers

Hidden Costs		
	Meals	Burger, chips and coke $7.48 3-course dinner $25 (Finnigan's)
	Kids' meal	$4.95–6.95 (Finnigan's and Lombard's Seafood Grill only)
	T-shirts	$17–30
	Souvenirs	$1.50–199
	Sundries	Portrait studio photo $24.95 and $28.95

flocking to the new Shrek 4-D film show in Production Central and the blockbuster Terminator 2: 3-D Battle Across Time show on Hollywood Boulevard to avoid the queues that build up here, then use Universal Express for the likes of Back To The Future and Men In Black.

Additionally, the opening in spring 2004 of the **Revenge Of The Mummy**, their latest high-energy ride, is likely to become a major crowd draw, so if the undoubted thrills of this attraction appeal to you, head here first, then continue to Earthquake, Jaws and Men In Black. Here's a full blow-by-blow guide to the Studios. For the rundown on CityWalk, see Chapter 9, page 241.

Production Central

Coming straight through the gates brings you immediately into the administrative centre, with a couple of large gift stores (have a look at these in mid-afternoon) plus The Fudge Shoppe. Call at **Guest Services** here for guides for disabled visitors, TDD and assisted listening devices, and to make restaurant bookings. If you are here early, you can sign up to be in the audience for one of Universal's TV shows at the **Studio Audience Center**. First aid is available here (and on Canal Street between New York and San Francisco), while there are facilities for nursing mothers at **Family Services** by the bank through the gates on the right. Coming to the top of the Plaza of the Stars brings you eventually to the business end of the park.

Shrek 4-D: replacing the old Alfred Hitchcock Theater, this adds a whole new dimension to the genre of 3-D film shows as the original cast of the Oscar-winning *Shrek* movie (Mike Myers, Eddie Murphy, Cameron Diaz and John Lithgow) returns for a 13-minute fun-fest that picks up where the original left off. The evil but vertically challenged Lord Farquaad is back in ghost form to welcome visitors to his 'dungeons' and reveal his plan to ruin the honeymoon of swamp-dwelling Shrek and Princess Fiona. The amusing 7-minute pre-show then leads into the 500-seat main theatre, where you don your 'OgreVision' 3-D glasses and prepare to enter a whole new technological world. The film is funny enough (and acts as a bridge between the original and *Shrek 2*, out in summer 2004) as Shrek and Donkey have to rescue the Princess, but the addition of a host of special effects (watch out for the 'spiders'!) and 'moving' seats mean this is almost a ride as much as a show, and the effect is both startling and hugely entertaining. State-of-the-art digital projection and audio systems, lighting effects, fog and smoke (plus a hilarious finale featuring an out-of-control Tinkerbell) ensure high quality all

round. It should appeal to all the family and is already a major draw, so go first thing in the day, take advantage of the Universal Express here or expect waits well in excess of an hour. AAAAA+ (UE).

Nickelodeon Studios: a lot of this American kids' TV series will be lost on us (although it's on satellite TV in Britain) as visitors go behind the scenes into the production set. Most kids will welcome the chance to get gunged in green slime by the Gakmeister! And they'll love the restrooms which feature green slime 'soap' and sirens when you flush the loo. Long queues build up quickly. AAAA (for children only) (UE).

Jimmy Neutron's Nicktoon Blast: anyone not familiar with the cartoon antics of Jimmy Neutron (Boy Genius) and other members of the Nicktoon stable (Rugrats, the Fairly Odd Parents and SpongeBob Squarepants) might be left bemused by the antics here in this rather noisy simulator ride experience. It revolves around Jimmy tangling once again with the evil (but hapless) emperor Ooblar and battling to save the world, with the help of his zany inventions and his cartoon friends. It is a big hit with under 10s and the ride is quite dynamic (although similar to the Hanna-Barbera ride which it replaced), and it quickly draws a queue as it is one of the first you encounter through the gates. There is no height restriction as long as a child can sit unassisted, but it is not recommended for anyone with heart, neck or back problems. TTTT (UE).

The main eating outlet here is the magnificently themed **Monsters Café**, specialising in salads, pasta, pizza and chicken. The counter-service area is done up like Frankenstein's lab, with the dining areas sub-divided into Swamp, Space, Crypt and Mansion Dining, all to the accompaniment of old black and white horror film clips on

6

the many video screens. There is also monster face painting for kids ($8–17). Shopping includes **On Location** (film, sundries, apparel, 2-way radio rentals), **Studio Sweets**, **Nickstuff** (Toon merchandise with Jimmy Neutron, SpongeBob Squarepants and Dora the Explorer), **Mardi Hut** (Mardi Gras apparel and accessories) and **It's A Wrap** (last-minute souvenirs).

New York

From Production Central you head on to New York and some great scene-setting in the architecture and detail of the buildings and streets. It's far too clean to be authentic, but the façades are first class.

Twister: this experience, based on the hit film, brings audiences 'up close and personal' with the awesome destructive forces of a tornado. The 5-storey terror will shatter everything in its path (okay, so it's pretty tame compared with the real thing), building to a shattering climax of destruction (watch out for the flying cow!). The noise is

The 5-storey tornado at Twister

stunning, but it's a bit much for young children (parental discretion advised for under 13s). The pre-show area is almost a work of art but, unless you can get here early, save this for late in the day. TTT (UE)

Revenge of the Mummy: this awesome new offering in Orlando's roller-coaster catalogue is due to open in spring 2004. A high-tech, high-thrill, high-fun journey into the highly successful world of *The Mummy* film series, it has replaced the old King Kong attraction. Revenge features an indoor spin into Ancient Egypt that fuses brand new coaster technology with space-age robotics and live pyrotechnic special effects. Your ride vehicle will move both backwards and forwards as you brave the menace of the Mummy and his skeleton warriors (prepare for a seriously close encounter here!), you will pass under the 'ceiling of flame' and experience the shadowy, curse-ridden interior of Hamunaptra, The City of the Dead. Mummy writer-director Stephen Sommers has added his design concepts to the project (another first for Universal), and he says: 'This is really a thrill for me. I am really energised to have the world of *The Mummy* films turned into a thrilling, scary, screamworthy ride. This is, in many ways, the next sequel of *The Mummy*, and one I can't wait to experience first-hand.' It is NOT a ride for younger children – or those of a nervous disposition! But it's expected to be an absolute knockout both for coaster addicts and those keen on the ghost train ride genre, as well as film fans. Check your park map for height restrictions, etc. TTTTT (expected; UE).

The Blues Brothers: fans of the film will not want to miss this live show as Jake and Elwood Blues (well, pretty good doubles, anyway) put on a stormin' performance on New York's Delancey Street 4–5 times a day. They cruise up in their Bluesmobile and go through a selection of the film's hits before heading off into the sunset, stopping only to sign a few autographs. Terrific entertainment. AAAA.

For dining, you have the choice of two contrasting restaurants. **Finnegan's Bar and Grill** offers the likes of shepherd's pie, fish and chips, corned beef and cabbage along with more traditional New York fare like prime rib, burgers, fries and a good range of beers, as well as live Irish-tinged entertainment and Happy Hour from 3–5pm (half-price beer and wine). **Louie's Italian Restaurant** has counter-service pizza and pasta, Italian ice cream and tiramisu. For shops you have **Safari Outfitters Ltd** (and the chance to have your picture taken in the grip of King Kong!), **The Aftermath** for Twister souvenirs, and **Second Hand Rose** for Coca-Cola™ merchandise and sweets. New York also boasts a noisy – and therefore kid-friendly – amusement arcade.

San Francisco/Amity

Crossing Canal Street brings you all the way across America to San Francisco/Amity and two of the biggest queues in the park.
Earthquake – The Big One: this 3-part adventure has them lining up from first thing in the morning until late. Go behind the scenes first to two stage sets where, with audience help, some of the special effects of the Charlton Heston film are explained. Then you enter the Bay Area Rapid Transit underground and arrive in the middle of a full-scale earthquake that shakes you to your boots. Tremble as the walls and ceilings collapse, trains collide, cars fall in on you and fire erupts all around, followed by a seeming tidal wave of water. It's not for the faint-

Men in Black – Alien Attack

hearted (or small children), while those who have bad backs or necks, or are pregnant, are advised not to ride. Restrictions: 4ft/122cm (unless accompanied by an adult, with parental discretion). TTTT (UE).
Jaws: the technological wizardry alone will amaze you here, and queues of an hour are common at peak times. The man-made lagoon holds 5 million gallons (23 million litres) of water; nearly 2,000 miles (3,219 metres) of wire run throughout the 7-acre (3-ha) site, which required 10,000cu yd (7,646cu metres) of concrete and 7,500 tons of steel; and the 32-ft (10-metre) monster shark attacks with a thrust equal to a Boeing 727 jet engine! Yes, this is no ordinary ride, and its

6-minute duration will seem a lot longer as your hapless boat guide steers you through an ever more spectacular series of stunts, explosions and menace from the Great White. Yes, of course it's only a model, but I defy you not to be impressed – and just a little scared! TTTT (UE).

All-New Beetlejuice Revue: Disney-MGM Studios has *Beauty and the Beast* and *The Little Mermaid*, Universal goes for *Dracula*, *Frankenstein*, *The Wolfman* and *Frankenstein's Bride* in this recently revamped, 20-minute shock 'n roll extravaganza, compered by Beetlejuice himself. It eschews the twee prettiness of Disney's attractions yet still comes up with a fun family show with lots of laughs, as the 'Graveyard' characters perform versions of hits like *Wild Thing* and *Great Balls Of Fire* in a spectacular setting. AAAA (UE).

The Wild, Wild, Wild West Stunt Show: corny gags, fistfights, explosions, high-level falls and dramatic shootouts all add up to 15 minutes of rootin', tootin' Wild West adventure, Universal Studios style. A hilarious finale and some very loud bangs (not good for small children) are accompanied by large crowds, but the auditorium seats almost 2,000 so there is usually no serious queuing here. NB: this attraction is due to close in late 2003. AAAA (UE).

San Francisco also has the park's best dining choice, with **Lombard's Seafood Grill** the highlight (reservations accepted). Great seafood, pasta and sandwiches are accompanied by a good view over the main lagoon, and there's a separate pastry shop for desserts and coffee. **Richter's Burger Co** offers a few interesting burger variations. For a quick snack, **Chez Alcatraz** provides shrimp cocktails, clam chowder and speciality hot sandwiches.

For shopping, try **Quint's Surf Shack** (men's and women's clothing) and **Shaiken's Souvenirs** for more upmarket mementoes and apparel. The added attraction of this area is a boardwalk of fairground games (which cost an extra few dollars to play), including a Guess Your Weight stall which usually attracts a good crowd for the fun patter of the person in charge.

World Expo

Crossing the bridge from Amity brings you to a rather nondescript area, but home to the park's other 5-star thrill attraction.

Back To The Future… The Ride: simulators just do not come more realistic than this journey through space and time in Dr Emmit Brown's time-travelling De Lorean. The queues are immense, but a lot of the time is taken up by some attention-grabbing pre-ride info on the TV screens above your head. Once you reach the front, there is still more information to digest and clever surroundings to convince you of the scientific nature of it all. Then it's into your time-travelling car and off in hot pursuit of baddie Biff, who has stolen another time-car. The huge, wraparound screen and violent movements of your vehicle bring the realism of the ride to a peak, and it all adds up to a huge experience. Restrictions: 3ft 4in/101cm. TTTTT (UE).

Men In Black – Alien Attack: new in 2000 and huge fun (especially for kids) is this combination thrill/scenic ride which takes up where the original hit film, starring Will Smith, left off. Visitors are secretly introduced to the MIB Institute in a wonderfully inventive mock-futuristic setting and enrolled as trainees for a battle around the streets of New York with a horde of escaped aliens. Your 6-person car is equipped with laser zappers for an interactive shoot-out that is like a real-life arcade game, as the aliens can also shoot back and send your car spinning out of control. The finale features a close encounter with a 30-ft (9-metre) bug that is all mouth – will you survive? Only your collective shooting skills can save the day, and there are numerous ride variations according to your accuracy as each rider's score is totted up. Will Smith and Rip Torn are your on-screen hosts, and Will returns at the end to reveal if your score makes you Galaxy Defenders, Cosmically Average or Bug Bait! Fast, frantic and a bit confusing, this will have you coming back for more until you can score more than

> BRIT TIP: For a big score in Men in Black, when you meet the Big Bug – push the big red button!

250,000 (Defender status). Restrictions: 3ft 6in/106cm. TTTT. (Beat my best score – 265,550!)

The **International Food and Film Festival** here is a food court-style indoor diner offering burgers, sandwiches, meatball subs and salads (and in air-conditioned comfort).

Woody Woodpecker's KidZone

Animal Planet Live!: new in 2001, replacing the old Animal Actors Stage, is this highly amusing show version of the Animal Planet satellite TV channel. Several children are invited to take part as your hosts and present a series of unlikely feats and stunts featuring a whole range of fairly tame wildlife, from a racoon to a python, and on to domestic cats and dogs. Many have been rescued

> BRIT TIP: Along the lagoon in the World Expo/ KidZone area is Central Park, a quiet area where you can escape the theme park whirl for a while.

from animal shelters and have gone on to feature in films before finding a home at Universal. It's a big theatre, too, and is handy for avoiding the afternoon crowds. AAAA (UE).

Fievel's Playland: strictly for kids but also a big hit with parents for taking them off their hands for a good half-hour or so, this playground, based on the enlarged world of the cartoon mouse, offers youngsters the chance to bounce under a 1,000-gallon hat, crawl through a giant cowboy boot, climb a 30-ft (9-metre) spider's web and shoot the rapids (a 200-ft/61-metre water-slide) in Fievel's sardine can. TTTT (young 'uns only!).

A Day in the Park with Barney: again, this is strictly for the younger set (ages 2–5) as the purple dinosaur from the popular kids' TV show is brought to Super-Dee-Duper life on stage in a 65,000 sq-ft (6,045sq-metre) arena that features a pre-show before the 15-minute main event, plus an interactive post-show area. Guaranteed to make parents cringe, but the youngsters love it. NB: check out the amazing state-of-the-art restrooms! AAA (AAAAA under 5s) (UE).

ET Adventure: this is as glorious as scenic rides come, with a picturesque queuing area like the pine woods from the film and then a spectacular leap on the trademark flying bicycles to save ET's home planet. Steven Spielberg (Universal's creative consultant) has added some special effects and characters, and the whole experience is a huge hit

6

with all the family (especially for your individual ET greeting at the end!). Queues here touch 2 hours at peak periods, so try to do this one either early or late (or, again, through UE). There is a height restriction of 4ft/122cm, but smaller children can ride with parents. AAAAA (UE).

Woody Woodpecker's Nuthouse Coaster: anchoring this excellent under-10s' adventure land is this child-sized but still quite racy roller-coaster. The brilliant red 800-ft (244-metre) track reaches only 28-ft high (8 metres) and 22mph (35kph), but it seems the real deal to youngsters. There is still a height restriction of 3ft/91cm, however, for the ride. TTTT (juniors only).

Curious George Goes to Town: this American children's book character means little to me, but kids of all ages just love this amazing adventure playground with its huge range of activities – and plenty of opportunities to get wet (bring swimsuits or a change of clothing for them here). It combines toddler play, water-based play stations and a hands-on interactive ball area, and adds up to a real boon to harassed parents. The town theme, on which Curious George has wreaked havoc, includes buildings to climb, pumps and hoses to spray water, a ball factory in which to shoot, dump and blast thousands of foam balls and – the tour de force – two 500-gallon (2,275-litre) buckets of water on the clock tower balconies which regularly dump their contents in spectacular fashion on the street below. TTTTT (under 12s).

Curious George himself roams the KidZone from time to time, while other characters make regular appearances. For snacks, **Animal Crackers** offers hot-dogs, chicken fingers, smoked sausage hoagies and frozen yoghurt. Shop at the **Cartoon Store, Barney Store** or **ET's Toy Closet** and **Photo Spot**.

The Terminator

Hollywood

Finally, your circular tour of Universal brings you back towards the main entrance via Hollywood (where else?). Here, you'll find **Universal's Horror Make-Up Show** (not recommended for under 12s) which demonstrates some of the often amusing ways in which films have attempted to terrorise us. It's a 20-minute show, queues are rarely long and the secrets of the special effects are well worth finding out about. AAA (UE).

Terminator 2: 3-D Battle Across Time: another first-of-its-kind attraction, this is hard to describe. Part film, part show, part experience but all action, it cost a staggering $60 million to produce and is guaranteed to leave its audience stunned and awed. The 'Wow!' factor works overtime as you go through a 10-minute pre-show that represents a trip into the workshops of the Cyberdyne Systems, from the *Terminator* films, and then into a 700-seater auditorium for a 'presentation' on their latest robot creations.

Needless to say, nothing runs to plan and the audience is subjected to a mind-boggling array of (loud) special effects, including indoor pyrotechnics, real actors interacting with the screen and the audience, and a climactic 3-D film finale that takes the *Terminator* story a step further. The original cast, including Arnold Schwarzenegger and director James Cameron, all collaborated on the 12-minute movie (which, at $24 million, is some of the most expensive frame-for-frame film ever made) and the overall effect of this technological marvel is dazzling. However, you need to arrive early or expect queues in excess of an hour all day (parental discretion for under 12s). TTTTT (UE).

The last attraction (or first, depending on which way you go round the park) is **Lucy: A Tribute**, which will mean little to all but devoted fans of the late Lucille Ball and her 1960s' TV comedy *The Lucy Show*. Classic shows, home movies, costumes and scripts are all paraded for close viewing, but youngsters will find it tedious. AA.

If you haven't eaten by now there is a choice of four contrasting but highly enjoyable eateries. **Mel's Drive-In**, a re-creation from the film *American Graffiti*, serves all manner of burgers, hot dogs and milkshakes, while **Café La Bamba**, offers rotisserie chicken, ribs, salad and burgers, plus Margaritas and beer (Happy Hour 3–5pm). **Schwab's Pharmacy** provides sandwiches, old-fashioned milkshakes, sundaes and ice cream and the **Beverly Hills Boulangerie** does baked breakfast treats, pastries,

6

Curious George Goes to Town

juices and coffee. Shop for hats in the **Brown Derby**, for *Terminator* gifts and clothing in **Cyber Image**, and, for movie memorabilia (especially Lucille Ball), at **Silver Screen Collectibles**.

Street Entertainment

In addition to all the set-piece action, watch out for various interactive street shows around the park. Check out **The Swashbucklers**, who engage in some amusing swordplay and stunts (eventually including the guests); **Extreme Ghostbusters: The Great Fright Way**, starring Beetlejuice and the Ghostbusters in a clever song and dance act; **Lucy and Ricky**, the 'stars' of a 7-piece Latin band who insist on starting a conga line (with you, of course!); and **Sarita and Rico**, who are another over-the-top Latin duo. More entertainment is provided by the **MIB Agents** show (enrolling YOU in a humorous screen test), the **Street Breaks** dancers, and *a capella* group **Double Date**.

Special programmes

The park features some brilliant extra seasonal entertainment for Mardi Gras (a major parade, plus music, street entertainment and authentic New Orleans food each night at 6pm from mid-February to April 1), as well as a major party for **New Year's Eve** and the **4th of July**, when the park swings into full fiesta mode.
NB: Universal's trademark Halloween Horror Nights programme has now moved from the Studios to Islands of Adventure. And don't forget to check their website www.universalorlando.com for the latest info.

UNIVERSAL STUDIOS with children

Our guide to the rides which generally appeal to the different age groups:
Under 5s
Nickelodeon Studios, Animal Planet Live!, A Day In The Park With Barney, Curious George Goes To Town, Fievel's Playland, ET Adventure.
5–8s
Nickelodeon Studios, Animal Planet Live!, Curious George Goes To Town, Fievel's Playland, ET Adventure, Woody Woodpecker's Nuthouse Coaster, Jimmy Neutron's Nicktoon Blast, Wild, Wild, Wild West Stunt Show, Shrek 4-D, Men In Black, as well as Earthquake – The Big One (with parental discretion).
9–12s
Jimmy Neutron's Nicktoon Blast, Shrek 4-D, Terminator 2, Twister, Earthquake – The Big One, Animal Planet Live!, Curious George Goes to Town, Woody Woodpecker's Nuthouse Coaster, Wild, Wild, Wild West Stunt Show, ET Adventure, All-New Beetlejuice Revue, Jaws, Men In Black, Back To The Future… The Ride, plus Revenge of the Mummy (with parental discretion).
Over 12s
Terminator 2, Universal's Horror Make-Up Show, Jimmy Neutron's Nicktoon Blast, Shrek 4-D, Twister, Revenge of the Mummy, Earthquake – The Big One, The Blues Brothers, ET Adventure, All-New Beetlejuice Revue, Jaws, Wild, Wild, Wild West Stunt Show, Men In Black, Back To The Future… The Ride.

Islands of Adventure

In May 1999, Universal's creative consultant Steven Spielberg officially opened the £1 billion Islands of Adventure, or IoA as the park is known, with the words: 'These are not just theme park rides, these are entertainment achievements beyond anything I have ever seen anywhere else in the world.'

And that's only the beginning. Here is the most complete and thrilling theme park on offer. Complete, because the park is a genuinely rounded and consistent concept that has been carried through to the full extent of its designers' aims. And thrilling because it contains more T-rides per

Islands of Adventure at a glance

Location	Off Exits 75A and 74B from I-4; Universal Boulevard and Kirkman Road
Size	110 acres (45ha) in 6 'islands'
Hours	9am–7pm off peak; 9am–10pm high season (Washington's Birthday, Easter, summer holidays, Thanksgiving, Christmas)
Admission	Under 3 free; 3–9 $42.95 (1-Day Ticket), $83.95 (2-Day Ticket), $96.95 (3-Day Ticket), $142.95 (4-Park FlexTicket), $175.95 (5-Park FlexTicket); adult (10+) $51.95, $96.95, $111.95, $175.95, $209.95; Universal Bonus Pass (5 consecutive days, online sales only) $76.95 and $89.95.
Parking	$8
Lockers	Yes; immediately to left through main gates; $6 and $9.
Pushchairs	$9 and $15; next to locker hire
Wheelchairs	$8 and $40 (with photo ID as deposit); same location as pushchairs
Top Attractions	Amazing Adventures of Spider-Man, Dueling Dragons, Incredible Hulk Coaster, Jurassic Park River Adventure, Dudley Do-Right's Ripsaw Falls
Don't Miss	Eighth Voyage of Sindbad, Jurassic Park Discovery Centre, If I Ran the Zoo playground (for kids), Firework Finale (high season only), dining at Mythos

Hidden Costs	Meals	Burger, chips and coke $7.58 3-course dinner $29 (Confiscos)
	Kids' meal	$5.95–6.99
	T-shirts	$18–30
	Souvenirs	$2.50–310
	Sundries	Dr Seuss character photos $12.95 and $17.95

6

PORT OF ENTRY
1 Ocean Trader Market
2 Confisco Grille

MARVEL SUPER-HERO ISLAND
3 Incredible Hulk Coaster
4 Doctor Doom's Fearfall
5 Café 4
6 Captain America Diner
7 The Amazing Adventures Of Spider-Man
8 Storm Force Accelatron

TOON LAGOON
9 Me Ship, The Olive
10 Popeye & Bluto's Bilge-Rat Barges
11 Dudley Do-Right's Ripsaw Falls
12 Comic Strip Café
13 Mat Hoffman's Crazy Freakin' Stunt Show
14 Toon Lagoon Beach Bash

JURASSIC PARK
15 Jurassic Park River Adventure
16 Camp Jurassic
17 Pteranodon Flyers
18 Triceratops Encounter
19 Discovery Center
20 Thunder Falls Terrace

THE LOST CONTINENT
21 Dueling Dragons
22 The Flying Unicorn
23 The Eighth Voyage of Sindbad
24 Poseidon's Fury
25 The Enchanted Oak Tavern (and Alchemy Bar)
26 Mythos Restaurant
27 The Mystic Fountain

SEUSS LANDING
28 Caro-Seuss-el
29 One Fish, Two Fish, Red Fish, Blue Fish
30 The Cat In The Hat
31 If I Ran The Zoo
32 Circus McGurkus Café Stoo-pendous
33 Green Eggs and Ham Café
34 Guest Services

ISLANDS OF ADVENTURE

One Fish, Two Fish

square inch than almost all the others combined.

It has a full range of attractions from the real adrenalin overloads to pure family entertainment. The shopping and eating opportunities are above average and it even *sounds* good – with some 40 pieces of original music, you can buy the CD of the theme park!

Okay, so they are not really islands (the six themed 'lands' form a chain around the central lagoon), but that's the only illusion. And you get a lot for your money here, unless you have extremely timid children or under 5s, in which case the *Magic Kingdom* is still your best bet. However, Seuss

Landing will keep them amused for several hours while Camp Jurassic is a clever adventure playground for the 5–12s, but the rest of the park, with its seven 5-star thrill rides and other standout attractions, is primarily geared to kids of 8-plus, their parents and especially teenagers. There are five elements that look truly alarming (two of which produce moments of supreme terror), but don't be put off – they all deliver immense fun. There is also great spectator value here!

If there is one ride that sums up IoA, it is the Amazing Adventures of Spider-Man, the world's first moving 3-D simulator ride. It is sure to leave you in awe of its technological wizardry and imagination, and it is the only ride I have seen where people applaud at the end!

Port of Entry

You arrive for IoA as you do for Universal Studios Florida® in the big multi-storey car parks ($8) off Universal Boulevard and either walk or ride the moving walkways into CityWalk, where you continue through to the entrance plaza (head for the 130ft- (40 metre) high Pharos Lighthouse).

Once through the gates, the

6

Night lights at Islands of Adventure

lockers, pushchair and wheelchair hire are all immediately to your left as the **Port of Entry** opens up before you. This elaborate 'village' consists of shops and eateries, so push straight on until you hit the main lagoon. Later in the day, you can return to check out the fully themed retail experience at places like the **IoA Trading Company** and **Ocean Trader Market**. Enjoy a snack from **Cinnabon** (cinnamon rolls and pastries) or the **Croissant Moon Bakery**, or chill out with a soft drink or ice cream from **Arctic Express**. Alternatively, sit down for lunch or dinner (great steak, pasta, burgers and salads) at **Confisco Grille** and grab a beverage at the **Backwater Bar** (Happy Hour 3–5pm). Above all, take a closer look at the wonderful architecture, which borrows from Middle East, Far East and African themes and includes odd bits of bric-a-brac from all over the world.

When you come to the end of the Port thoroughfare, you are faced with three choices, and this is where you need a plan of campaign. There are five attractions where the queues build up quickly and remain that way. If you are here for the big thrill rides, turn left into Marvel Super-Hero Island and head straight to Spider-Man, then do Dr Doom's Fearfall and the Incredible Hulk Coaster, taking advantage of the Universal Express (UE) system.

Alternatively, dinosaur fans should head straight around the lagoon to Jurassic Park, where you should be able to do the Triceratops Encounter and River Adventure before the majority arrive. Once you are nice and wet, you might as well go to Toon Lagoon and get Ripsaw Falls and the Bilge-Rat Barges under your belt. If you have younger children, turn right into the amazing multi-coloured world of Seuss Landing and enjoy the Cat In The Hat and other family-type rides prior to the crowd build-up.

BRIT TIP: At the Incredible Hulk Coaster keep left where the queue splits up and you will be in line for the front car for an even more extreme Hulk experience.

Marvel Super-Hero Island

Taking the journey clockwise, you arrive first in the elaborate comic-book pages of the super-heroes. As with all the islands, the experience is total immersion. The amazing façades of this world surround you with an utterly credible alternative reality that is one of the park's triumphs – and that's before you have even tried the rides.

The Incredible Hulk Coaster: roller-coasters don't come any more dramatic than this giant green edifice that soars over the lagoon, blasting 0–40mph (64kph) in 2 seconds and reaches a top speed of 65mph (105kph). It looks awesome, sounds stunning and rides like a demon as you enter the gamma-ray world of Dr David Banner, aka the Incredible Hulk. You zoom into a weightless inversion 100ft (30 metres) up, and it keeps getting better!

Just watching is quite mind-boggling, and the after-effects are distinctly brain-scrambling. You will need to deposit ANY loose articles (sunglasses, cameras, coins, etc) in the lockers at the front of the building as the ride is guaranteed to shake just about anything free from your pockets. Crowds build up rapidly, but the queues seem to move quite quickly. Restrictions: 4ft 6in/137cm. TTTTT+ (UE).

Dr Doom's Fearfall: stand by for one of those two moments of supreme terror I mentioned earlier. This is where, O hapless visitor, you wander into the lair of the evil Dr

Doom – arch-enemy of the Fantastic Four – and his sinister cohorts. His latest creation is the Fearfall, a device for sucking every ounce of fear out of his victims, and YOU are about to test it. Four riders at a time are strapped into chairs at the bottom of a 200-ft (60-metre) tower, the dry ice rolls, and whooooosh! Up you go at breakneck speed, only to plummet back seemingly even faster, with an amazing split second in between when you feel suspended in mid air. Summon up the courage to do this and I promise a truly astonishing (if brief!) experience. Queues are substantial during the main part of the day. Restrictions: 4ft 4in/132cm, and I reckon this is way too scary for under 10s. TTTTT+ (UE).

You exit Fearfall into the inevitable high-energy video arcade, or you may prefer to calm your nerves with a meal at the Italian buffeteria **Café 4** (pizza, spaghetti, sandwiches and salads) or a burger at the **Captain America Diner**.

For shopping, each of the rides has its own character merchandise for sale, while the **Comics Shop** and **Marvel Alterniverse** sell other souvenirs.

The Amazing Adventures of Spider-Man: just queuing is a novel experience as your visit to the *Daily Bugle*, home of ace reporter Peter Parker (or Spider-Man to his enemies), unravels into a reporting secondment in one of the 'Scoop' vehicles. Prepare for an audio-visual extravaganza as the combination of 3-D and motion simulator takes you into a battle between Spidey and arch-villains like Dr Octopus with his anti-gravity gun, culminating in a 400-ft (122-metre) sensory drop off a skyscraper, as the contest literally hots up. There are numerous jaw-dropping special effects and you will probably need to ride at least twice to appreciate it all. In fact, you'll see it and you still won't believe it. Ride

early on or leave it till late in the day – queues usually top an hour. Restrictions: 3ft 4in/101cm. TTTTT+ (UE).

Storm Force Accelatron: this ride, aimed primarily at youngsters, puts you in the middle of a whirling, twirling battle between X-Men super-heroine Storm and arch-nemesis Magneto, with a range of special effects. It is basically an updated version of a fairground spinning-cup ride, but with some neat twists (there is a 3-way rotation when the cars look set to collide at any moment!). TTT (TTTTT under 12s) (UE).

You can also meet the **Marvel Super-Heroes** for autographs several times a day as they patrol around the island.

Toon Lagoon

The thrills continue here with a watery theme and more comic-book elements as the (American) newspaper cartoon characters take a bow. Children will love the chance to play with the fountains, squirt pools and overflowing fire hydrants, plus a purpose-built playland **Me Ship, The Olive**, a 3-storey boat full of interactive fun and games, including slides, bells and water cannons (with which to squirt riders on the Bilge-Rat Barges below) in best Popeye style. TTTT (youngsters only).

Popeye and Bluto's Bilge-Rat Barges: every park seems to have a variation on the white-water raft ride, but none is as outrageously themed and downright wet as this. It's fast, bouncy and unpredictable, with water coming at you from every direction, a couple of sizeable drops and a whirl through the Octoplus Grotto that adds to the fun. If you don't want to get wet, don't ride, because there is no escaping the deluge here. This is also one of the top five rides for queues, but it's worth the wait. Restrictions: 4ft/122cm. TTTTT (UE).

> BRIT TIP: A change of clothes is often advisable after riding the Barges, unless it's so hot you need to cool down in a hurry. Bring a waterproof bag for your valuables, too.

Dudley Do-Right's Ripsaw Falls: Universal's designers have again taken an existing ride concept and given it a new spin, as this becomes the first flume ride to send its passengers through the water surface and out the other side at high speed. You join guileless mountie Dudley Do-Right in a bid to save girlfriend Nell from the evil Snidely Whiplash. The action builds to an 'explosive' showdown at the top of a 60-ft (18-metre) precipice that drops you through the roof of a ramshackle dynamite shack and into the lagoon below. Just awesome – as are the queues from mid-morning to late afternoon. Wet? You bet! Restrictions: 3ft 8in/111cm. TTTTT (UE)

Popeye and Bluto's Bilge-Rat Barges

Dr Doom's Fearfall

After you have dried off, take a walk along **Comic Strip Lane** to meet up with characters like Beetle Bailey, Hagar the Horrible, Krazy Kat and Blondie (some of whom will mean little to a British audience). Then prepare to meet **Mat Hoffman's Crazy Freakin' Stunt Show** in the circus amphitheatre, a daring cavalcade of stunt bikes and skateboards designed by the world bicycle stunt champ (T T̆T). There is the usual array of character shopping outlets, like **Gasoline Alley** and **Toon Extra**, while you can grab a truly humongous sandwich at **Blondie's: Home of the Dagwood**, a trademark hamburger or hot dog at **Wimpy's**, sample the **Comic Strip Café** food court (Mexican, Chinese, American and Italian) or tuck into something colder at **Cathy's Ice Cream**. Watch out for appearances of the **Toon Lagoon Beach Bash** for a meet-and-greet with the characters.

The Cat in the Hat

Jurassic Park

Leaving the comic-book lands behind, you travel back in time to the Cretaceous age and the credible make-believe dinosaur film world. Again, the immersive experience is first class and the lavish scenery will have you looking over your shoulder for dinos.

Jurassic Park River Adventure: the mood change from scenic splendour to hidden menace is startling as your journey into this magnificent waterborne realm brings you up close and personal with the most realistic dinosaurs created to date. Inevitably, your passage is diverted from the safe to the hazardous, and the danger increases as the 16-person raft climbs into the heights of the main building – with raptors loose everywhere. You are aware of something large lurking in the shadows – will you fall prey to the T-Rex, or will your boat take the 85-ft plunge to safety (with a good soaking for all concerned)? Queues usually move quite briskly here. Restrictions: 3ft 6in/106cm. TTTTT (UE).

Camp Jurassic: more excellent kids' fare here with the mountainous jungle giving way to an 'active' volcano for youngsters to explore, climb over and slide down. Squirt guns and 'Spitter' dinosaurs add to the fun. TTTT (children first, but parents may explore).

Pteranodon Flyers: the slow-moving queues are a major turn-off, especially for a fairly average ride, which glides gently over much of Jurassic Park. It is designed mainly for kids, though, and the height range of 3–4ft 8in (91–142cm) requires anyone OVER the upper limit (usually 11 or older) to be accompanied by a child of the right height! TT (TTTT under 9s).

Triceratops Encounter: a face-to-face meeting with the park's resident 4-ton, 24ft- (7 metre) long 'living' dinosaur, which reacts to both its handler and visitors. The spiel is amusing and educational and the 'Trike' pretty convincing, especially for children. It also draws a crowd and there is little shade (one of the few minus points), but the queues move steadily. AAAA. (UE).

Discovery Center: the designers' imagination has gone into overdrive here with terrific results. Interactive opportunities include creating a

The Dueling Dragons

dinosaur through DNA sequencing, mixing your own DNA with a dino via a computer touchscreen, seeing through the eyes of various large reptiles and even watching a baby raptor hatch, plus a host of other hands-on exhibits that are fun and educational. Air-conditioned, this is a good place to visit in the hotter part of the day. AAAA.

Best of the shopping is in the Discovery Center itself, while you can chow down at the **Burger Digs** there, visit the **Pizza Predattoria** or the **Watering Hole**, or go for the rotisserie chicken at the rustic **Thunder Falls Terrace** (counter service), which boasts a great view of the River Adventure.

The Lost Continent

This is one of my favourite lands for its theming, gentle contrast after Jurassic Park; superb attractions, great eating options and a few amusing 'extras'.

Dueling Dragons: there is no disguising the intense nature of this magnificent double coaster, with its 100-ft (30-metre) drop, multiple loops, twists and three near-miss encounters. There is a lot more, too, as the queuing area is a real mind-boggler – 1,060yd (969 metres), most of it along a dark tortuous path through the ancient castle that is the domain of the dragons, Fire and Ice. You are given their story while you stand in line, and Merlin arrives in time to cast a spell to ensure you survive. You choose which dragon to ride (the tracks differ slightly), and you can join an additional queue for the front seats. Unlike the Hulk, this is a suspended coaster, so your legs dangle free, and the initial drop is like going into free-fall (Supreme Terror moment Number 2!). Coaster aficionados reckon the best ride is in the back of the Ice (Blue) dragon, but it's all pretty amazing.

Restrictions: 4ft 6in/137cm, and you will need to leave all your loose belongings in the lockers provided to the left of the entrance. TTTTT+ (UE).

The Flying Unicorn: this junior-sized coaster is aimed primarily at youngsters and features a wizard's workshop, hidden in an enchanted wood, which is the gateway to a magical journey inspired by the Unicorn. There are no big drops, but it delivers a surprisingly fast-paced whirl. TTTTT (for 6–12s) (UE).

The Eighth Voyage of Sindbad: this stunt and special effects show is another marvel, as much for its elaborate staging as its performance. Mythical adventurer Sindbad and his sidekick Kabob (a name that's the cue for a truly awful pun) tackle the evil witch Miseria in a bid to rescue Princess Amoura, and the action springs up in surprising places. There are several loud bangs which could scare young children, but otherwise it is good, family fun. At peak times, arrive 15 minutes before showtime, but everyone usually gets in. TTT/AAAA (UE).

Poseidon's Fury: a walk-through show that puts its audience at the heart of the action as you journey in the company of a hapless young archaeologist (who ignores all the various 'warnings') beneath the sea to the lost temple of Poseidon. The route passes through an amazing water vortex and your 'expedition' takes a wrong turn, awakening an ancient demon. Again, there is an element of suspense, so I won't reveal any surprises, but the showdown between Poseidon and the demon is amazing as the arena seems to explode in water and fire. Queuing is tedious, but at least you are inside in summer. TTT (UE).

For an extra dollar or two, try the **Pitch and Skill Games**, or shop at **The Coin Mint** (coins forged and struck before your eyes), or visit **Historic Families** (explore the history of your family name and coat of arms in a medieval armoury), **Pearl Factory** (pick an oyster), and **The Dragon's Keep** (dragon apparel, games, and toys.

The **Fire-Eater's Grill** (sausages, fries and drinks) and **Frozen Desert** (sundaes and sodas) provide the snacks, while there is the magnificent, must-see **Enchanted Oak Tavern** (in the dark, cool interior of a vast, sculpted oak tree) and **Alchemy Bar** for counter-service meals (hickory-smoked chicken, ribs and salads). The elaborate **Mythos Restaurant** provides the best dining in IoA, though. Not only is the food first class (seafood, grills, pizza and pasta), but the setting, inside a dormant volcano with streams, fountains and clever lighting, is an attraction in its own right.

Finally, watch out for **The Mystic Fountain** in Sindbad's Village – it has the ability to get you very wet when you least expect it!

Seuss Landing

There is not a straight line to be seen in this vivid 3-D working of the books of Dr Seuss. The characters may not mean much to those unfamiliar with the children's stories, but everyone can relate to the fun here (although queues build up quickly). There is so much clever detail packed into the area, from squirt ponds to beach scenes, it can be easy to miss something, so take your time.

Caro-Seuss-el: this intricate carousel ride on some of the Seuss characters – like cowfish, elephant-birds and dog-a-lopes – has rider-activated features that are a big hit with the young ones. AAA (AAAA under 5s) (UE).

One Fish, Two Fish, Red Fish, Blue Fish: another fairground ride is given a twist as you pilot these Seussian fish up and down according to the rhyme that plays while you ride. Get it wrong and you get squirted! More guaranteed fun for the younger kids. TTT (TTTTT under 5s) (UE).

The Cat In The Hat: prepare for a ride with a difference as you board these crazy 6-passenger 'couches' to meet the world's most adventurous cat and his friends, Thing One and Thing Two. You literally go for a spin through this storybook world, and it may be a bit too much for very young children. The slow-moving queues are a bit of a drag, so try to get here early or leave it until much later in the day (or use the UE system). AAAA/TTT) (UE).

If I Ran The Zoo: interactive playgrounds don't get much more fun for the pre-school brigade than with the 19 different Seuss character scenarios, most of which can get them quite wet. Hugely imaginative and great fun just to watch. TTTTT (young 'uns only).

If you have been captivated by the land, you can buy the book at **Dr Seuss' All The Books You Can Read** store, or visit the **Mulberry Street Store** for all the characters. **Snookers & Snookers Sweet Candy Cookers** is a super sweet shop, while snacks and drinks can be had at **Hop on Pop Ice Cream Shop** and **Moose Juice Goose Juice**. The **Circus McGurkus Café Stoo-pendous** is a mind-boggling cafeteria for fried chicken, lasagne, pizza and spaghetti, complete with clowns and pipe organs, while **Green Eggs and Ham Café** is a must for all Seuss fans to try the meal of the same name (and the eggs ARE green!).

Private nursing facilities, an open area for feeding and resting (with high-chairs) and nappy-changing stations can be found at the **Family Service Facility** at Guest Services (to the right inside the main gates), while ALL restrooms throughout the park are equipped with **nappy-**

changing facilities. **First aid** is provided in Sindbad's Village in the Lost Continent, just across from Oasis Coolers.

In high season, there is a nightly **firework show** on the Lagoon that provides a fitting and spectacular finale to the day.

The Flying Unicorn

Halloween Horror Nights

Moving over from the Studios park is Universal's massively popular Halloween celebration throughout October each year. The Horror Nights have become a real trademark hereabouts and add a wonderfully bloodthirsty touch (although there is an extra charge – $49.95, or an extra $19.95–36.95 if you upgrade your park ticket on the day). The islands are transformed with some highly imaginative re-creations and set-pieces from various horror movies, with a parade and shows that include live (terrifyingly so, in some cases!)

character interaction. The rides are also all open (anyone for The Hulk and Dueling Dragons in the dark?!), adding more novelty to the park experience, but this over-the-top (and occasionally downright grisly) extravaganza is definitely not for kids. It goes down a treat with adults with the right sense of humour, though, and begins every evening at 7.30pm.

And that, folks, is the full low-down on arguably the world's best theme park to date. Miss it at your peril.

ISLANDS OF ADVENTURE with children

Our guide to the rides which generally appeal to the different age groups:

Under 5s
Caro-Seuss-el, If I Ran The Zoo, The Cat In The Hat, One Fish, Two Fish, Red Fish, Blue Fish, Eighth Voyage of Sindbad, Jurassic Park Discovery Center, Me Ship, The Olive.

5–8s
All the above, plus Flying Unicorn, Triceratops Encounter, Pteranodon Flyers, Camp Jurassic, Amazing Adventures of Spider-Man, Storm Force Accelatron, and Jurassic Park River Adventure (with parental discretion).

9–12s
The Cat In The Hat, Flying Unicorn, Dueling Dragons, Eighth Voyage of Sindbad, Camp Jurassic, Pteranodon Flyers, Jurassic Park River Adventure, Triceratops Encounter, Jurassic Park Discovery Center, Dudley Do-Right's Ripsaw Falls, Popeye and Bluto's Bilge-Rat Barges, Amazing Adventures of Spider-Man, Dr Doom's Fearfall, Storm Force Accelatron, Incredible Hulk Coaster.

Over 12s
Dueling Dragons, Eighth Voyage of Sindbad, Jurassic Park River Adventure, Jurassic Park Discovery Center, Dudley Do-Right's Ripsaw Falls, Popeye and Bluto's Bilge-Rat Barges, Amazing Adventures of Spider-Man, Dr Doom's Fearfall, Storm Force Accelatron, Incredible Hulk Coaster.

SeaWorld Adventure Park

SeaWorld is firmly established as one of the most popular parks with British visitors for its more peaceful and naturalistic aspect, the change of pace it offers and the general lack of substantial queues. It is a big hit with families in particular, but also possesses some dramatic rides and attractions.

An extensive development programme by owners Anheuser-Busch has given it the big-park treatment in recent years, with an impressive 12-acre (5-ha) entrance plaza and rebranding as an Adventure Park, and it now demands a full day's attention. The opening, in summer 2000, of an exclusive sister park – Discovery Cove, an exotic tropical island with dolphin, stingray and snorkelling adventures – has added still more.

Happily, the queues and crowds have yet to reach the monster proportions of elsewhere, so this is a park where you can still proceed at a relatively leisurely pace, see what you want without too much jostling and yet feel you have been superbly entertained (even if mealtimes do get rather crowded in the restaurants).

SeaWorld is also a good starting point if this is your first visit to Orlando as it will give you the hang of negotiating the vast areas, navigating by the various maps and learning to plan around the showtimes. This park has a strong educational and environmental message, plus three hour-long, behind-the-scenes tours (book up as soon as you enter), which provide a greater insight into SeaWorld's marine conservation, rescue and research programme, as well as their entertainment resources. The **Polar Expedition** provides a close-up of the penguin and polar bear environments, **To the Rescue** showcases the park's animal rescue and rehabilitation programme, and **Predators!** offers a backstage view of Shark Encounter. You pay an extra $15 ($14 for 3–9s) for these tours, but they are worth it and, if you take one early on, it will increase your appreciation of the park. You can also SAVE 10% on single-day tickets by booking online at www.seaworld.com, where you print your own tickets and save waiting in the queues.

The new Waterfront at SeaWorld

Five additional programmes provide unique insights and experiences of the park's activities. The 6-hour **Adventure Express Tour** offers visitors their own guide to tour the park, with back-door access to the rides, reserved seating at shows and animal feeding opportunities (an extra $80 for adults, $75 for 3–9s; book up first thing at the Guided Tours counter or call 1-800 406 2244); **Trainer For A Day** is an 8-hour programme open to just 3 people (at least 13 years old and in good physical condition) each day, which shows how SeaWorld trainers care for and train their animals (cost is $389, including T-shirt, waterproof disposable camera and lunch with trainers; for reservations, call 407 370 1382); the new **SeaWorld Whale Swim Adventure** programme is a 2-hour opportunity for 4 people (at least 13 and 4ft 4in/132cm tall) daily to join the trainers at the Whale and Dolphin Stadium and help feed their wonderful animals and learn some of the training techniques (including

SeaWorld Adventure Park at a glance

Location	7007 SeaWorld Drive, off Central Florida Parkway (Junctions 71 and 72 off I-4)
Size	More than 200 acres (81ha), incorporating 25 attractions
Hours	9am–7pm off peak; 9am–10pm high season (Easter, summer holidays, Thanksgiving, Christmas)
Admission	Under 3 free; 3–9 $42.95 (1-Day Ticket), $142.95 (4-Park Orlando FlexTicket), $175.95 (5-Park FlexTicket), $80.90 (SeaWorld/Busch Gardens Combo ticket); adult (10+) $51.95, $175.95, $209.95, $85.95.
Parking	$7
Lockers	Yes, by main entrance; $1.50
Pushchairs	$10 and $17 ($2 refundable; from Information Centre, to left of main entrance)
Wheelchairs	$8 and $32 (no refunds); with pushchairs
Top Attractions	Shamu Stadium, Shark Encounter, Journey to Atlantis, Kraken, Wild Arctic
Don't Miss	Fireworks at The Waterfront (high season), Manatees: The Last Generation?, Behind-the-Scenes Tours, Odyssea show, dining at Sharks Underwater Grill

Hidden Costs		
	Meals	Burger, chips and coke $8.69
	Kids' meal	$5.29
		3-course lunch (Sharks Grill) $22
	T-shirts	$16.99–26.95
	Souvenirs	99 cents–$1,535
	Sundries	Face painting $6–12

lunch, T-shirt and souvenir photo PLUS a 7-day SeaWorld ticket; $200/person); and **SeaWorld's Marine Mammal Keeper Experience** which is another new option for 2 visitors daily (aged 13 or above) to find out about the intensive care necessary to rehabilitate injured manatees, plus bottle-feed some of them, meet the seals and walruses and prepare meals for the beluga whales. It starts at 6.30am and lasts around 8 hours for $389/person (including lunch at the the Shark Encounter, T-shirt, special book, souvenir photo and 7-day SeaWorld pass). Finally, **Sharks Deep Dive** is the most original and captivating experience of all, a chance to suit up and dive in a specially constructed cage into the huge shark aquarium, and spend half an hour up close and personal with these deadly but amazing creatures. The 2-hour programme includes a full and educational induction into the world of sharks, what they are and what makes them tick (with important pointers like never wear jewellery in the sea – sharks can be attracted by the glitter, mistaking it for the reflection off fish scales). Then you are equipped for the dive with wetsuit (the water IS chilly), gloves, dive belt and either mask and snorkel or air tank (if you can show a scuba certification) for the reinforced steel cage, that glides slowly from one end of the 125ft- (38 metre) long tank to the other and back. Getting a fish-eye view of these creatures is truly an astounding experience, and you never tire of the underwater panorama (which includes waving to folks walking through the shark tunnel!). It is an eye-opening and addictive programme, but the best part is you get to wear a really cool wetsuit with 'Scubapro' on the front! It costs $150 for the scuba experience or $125 to snorkel (including 2-day park admission, a neat souvenir T-shirt and shark book; participants must be aged at least 10).

Location

SeaWorld is located off Central Florida Parkway, between I-4 (Exit 71 going east or 72 heading west) and I-Drive, and the parking fee is $7. It is still a good idea to arrive a bit before the officially scheduled opening time so you're in good position to book one of the backstage tours or scamper off to one of the few attractions that does draw crowds, like Journey to Atlantis.

The park covers in excess of 200 acres (81ha), with nine shows (10 with the nightly **Makahiki Luau** dinner show at the Seafire Inn which costs $37.95 for adults, $27.95 for 3–9s; nightly 6.30–8.45pm, call 407 351 3600 or book online), nine large-scale continuous viewing attractions and nine smaller ones, plus the eye-catching new **Waterfront area**, relaxing gardens, a kids' play area and a smart range of shops (a noticeable feature of Anheuser-Busch parks). Their hire pushchairs (strollers) are also the most amusing – shaped like baby dolphins. Be warned, though, the size of the park will take you by surprise and requires a lot of to-ing and fro-ing to catch the various shows. Keep a close grip on your map and entertainment schedule and try to establish your own programme that gives you regular breaks to sit and enjoy some of the quieter spots.

For something different, you can sign up for the free 35-minute Anheuser-Busch **Beer School** at the Hospitality Center for a glimpse into beer-making (and tasting!).

The main attractions

Wild Arctic: this interactive ride-and-view experience provides a realistic environment that is both educational and thrilling. It consists of an exciting simulator jet

1 Information
2 Wild Arctic
3 Shamu Stadium
4 Dine with Shamu
5 Sea Lion and Otter Stadium
6 Key West Dolphin Fest
7 Atlantis Bayside Stadium
8 The Waterfront
9 Seaport Theater
10 Nautilus Theatre – Odyssea
11 Clydesdale Hamlet
12 Anheuser-Busch Hospitality
   Center
13 Manatees: The Last Generation?
14 Pacific Point Preserve
15 Shamu's Happy Harbor
16 Shark Encounter
17 Sharks Underwater Grill
18 Tropical Reef
19 Penguin Encounter
20 Key West At SeaWorld
21 Stingray Lagoon
22 Turtle Point
23 Dolphin Cove
24 Journey To Atlantis
25 Kraken
26 Dolphin Nursery

SEA WORLD

helicopter journey into the Arctic wilderness arriving at a clever research base, Base Station Wild Arctic, where the 'passengers' are disgorged into a frozen wonderland to meet polar bears, beluga whales and walruses. The imaginative detail includes a replica sunken galleon and other nautical touches, as well as some scientific research. This one is not to be missed (but not just after a Shamu show when the hordes descend). Restrictions: 3ft 6in/ 106cm. TTTT plus AAAAA. Those who don't want to ride can just walk through to the Base Station.

Shamu Stadium: SeaWorld has long since outgrown its tag as just the place to see killer whales, but the Shamu show is still one of its most amazing sights. Watch the killer whales and their trainers pull off some spectacular stunts, as well as hearing everything you need to know about these majestic creatures.

> BRIT TIP: Reader David Snelling from Cheshire, warns, 'Gentlemen, do not volunteer to participate in the Shamu display – it will be chauvinistically humiliating.'

There are two distinct shows, the more humorous *Shamu Adventure* during the day (25 minutes) and the louder *Shamu Rocks America* at night (20 minutes). Both are worth seeing, and are easily the park's most popular events, so do make an effort to arrive early (especially as there is an amusing pre-show). Also, the first 14 rows get VERY wet (watch out for your cameras) – when a killer whale leaps into the air in front of you, it displaces a LOT of water on landing! AAAAA.

Dine with Shamu: this new offering gives guests a VIP

experience 'backstage' with the killer whales and their trainers. An all-you-can-eat buffet on a covered terrace right alongside the main whale pool is accompanied by the chance to ask questions of the trainers and watch some of the training sessions. It costs $32 for adults and $18 for children, there are two seatings daily (at 4.45 and 7.30pm) and it's advisable to book in advance on 407 351 3600. All guests can take advantage of the **Underwater Viewing** area for the wonderful whales.

Sea Lion and Otter Stadium: the venue for a wonderful show, *Clyde and Seamore Take Pirate Island*, it features the resident sea lions who, with their pals the otter and walrus (plus a couple of humans as the fall guys!), put on a hilarious 25-minute performance of watery stunts and gags. Arrive early for some first-class audience mickey-taking from the resident pirate mimic. AAAA.

Key West Dolphin Fest: more breathtaking marine mammal stunts and tricks in a funky beach theme, with the accent again on informing and educating in a gentle manner on the current state of research into dolphins and false killer whales and the dangers they face. The show lasts almost 20 minutes and is rarely over-subscribed, but once again the first few rows face a soaking. AAAA.

Atlantis Bayside Stadium: this arena is host to various special events

6

Shamu the killer whale

BRIT TIP: The weather may occasionally mean the outdoor entertainment is cancelled, but don't let it stop you enjoying yourself. Cheap, plastic ponchos will appear in the shops at the first sign of rain!

and is a great place from which to watch the nightly firework show (in high season only) over The Waterfront. NB: The old ski show here has been discontinued.

The Waterfront: not so much an attraction as a new 5-acre (2-ha) 'village' at the heart of SeaWorld, offering fine dining, smart shops, several shows and street entertainment. This area forms an arc around part of the central lake, is themed like an eclectic harbour and offers two excellent eateries (the **Seafire Inn**, for gourmet steak burgers, salads and coconut-fried shrimp, and the superb **Voyagers** for wood-fired pizzas, pasta and sandwiches; not cheap but quite delicious), two snack bars (**Café de Mar** for pastries, coffees and soft drinks, and **Freezas** for frozen yoghurt and other drinks), four interlinked boutique-style shops (with some stylish souvenirs – check out **Allura's Treasure Trove** and **Under The Sun**) and some highly amusing street performers. Look out in particular for the feline antics of **Kat 'n' Kaboodle** (an incredible display of pure-bred cats), the zany **Aquanuts** (a pair of hapless longshoremen who make Laurel and Hardy look competent!) and the percussive pots-and-pans rhythms of the **Groove Chefs**. The Seafire Inn is also home to **Rico and Roza's Musical Feast**, a rather uneven 25-minute song and dance show, as well as the nightly – and much more vibrant – Luau. Finally, in best

fortress style, **The Tower** is the centrepiece of The Waterfront, with a 400-ft (122-metre) landmark offering slowly rotating rides (at an extra $4) up for a bird's eye view of the park. Here you will also find the **SandBar**, a lovely water's edge cocktail bar with live musicians throughout the day, and snacks like sushi, cheese plates, fresh fruit and shrimp cocktail. It's the perfect place to watch the sun go down (and the fireworks go up!). Kids can play in the two **squirt fountains** (remember those swimming trunks) and the whole scene is characterised by lovely landscaping and even some ocean sound effects. AAAA.

Seaport Theater: just inside the Waterfront, this air-conditioned haven (during the hottest part of the day) hosts the *Pets Ahoy!* show, a genuinely cute 25-minute giggle featuring the unlikely talents of a menagerie of dogs, cats, birds, rats, pot-bellied pigs and others, the majority of which have been rescued from animal shelters. AAA.

Nautilus Theater – Odyssea: fans of the old Cirque de la Mer show here will be sad to know it has gone – but happy that it has been replaced by something even smarter and equally as captivating. Odyssea is their latest creation (opened in July 2003), a 30-minute fantasy featuring some mind-boggling acrobatic feats, engaging live music, clever lighting and a host of in-theatre special effects. The show tells the spectacular, if stylised, story of a seaman who falls into the ocean and descends through various levels to the sea bed, encountering various creatures along the way. Think of a watery version of Cirque du Soleil and you are not far wrong. When it's hot or wet, this is a great place to head for! AAAAA.

Clydesdale Hamlet: these massive stables are home to the Anheuser-Busch trademark Clydesdale dray horses. They make great photo opportunities when fully harnessed, and there is a life-size statue outside on which to sit the kids to take their picture. The Hitching Barn shows how the horses are prepared for the twice-daily parade, including washing, grooming and braiding. AA.

Anheuser-Busch Hospitality Center: adjoining Clydesdale Hamlet, this offers the chance to sample the company's most famous product, beer (in fact, the world's No 1 bottled beer, Budweiser, and its cousins). Sadly, it's only three small samples per visitor aged 21 or over, but it still makes a nice gesture, and you can take your free drink and sit on the outdoor terrace, which provides a pleasant break from all the usual theme park hustle and bustle. AAA. You'll also find the Beer School, here, while **The Deli** restaurant is an attractive proposition, serving fresh-carved turkey and beef, German sausage, sauerkraut, fresh-baked breads and delicious desserts.

Manatees: The Last Generation?: here is an exhibit that will really tug at your heartstrings as you learn of the tragic plight of this endangered species of Florida's waterways. Watch these lazy-looking creatures (half walrus, half hippo?) lounge around their manmade lagoon from above, then walk down the ramp to the special circular theatre where a 5-minute film with amazing 3-D effects will reveal the full dangers facing the harmless manatee. Then pass into the underwater viewing section, with hands-on TV screens offering more information. It's a magnificent exhibit and often provokes a few tears at the animals' uncertain future. It is also right behind the Key West Dolphin Fest, so DON'T go just after one of the shows there. AAAAA.

Pacific Point Preserve: another SeaWorld first, this carefully re-created rocky coast habitat shows the park's seals and sea lions at their most natural. A hidden wave-making machine adds the perfect touch, while park attendants provide informative talks at regular intervals. You can also buy small packs of smelt to throw to the ever-hungry sea mammals. AAAA.

Shamu's Happy Harbor: 3 acres (1.2ha) of brilliantly designed adventure playground await youngsters of all ages here, with all things climbable or crawlable. Activities include a 4-storey net climb, two tented 'ball rooms' to wade through, and a giant 'trampoline' tent. It does get busy in mid-afternoon, but the kids seem to love it at any time. Next door is the clever **Shamu Splash Attack** (water-balloon catapults), the inevitable video arcade and some funfair games for a few extra dollars. TTTTT.

Shark Encounter: the world's largest collection of dangerous sea creatures can be found here, brought vividly and dramatically to life by the walk-through tubes that surround you with more than 50 prowling sharks (including sand tigers, black tips, nurse sharks and sand bars), sawfish, tropical fish and two gigantic groupers. It's an eerie experience (and perhaps too intense for small children), but brilliantly presented and, again, highly informative. You can also watch the intrepid souls in the Sharks Deep Dive cage as it traverses the aquarium (see page 159). Queues do build up here at peak times, though. AAAA or TTTT (take your pick!).

Once you have ridden the moving walkway, head for the best restaurant in the park for another close-up at the new **Sharks Underwater Grill**. Not only do you have an amazing backdrop for your meal in a clever, subterranean environment (check out the incredible bar for a source of fascination – it is a mini-aquarium!), but the upscale, full-service

BRIT TIP: If the main adult portions look too big at the Sharks Underwater Grill – and they are pretty hefty – you can order from the Young Adults menu for smaller portions of four regular dishes. Check out the kids' dessert menu, too!

restaurant features a hugely appetising 'Floribbean'-style menu, blending both local and spicy Caribbean fare. The emphasis is on seafood – and wonderful creations with scallops, jumbo shrimp, grouper and sea bass – plus pasta, oak-grilled filet mignon, chicken and pork, and a dessert menu to die for. Some refreshing (non-alcoholic!) cocktails and menus for under 10s and teens round out an excellent picture here, and it is a real treat – especially on a hot day. Open daily from 11am to park closing (it gets VERY busy for lunch but quieter in later afternoon), it is highly advisable to book at the restaurant itself or on 407 351 3600 in advance. A 3-course meal will cost around $31.

Tropical Reef: after the dramas and amusements elsewhere, this may seem a little tame, but stick with it. Literally thousands of colourful fish inhabit the centrepiece 160,000-gallon (728,000-litre) tropical reef, while smaller tanks show off other intriguing species. AAA.

Penguin Encounter: always a hit with all the family (and hence one of the more crowded exhibits at peak periods), the eternally comical penguins are in this brilliantly presented (if decidedly chilly) showpiece. You have the choice of going close and using the moving walkway along the whole of the display or standing back and watching from a non-moving position. Both positions afford views of how the 17 different species are so breathtaking under water. Feeding time is the most popular time for visitors, so arrive early if you want a prime position. There is also a special question-and-answer session at 2pm every day – the winner gets to pet a penguin. AAAA.

Key West at SeaWorld: a whole collection of exhibits are grouped together here under the clever Key West theme. **Stingray Lagoon**, where you can feed and touch fully grown rays, includes a nursery for newborn rays, while the park's rescued and rehabilitated sea turtles can be seen at **Turtle Point**, which helps to explain the dangers to these saltwater reptiles. The centrepiece exhibit, the 2.1-acre (0.8-ha) **Dolphin Cove**, is a more spectacular, naturalistic development and offers visitors the chance to get right up close and feed this friendly community of frisky Atlantic bottlenose dolphins. There is an excellent underwater viewing area to the lagoon, which features waves, a sandy beach and a reproduced coral reef. The park's photographers also patrol here, ready to snap you at play with the dolphins, and a 2-photo

Makahiki Luau at The Waterfront

BRIT TIP: Touching the rays and dolphins is an experience at SeaWorld you won't easily forget.

Beluga whales at Wild Arctic

package (in a 5 x 7in/127 x 178mm stand-up frame) will set you back $22.99.

The whole area is designed in the tropical, seaside flavour of America's southernmost city, Key West, with beach huts, lifeguard chairs, dune buggies, themed shops and other eclectic lookalike elements, but it also underlines the environmental message of conservation through a series of interactive graphics and video displays adjacent to the animal habitats, and children of all ages will find it a fun, educational experience. The shops here are above average, too. AAAA.

Journey to Atlantis: unique in Orlando, this terrific 'water-coaster' gave SeaWorld its first 5-star thrill attraction in 1998. The combination of extra elements here ultimately makes it unique, with a series of illusionary special effects giving way to a high-speed water ride that becomes a runaway roller-coaster. An amusing TV show preamble about the 'discovery' of Atlantis opens the way to your 8-passenger Greek fishing boat, which sets off gently through the lost city. The evil spirit Allura takes over and riders plunge into a dash through Atlantis, dodging gushing fountains and water cannons, with hundreds of dazzling holographic and laser-generated illusions, before the heart-stopping 60-ft (18-metre) drop, which is merely the entry to the roller-coaster finale back in the candle-filled catacombs. An amazing

creation. Once again, be prepared to get seriously wet (soaked) in the course of the ride, which is great in the heat of the summer but not so clever first thing in the morning in winter. Restrictions: 3ft 6in/106cm. TTTTT. Riders exit into the **Sea Aquarium Gallery**, a combination gift shop and huge aquarium full of sharks, stingrays and tropical fish (don't forget to look up!).

Kraken: new in 2000, this addition to the coaster family is the longest, fastest and highest in central Florida. Based on the mythical sea monster, Kraken is an innovative pedestal ride (you are effectively sitting in a chair without a floor – pretty exposed!) that plunges an initial 144ft (44 metres), hits 65mph (105kph), dives underground three times, adds seven inversions (including a 119-ft/36-metre vertical loop, a 101-ft/31-metre diving loop, a zero-gravity roll and a cobra roll) and a flat spin before riders escape the beast's lair. The ride from the front row, especially down that opening drop at an angle best described as ludicrous, is positively blood-curdling, and the rear seats are pretty amazing, too. Restrictions: 4ft 6in/137cm. TTTTT+.

SeaWorld Specials

For extra fun, there is live entertainment daily around the Key West attractions, including the trademark **Sunset Celebration**

SeaWorld main entrance

street party. Throughout the summer, when the park tends to stay open until at least 9pm, there are often other live elements, with outdoor DJs, music, dancers and games, plus a teens' music scene, **Club Shamu**, next to Kraken.

As well as all the main set-pieces, several smaller ones can be equally rewarding for their more personal touch. The **Dolphin Nursery** provides more close encounters with the park's (younger) dolphins, and then there are the **Flamingo, Pelican and Spoonbill Exhibits**. The **Tide Pool** is another hands-on experience with starfish and sea anemones.

The flamingo pedal-boats, which rent for $6 per half-hour (for 2 people) in one corner of the lagoon, are also fun to do. Look out, too, for the best photo opportunity of the day as a big, cuddly Shamu will greet the kids just inside the main entrance.

You can choose to eat from a further 10 different places, with the best of the bunch being the **Dockside Cafe** (barbecued, mesquite-grilled chicken and beef, chicken fingers and hot dogs), **The Deli** (in the Anheuser-Busch Hospitality Center, see page163),

Mama Stella's Italian Kitchen (pizza, pasta and salads), **Smoky Creek Grill** (a Texas-style barbecue) and **Mango Joe's Café** (delicious grilled fajitas, speciality salads and sandwiches). As in the other main parks, try to eat before midday or after 2.30pm for a crowd-free lunch, and before 5.30pm if you want a leisurely dinner.

Your wallet will also be in severe peril in any of the 24 additional shops and photo kiosks. Make sure you visit at least **Shamu's Emporium** (for a full range of cuddly Shamu toys and souvenirs), **Manatee Cove** (more cuddlies), **Friends of the Wild** (dedicated to animal lovers everywhere) and **The Label Stable** for Anheuser-Busch gifts and merchandise (some of it extremely smart). Your purchases can be forwarded to Package Pick-up in Shamu's Emporium, to collect on your way out of the park, provided you leave at least an hour for this service to work.

Finally, non-drivers will want to make a note of the special daily bus service from SeaWorld (and other points on I-Drive) direct to sister park Busch Gardens (see page 170), which you can book outside at Guest Relations.

SEAWORLD with children

The following gives a general idea of the appeal of SeaWorld's attractions to the different age groups:

Under 5s
Shamu Adventure Show, Key West Dolphin Fest, Clyde & Seamore Take Treasure Island, Pets Ahoy!, Wild Arctic (without the ride), Manatees: Last Generation?, Penguin Encounter, Tropical Reef, Pacific Point Preserve, Clydesdale Hamlet, Waterfront entertainment.

5–8s
All the above, plus Wild Arctic (with the ride), Odyssea, fireworks, Shark Encounter, Shamu's Happy Harbor.

9–12s
All the above, plus Kraken.

Over 12s
Kraken, Journey to Atlantis, Wild Arctic, Shark Encounter, Shamu Adventure Show, Clyde & Seamore Take Treasure Island, Odyssea, fireworks.

Discovery Cove

Fancy a day in your own tropical paradise, with the chance to swim with dolphins, encounter sharks, snorkel in a coral reef and dive through a waterfall into a tropical aviary? Well, Discovery Cove is all that and more. The only drawback is the price. This mini theme park comes at a premium because it is restricted to just 1,000 guests a day, creating an exclusive experience, and the admission fee reflects that. The flat rate entrance fee is $229 and the only reduction is to $129 for those not wishing to do the Dolphin Swim and for 3–5s; under 3s are free.

A new **Trainer For A Day** programme adds the exciting opportunity to go behind the scenes into the training, feeding, health and welfare of the park's animals. You get to work with the experts as they interact with dolphins, birds, sharks, stingrays and tropical fish. The experience includes a behavioural training class, souvenir shirt, dolphin book and waterproof camera, and participants must be aged at least 6 and in good health. You need to book well ahead on 0208 668 4218 or online at www.discoverycove.com. The cost? A healthy $399, including the main entrance fee, plus tax.

So, just what do you get for your money at Discovery Cove? Well, as you would expect, it is a supremely personal park. You check in as you would for a hotel rather than a theme park (the entrance lobby is wonderfully impressive), and you have a guide to take you in and get you set for the day.

All your basic requirements – towel, mask, snorkel, wet-jacket, lockers, beach umbrellas and lunch – are included in the price, and the level of service is excellent. A valuable 7-day pass for SeaWorld is also included. The lunch provided at the buffet-style **Laguna Grill** is

pretty good, but you have to pay for any further snacks and drinks around the park, while the gift shop and photographic prices reflect the entrance fee – expensive.

Location

Situated on Central Florida Parkway, almost opposite the SeaWorld entrance (open year-round from 8.30am–5.30pm. Parking is free), the whole of the 30-acre (12-ha) park is magnificently landscaped, with lovely thatched buildings, palm trees, lush vegetation, brilliant white-sand beaches, gurgling streams and even hammocks. The overall effect is as if you have been transported to some Caribbean or South Seas oasis.

The usual tourist hurly-burly is left far behind. The 5-star resort feel is enhanced by a high staff-to-guest ratio (the lifeguards can outnumber guests at times, it seems). There should be no queues for anything (okay, the buffet-service restaurant may get busy at lunch) and the highlight dolphin encounter is world class. The ultimate effect is total relaxation, a holiday from your holiday, and a real feeling of escape.

Visitors with disabilities are well catered for, with special wheelchairs that can move across the sand and into shallow water, with an area of the Dolphin Lagoon to allow those who can't enter the water still to be able to touch the dolphins.

The essence of a day here involves close encounters with all the animals – although not too close in the case of the sharks – plus a strong underlying conservation message.

The main attractions

Coral Reef: a huge rocky pool, filled with several thousand tropical

The famous dolphin encounter

fish, offers the most amazing man-made snorkelling experience you'll find. The water teems with silverjacks, angelfish and yellowtail snapper and, even if the 'coral' is hand-painted concrete, it is a clever environment. Some of the larger stingrays inhabiting the bottom of the reef are fascinating to watch. Swimmers also come within inches of sharks and barracuda – all safely behind a Plexiglass partition – which adds another novel element. If you stay reasonably still in the water, many of the fish will crowd around to inspect their latest pool-mate! AAAA.

Ray Lagoon: another carefully sculpted pool provides the opportunity to paddle among several dozen southern and cownose rays, quite harmless, but with just a hint of menace to the fascination. AAAA.

Tropical River: this 800-yd (732-metre) circuit of gently flowing bath-warm water is a variation on the lazy river feature of many of the water parks, although with a far more naturalistic aspect and none of the inner tubes. It is primarily designed for snorkellers and features rocky lagoons, caves, a beach section, a tropical forest segment, sunken ruins and an underwater viewing window into the Coral Reef. The lack of fish makes it seem a bit bland after the Tropical Reef and Ray Lagoon, but again, it is as much about relaxing as having fun. AAA.

Aviary: this recently enhanced 3-part adventure is both an area in its own right and a 40-yd (37-metre) section of the Tropical River. You can walk in off the beach or swim in through one of the two impressive waterfalls which guard each end, a beautifully scenic touch and fun for snorkellers. Some 200 tropical birds (plus two tiny Muntjac deer) fill the main 30ft- (9 metre) high enclosure and, if you stand still for a while, they are likely to use you for a perch. An expansion in 2002 effectively doubled the size of the aviary by adding a small-bird sanctuary – full of finches, honeycreepers and hummingbirds – and a large-bird enclosure, featuring toucans and the red-legged seriema. Guides will introduce you to specific birds (which you can hand-feed) and tell you about their habits, habitats and conservation issues. AAAAA.

Dolphin Swim: the headline attraction at Discovery Cove is the encounter with the park's Atlantic bottlenose dolphin community. A 20-minute orientation programme in one of the four thatched beach cabanas, with a film and instruction from two of the animal trainers, sets you up for this deeply thrilling experience. Groups of 6–8 go into the huge lagoon with careful supervision from the trainers and, starting off by standing in the waist-deep (and slightly chilly) water as one of the dolphins comes to you, you gradually become more adventurous until you are swimming next to them. Timid swimmers are catered for and there are life-jackets for those who feel they need them, but the lagoon is up to 12ft (3.6 metres) deep so there is a feeling of really being in the dolphins' environment. You will learn how trainers use hand signals and positive reinforcement to communicate with them, and get the chance to stroke, feed and even kiss (!) your dolphin. The encounter comes to a dramatic conclusion as you are towed back to shore by one of these awesome animals, which can weigh from 300–600lb (136–272kg), although the activities vary according to the dolphins' own attention span. You spend around 30 minutes in the water and it is genuinely unforgettable. Under 6s are not allowed into the dolphin lagoon. TTTTT+.

Truly, Discovery Park is an attraction with huge style and appeal – not to mention the stuff of which cherished memories are made – but it will take a big bite out of your holiday budget. A family of four, with children of 6 or older who want to do the Dolphin Swim, would pay $928.56 (including tax; $970.96 after March 2004) for the day and that's not including the Trainer for a Day programme. Even with the 7-day SeaWorld pass included, it is a massive outlay. The charge for 3- to 5-year-olds is also pretty steep, in my opinion. Your sundries are likely to add up, too. A 5 x 7in (127 x 178mm) photo is $15.99 and an 8 x 10in (200 x 254mm) is $28.99. Then there are various photo packages at $29.99, $59.99 and $99.99, while the video of your experience (which includes 30 minutes of highlights of the whole park) costs $59.99.

The weather can get distinctly cool in the winter months, but the water is always heated (apart from the dolphin lagoon, which remains at 72°F/22°C) and full wetsuits are also available to keep out the chill. In the winter of 2000/2001, when the temperature in Florida hit freak lows (almost freezing at night), Discovery Cove came to its visitors' aid by providing temporary heaters around the park and complimentary coffee and hot chocolate! Their attention to detail is really that good, and guest satisfaction ratings remain extremely high (it is hugely popular with British visitors – up to 40% of the daily attendance at times).

However, if any element falls below expectations, it is worth bringing it to the attention of the park managers as they are always keen to rectify any apparent oversights.

Special occasions

Want an extra special birthday or anniversary occasion, or somewhere to make that unique marriage proposal? Discovery Cove has a range of options here, involving extra dolphin interaction, private beach cabanas, champagne and keepsakes. The **Premium Package** (at an extra $474.95 per couple) includes sharing your special moment with a dolphin, who delivers a specialised message buoy, a private tent on the beach, Dom Perignon champagne, a dozen roses, chocolate-dipped strawberries, disposable waterproof camera, keepsake photo and frame, and a video of the occasion. The **Golden Ring Package** (at $224.95 per couple) and **Sweetheart Package** ($149.95), are scaled-down versions of the same. The **Birthday Package** ($74.95) includes dolphin activity, cake, photo and souvenir buoy, plus T-shirt and video, and a **Premium** version ($174.95) offers a T-shirt and video of the occasion.

For more details, look up www.discoverycove.com. You can book online – and it is advisable to do so at least three months in advance at busy times – or call 407 370 1280.

Snorkelling in the Coral Reef

Busch Gardens

Question: when is a zoo not a zoo? Answer: when it is also a theme park like the 335-acre (136-ha) Busch Gardens in nearby Tampa.

Busch Gardens, the second big Anheuser-Busch park in the area, started life as a mini-menagerie for the wildlife collection of the brewery-owning Busch family (Budweiser). In 1959, they opened a small, tropical-themed hospitality centre next to the brewery and things have mushroomed ever since. Now, it is a major, multi-faceted family attraction, the biggest on Florida's west coast and a little more than an hour from Orlando.

Busch Gardens is rated among the top four zoos in America, with more than 2,700 animals representing more than 320 species of mammals, birds, reptiles, amphibians and spiders. But that's just the start. It boasts a safari-like section of Africa

Busch Gardens at a glance

Location	Busch Boulevard, Tampa; 75–90 minutes drive from Orlando
Size	335 acres (136ha) in 11 themed areas
Hours	9.30 or 10am–6pm off peak; 9am–9pm high season (Easter, summer holidays, Thanksgiving, Christmas)
Admission	Under 3 free; 3–9 $42.95 (1-Day Ticket), $72.95 (Busch/SeaWorld Combo ticket), $175.95 (5-Park FlexTicket, including Universal Studios, SeaWorld and Wet 'n Wild); adults (10+) $51.95, $85.95, $209.95
Parking	$7
Lockers	Yes; in Morocco, Congo, Egypt and Stanleyville; $1
Pushchairs	$11 and $15 ($2 gift card refund; in Morocco)
Wheelchairs	$9 ($2 gift card refund) and $32, with pushchairs
Top Attractions	Rhino Rally, Gwazi, Kumba, Montu, Congo River Rapids, Tanganyika Tidal Wave, RL Stine's Haunted Lighthouse
Don't Miss	*World Rhythms on Ice*, Myombe Reserve, Edge of Africa, Elephant Wash, Mystic Sheikhs band
Hidden Costs	**Meals** — Burger, chips and Pepsi $8.18; 3-course meal $16–23; family-style dinner $10.95 and $5.95 (Crown Colony House)
	Kids' meal — $3.99 ($5.49 with souvenir bucket)
	T-shirts — $9.79–24.99
	Souvenirs — 99 cents–$1,950
	Sundries — Ride photos $8.99

spread over 65 acres (26ha) of grassy veldt, with special tours to hand-feed some of the animals.

Interspersed among the animals are more than 20 bona fide theme park rides, including the mind-numbing roller-coasters **Kumba, Montu** and **Gwazi**, which guarantee a new experience for coaster addicts, and yet another in the series of simulator rides, the amusing and novel **Akbar's Adventure Tours**; plus animal shows, comedians, musicians, strolling players and a family show extravaganza in the impressive Moroccan Palace Theater, *World Rhythms on Ice*.

The overall theme is Africa, hence the park is subdivided into areas like Nairobi and the Congo, and the dining and shopping facilities are equal to most of the other theme parks. It doesn't quite have the pizzazz of an *Epcot* or Universal, and the staff are a bit more laid back. In a way, it is like the big brother of the Chessington World of Adventures in Surrey, although admittedly on a much grander scale (and in a better climate). But it has guaranteed, 5-star family appeal, especially with its selection of rides just for kids, and it is a big hit with the Brits.

Busch is the only park to offer with 1-Day Tickets a **Rain Guarantee**, which means if you get rained out on your visit, you can return FREE within 7 days.

Location

Busch Gardens is the hardest place to locate on the sketchy local maps and the signposting is not as sharp as it could be but, from Orlando, the directions are pretty simple. Head west on I-4 for almost an hour (it is 55 miles/88km from I-4's junction with Highway 192) until you hit the intersecting motorway I-75. Take I-75 north for 3½ miles (5.5km) until you see the exit for Fowler Avenue (Highway 582). Continue west on Fowler for another 3½ miles (5.5km), then just past the University of South Florida on your right, turn LEFT into McKinley Drive. A mile (1.6km) down McKinley Drive, Busch Gardens' car park entrance will be on your left, where it costs $7 to park.

Those without a car can use the brilliant daily **Busch Gardens Shuttle Express** bus service, which makes several round trips a day from Orlando at $5 a time (free if you have a 5-Park FlexTicket). You board the Shuttle at SeaWorld, The Mercado, Orlando Premium Outlets, Universal Studios or Old Town in Kissimmee and pick-up times range from 8–10.15am, returning at 6 or 7pm. Book at the **Guest Services** window at SeaWorld or call 1-800 221 1339.

You may think you have left the crowds behind in Orlando but, unfortunately, in high season you'd be wrong. It is still advisable to be here in time for opening, if only to be first in line to ride the amazing Rhino Rally or the dazzling roller-coasters Gwazi, Kumba and Montu, which all draw queues of up to an hour. The Congo River Rapids, Stanley Falls Log Flume ride and Tanganyika Tidal Wave (all opportunities to get wet!) are also prime rides, as is Akbar's Adventure Tours and the other two roller-coasters, Python and Scorpion. New in 2003 was **RL Stine's Haunted Lighthouse**, a 3-D film show, which was also proving popular. The queues take longer to build up here, so for the first few hours at least you can enjoy a relatively crowd-free experience.

On your right as you approach the main entrance gates is the **Tours Centre** window, and you need to visit here first thing (or book in advance on 813 984 4043 or email BGT.VIPTours@Buschgardens.com) if you'd like to do their wonderful

MOROCCO
1 Zagora Café
2 Marrakesh Theater
3 Moroccan Palace Theater
CROWN COLONY
4 Skyride Station
5 Clydesdale Hamlet
6 Crown Colony Restaurant and Hospitality
   Center
SERENGETI PLAIN
7 Edge of Africa
NAIROBI
8 Myombe Reserve
9 Rhino Rally
TIMBUKTU
10 Scorpion
11 The Phoenix
12 Sandstorm
13 Crazy Camel
14 Kiddie Rides
15 Carousel Caravan
16 Desert Grill
17 RL Stine's Haunted Lighthouse
CONGO
18 Kumba
19 Congo River Rapids
20 Ubanga-Banga Bumper Cars
21 Python
STANLEYVILLE
22 Stanley Falls Log Flume
23 Tanganyika Tidal Wave
24 Stanleyville Theater
LAND OF THE DRAGONS
25 Dragon's Tale Theater
BIRD GARDENS
26 Bird Show Theater
27 Lory Landing
28 Aviary
29 Hospitality House/Beer School
30 Gwazi
EGYPT
31 Montu
32 Akbar's Adventure Tours
33 Tut's Tomb
34 Train Stations

BUSCH GARDENS

Main Entrance

Congo River Rapids

Serengeti Safari or one of their other Adventure Tours (see page 179). Busch Gardens is divided into 11 main sections, with the major rides all a bit of a hike from the main entrance. **Rhino Rally**, which opened in summer 2001, is one of the prime attractions, so I would definitely head here first (especially as the animals are more visible early in the day). Bear right through Morocco, turn left into Nairobi, pass the train station and the Rally entrance is opposite the elephant habitat. **Gwazi**, the fabulous wooden double-coaster, is another to draw a crowd relatively quickly, so, if you are tempted by this first, bear left through Morocco past the Zagora Café and you will soon arrive in its own purpose-built area. Then go through Stanleyville to Congo for **Kumba**, and retrace your steps to do **Congo River Rapids**, the **Python** and the other two water rides. Alternatively, turn right through the main entrance and visit Egypt for **Montu** and **Akbar's**. Here is the full park layout going anti-clockwise.

Morocco

Coming through the main gates brings you first into **Morocco**, home of all the main guest services and a lot of the best shops. *Epcot*'s Moroccan pavilion sets the scene rather better, but the architecture is still impressive and this version won't overtax your wallet quite as much as Disney does! For a quick meal try the **Zagora Café**, especially at breakfast when the marching, dancing, 8-piece brass band **Mystic Sheikhs** swings into action to entertain the early crowds. Alternatively, the wonderfully enticing **Sultan's Sweets** serves coffee and pastries. Watch out, too, for the strolling Men of Note, a scintillating 4-piece *a cappella* group, and the costumed characters like TJ the Tiger and Hilda Hippo.

Turning the corner brings you to the first animal encounter, the alligator pen. Morocco is also home to two of the park's biggest shows. The **Marrakesh Theater** offers the 25-minute *Moroccan Roll* song and dance show, with live musicians, top-notch singers and energetic dancers all in an amusing pastiche of pop and rock with a desert theme (hence songs like *Midnight At The Oasis* and *Rock The Casbah*). AAA.

Moroccan Palace Theater: the award-winning and unmissable *World Rhythms on Ice* show is performed here (although there are rumours of a new, non-ice show taking over in 2004). Even if the thought of an ice show doesn't immediately appeal to you, think again, because this is a surprising and highly entertaining 30-minute spectacular celebrating different cultures around the world. The costumes (some 95 of them) are terrific, the music is vibrant and

The Scorpion in Timbuktu

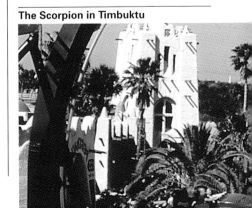

6

enhanced by video screens at either side of the stage, and some breathtaking special effects sum up a brilliant concept here. It is also air-conditioned, a welcome relief in summer (you should arrive a little early as the doors close right on time). AAAAA.

Crown Colony

This area sits in the park's bottom right corner and has five distinct components. Here, you can take the **Skyride** cable car (AAA) on a 1-way trip to The Congo (and providing a great look at Rhino Rally). The **Clydesdale Hamlet** is also here, but if you've seen the massive dray horses and their stables at SeaWorld, the set-up is pretty similar (AA). The **Showjumping Hall of Fame** will interest equine devotees.

The **Crown Colony Restaurant and Hospitality Center** is a large Victorian-styled building overlooking the Serengeti Plain. It offers counter-service salads, sandwiches and pizzas (downstairs) or a full-service restaurant upstairs with magnificent views of the animals roaming the plain. For a memorable meal (11.30am until an hour before park closing), head here for lunch (they don't take bookings) or, better still, come back for dinner in the early evening and see the animals come down to the waterhole for an evening drink.

Serengeti Plain

The Serengeti Plain itself is a 49-acre (20-ha) spread of African savannah that is home to buffalo, antelope, zebra, giraffe, wildebeest, ostriches, hippos, rhinos and many exotic birds, and can be viewed for much of the journey on the **Serengeti Express Railway**, a full-size, open-car steam train that chugs slowly from its main station in

Nairobi to Egypt and all the way round to Congo, Stanleyville and back. It is a good ride to take during the main part of the day when queues build up at the thrill rides. AAA.

Edge of Africa: a 15-acre (6-ha) safari experience that guarantees a close-up encounter almost as good as the real thing. The walk-through attraction puts you in an authentic setting of natural wilds and native villages (right down to the imported plants and even the smells), from which you can view giraffes, lions, baboons, meerkats, crocodiles, hyenas, vultures and even get an underwater view of a specially designed hippopotamus habitat. Look out for the abandoned jeep – you can sit in the front cab while lions lounge in the back! Wandering 'safari guides' and naturalists offer informal talks, and the attention to detail is wonderful. AAAAA.

> BRIT TIP: Edge of Africa offers some fantastic photo opportunities but, in the hot months, come here early in the day as many animals seek refuge from the heat later.

Nairobi

Nairobi is home to the awesome **Myombe Reserve**, one of the largest and most realistic habitats for the threatened highland gorillas and chimpanzees of central Africa. This 3-acre (1.2-ha) walk-through has a superb tropical setting where the temperature is kept artificially high and convincing with the aid of lush forest landscaping and hidden water mist sprays. Take your time, especially as there are good, seated vantage points, and be patient to catch these magnificent creatures going about their daily routine. It is also highly informative, with attendants usually on hand to answer any questions. AAAAA.

Rhino Rally: new in summer 2001, this wonderfully dramatic and scenic ride starts out as an off-road jeep safari and changes into an innovative raft adventure as your 17-passenger vehicle gets caught in a flash flood. The blockbuster 8-minute whirl through the wilds of Africa includes encounters with elephants, rhinos, crocodiles, antelope and more, as the off-road part of the ride is just about as 'real' as they can make it. Your driver adds to the fun with some amusing spiel about the rally and your purpose-built (by Land-Rover) vehicle, but it soon becomes clear your 'navigator' (the front seat passenger) has led you into a blind gully. An unused pontoon bridge is your only way out, but 'fate' has a unique twist in store, which opens the way to part two of the ride and the thrilling raging river section that is unlike any attraction to date. Check this out (but get here early to beat the queues). Height restriction is just 3ft 3in/99cm. TTTT and AAAAA.

Back at **Myombe Gifts** you can buy your own cuddly baby gorilla (a toy, of course!) and you can get a snack or soft drink at the **Kenya Kanteen**. This is also the place to see the Asian elephants (check the advertised times for the **Elephant Wash**) and the **Nairobi Field Station**, an animal nursery and care centre which houses all manner of rehabilitating and hand-reared creatures.

Continuing round the nursery brings you to the **Reptile House** and **Tortoise Habitat**. The **Curiosity Caverns**, just to the left of the nursery, are easy to miss but don't if you want to catch a glimpse of nocturnal and rarely seen creatures in a clever, cave-like setting.

Timbuktu

Passing through Nairobi brings you to the more ride-dominated area of the park, starting with Timbuktu. Here in a North African desert setting you will find many of the elements of a traditional funfair, with a couple of brain-scrambling rides and two good shows.

Scorpion: a 50mph (80kph) roller-coaster, this features a 62-ft (19-metre) drop and a 360-degree loop that is guaranteed to dial D for Dizzy for a while! The ride lasts just 120 seconds, but it seems longer! The queues build up here from late morning to mid afternoon, and you have to be at least 3ft 6in/106cm to ride. TTTT.

Other rides include **The Phoenix**, a positively evil invention, that involves sitting in a gigantic, boat-shaped swing which eventually performs a 360-degree rotation in dramatic, slow-motion style. Don't eat just before this one! Height restriction: 4ft/122cm; TTTT. **Sandstorm** is a fairly routine whirligig contraption that spins and levitates at fairly high speed (hold on to your stomach). Height restriction 3ft 6in/106cm; TTT. The **Crazy Camel** is an odd sort of ride resembling a giant sombrero that spins and tilts its riders into a state of dizziness. Height restriction 3ft 6in/106cm; TT.

A series of scaled-down **Kiddie Rides** are usually a hit with the under 10s (and give Mum and Dad a break as well). The **Carousel Caravan** offers the opportunity to ride a genuine Mary Poppins-type carousel, while there is also the inevitable **Electronic Arcade** and a **Games Area** of side shows and stalls that require a few extra dollars to play.

Desert Grill is a new African-themed buffet diner here (offering large sandwiches, Italian sausage with grilled vegetables, salads and

6

pasta, plus kids meals in a souvenir bucket) set in a huge hall that provides some serious stage entertainment too. Watch out for the reggae sounds and fun of **We Be Jammin'** and a neat Country & Western combo. AAA.

RL Stine's Haunted Lighthouse: the final element and a thoroughly fun 3-D film romp in the company of Christopher Lloyd that will appeal especially to children of all ages (although it may be a touch spooky for the youngest). The story centres on the two 'ghost children' of the Haunted Lighthouse and the real children who inadvertently come to visit. Cue a riot of 3-D visuals plus many clever (and hilarious) special effects (prepare to duck when Lloyd drinks a beer!). It also uses fog and wind effects, plus strobe lighting and a few 'surprises.' Based on a story by American kids' mock-horror writer RL Stine (of Goosebumps fame), it is an extremely well made 22-minute movie, with full surround-sound, that draws a good crowd through the main part of the day, so go early or leave it until later on. AAAA.

Congo

You're into serious ride territory here, with the unmistakable giant turquoise structure of **Kumba** looming over the area. First of all, it's one of the largest and fastest

RL Stine's Haunted Lighthouse

roller-coasters in the south-east United States and, at 60mph (97kph), it features three unique elements: a diving loop which plunges the riders a full 110ft (33 metres), a camelback, with a 360-degree spiral that induces a weightless feeling for 3 seconds, and a 108-ft (33-metre) vertical loop. For good measure, it dives underground at one point! It looks terrifying close up, but it is absolutely exhilarating, even for non-coaster fans. Restrictions: 4ft 6in/137cm. TTTTT.

Congo River Rapids: these look pretty tame after that, but don't be fooled. These giant rubber tyres will bounce you down some of the most convincing rapids outside of the Rockies, and you will end up with a fair soaking for good measure. Restrictions: 3ft 6in/106cm. TTTT.

Ubanga-Banga Bumper Cars: they are just that, typical fairground dodgems (height restriction: 3ft 6in/106cm; TT), and you won't miss anything by passing them by for the more daring **Python**, the fourth of Busch Gardens' roller-coasters, with this one featuring a double spiral corkscrew at 50mph (80kph) from 70ft (21 metres) up. Height restriction is 4ft/122cm, and the whole ride lasts just 70 seconds, but it's a blast. TTTT.

More **Kiddie Rides** are available for the smaller visitors. The **Vivi Restaurant** offers chicken fajitas, club sandwiches, salads and desserts, and there are two gift shops, including the **Tiger's Den**.

Stanleyville

You pass over Claw Island, home to the park's spectacular rare white **Bengal tigers**, to get to Stanleyville, which seems to merge into one area from the Congo. Here there are more watery rides, with the popular **Stanley Falls Log Flume** ride (almost identical to the ones at Chessington, Legoland, Thorpe Park and Alton Towers), which guarantees a good soaking at the final drop (height restriction: 3ft 10in/116cm; TTT) and the distinctly cleverer **Tanganyika Tidal Wave**, which takes you on a scenic ride along 'uncharted' African waters before tipping you down a 2-stage drop that really does land with tidal-wave force. Height restriction: 4ft/122cm. TTTT.

Stanleyville Theater: a good place to relax and put your feet up for a while as you watch the unusual *Mapapa Acrobats*, a troupe of fun-loving African entertainers who will enthral you with their offbeat gymnastics (including the lowest limbo you can ever imagine and some stunning tumbling feats). It starts off slow but quickly builds to a resounding series of clever acrobatics and balancing tricks that will send you out after 30 minutes with a smile as broad as the performers themselves. AAA½.

For a hearty, if messy, meal visit the **Stanleyville Smokehouse** – their wood-smoked ribs platter is a delight. As you leave Stanleyville behind, say hello to the Muntjac deer and orang-utans (who are rarely active during the day) in the large pens either side of the Train Station.

Land of the Dragons

Parents will want to know about this large, wonderfully clever area of activities, entertainment, rides and attractions purely for the young 'uns. It features a 3-storey treehouse complete with towers and maze-like

> BRIT TIP: Don't stand on the bridge into Orchid Canyon unless you want to catch the full weight of the Tidal Wave!

stairways, a rope climb, ball crawl and outdoor **Dragon's Tale Theater**, which presents the 15-minute show *Dumphrey's Special Day* – a birthday special with the resident cuddly dragon. It is all good, knockabout, well-supervised stuff, and some of the kiddie rides are superbly inventive, as well as offering plenty of opportunity to get wet. TTTTT (youngsters only – but mums and dads can watch!).

Bird Gardens

Your anti-clockwise route now brings you to the most peaceful area, and the original starting point of the park in 1959, the **Bird Gardens**. Here it is possible to unwind from the usual theme park hurly-burly. The exhibits and shows are all family-orientated, too, with the 30-minute *Wild Wings of Africa* presented in the **Bird Show Theater** (AAA) and the **Hospitality Patio**, where the resident band plays a mix of musical favourites, past and present. **Lory Landing** is a desert island-themed walk-through bird encounter featuring lorikeets, hornbills, parrots and more, with the chance to become a human perch and feed the friendly lorikeets (or have your ear nibbled!). A cup of nectar costs $1, but is a great investment for a memorable photo. Take a slow walk round to appreciate the lush, tropical foliage, and special

Land of the Dragons

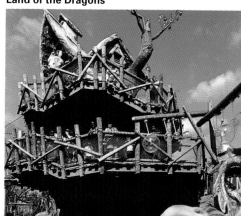

6

displays such as the walk-through **Aviary, Flamingo Island, Eagle Canyon**, plus the emus and kangaroos. AAA.

A free taste of Anheuser-Busch products is on offer in **Hospitality House**, where you can enroll for the **Beer School**, a 40-minute session in the process of beer-making. It offers a fascinating glimpse into the brewery world, and is excellently explained, with the bonus of some tasting! You will also be presented with a Brewery Master certificate. AAA (21 and over only).

Gwazi: this is Busch's most recent roller-coaster, a massive 'duelling' wooden creation in the classic mould (i.e. no going upside down). The two sets of cars, the Gwazi Lion and Gwazi Tiger, each top 50mph (80kph) and generate a G-force of up to 3.5 as they career around nearly 7,000ft (2,134 metres) of track with six fly-by encounters. You get to choose your ride in the intricately themed 8-acre (3-ha) village plaza and then you are off up the 90-ft (27-metre) lift for a breathtaking 2½ minutes. The shake, rattle 'n roll effect of a classic coaster is cleverly re-created and the Lion and Tiger rides are slightly different, so you need to do both. Even if you don't like coasters, try this one. Height restriction: 4ft/122cm. TTTTT.

Next door is the **River Rumble** game for kids, a series of catapults that fire water-filled balloons guaranteed to get everyone wet. TTTT (for under 12s). This actually costs an extra $3 for a bucket of 9 balloons (or $5 for two buckets). Children can also try the **bungee trampoline** and the **rock-climbing wall** at $6 each or $9 for both.

Egypt

The final area of Busch Gardens is tucked away through the Crown Colony, so it is best visited either first thing or late in the day. **Egypt** is 8 acres (3ha) of carefully re-created pharaoh country, dominated by the trademark roller-coaster Montu, named after an ancient Egyptian warrior god.

Montu: a truly breathtaking creation, this is one of the world's tallest and longest inverted coasters, covering nearly 4,000ft (1,219 metres) of track at speeds topping 60mph (97kph) and peaking with a G-force of 3.85! Like Kumba, it looks terrifying, but in reality it is an absolute 5-star thrill as it leaves your legs dangling and swoops and plunges (underground at two points) for almost 3 minutes of brain-scrambling fun. Height restriction: 4ft 6in/137cm. TTTTT.

Akbar's Adventure Tours: this is actually located in Crown Colony because it replaced the Questor ride in 1998. Another in the array of simulator rides, it relies as much on fun as thrills. The TV pre-show leads its audience into the world of down-at-heel Akbar (brilliantly played by comedian Martin Short) and his home-made (and untried) excursion machine. It explores, in unconventional fashion, the secrets and treasures of ancient Egypt, but don't expect a smooth ride – a mysterious force takes control in the forbidden tomb and the trip takes a high-speed turn for the unexpected! It is not recommended for anyone with back or neck problems or expectant mothers, while the height restriction is 3ft 6in/106cm. TTTT.

You can travel back in time on a tour of **Tut's Tomb**, as it was discovered by archaeologist Howard Carter, with clever lighting, audio and even aroma effects. AAA. Youngsters can also make their own excavations in a neat **Sand Pit** (with some little 'treasures' to be found!), while the shopping at **Golden Scarab** takes on a high-quality air with its hand-blown glass items, elaborate sculptures and authentic cartouche paintings.

You should finally return to Morocco for a spot of shopping in the area's tempting bazaars. Middle Eastern brass, pottery and carpets will all tempt you into opening your wallet yet again at **Casablanca Outfitters**, **Genie's Bottle** and **Marrakesh Market**, while there is a full range of Anheuser-Busch products and gift ideas at the **Emporium** and **Label Stable**, if you haven't already fallen prey to the array of shops and cuddly-toy outlets around the park.

In addition...

The **Serengeti Safari** tour is a 30-minute excursion (5 times a day, taking 20 people at a time) aboard flat-bed trucks that take you to meet the Serengeti Plain's giraffes, zebras, ostriches and rhinos close up and learn more about the park's environmental efforts. You book up at the Tour Office window just outside the main entrance, or at the kiosk in front of Casablanca Outfitters, for an extra $29.99, and places tend to fill up very quickly (children must be at least 5 to take part, and 5–15s must be accompanied by an adult).

The **Guided Adventure Tours** takes 15 at a time on a VIP park trek (lasting 4–5 hours), with your own guide, reserved seating at *World Rhythms on Ice*, front-of-line access for a number of rides (including Gwazi and Rhino Rally), counter-service lunch at Crown Colony and an up-close animal encounter with many of the animals and their staff, including the Serengeti Safari. They cost $69.99 ($64.99 for children) in advance or $74.99 ($69.99) on the day in addition to park entry. The new **Adventure Thrill Tours** are similar but substitute more rides – including the water rides – for the animal encounters ($59.99 and $54.99 in advance; $69.99 and

$64.99 on the day). The 2-hour **Animal Adventures Tour** is a personal animal experience for 7–10 people a day. The next best thing to becoming a park zookeeper, it provides close encounters with the Budweiser Clydesdales, black rhinos, hippos, giraffes and elephants, plus participation in various animal behavioural sessions. It is $99.99 per person in addition to daily admission.

Finally, the **Elite Adventure Tour** offers a personal, exclusive park tour, with front-of-line access to all rides, the Serengeti Safari, reserved seating at shows, free bottled water throughout, continental breakfast, lunch at the Crown Colony Restaurant, free parking and a free Fujifilm camera – all for an extra $149.99/person. Once again, all tours can be booked in advance on 813 984 4043.

For a full family day out, you can combine Busch Gardens with the next-door water park **Adventure Island** (on McKinley Drive) which is particularly welcome when it hots up (provided you plaster on the sun cream). The 25 acres (10ha) of watery fun, in a Key West theme, offer a full range of slides and rides, like the **Wahoo Run** adventure ride, the 76-ft (23-metre) free-fall plunge of the **Tampa Typhoon** and the spiralling **Calypso Coaster**, kids' playground, cafés, gift shops, arcades and volleyball, plus the wonderful **Splash Attack** adventure, a water activity maze culminating in a 1,000-gallon (4,550-litre) bucket dump on the unwary! Adventure Island is open from mid-February to late October (weekends only February to March and September to October) 10am–5pm (later in high season) and a combined Busch Gardens ticket costs $61.95 for adults and $52.95 for 3–9s.

Well, that's the full low-down on all the main theme parks now, but there are still plenty of other attractions to discover…

7 The Other Attractions

(or, One Giant Leap for Tourist Kind)

If you think you have seen everything Orlando has to offer by simply sticking to the theme parks, in the words of the song, 'You ain't seen nothin' yet'. It would be relatively easy to add the Kennedy Space Center to Chapter 6 because, although it's not strictly a theme park, it is adding new attractions all the time and is fast becoming a full day's excursion from Orlando to the east or 'space' coast.

Silver Springs and Historic Bok Sanctuary will give you a taste of the more natural things Florida has to offer. The Kissimmee attraction Splendid China provides a completely different park experience, as does the mind-boggling Gatorland, with its alligators, crocs and gator shows (great value, too), and the one-off family centres like WonderWorks, the Orlando Science Center and Ripley's Believe It Or Not.

For more individual attractions, you have the unique aviation experience of Fantasy of Flight, the hair-raising haunted house walk-through of Skull Kingdom plus a magnificent array of water fun parks.

The choice is yours, but it is an immense selection. Let's start here with One Giant Leap for Mankind.

Kennedy Space Center

The recent change to a fully ticketed entrance fee is a reflection of the massive amount of new development that has taken place at the home of NASA's space programme. More than $120 million has been spent on revamping the Kennedy Space Center's Visitor Complex in the last few years and, while it was always a great visit in the past, now it is simply unmissable, in my opinion, for its hugely imaginative depiction of the past, present and future of space exploration. The KSC also now owns the neighbouring Astronaut Hall of Fame, and a new Maximum Access Pass provides entry to that as well.

There are five continually running shows or exhibitions, four static showcases, a kids' play area (and a new show designed specifically for them), an art gallery, the Astronaut Encounter, two splendid IMAX films and a full bus tour of the Space Center, which adds up to great value for the entrance fee.

You enter through the futuristic ticket plaza and can spend several hours wandering around the exhibits and presentations of the 70-acre (28-ha) complex itself.

Robot Scouts is a walk-through display-and-show in the company of Starquester 2000, your robot host

Kennedy Space Center

ORLANDO'S OTHER ATTRACTIONS

A	Winter Park	T	Horse World Riding Stables
B	Aquatic Wonders Boat Tours	U	Pirates Dinner Adventure
C	Boggy Creek Airboat Rides	V	TD Waterhouse Center
D	Port Canaveral	W	Citrus Bowl Stadium
E	Leu Gardens	X	Osceola County Stadium
F	Flying Tigers Warbird Museum	Y	Central Florida Zoo
G	Green Meadows Petting Farm	Z	Sak Comedy Lab
H	Sanford-Rivership Romance	A1	Sleuth's Mystery Dinner Shows
I	WonderWorks	B1	Arabian Nights
J	Trainland Inc	C1	Florida Eco-Safaris
K	Disney's Wilderness Preserve	D1	Orlando Science Center
L	Marriott's Orlando World Center	E1	Orange County History Center
M	West Orange Trail Bikes	F1	Lake Eola
N	Kissimmee Rodeo	G1	Medieval Times
O	Richard Petty Driving Experience	H1	Hard Rock Vault/Titanic Exhibition
P	Black Hammock Fish Camp	J1	Skull Kingdom
Q	Dave's Ski School	K1	WayFun Kayak Adventures
R	Dolly Parton's Dixie Stampede	L1	Sanford Museum
S	Grand Cypress Equestrian Center	M1	Soulfire Theatre Dinner Experience

who will explain the history of NASA's unmanned space probes in a surprising and often amusing style. Next door, the **Quest for Life** film – narrated by *Deep Space Nine* star Avery Brooks – provides another illuminating view in the Universe Theater. Head on out and see some of the hardware of space flight in the completely revamped **Rocket Garden**, which has a kids' water fountain and an Apollo space capsule gantry, to give you the feel of that last earthbound walk before the astronauts boarded the *Saturn V* rocket. Free guided tours are given twice a day. And don't forget to stop by the **Astronaut Memorial**, a stark, sombre but very moving tribute to the men and women who have died in advancing the space programme. **Shuttle Explorer** allows you to inspect a full-size replica space shuttle, while the **Launch Status Center** displays actual flight hardware, plus live mission briefings (once the programme is active again following the tragedy of the *Columbia*). Free walking tours are available several times a day.

Early Space Exploration is a clever and coherent walk-through trip into the recent past of the space programme, including the *Hall of Discovery*, the *Mercury Mission Control Room* – the original consoles from America's first manned space flights – and the *Hall of History*. The futuristic **Exploration in the New Millennium** exhibit provides more appeal for youngsters, with a fun educational element from the spaceship-like *Exploring Gallery*, the *Mars Rock* exhibit and a series of interactive panels. New in 2001 was the kid-friendly **Mad Mission To Mars 2025** show, a mix of educational messages and pure fun theatricals, with lots of special effects, audience participation and even its own hip-hop song, The *Newton Rap*. Children aged 8 and up should have a laugh or two here.

Also here is **Nature and Technology** (which showcases the unique balance the Center maintains with the local environment), the **Center for Space Education** (an interactive learning and Teacher Resource Center), the **Space Walk of Honor**, and **NASA Art Gallery** (space exhibits and artwork).

Perhaps the most innovative feature, though, is the **Astronaut Encounter**, with personal briefings, Q&A sessions, video footage and anecdotes from various veterans of the Mercury, Gemini and Apollo programmes, plus several space shuttle astronauts. It is an amazingly insightful, inspirational and engrossing feature, and takes place up to three times a day at the Center Plaza. You can even take things a step further with the new **Dine with an Astronaut** opportunity (1pm, Mon–Sat only), whereby a small group gets to have lunch with the astronaut of the day. The featured astronaut will also give a special briefing adding extra insight into their space missions. Various packages are available, starting at $29.95 for adults and $19.95 for children aged 3–11, and tickets may be purchased online (see below) or by phone at 321 449 4444. Kids have their own playground, too, the **Children's Play Dome**, complete with a one-fifth scale space shuttle.

The air-conditioned **Coach Tour** (departures every 15 minutes), fully narrated throughout, makes two important stops in addition to driving around much of the working area of the Space Center, including the truly massive Vehicle Assembly Building. The first stop is the **LC39 Observation Gantry**, just 1 mile (1.6km) from shuttle launch pad 39A, a combination 4-storey observation deck and exhibition centre. The exhibits consist of a 10-minute film on the preparation of a shuttle for launch, models and videos of a launch countdown and touch-screen information on the shuttle programme.

Next is the awesome **Apollo/Saturn V Center**, one of the area's truly great exhibits, where you can easily spend 90 minutes. It highlights the Apollo programme and first moon landing with two deeply impressive theatrical presentations on the risks and triumphs, with an actual 363-ft (111-metre) *Saturn V* rocket and a hands-on gallery that brings the past, present and future of space exploration into sharp focus. It is also quite a humbling experience. A third stop for the **International Space Station Center** had been discontinued due to extra security considerations after September 11. You should allow a good 2–3 hours to do the tour justice. Additional tours are available at an extra $20 per person (adult or child).

Cape Canaveral: Then and Now is a 2-hour-plus in-depth journey (security considerations permitting) into the early days of space exploration around the older part of the facility. Highlights include the Air Force Space Museum, Mercury launch sites and Memorial, original astronaut training facility and several active launch pads, all of which are otherwise off-limits. The 90-minute **NASA Up Close** takes visitors along the astronaut's launch day routine, with a look at both launch pads, the VAB and the gigantic crawler transports.

Equally impressive are the IMAX cinemas – 55-ft (17-metre) screens that give the impression of sitting on top of the action. The 37-minute film **'The Dream Is Alive'** puts you inside a space shuttle mission, while the new 3-D **Space Station** (narrated by Tom Cruise) is a breathtaking slice of science fact, living with the crew of the International Space Station as it comes together, and affording a

heart-stopping look at the construction process. Both films are included in the admission price.

The Visitor Complex boasts an excellent **Space Shop**, four restaurants, including the full-service **Mila's**, and three snack counters. Even the Apollo/Saturn V Center has its own café where you can sit and marvel at it all.

Owners Delaware North Parks Services have lavished a fortune on upgrading the Center and, for my money, it's an essential experience for all but pre-school children.

Getting there: for the Kennedy Space Center, take the Beeline Expressway out of Orlando (Route 528, and it's a toll road, remember) for about 45 minutes, then bear left on the SR 407 (Don't follow the signs to Cape Canaveral or Cocoa Beach at this point) and turn right at the T-junction on to SR 405. The Space Center's Visitor Center is located 6 miles (10km) along SR 405 on the right-hand side. Opening hours are 9am to dusk every day except Christmas Day, and it is busiest around lunchtime.

Admission to the complex is $28 for adults and $18 for children 3–11, including the Bus Tour and IMAX films. The new Maximum Access Pass ($33 adults, $23 children) adds admission to the Astronaut Hall of Fame. Parking is free. It is open daily (but not on shuttle launch days – call 321 449 4444 to check when those are) from 9am and the first tours and IMAX presentations start at 9.30am, while the final tour of the day is 2 hours before dark. For more details, log on to their website at www.kennedyspacecenter.com. Total attraction rating: AAAAA.

The greatest thrill of all is watching an actual **shuttle launch**, of which there are six or seven a year. You can call the number above for information and Launch Transportation Tickets to a viewing area just 6 miles (10 km) from the

7

BRIT TIP: Reader Les Watson advises: 'Head to Port Canaveral, and there is a recreation area called Jetty Park. It has a wooden jetty about 100yd (100 metres) long brilliant for watching Shuttle launches. What an experience.'

launch pad or buy them online via the Space Center's website. Adult tickets cost $45.50 (33.50 for children), including admission to the Visitor Complex, or $15 a head for the launch-viewing site only. However, in the event of a launch cancellation, there are NO refunds, and the traffic in the area is usually humongous, taking anything up to 3 hours to get here from Orlando. Alternatively, prime viewing sites are available outside the Space Center along Highway 1 in Titusville and Highway A1A through Cape Canaveral and Cocoa Beach. To be on hand for a shuttle launch is certainly an awe-inspiring experience.

Astronaut Hall of Fame

While the Space Center tells you primarily about the machinery of putting men and women in space, the Astronaut Hall of Fame (on SR 405, just before the main entrance to the KSC) gives you the low-down on the people involved. This museum to the space programme houses fascinating memorabilia, interactive exhibits and engaging explanations of the people behind the spacesuits. A chronologically coherent approach divides the Hall of Fame into six main sections. The **Entry Experience** introduces the visions of space flight, with an 8-minute video of the astronauts as modern explorers, and leads into **Race to the Moon**, the stories of the Mercury, Gemini and Apollo missions. The **New Frontier** opens the way for Skylab and shuttle missions, adjacent to the **Astronaut Hall of Fame**, the museum's heart and soul. **Space Explorers Today and Tomorrow** includes an audio-visual experience aboard a replica shuttle, before introducing the hands-on **Astronaut Adventure** with its working models, G-force and flight simulators (a cabin that does six 360-degree rolls!), space-walk 'chairs', moon exploration, interactive computers and Mars Mission experience.

Admission is now part of the Maximum Access Pass for the Kennedy Space Center (see page 183). There is a gift shop and refreshments are provided by the **Cosmic Café**. If you enjoyed the KSC, try to spend a couple of hours here. AAAA.

Cypress Gardens

(Closed 2003)
Turning from the futuristic to the more natural, it is sad to report Florida's oldest 'theme park', Cypress Gardens in Winter Haven, shut its gates, probably permanently, in 2003. The more than 200 acres (80ha) of immaculate botanical gardens, flower festivals, water-ski shows and good ol' southern hospitality, not to mention animal exhibits, mini water park and boat

Chalet Suzanne in Lake Wales

View of the top of the Singing Tower

rides, look to have lost the struggle with Disney and Co and given in to the economics of falling attendances, to the detriment of the local scene, tourist and otherwise. At the time of writing, there was a local campaign to get the State to put together a rescue package, but it seemed unlikely. For the latest on the salvage bid, look up www.friendsofcypressgardens.org.

Historic Bok Sanctuary

For those wishing to experience the genuine peace, tranquillity and floral ambience of Florida, there is no better recommendation than this national monument and natural garden centre at Lake Wales, 50 miles (80km) to the south-west of Orlando. With one of the most extraordinary attractions in the state – the majestic 205-ft (62.5-metre) pink-and-grey marble Carillon tower – set in 250 acres (101ha) of unique parkland, this is a feast for the eyes and soul.

The centrepiece is the **Singing Tower**, the 1920s-built carillon that still gives recitals every day at 3pm. A carillon is the largest musical instrument of them all, a series of cast bronze bells which are played by a keyboard, or clavier. There are only around 400 in the world, and Bok Sanctuary's version consists of 60 bells (crafted in Loughborough, England) ranging from 16lb (7.2kg) to nearly 12 tons. The park has its own resident player, or carilloneur, and his daily recital is an undoubted highlight. The tower is also a work of art, consisting of a neo-Gothic and art deco mix crafted from coquina stone and marble, with some stunning sculptural elements at various stages. It is wonderfully photogenic and, on a cloudless day, the combination of sight and sound is utterly captivating.

Around the tower is a 15-ft (4.5-metre) wide moat, a long pond and a series of semi-formal gardens. The view, from the highest point on peninsular Florida (all of 298ft/90 metres above sea level), is both uncluttered and inspiring, and retains an inherent peace and solitude which persuaded founder and philanthropist Edward W Bok to grant the estate to the local people almost 75 years ago.

The **gardens** themselves provide a wildlife observatory (the Window by the Pond, where you can see up to 126 species of birds, plus reptiles, butterflies, local squirrels, turtles, rabbits and armadillos, as well as the endangered gopher tortoise), nature trails, an endangered plant exhibit,

Pinewood Estate exterior

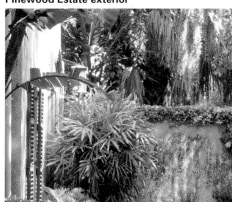

butterfly and woodland gardens, and pine forests. The acres of ferns, palms, oaks and pines create a surprisingly lush backdrop for the spectacular seasonal bursts of azaleas, camellias, magnolias and other flowering shrubs.

The award-winning **Education and Visitor Center** illustrates the story of Edward W Bok (don't miss the orientation film about him and his impact on American society), his vision for the gardens, the carillon and tower architecture (with a close-up look at the bells themselves), the landscape design and the ecology of Florida. The **Carillon Café** then adds a pleasant opportunity to grab a light lunch and other refreshments (in the open air when it's not too hot – and there always seems to be a pleasant breeze up here), while the **Tower & Garden Gift Shop** offers some unique gift and souvenir items.

For an additional fee ($5 for adults, $4 for seniors and $3 for 5–12s; daily at 11am and 1.30pm), you can tour the **Pinewood Estate**, one of the finest examples of Mediterranean revival architecture in Florida. This 20-room mansion was built as a winter retreat for a Pennsylvania steel tycoon in the early 1930s, and has been lovingly maintained to demonstrate a real slice of period opulence.

With this genuine sanctuary being situated somewhat off the beaten track yet an easy drive from Orlando (around 45–50 minutes), it makes for a thoroughly worthwhile day out with some of the other attractions of Lake Wales.

Getting there: Historic Bok Sanctuary can be found off US Highway 27 on Burns Avenue. Take I-4 west to Exit 55, then head south on US 27 for 25 miles (40km), turn left on Mountain Lake Cutoff Road (two traffic lights past Eagle Ridge Mall) and follow the signs.

Admission is $6 for adults, $2 for 5–12s (under 5 free), apart from occasional specially-ticketed events (mainly carillon festivals and recitals) and it is open 8am–6pm daily (last entry at 5pm), With the demise of Cypress Gardens and its 300 weddings a year, this is also an extremely attractive wedding venue. Call 863 676 1408 for more info, or visit www.boktower.org. AAAA.

High on the list of other must-see places around here is **Chalet Suzanne**, a wonderfully eclectic yet classy little country inn and restaurant, quietly famous throughout Florida. This family-run delight (since 1931) is a 100-acre (40.5-ha) estate featuring 30 individual and quite striking guest rooms, a tropical sunken wedding garden, a pottery and antique store, swimming pool and private lake, plus, wait for it, a soup cannery which sent its produce to the moon! In fact, Chalet Suzanne is such a sought-after hideaway, it has its own airstrip.

Its other claim to fame is its restaurant – voted one of Florida's Top 20 for more than 30 years, and a truly amazing venue before you even get to the menu. Consisting of various cast-off buildings (a wing of stable here, a chicken house there) that have been lovingly restored and melded together, it provides a series of dining rooms with 14 different levels!

Eclectic is something of an understatement. The food is another highlight, gourmet cuisine of the highest order but with a semi-set menu which barely changes year by year. Specialities include broiled grapefruit, baked sugar cured ham, Chicken Suzanne, and their own signature soup, Romaine Soup – such a favourite of *Apollo 15* lunar module pilot James Irwin, he persuaded NASA to take it on the mission with them, hence it became known as Moon Soup! The traditional set luncheon is $19 a head ($14 for under 12s), while dinner varies from $59–79 ($19 for under 12s), depending on your main course choice (which includes filet mignon, lobster and crab thermidor). But, even if you don't stop to eat, or stay in one of their remarkable Swiss-style cottage rooms (which go from $169–229 per night, plus tax), it is worthwhile visiting to experience the unique charm and style, learn the family story of the owning Hinshaws – and have a tour of that truly one-off soup cannery! Apart from anything else, a gift pack here is one of the most original souvenirs you will ever bring back from Florida. Call 863 676 6011 to book (always essential) or visit www.chaletsuzanne.com.

Getting there: Chalet Suzanne can be found just outside Lake Wales, off Highway 27 on Chalet Suzanne Road.

Head into the quaint town of **Lake Wales** and you will discover Spook Hill (where cars mysteriously roll uphill!), Grove House Visitor Center (home of Florida's natural fruit juice products – as fresh as it gets) and the quaint Museum & Cultural Center (set in a restored 1928 Atlantic Coast Line railroad station), as well as the world's sky-diving capital (from Lake Wales Airport – every kind of parachuting known to man). For more information, call Lake Wales Chamber of Commerce on 863 676 3445 or visit www.lakewaleschamber.com.

Silver Springs

Continuing the theme of natural attractions, we have Silver Springs, just under 2 hours' drive to the north of Orlando. This peaceful 350-acre (142-ha) nature park (don't worry, you won't have to walk round all of it) surrounds the headwaters of the crystal-clear Silver River. Glass-bottomed boats take you to watch the artesian springs (the largest in the world) that bubble up here, along with plenty of wildlife. Expect

BRIT TIP: Silver Springs and Wild Waters are both busy at the weekends, but you shouldn't encounter many queues here during the rest of the week.

close encounters with alligators, turtles, raccoons and lots of waterfowl, while the park also contains a collection of more exotic animals, like bears, panthers, giraffes, camels and zebras that can be viewed from either land or water.

Four animal shows, an alligator and crocodile encounter, the world's largest bear exhibit, a petting zoo, a kids' adventure playground and a white alligator exhibit complete the attractions. To ruin a few more illusions of the film industry, this was the setting for the 1930s' and 1940s' *Tarzan* films starring Johnny Weissmuller. And, once you have absorbed the timeless tropical nature of the landscape, you will understand why they decided to save on the cost of shipping the film crew to Africa.

The park's main attraction (dating back to 1878) is the **Glass-bottomed Boat Ride**, a 20-minute tour which goes down well with all the family and gives a first-class view of the seven different springs and a host of water life. Similarly, the **Lost River Voyage** is another 20-minute boat trip down one of the unspoilt stretches of the Silver River, including a visit to the park's animal hospital where the local park ranger introduces you to all his current charges. The third boat trip, the **Jungle Cruise**, is a water safari, where animals from six continents, including giraffes, ostriches and antelope, are arranged in natural settings along the riverbanks.

As an alternative to messing about on the river, the **Jeep Safari** is a 15-minute ride in the back of an

7

open trailer through a natural forest habitat, home to more animals from other corners of the world, such as tapirs, marmosets, antelope and vultures (plus a drive-through alligator pond!). Then there are the three **Ross Allen Island Animal Shows,** each one lasting 15 minutes and featuring an entertaining – and occasionally hair-raising – look at the worlds of reptiles, birds (including comical parrots, macaws and cockatoos) and creepy crawlies. The hair-raising part occurs only if you are the unlucky victim chosen to display a large tarantula, giant cockroach or scorpion.

As you exit the animal shows take time to wander round **Big Gator Lagoon** and the **Crocodile Encounter** in a cypress swamp habitat, viewed from a raised boardwalk. See the largest American crocodile in captivity, the 16-ft (5-metre), 2,000-lb (900-kg) Sobek, as well as a collection of alligators, turtles and Galapagos tortoises. The **Florida Natives** attraction features a collection of snakes, turtles, spiders, otters and other denizens of the state. The **Botanical Gardens** then provide a peaceful haven to sit and watch the world go by for a while.

Other large-scale exhibits are the **World of Bears,** an educational presentation including conservation information in a 2-acre (0.8-ha) spread devoted to bears of all kinds (including the largest of its type in the world), from grizzly to spectacled and black bears, and the **Panther Prowl,** with a unique look at the endangered Florida panther and Western cougar. Both of these have educational presentations on their welfare several times daily.

Birds of Prey is a 30-minute show in the Silver River Showcase arena, highlighting the strengths, beauty and conservation issues of the park's collection of hawks, eagles, owls, falcons and vultures in a dramatic free-flight demonstration.

Silver Springs glass-bottomed boat

Children are not forgotten, either. **The Kids Ahoy!** playland, with its centrepiece riverboat featuring slides, rides, an air bounce, ball crawl, 3-D net maze, carousel, bumper boats and games, and **Doolittle's Petting Zoo,** with deer and goats, are big draws for the young 'uns.

The usual collection of shops and eateries are fairly ordinary here, in contrast to the slick appeal of Orlando's parks, although the **Deli** offers some pleasant sandwich alternatives and the **Springside Restaurant** is above average. In all, you would probably want to spend a good half day here, with the possibility of a few hours in the neighbouring 9-acre (4-ha) water park of **Wild Waters,** which offers slides like the Twin Twister, a pair of 60-ft (18-metre) high flumes, the free-fall Thunderbolt, the twin-tunnelled Tornado, the 220-ft (67-metre) Silver Bullet and the helter-skelter Osceola's Revenge, as well as a 400-ft (122-metre) tube ride on the turbo-charged Hurricane, a huge wave pool, and various kid-sized fun in Cool Kids Cove and Caribbean Sprayground.

Getting there: Silver Springs is located on SR 40 just through the town of Ocala, 72 miles (116km) to the north of Orlando. Take the Florida Turnpike north (it's a toll road, remember) until it turns into I-75 and, 28 miles (45km) further north, you turn off and head east on SR 40. Another 10 miles (16km) brings you to Silver Springs, just past the Wild Waters water park on your right.

Admission fees are $32.99 for adults, $29.99 for seniors (55+) and $23.99 for children under 4ft (122cm) tall (under 3s free). A joint ticket (Silver Springs and Wild Waters) is $36.99 and $27.99. Parking is $5. Open 10am–5pm, 7 days a week. Visit www.silversprings.com for more info or call 352 236 2121. AAAA.

Splendid China

New in 1994 and still expanding and modifying its various displays and exhibits, Splendid China is unique to central Florida and a completely different type of attraction that has yet to be discovered by the masses. You won't find rides and other flights of fancy, but you will be taken on a fascinating journey through one of the biggest and most mysterious countries in the world.

This 76-acre (30-ha) park offers a range of intricate, miniaturised features like the Great Wall of China, the Forbidden City and the Stone Forest, some fascinating full-size exhibits, thrilling acrobats and martial arts experts and, naturally enough, some great food. There is a play area for young children but, realistically, this will not hold their attention for long and, in summer, there is little escape from the relentless heat. But where it scores impressively is in its amazing eye for detail, its air of authenticity (Chinese craftsmen were brought in to hand-build every miniature) and its peaceful atmosphere – quite an achievement in the tourist bustle of Orlando!

You need at least 4 hours, to take in all the different shows and attractions. Here's how its 10,000-mile (16,100km) journey through 5,000 years of history works. The four elements are:

The exhibits: more than 60 painstakingly recreated scale models of China's greatest buildings, statues and landmarks. The **Great Wall** is one of the most striking, at half a mile (almost 1km) long and up to 5½ ft (almost 2 metres) high. It is constructed of more than 6 million tiny bricks, all faithfully put into place by hand. Other highlights include Beijing's **Imperial Palace and Forbidden City**, the 26-storey **Grand Buddha of Leshan** (reduced to a 'mere' 36ft/11 metres tall), and the **Mausoleum of Genghis Khan**. The stairs by the side of the **Mausoleum of Dr Sun Yat Sen** afford a wonderful high-rise overview of the park, while the famous **Terracotta Warriors** exhibit offers a chance to get in the air-conditioned cool. Splendid China is three-quarters the size of the *Magic Kingdom Park*, so it still demands a fair amount of leg work to take it all in.

The shows: There is one main centre for the performing arts here, which showcases the talents of some

7

Splendid China

top musicians, artists, acrobats and martial arts exponents, plus three other venues which can be used when the park is (occasionally) busy (first show each day at 1.30pm). The **Golden Peacock Theater** is actually right outside the main turnstile entrance, inside the Suzhou Gardens. During the day, dance and folk costume shows are presented, and, in the evening (not Mondays), it features the 90-minute spectacular *Mysterious Kingdom of the Orient*, which showcases the amazing talents of some 50 dancers, acrobats and martial artists in magnificent costumes. The **Temple of Light Theatre, Pagoda Gardens**, and **Imperial Bell Theatre** all see occasional use for music in the park.

You need to get your entry ticket validated if you leave the park early and want to return for the *Mysterious Kingdom* show, or you can pay the $14.95 for the show on its own, which includes a buffet-style meal either before or after the show.

The restaurants: the park sets great store by its food, whether it be in its sumptuous 5-star restaurant or its cafeteria-style buffet. The jewel in the crown is the elegant **Suzhou Pearl Restaurant** for full-service, gourmet cuisine (park entry not required here), while more budget-priced is the **Seven Flavors**, a cafeteria-style diner offering American as well as Chinese dishes.

The shops: unlike the other theme parks, Splendid China's shopping opportunities are all located in the Chinatown front area of the park, the **Suzhou Gardens**, which is open without park admission. The 10 gift shops are also one up on their counterparts by stocking a more upmarket and distinctive range of goods, from Bonsai trees to furniture, jewellery to T-shirts, silk and satin clothing to children's toys, and antique curios to contemporary artefacts. You can also watch Chinese artisans at work here.

The mixture of Chinese and Floridian staff adds to the friendly atmosphere of the park, but ultimately it is a difficult concept to describe so it's best to see it for yourself.

Getting there: Splendid China is located at the western end of the main tourist drag of Highway 192, just 3 miles (5km) west of its junction with I-4, off the main road opposite the big Key W Kool Restaurant, on Splendid China Boulevard.

Admission is $28.88 for adults and $18.18 for children (5–12; under 5s free). You can also take a highly recommended guided tour for an extra $9/person. Opening hours are 9.30am–6pm, 7 days a week and parking is free. AAAA.

Gatorland

For another taste of the 'real' Florida, this is as authentic as it gets when it comes to the wildlife, and consequently it is popular with children of all ages. When the wildlife consists of several thousand menacing alligators and crocodiles in various natural habitats and four fascinating shows, you know you're in for a different experience. 'The Alligator Capital of the World' was founded in 1949 and is still family-owned, hence it possesses a home-spun charm and naturalism which few of its big-money competitors can match.

Start by taking the 15-minute **Gatorland Express** railway around the park to get an idea of its

> BRIT TIP: If you have an evening flight home, Gatorland is handy to visit on your final day. Conveniently located for the airport, it is the ideal place to soak up half a day.

BRIT TIP: If you are at Gatorland first thing, take the Swamp Walk straight away. There will be far more wildlife activity then and the peaceful ambience is quite invigorating.

110-acre (45-ha) expanse. This costs an extra $1 but is good for multiple rides, is fully narrated (usually in amusing style) and is especially fun for kids. You also get a good look at the native Florida animal habitat, which features whitetail deer, wild turkey and quail. Wander through the natural beauty of the 2,000ft-(610-metre) long **Swamp Walk**, as well as the **Alligator Breeding Marsh Walkway**, with its 3-storey observation tower, and get a close-up view of these great reptiles, who seem to hang around the walkway in the hope someone might 'drop in' for lunch.

Breeding pens, baby alligator nurseries and rearing ponds are also situated throughout the park to provide an idea of the growth cycle of the Florida gator and enhance the overall feeling that it is the visitor behind bars here, not the animals. Many of the small-scale attractions have been designed with kids in mind and there is plenty to keep even the youngest amused, notably at **Lilly's Pad**, an imaginative water playground guaranteed to get them good and wet (swimming costumes advisable). **Allie's Barnyard** is the petting zoo, while you can feed some friendly lorikeets at the **Birds of Florida**. Other animals on view include bats, iguanas, turtles, turkey vultures, tortoises, snakes, flamingos, emus, a Florida bear and deer.

However, the gators and crocs are the main attraction and it is the three shows which are the real draw

(although you will never find yourself on the end of a queue here). The 800-seat **Wrestling Stadium** sets the scene for some real Cracker-style feats (a Cracker is the local term for a Florida cowboy) as Gatorland's resident 'wranglers' catch themselves a 7–8ft-(2–3-metre) long gator and proceed to point out the animal's various survival features, with the aid of some daredevil stunts that will have you questioning the cowboys' sanity.

The **Gator Jumparoo** is another eye-opening spectacle as some of the park's biggest creatures use their tails to 'jump' out of the water and be hand-fed tasty morsels, like whole chickens! Gatorland has been working on different aspects of this show to provide new looks at the animals, and even some audience participation! **Jungle Crocs of the World** features some of the deadliest animals of Egypt, Australia and Cuba, with authentic lairs and brilliant presentation, while the show element has its scare-raising moments as the highly knowledgeable guides enter the pens to tell you all about the inhabitants. The revamped **Upclose Animal Encounters** is another entertaining and highly amusing showcase of various creatures, from the obvious snakes to less obvious scorpions and cockroaches. Brave children can provide some great photo opportunities here!

Obviously, face-to-face encounters with the park's living dinosaurs are not everyone's cup of tea, but it's an experience you're unlikely to repeat anywhere else. In addition, you can dine on smoked alligator ribs and deep-fried gator nuggets (as well as burgers and hot dogs) at **Pearl's Smokehouse**, with excellent kids' meals at $3.99.

The park is also home to hundreds of nesting herons and egrets, providing a fascinating close-up of the nests from March to

7

August. Gatorland is actually Central Florida's largest wading bird sanctuary and it adds an extraordinary ecological and environmental aspect to this very user-friendly park.

A recent venture is Gatorland's **Cypress Glades Adventure Tours**, providing more hands-on wildlife opportunities and sightseeing, including *Trainer for a Day* (must be at least 12 and book at least a day in advance; wear 'working' clothes – nothing baggy; $190 per person) and *Gator Egg Collecting* (12 and up, 'working' clothes, June and July only; $49 per person).

Getting there: Gatorland is located on the South Orange Blossom Trail, 2 miles (3km) south of its junction with the Central Florida Greeneway and 3 miles (5km) north of Highway 192.

Admission: Gatorland also scores on its great value for money, with adult tickets at $19.95 children 3–12, $9.95. There is also a highly worthwhile $6 Walkabout Tour several times a day, offering more insight into the park's history and behind-the-scenes areas, including an encounter with a baby gator. Hours are 9am–dusk and parking is free. Visit www.gatorland.com for more info. AAAA.

Fantasy of Flight

Another wonderful and fresh alternative on the Central Florida scene is this aviation museum attraction which is an absolute must, even for anyone not usually interested in the history of flight or the glamour of the Golden Age of flying. Fantasy of Flight is a 5-part adventure featuring the world's largest private collection of vintage aircraft.

You start by entering the **History of Flight**, a series of expertly recreated 'immersion experiences' into memorable moments in aviation history. The entrance alone is eye-opening – you enter the fuselage of a DC-3 Dakota as if for a parachute drop, and step out into a moonlit night. Then you visit set-pieces like a dogfight over the trenches in World War One and a bomber mission with a Flying Fortress in World War Two. Audio-visual effects and film clips enhance the experience and give everything an awe-inspiring feeling of authenticity.

You exit into the **Vintage Aircraft** displays in two huge hangers, with the exhibits ranging from a replica Wright Flyer, to a Ford Tri-Motor, a Mk-XVI Spitfire and the world's only fully working Short Sunderland

A Gatorland denzien

Fantasy of Flight main hangar

flying boat. From the museum's collection of 40 or so vintage planes, one is selected each day as the **Aircraft of the Day**, with a pilot holding a question-and-answer session about that plane before performing an aerial demonstration over Fantasy of Flight. Two **Guided Tours** are given each day, one taking visitors into the Backlot and the other visiting the Restoration Shop, highlighting what it takes to restore and maintain these magnificent machines. Finally, **Fightertown** features eight realistic fighter simulators that take you through a World War Two aerial battle. You get a pre-flight briefing on how to handle your 'plane' (a Vought Corsair), and then climb into the totally enclosed cockpit to do battle with the Japanese Air Force. It's difficult, absorbing, fun and totally addictive.

The whole experience is crafted in 1930s' art deco style, including a full-service diner (the excellent **Compass Rose**) and original gift shop. There is strong British appeal, too, with the war portrayals and exhibits.

Getting there: just 25 minutes down I-4 towards Tampa (take Exit 44, Polk City, go north on SR 559 for half a mile, then turn left into the main entrance.

Admission: $24.95 for adults, $22.95 for seniors (60+) and $13.95 for kids 5–12 (under 5s free). It is open 9am–5pm and parking is free.

Additionally, you can take a vintage **biplane ride** here with Waldo Wright's Flying service in an open-cockpit 1929 New Standard D-25 for $49/person (up to 4 passengers a time) or try the Fantasy of Flight 3-hour **balloon ride** experience for $160 (up to 3 passengers). Both operate seasonally and reservations are required.

Fantasy of Flight is the brainchild of American entrepreneur and aviation whiz Kermit Weeks and I have yet to encounter an attraction put together with more genuine affection. In fact, it is as much a work of art as a tourist attraction, and the masses have yet to discover it, too. For more info, call 863 984 3500 or visit www.fantasyofflight.com. AAAA.

International Drive Area

The long tourist corridor of I-Drive continues to be a fast-developing source of hotels, restaurants, shopping and, more importantly, fun. It now has its own development council, advertising 'Orlando's Most Dynamic Destination', to emphasise its attractions. The I-Ride trolley brings it all together in transport terms and the website www.InternationalDriveOrlando.com highlights all the options. There is an Official Visitors Guide with an I-Ride map and valuable money-off coupons (which they will mail to the UK), and a freephone number – 1-866 2437 483 – to steer people in the right direction. Here's a look at the top attractions (see also chapters 9 and 11 – Orlando By Night and Shopping – to complete the picture):

Ripley's Believe It Or Not

You can't miss this particular attraction, next to The Mercado shopping village on I-Drive, as its extraordinary tilted appearance makes it seem as though it was designed by an architect with an aversion to the horizontal. However, once inside you soon get back on the level and, for an hour or two, you can wander through this museum dedicated to the weird and wonderful.

Robert L Ripley was an eccentric and energetic explorer and collector who, for 40 years, travelled the world in his bid to assemble a collection of the greatest oddities known to man. The Orlando branch of this chain features 8,900sq ft (830sq metres) of displays, including authentic artefacts, video presentations, illusions, interactive exhibits and music. The elaborate re-creation of an Egyptian tomb showcases a mummy and three rare mummified animals, while the Primitive Gallery contains artefacts from tribal societies around the world (some quite gruesome). Human and Animal Oddities, Big and Little galleries, Illusions and Dinosaurs all boast some recent up-dates and extra interactive elements.

The collection of miniatures includes the world's smallest violin and a single grain of rice hand-painted with a tropical sunset. Larger-scale exhibits include a portion of the Berlin Wall, a two-thirds scale 1907 Rolls Royce built entirely out of matchsticks and a version of the *Mona Lisa* textured completely from toast! **Admission:** $15.95 for adults and $10.95 for 4–12s and it is open 9am–1am daily (last ticket sold at midnight). AAA.

> BRIT TIP: Ripley's, Hard Rock Vault and WonderWorks are all handy retreats to keep in mind for places to visit on the occasional rainy day.

Titanic

A new attraction in 1999 inside The Mercado was **Titanic - The Exhibition**, the first permanent exhibit to the great maritime disaster of 1912. With a mixture of genuine artefacts, full-scale re-creations of the ship's interior, several clever scene-setting presentations, film memorabilia from *Titanic* and *A Night to Remember*, plus live interpretations by storytellers in period costume, you will see, hear and feel just about everything there is to know about the *Titanic* and her tragic fate. The full experience takes at least an hour. Entry is $16.95 for adults and $11.95 for 6–12s (5 and under free). It is open 10am–8pm daily (first guided tour at 10.30am). Attraction rating: AAAA.

Hard Rock Vault

Newly opened (in December 2002), this is a wonderfully creative interactive rock 'n roll 'Hall of fame' type museum from the worldwide and innovative restaurant chain. After the success of their Hard Rock Live venue at Universal's CityWalk and the Hard Rock Hotel, this is another exercise in rock chic, with 17,000sq ft (1,580sq metres) of dedicated space paying homage to the past and present of rock 'n roll. There are both guided and self-guided tours through a 'living timeline', or chronological review, of music and its effect on society, era by era, from the 1950s on.

The Vault also features some of the most prized pieces from the Hard Rock collection from all over the world (more than 100 HR Cafés in more than 40 countries), as well as material which has never been seen before. The highlight is the guided Total Immersion Tour through five galleries of recreated period history, from The Beatles and Rolling Stones (The Light and the Dark) to

Punk Rock (The Back Alley), and Elvis (The King's Chamber) to the Grateful Dead (The Psychedelic Meltdown). The stories unfold through video, artefacts, music and instruments, while the tour guides play a highly individual and distinctive part in bringing it all to life. There is a listening room, with a show of its own (The Sound Asylum), a snack bar and an eye-catching Hard Rock merchandise shop. Spend time wandering around The Hub and you will come across showcases of such rock luminaries as Eric Clapton (whose guitar, donated to the London Hard Rock, actually began the whole memorabilia phenomenon back in the 1970s), The Beach Boys, Led Zeppelin and Bruce Springsteen, plus the Blues Masters who originated the whole rock idiom. There are almost 1,000 original items on show, including more than 40 stars' guitars, and rock devotees will want to spend at least 2 hours here.

Admission: $14.99 for adults and $9.99 for children aged 5+ (under 5s free). For more info, visit www.hardrock.com. Call 407 445 7625 or visit the website for more details. AAAA.

Skull Kingdom

The walk-through haunted house idea takes on a new dimension here. Not content with a house, this is a full-blown castle on I-Drive (opposite Wet 'n Wild) dedicated to frights, horrors and grisly goings-on at every turn. The setting and lavishness of the Kingdom of the Skull Lord marks it out as way above average, and the combination of elaborate light and sound effects, robotics and the scream-inducingly brilliant live actors (who are kept suitably creepy by full-time make-up artists) provides a hair-raising experience. The shock tactics are

> BRIT TIP: Friday and Saturday evenings are peak periods for Skull Kingdom, with queues of up to 30 minutes.

state of the art, with the best elements of horror films and haunted houses well maintained over the 2-storey spread of mazes, caverns and other demonic challenges (watch out for the monster spit!).

The Haunted Gift Shop and Ghoulish Arcade Games await you at the end of your 20–30-minute (depending on how much you 'enjoy' the experience!) Skull Kingdom immersion.

Admission: it is open 6pm–11pm Mon–Thur, noon–midnight Fri–Sun, with extended hours in peak season, and costs $14.95 per person (www.skullkingdom.com). Go with a few friends, or have a drink or three first! TTTTT (not recommended for under 12s).

Fun Spot

Here is another choice for full-scale, family-sized fun, just off I-Drive on Del Verde Way (look for the 102-ft (31-metre) big wheel past the junction with Kirkman Road). With four different and highly challenging go-kart tracks, bumper cars and boats, four daring fairground-type rides (check out the Spyder and Paratrooper), an impressive 2-storey video arcade (one of the largest in Florida) and food court, plus five Kid Spot rides for the little ones, the 4.7-acre (2-ha) park promises several hours of fun.

Admission and parking are free, but you must buy tickets for the rides, which are $3 each (or $22 for eight). Go-karts require 2 tickets, while the other rides are a ticket

BRIT TIP: WonderWorks and Fun Spot are both open until midnight in high season, long after most theme parks are shut, meaning you can have a day at the park, then let the kids loose here for a while to really tire them out!

Ripley's Believe It Or Not

apiece. However, if you are planning on a visit of an hour or longer, their 'armband' tickets are better value. The Adult Armband (for ages 10+) includes all-day privileges on all Tracks and Rides for $29.95, while the Child Armband (2–9) allows all-day access to the 6 rides geared towards younger kids, for $9.95. The Rides Armband allows unlimited rides on the 13 Family and Thrill Rides for only $19.95. It is $6 for an all-day ticket to the Freeplay Arcade, which contains 37 classic arcade games and a spread of more than 100 token-driven games (some of them state-of-the-art). It opens 10am–midnight (high season), or 2pm–11pm Mon–Fri, 10am–midnight Sat and noon–11pm Sun in low season. Call 407 363 3867 or log on to www.fun-spot.com for more information. TTTT.

In a similar vein, **Magical Midway** on I-Drive (just north of Sand Lake Road) offers more go-karts, games, laser tag and thrill

Back Alley at Hard Rock Vault

rides (including 0–230ft/70 metres in 3 seconds on the Space Shot Tower!). The two elevated kart tracks (the double uphill corkscrew of *The Avalanche* – you must be at least 14 and 4ft 10in/146cm tall to drive and at least 4 and 3ft 6in/107cm to be a passenger – and the sharply banked *Alpine Jump*, for which you must be at least 10 and 4ft 6in/137cm to drive and at least 4 and 3ft 6in/107cm to be a passenger) are both highly challenging. And then there are bumper cars, a giant slide, Lazer Runner laser tag, bumper boats, four more fairground-type rides and a large arcade.

Admission: their $28.95 Play All Day ticket includes unlimited go-karts, other rides and two laser tag games; the $24.95 Play Pass is just unlimited go-karts and other rides for 3 hours; the $14.95 Midway Pass gives unlimited rides all day (but not go-karts); individual ride tickets are $6 (go-karts), $5 (Space Shot) and $3 (all other rides); Laser Tag is $3.95 per game. Parking is free and it is open daily from 10am–midnight. Call 407 370 5353 or visit www.magicalmidway.com. TTT½.

WonderWorks

I-Drive's most unmistakable landmark is the 'interactive entertainment centre' of **WonderWorks**, a 3-storey chamber of real family fun with a host of novel elements. Unmistakable? You

Skull Kingdom

bet – how many buildings do you know that are upside down? That's right, all of the 82-ft (25-metre) edifice is constructed from the roof up! The basic premise (working on the theory that every attraction has to have a story behind it) is that WonderWorks is a secret research facility into unexplained phenomena that got uprooted by a tornado experiment and dumped in topsy-turvy fashion in the heart of this busy tourist district (yeah, right!). Well, you have to give them full marks for imagination and, if the interior attractions aren't quite as entertaining as the exterior façade, there is still a lot here, especially for the 6–12 age group.

You enter through an 'inversion tunnel' that orientates you the same way round as the building (look out of the window to check!) and progress to chambers of entertaining and mildly educational hands-on experiences that demand several hours to explore fully. Without ever using the words 'science' or 'museum', WonderWorks steers you through five 'labs' of interactive activities, including the **Bermuda Triangle Corridor**, the **Mystery Lab** (experience earthquakes and hurricanes and see famous disasters on a bank of computer monitors), **Physical Challenge Lab** (virtual basketball, table tennis, hang-gliding

and even horse racing, a baseball test, health and lifestyle quizzes and the wonderfully creepy Shocker Chair, a high-voltage simulation that gives you the feeling of 2,000 jolts rather than volts – it's weird!), **Illusions Lab** (with the Bridge of Fire static electricity generator, a computer ageing process and 'elastic surgery', hall of mirrors and bubble table), plus the **WonderWorks Emporium** gift shop, souvenirs and **Mazzarella's Pizzeria**. A Lazer Tag game on the top floor adds even more appeal for youngsters.

On no account miss the two virtual roller-coasters, a pair of amazing enclosed 'pods' which let you design and ride your own coaster. If you have already been to *DisneyQuest*, this may seem tame, while it isn't as educational as the Orlando Science Center. WonderWorks offers a fun new dinner-show option, **The Outta Control Magic Show** (see Orlando By Night, page 248), with a good value combination ticket.

Admission: $16.95 for adults, $12.95 for seniors (55+) and children 4–11; $4.95 for the Lazer Tag; $17.95 and $14.95 for the Magic Show on its own; $31.95 and $25.95 for the WonderWorks/dinner-show combo; $19.95 and $15.95 for WonderWorks/Lazer Tag; and $32.95 and $26.95 for all three elements. Open 9am–midnight daily. Visit www.wonderworksonline.com for more info. AAA/TTT.

WonderWorks

Trainland Inc

The large-scale steam engine around the outside of the building (just south of the huge Race Rock restaurant) marks this out as a must for all train and model railway enthusiasts. New in 2001 and still developing, Trainland features a 4,000sq ft (370sq metre) G-gauge layout inside, beautifully crafted and with three main, highly elaborate sections – the Pennsylvania Backwoods, the Town, and the Industrial Area. The mountains, bridges, streets and buildings, coal mines, lakes, rivers and waterfalls have all been painstakingly hand-built from scratch, and some 8–14 trains are constantly on the go, with the longest track completing a mazy, 960-ft (293-metre) circuit of the whole premises. A scavenger hunt will keep children amused while they wander round, and birthday parties can also be held here (call 407 363 9002 for details).

The gift shop stocks a huge range of model trains, tracks and accessories and has a Thomas the Tank Engine play area for young 'uns. The purpose-built outdoor locomotive Lady Liberty (with two open-sided – and wheelchair accessible – passenger cars) on the narrow-gauge line is likely to be a magnet for children of the right age. The ¼-mile (400-metre) route around the museum lasts just 5 minutes, but a ticket is valid all day which means youngsters can ride as often as they like.

Admission: the museum itself costs $6.95 for adults, $5.95 seniors and $4.95 children, while the combination pass (museum and outdoor rides) is $8.95, $7.95 and $6.95. For the train ride alone, the fee is $3 for adults and seniors and $2 for children. Opening hours are 10am–6pm (noon–6pm, Sun), with extended opening at peak periods. For more info call 407 363 9002, or visit www.trainland.net. AAA.

Downtown Orlando

The last couple of years have seen a significant move towards regenerating the city centre – the 'downtown' area – with new offices, apartments, shops and restaurants. This has also brought several significant tourist developments.

And, because this is Orlando, there is no such thing as a simple museum or science centre. Everything must be all-singing, all-dancing just to compete. Hence, the **Orlando Science Center** is more than a mere museum and far more fun than the average science centre. Here, you get a series of hands-on experiences and habitats that entertain as well as inform, and school-age children in particular will get a lot from it.

The Science Center has nine main components, plus an inviting café, a night sky observatory and an IMAX cinema. **Natureworks** is an immersion-style exhibit creating a number of typical Florida habitats (with several shows like the *Circle of Life Game* and a series of hands-on field stations). **Science City** introduces fun ways to understand and use physical science and maths (including some mind-bending puzzles and challenges, notably in the Power Station), while the **Cosmic Tourist** offers a trip around our solar system with an amusing travel theme. **Bodyzone** provides some fascinating insights into the human body, with an interactive element called Measure Me which explores your size, strength, flexibility, agility and sensory abilities. A Healthy Lifestyles exhibit shows how bad habits like smoking affect a healthy body. Next door, **TechWorks** is a four-part adventure into light, imaginary landscapes, showbiz science and a micro-world of microscopic investigation.

For those a bit too young for the educational element, **KidsTown** has plenty of junior-sized fun and games for under 8s. You'll be amazed at how much they learn in the course of having fun. **DinoDigs: Mysteries Unearthed** was a gift from the Walt Disney Company of their former Dinosaur Jubilee exhibit in the DinoLand USA area of *Disney's Animal Kingdom*. It has been recreated in the OSC as a palaeontological excavation site, complete with eight full dinosaur skeleton replicas and a number of

> BRIT TIP: The CineDome film and laser show can operate until midnight on Friday and Saturday for a show independent of the Orlando Science Center.

genuine fossils. **Wired Science** was new in 2002, a series of networked multimedia information kiosks introduced by wacky characters, it illustrates basic scientific principles and supports other exhibits around the Center. The **Darden Adventure Theater** features science-themed musical comedy shows and demos, like PreHisto Rock (fun for all would-be palaeontologists) and the audience participation Science Spectrum.

In addition, the Center has two separate programmes in the **Dr Phillips CineDome**, a 310-seat cinema that practically surrounds its audience with large-format films, digital planetarium shows (a virtual tour of the universe, anyone?) and laser shows. It also boasts a 28,000-watt digital sound system that makes the experience unforgettable.

Getting there: the Science Center is on Princeton Street in downtown Orlando, just off Exit 85 of I-4 (as you go east on Princeton, the Center will be on your left but

the multi-storey car park is on the right), and is open 9am–5pm Tue–Thur, 9am–9pm Fri and Sat, and noon–5pm Sun (closed Mon, except school holidays).

Admission: $10 for adults, $9 for seniors (55+) and $7.50 for 3–11s; or $13, $12 and $10.50 with one CineDome show (film or planetarium) and $16, $15, and $13.50 with two shows; the CineDome only is $7, $6, and $5 for one film. Parking is $3.50. It is closed on Thanksgiving Day in November, Christmas Eve and Christmas Day. See www.osc.org for more info. AAAA.

Orange County History Center

This relatively recent addition offers an imaginative journey into central Florida history, from the wildlife and Native Americans to today's tourist issues and the space programme. Again, the accent is on the interactive, with hands-on exhibits and audio-visual presentations, and it is very much a journey through time, starting outside in renovated Heritage Square, complete with cypress trees and fountains. The History Center itself is in the former 1927 Orange County Courthouse, with the foyer converted into a dome featuring more than 150 icons unique to central Florida (see how many you can identify before and after your tour).

The 4-storey adventure starts at the top with the **Orientation Theater's** 14-minute multimedia presentation as you sit in rocking chairs on the 'front porch'. Then you visit the Natural Environment and First Peoples exhibits (12,000 years ago), before First Contact brings in the European element. Jump into the 1800s and you visit a Seminole settlement, a Pioneer Cracker home (the first true

BRIT TIP: Combine a visit to the History Center with lunch at the wonderfully eclectic Globe restaurant on the corner of the square.

'cowboys'), hear tales of the old cattle-ranching days and learn about the citrus industry.

The early 20th century brings the story of Transportation, Tin Can Tourists, Aviation and the great land boom, Selling Central Florida. Then witness how the region dramatically altered with the development of the Space Programme and the arrival of a certain Walter Elias Disney in The Day We Changed. From there, you move on to the beautifully restored Courtroom B for some more real-life Orlando history. Finally, you hit the present in the Community exhibit, a spotlight on famous places, people and activities in the area, and a chance to view the dome from the top, testing all your new-found knowledge of the icons. A new exhibit here in 2003 was African American history in Florida, featuring the achievements and tragedies of central Florida's African American community. You will also find periodical travelling exhibits here (the story of World War Two in Florida was on show during summer 2003), as well as the **Historium** gift shop.

Getting there: the History Center can be found off Central Boulevard and Magnolia Avenue downtown (Exit 82C off I-4, left on to Magnolia, right on to Central Boulevard). Best place to park is the Orlando Public Library multi-storey car park on Central Boulevard (History Center admission includes 2 hours free parking there if you show your ticket).

Admission: $7 for adults, $3.50 for 3–12s and $6.50 for seniors (60+), and it is open 10am–5pm Mon–Sat and noon–5pm Sun. For more info, call 407 836 8500 or visit www.thehistorycenter.org. AAA.

Other downtown developments include the free **Lymmo** bus service which connects the central stretch along Magnolia Avenue, from South Street to the **TD Waterhouse Center** (formerly the Orlando Arena for sports and concerts) on Amelia Street, the **Downtown Arts District** and **Arts Market** (on Wall Street, off Orange Avenue, second Saturday every month; 11am–9pm Oct–April), seasonal concerts and firework shows, plus new shops and restaurants around **Lake Eola**.

The **Cultural Corridor** links the Downtown Arts District (which includes the Bob Carr Performing Arts Center and the Centroplex), with the Loch Haven area (where you can find the Orlando Museum of Art, Mennello Museum of American Folk Art, Orlando Philharmonic Orchestra and the Orlando-UCF Shakespeare Festival), via the **Dr Phillips Performing Arts Center**, which is home of the Orlando Opera and Orlando Ballet.

The Saturday **Farmers' Market** (7am–1pm) has become a real downtown focal point (in the park area just outside the Orange County History Center), with vendors now including local artisans, such as glass and dressmakers, as well as wonderful fresh produce. The

Orlando Science Center

Thornton Park area is currently the most happening part of Orlando, with the new Thornton Park Central (at the junction of Summerlin Avenue and Central Boulevard, just south-east of Lake Eola) offering a mix of unique small boutiques and trendy restaurants, with the monthly Third Thursday street party (5–10pm) attracting sizeable crowds. Visit www.downtownorlando.com for the latest info (see also Chapter 9, Orlando By Night).

The Holy Land Experience

Not so much a conventional attraction but right in the heart of the tourist mainstream is this 15-acre (6-ha) 'living Biblical museum', which sets out to recreate in great detail the city of Jerusalem and its religious significance from 1450BC to AD66 and provide an explanation and celebration of the Christian faith.

The staff are all in period costume, the architecture and landscaping are impressive and the background music in both the indoor and outdoor areas is all original and suitably atmospheric. From the **Jerusalem Street Market** entrance to the **Qumran Dead Sea Caves, Calvary's Garden Tomb** and on to the highly impressive **Temple of the Great King** (destroyed by the Romans in AD70), everything is portrayed in literal Biblical terms. **The Theater of Life** shows a 25-minute film of Bible landmarks, from Adam and Eve to the Crucifixion, while the **Wilderness Tabernacle** is a 25-minute theatrical portrayal of Old Testament worship, featuring the Holy Ark with lasers and pyrotechnics. A huge replica Jerusalem Model – which took more than a year to build – is explained in

BRIT TIP: Reader Peter Crumpler suggests: 'The Holy Land is an unusual cross between a theme park and an educational tour, but I'd say British Christians would find it fascinating – both for learning more about the Bible and for seeing their livelier American cousins in action.'

great detail several times a day in the form of a guided tour. Live performances include the *Garden Tomb Music & Drama* celebrating the Resurrection and an original musical drama *Today's The Day*, which plays out in the Plaza of Nations. There is even a Middle Eastern-style café where you can eat a Goliath Burger.

Recently opened is the **Scriptorium** centre for Biblical antiquities, another themed environment showcasing various rare artefacts. It is a thoroughly unusual 'attraction' (although they don't call it that), and sits rather awkwardly among the main tourist offerings, but it may well pique the interest of some.

Getting there: The Holy Land Experience can be found immediately off Exit 78 of I-4, on the junction of Conroy and Vineland Roads (just north of Universal Orlando).

Disney's Typhoon Lagoon

© Disney

Admission: $29.99 for adults and $19.75 for children 4–12. Parking is free. It is open 10am–6pm Mon–Fri, 9am–6pm Sat, and noon–6pm Sun. Call 407 367 2065 for more info or check out their website at www.theholylandexperience.com. AAA.

THE WATER PARKS

If anyone has been down the slides and flumes at the local leisure centre, they will have an inkling of what Orlando's four big water parks are all about. Predictably, Disney has the two most elaborate ones, but the Universal-owned Wet 'n Wild and Water Mania are equally adept at providing hours of fun in a variety of styles that owe much to the flair of the theme park creators.

All four require at least half a day of splashing, sliding and riding to get full value from their rather high prices but, if you prefer to get your kicks in watery rather than land-borne fashion, these are definitely for you. Lockers are provided for valuables and you can hire towels.

Disney's Typhoon Lagoon Water Park

Until *Disney's Blizzard Beach* water park opened in 1995, *Disney's Typhoon Lagoon* was the biggest and finest example of Florida's water parks. In high season, it is also the busiest, so be prepared to run into more queues. The park's 56 acres

BRIT TIP: While water parks are a great way of cooling down, it is easy to pick up a 5-star case of sunburn. So don't forget the high-factor, waterproof suntan lotion.

BRIT TIP: As the busiest of the water parks, *Disney's Typhoon Lagoon* can hit capacity quite early in the day in the summer. Call 407 824 4321 in advance to check on the crowds.

(23-ha) are spread out around the 2½-acre (1-ha) lagoon fringed with palm trees and white-sand beaches. If it wasn't for the high-season crowds, you could easily convince yourself you had been washed up on some tropical island paradise. *Disney's Typhoon Lagoon* also goes in for some of the most extravagant landscaping and introduces some unique and clever details. The walk up Mount Mayday, for instance, provides a terrific overview of the park as well as adding scenic touches like rope bridges and tropical flowers. Sun loungers, chairs, picnic tables and even a few hammocks are provided to add to the comfort and convenience of restful areas like Getaway Glen. However, you need to arrive early to bag a decent spot with some shade.

The park is overlooked by the 90-ft (27-metre) Mount Mayday, on top of which is perched the luckless *Miss Tilly*, a shrimp boat that legend has it landed here during the typhoon that gave the park its name. Watch for the water fountains that shoot from Miss Tilly's funnel at regular intervals, accompanied by the ship's hooter, which signal another round of 6ft-high waves in the **Surf Pool** (you can hire inner-tubes to bob around on or just try body-surfing). Circling the lagoon is **Castaway Creek**, a 3ft (1 metre) deep, lazy flowing river that offers the chance to float happily along on rubber tyres.

The series of slides and rides are all clustered around Mount Mayday and vary from the breathtaking three body slides of **Humunga Kowabunga**, which drop you 214ft (65 metres) at up to 30mph (48kph) down some of the steepest inclines in waterdom (make sure your swimming costume is SECURELY fastened!), to **Ketchakiddee Creek**, which offers a selection of slides and fun pools for all youngsters under 4ft (122cm) tall. In between, you have the three **Storm Slides**, more body slides which twist and turn through caves, tunnels and waterfalls, **Mayday Falls**, a 460-ft (140-metre) inner-tube ride down a series of banked drops, **Keel Haul Falls**, an alternative tube ride that takes slightly longer, and **Gangplank Falls**, a group or family ride whose tubes take up to 4 people down 300ft (90 metres) of mock rapids. The hugely imaginative (but chilly) **Shark Reef** is an upturned wreck and coral reef, which you can snorkel around among 4,000 tropical fish and a number of real, but quite harmless, nurse sharks. Like all the areas, this is carefully supervised, and those who aren't quite brave enough to dive in can still get a close-up of the fish through the underwater portholes of the sunken ship (the Reef is closed during the coldest winter months).

There are height and health restrictions on Humunga Kowabunga (it's not suitable for anyone with a bad back or neck, or for pregnant women), while the

> BRIT TIP: 'Buy a disposable waterproof camera to tie around our wrist when you visit the water parks. We bought one cheap at Wal-Mart and have some lovely photos from *Typhoon Lagoon*,' says Judith Bingham.

> BRIT TIP: Ladies, please remember, down some of the whizziest slides it is advisable to wear a one-piece swimsuit rather than a bikini. Your modesty could be at stake here!

queues for this slide, plus the Storm Slides and Shark Reef, can touch an arduous hour at times, which can take a lot of the fun out of it. Getting out of the sun can also be slightly problematic as the provision of shaded areas is not overwhelming, but a quick plunge into Castaway Creek usually sorts out any overheating.

For snacks and meals, **Lowtide Lou's** and **Let's Go Slurpin'** both offer snacks and drinks while **Typhoon Tilly's** and **Leaning Palms** serve a mixture of burgers, sandwiches, salads and ice cream. It is essential to avoid main mealtimes here if you want to eat in relative comfort. You can, however, bring your own picnic (unlike the main theme parks) which you can eat in special scenic areas (but no alcohol or glass containers are allowed). You CAN'T bring your own snorkels, inner-tubes or rafts, but snorkels are provided at Shark Reef and you need to hire inner-tubes (if required) only for the lagoon. If you have forgotten a vital item like a sunhat or bucket and spade for the kids, or even your swimsuit, they are all available (along with gifts and souvenirs) at **Singapore Sal's**.

To avoid the worst of the summer crowds (when the park's 7,200 capacity is often reached), Monday morning is about the best time to visit (steer clear of weekends at all costs), while, on other days, arrive either 30 minutes before opening or in mid-afternoon, when many decide to dodge the daily rainstorm. Early

> BRIT TIP: You can save money on your day at the two Disney water parks by buying refillable drinks mugs – about $10.95 each – when you arrive and using them all day.

Cruisin Creek at Water Mania

evening is also extremely pleasant as the park lights up.

Getting there: on Buena Vista Drive, just half a mile from the *Downtown Disney* area.

Admission is $31.95 and $24.95 for 3–9s (under 3s free), or it is free as one of the options with the Park Hopper PLUS Tickets. Parking is free. It opens from 9am to dusk every day. TTTT/AAAAA.

Disney's Blizzard Beach Water Park

Ever imagined a skiing resort in the middle of Florida? You haven't? Well, Disney has, and this is the wonderful result. *Disney's Blizzard Beach* water park puts the rest in the shade for size as well as extravagant settings, with the whole park arranged as if it were in the Rocky Mountains rather than the sub-tropics. That means snow-effect scenery, Christmas trees and water slides cunningly converted to look like skiing pistes and toboggan runs. It delivers a real feast for water lovers and Disney admirers in general, and the basic premise of snow-surfin' USA is an unarguable 5-star knockout.

Disney's Blizzard Beach

Main features are **Mount Gushmore**, a 90-ft (27-metre) mountain down which all the main slides run (including the world's tallest free-fall speed slide, the terrifying 120-ft (37-metre) **Summit Plummet**, which rockets you down a 'ski jump' at up to 60mph (97kph)!), **Tike's Peak**, a kiddie-sized version of the park's slides and a mock snow-beach, and **Ski-Patrol Training Camp**, a series of slides and challenges for pre-teens. **Melt-Away Bay** is a 1-acre (0.4-ha) pool fed by 'melting snow' waterfalls (actually blissfully warm), and **Cross Country Creek** is a lazy-flowing half-mile river around the whole park which also floats guests through a chilly 'ice cave' (watch out for the mini-waterfalls of ice-cold water!).

A ski chair-lift operates to the top of Mount Gushmore, providing a magnificent view of the whole park and surrounding areas. Don't miss the outstanding rides – **Teamboat Springs**, a wild, family inner-tube adventure, Runoff Rapids, a 1-, 2- or 3-person tube plunge, and the **Snow Stormers**, a daring head-first 'toboggan' run. **Toboggan Racers** gives you the chance to speed down the 'slopes' against seven other head-first daredevils. All four go to new heights of water park imagination and provide good-sized thrills without overdoing the scare factor.

The **Downhill Double Dipper** is two side-by-side slides which send you down 230-ft (70-metre) tubes in a race that is timed on a big clock at the bottom, and which gives you a real jolt halfway down! For those not quite up to Summit Plummet lunacy, the wonderfully named **Slush Gusher** is a slightly less terrifying speed slide. There is a 'village' area with a **Beach Haus** shop and **Lottawatta Lodge** fast-food restaurant, offering diners a grandstand view of Mount Gushmore and Melt-Away Bay beach. Snacks are also available at **Avalunch** (ouch!), the **Warming Hut** and **Polar Pub & Frostbite Freddie's Frozen Refreshments**. Predictably, the crowds are suitably massive, so avoid the weekends and from mid-morning onwards on Wednesday to Friday.

Getting there: just north of *Disney's All-Star Resorts* off Buena Vista Drive.

Admission: $31.95 per adult and $24.95 per child (3–9); again it is one of the free optional extras with Hopper PLUS Tickets, with opening times from 9am to early evening. TTTTT/AAAAA.

Adjacent to *Disney's Blizzard Beach* is the amazing **Winter Summerland Miniature Golf Courses** (where Santa's elves hang out!), with two wonderfully elaborate courses that provide children with a great diversion. Watch out for a riot of visual gags and puns, as well as some tricky mini-golf.

Wet 'n Wild

If Disney scores highest marks for scenic content, Wet 'n Wild, the world's first water park back in 1977, goes full-tilt for thrills and spills of the highest quality. And this place will test the material of your swimsuit to the limit!

Wet 'n Wild is repeatedly one of the best-attended water parks in the

> **BRIT TIP:** The Children's Playground at Wet 'n Wild was built especially for those under 4ft (122cm) in height – right down to the only junior wave pool in the world.

country, and its location in the heart of I-Drive makes it a major draw. Consequently, you will again encounter some serious crowds here, although the 12 slides and rides, **Lazy River** attraction, an elaborate kids' park (with mini versions of many of the slides), **Surf Lagoon** and restaurant and picnic areas all manage to absorb a lot of punters before the queues develop. Amazingly, waits of more than half an hour at peak times are rare. Its popularity with locals means it is busiest at weekends, with July the month that attracts most crowds.

You are almost spoilt for choice with main rides, from the highly popular group inner-tube rides of the **Surge** and **Bubba Tub**, through the more demanding rides of **Raging Rapids** to the high-thrill factor of the 2-person **Black Hole** (like the *Magic Kingdom's* Space Mountain, but in water!), **Blue Niagara** (also enclosed, but this one's a body slide) and **Mach 5**, to the ultimate terror of **Der Stuka** and the **Bomb Bay**. The latter duo are definitely not for the faint-hearted. Basically, they are two 76ft-high body slides with a drop as near vertical as makes no difference. Der Stuka is the straightforward slide

Wet 'n Wild Fuji Flyer

version, while the Bomb Bay adds the extra terror of being allowed to free-fall on to the top of the slide. And they call it fun! Suffice it to say, your author has not put himself at risk on these particular contraptions, and has absolutely no intention of doing so! For some reason, only 15–25% of the park's visitors pluck up the courage to try it. Can't think why. Height restrictions of 4ft/122cm are in force on the Bomb Bay, Der Stuka and Blue Niagara, while older kids get their own chance for thrills on the huge, inflatable **Bubble Up**, which bounces them into 3ft (1 metre) of water.

> BRIT TIP: For all the water parks, it can be a good idea to bring a pair of deck shoes or sandals that can be worn in water.

The thrilling toboggan-like **Fuji Flyer** takes 4 passengers in 8ft (2-metre) in-line tubes which whoosh down more than 450ft (137 metres) of banked curves and speed-enhancing straights, and the bungee-like **Hydra Fighter** is a 2-person swing equipped with a fire-type hose that sends the contraption into mad gyrations as you increase the water pressure! New in 2001 was **The Storm**, a pair of identical circular slides billed as 'body coasters'! The enclosed tubes – complete with storm sound and light effects – send the rider plunging into a circular bowl, around which they spin at high speed before landing in the splash-pool below. Huge fun.

For those under 4ft (122cm) tall, the recently renovated **Kids Park** area has a full range of junior-sized slides, plus a new sandcastle structure with two semi-circular water slides and a giant bucket that fills and tips up at regular intervals. Uniquely, the children can use speciality tubes, beach chairs and tables designed specifically for their height.

The neighbouring lake is also part of the fun (although not in winter when its temperature drops below that of merely chilly), adding the opportunities to try the cable-operated **Knee Ski** and (for a nominal fee) ride the **Wild One** (large inner-tubes tied behind a speedboat). Alternatively, take a breather in the slow-flowing **Lazy River** or abandon the water altogether for one of several shaded picnic areas, although they are quickly snapped up. The energetic can play beach volleyball and ride the **Robo Surfer** at selected times, a watery version of the mechanical bucking bronco. Lockers, showers, tube and towel rentals are all available but, if you bring your own floating equipment, you must have it checked by one of the lifeguards.

For food, **Bubba's Bar-B-Q** serves chicken, ribs, fries and drinks, the **Surf Grill** features burgers, hot dogs, chicken and sandwiches and another seven snack bars offer similar fast-food fare, including a pizza bar and a kiddies' counter (peanut butter sandwiches, hot dogs and chips). Picnics can also be brought in, provided you don't include alcohol or glass containers.

Getting there: Wet 'n Wild is half a mile north of I-Drive's junction with Sand Lake Road at the intersection with Universal Boulevard and is open year-round (with heated pools in the cooler months) from 9am in peak periods (10am at other times) until variously 5, 6, 7, or 9pm.

Admission: $31.95 for adults, $25.95 for 3–9s and free for under 3s, alternatively, it is included with the Orlando FlexTicket. Tube rentals are $4 ($2 deposit), towels $2 and lockers $5 ($2 deposit), or $9 for all three ($4 deposit). Parking is $5. Visit www.wetnwild.com. TTTTT/AAA.

Water Mania

If Wet 'n Wild attracts the serious thrill seekers, Kissimmee's version, Water Mania, is more family-orientated and laid back, with the crowds highest at weekends when the locals flock in. That's not to say this park doesn't have its share of scary slides (or Wet 'n Wild doesn't cater for families), it's just their emphasis is slightly different and those looking to avoid the crowds often end up here. Where this 36-acre (15-ha) park scores a minor victory over its rivals is in the provision of 3 acres (1ha) of wooded picnic area where you can bring your own picnic (although no glass items).

Eight different slides, including a patented non-stop surfing challenge called **Wipe-Out**, the usual **Cruisin' Creek**, a 720,000-gallon (3,276,000-litre) **Wave Pool** (waves every 15 minutes, up to 4ft (122cm) high) and three separate kids' areas provide the main attractions – plenty to keep you occupied for at least half a day. Top of the list for those daring enough to throw themselves down things like Der Stuka is the **Screamer**, an aptly named 72-ft (22-metre) free-fall speed slide, and the **Abyss**, 380ft (116 metres) of enclosed-tube darkness. The **Anaconda** and **Banana Peel** both feature family-sized inner-tubes down long, twisting slides, while the **Double Berzerker** offers two different ways to be whooshed along and spat out into a foaming pool.

However, the outstanding feature, for both trying and watching, is the **Wipe-Out**, one of only two such attractions in the world. The challenge is to grab a body board and try to ride the continuous wave, risking going over the edge into another pool if you stray too wide, or being sent flying backwards if you lose your balance. A real blast!

When it comes to pint-sized fun for the children, Water Mania is one of the best. The **Rain Forest** is designed for the 2–10s, with a 5,000-sq ft (464-sq metre) pool ranging from 3in (7cm) to 2ft (60cm) deep and featuring a selection of mini-slides, fountains and water guns, all arranged around a wonderful large-scale pirate ship, with more chances to climb, jump and generally swashbuckle. Other innovative recent additions are the **Rain Train**, a near life-size locomotive that sprays water out of its stack in the centre of a shallow pool, with other interactive play features and more slides; and **Tot's Town** for the toddlers (and their parents who want to relax a little), which is a partly fenced playground with sand beach and paddling area, added shade and refreshment hut.

In addition to the cooling picnic areas, there are several snack bars, a mini-golf course, volleyball and basketball courts and a large shop.

Getting there: Water Mania is located on Highway 192, just a mile east of the I-4 intersection.

Admission: $19.95 for adults and $16.95 for children (3–9) and parking is $6. Open 10am–5pm daily from early March to the end of September, and 11am–5pm Thur–Sun only in October (hours are subject to change). Call 407 396 2626 for more details or www.watermania-florida.com. TTTT/AAA.

Okay, that sums up the main large-scale attractions, but many people are now looking for the 'something different' factor, so let's explore some alternatives to the mass-market experience…

BRIT TIP: Kids are again extremely well catered for, and Water Mania can even host birthday parties in Mr Kool's Party Land. Call 407 396 2626 for details.

Off the Beaten Track

(or, When you're All Theme-Parked Out)

After several days in the midst of the hectic tourist whirl of mainstream Orlando, you may be in need of a rest from the non-stop theme park activities. Or you may be a repeat visitor looking for a different experience. If either is the case, this chapter is for you.

Hopefully, you will already have noted the relatively tranquil offerings of Silver Springs and Historic Bok Sanctuary in the previous chapter but, to get away from it all more completely and to enhance your view of the area further, the following are guaranteed to take you well off the beaten tourist track. This chapter should really be subtitled 'A Taste of the Real Florida', as it introduces the areas of Winter Park and Seminole County, nature boat rides, eco-tours and journeys by airboat, balloon, ship, train and plane.

The Morse Museum of American Art

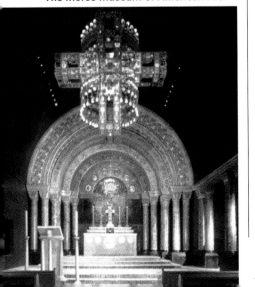

Winter Park

Foremost among the 'secret' hideaways is this elegant northern suburb of Orlando, little more than 20 minutes' drive from the hurly-burly of the likes of I-Drive and yet a million miles from the relentless commercialism. It offers several renowned museums and art galleries, fabulous shopping, numerous restaurants, several pleasant walking tours, a delightful 50-minute boat ride around the lakes and, above all, a chance to slow down.

The central area is **Park Avenue**, a classy street of fine shops, boutiques, two museums and a wonderfully shaded park. At one end of the avenue is Rollins College, a small but highly respected arts education centre which houses the **Cornell Fine Arts Museum**, with the oldest collection of paintings, sculpture and decorative arts in Florida (open 10am–5pm Tue–Fri, 1pm–5pm Sat–Sun, closed Mon and main holidays, admission free) and the **Annie Russell Theater** (visit www.Rollins.edu for more info).

The **Morse Museum of American Art** is a must for admirers of American art pottery, American and European glass, furniture and other decorative arts of the late 19th and early 20th centuries, as it includes one of the world's foremost collections of works by Louis Comfort Tiffany. The dazzling chapel restoration from the 1893 Chicago World Expo is now on display in its original form for the first time since the late 19th century and is worth the entrance fee alone.

The museum is open 9.30am–4pm Tues–Sat and 1–4pm Sun, admission $3, under 12s free (www.morsemuseum.org).

The **Albin Polasek Museum and Sculpture Gardens** are also worth a look for culture buffs and for the serene setting devoted to this Czech-American artist. Open 10am–4pm Wed–Sat, 1–4pm Sun, admission is free and it is a superb setting for weddings.

The **Scenic Boat Tour** is located at the east end of Morse Avenue and offers a charming, narrated 12-mile (19-km) tour of the 'Venice of America' around the lakes and canals for a fascinating glimpse of some of the most beautiful houses, boat houses and lakeside gardens (properties in the area start at $800,000 and several top $4 million!). Tours run 10am–4pm daily and cost $8 for adults and $4 for children 2–11, and it is one of the most relaxing hours you will spend in Orlando. Visit www.scenicboattours.com.

Alternatively, a trip with **Home Town Bicycle Tours** gives a gentle but unique overview of this picturesque neighbourhood, including several parks and Rollins College, with full guide narration ($50/hour for groups up to 10; i.e. $5/person/hour, plus $20 bike hire; call 407 332 8703 or e-mail hometownbicycletours@hotmail.com). You can also take the **Park Avenue Walking Tour**, with useful free maps provided by the Chamber of Commerce on New York Avenue.

The shops of Park Avenue are a cut above anything you will encounter elsewhere and, while you may find the prices equally distinctive, just browsing is an enjoyable experience with the charm of the area highlighted by the friendliness of everyone hereabouts. For shops that are both unique and fun, look out for **Panache** (jewellery), **Park Avenue Gallery**

(art), **Kendyl's Kloset** (children's clothes and toys) and **The Doggie Door** (for pets). Recent additions are **Winter Park Teddy Bear Co** (make and stuff your own soft toys), **Olive this Relish that** (a wonderful gourmet food store with Mediterranean specialities) and **Peter Brook Chocolatier**. Regular pavement craft fairs and art festivals (especially the Spring Art Festival in March/April, which is a big part of the social scene) add splashes of colour to an already inviting scenario. In addition to the **Park Plaza Gardens**, which specialises in continental cuisine (see Chapter 10, page 273), you can sample French, Italian and Thai cuisines, among others. The new **Zak's on Park Avenue** receives rave reviews from the locals for its sparkling New Orleans-flavoured menu. Watch out, too, for Dress Up Thursdays, where the best-dressed diner in each of six restaurants receives a goody bag of great items from Park Avenue merchants. Street parking here usually allows 2 hours free, but the Sun Trust Building on the corner of Comstock and Park Avenue is a better bet. Watch out, too, for the **Sidewalk Art Festival** every March (see page 17).

The **Central Park** area alongside Park Avenue, notable for its fountains and flowers, is due to be expanded in the near future, which should enhance things still further. Check out www.wpfl.org and www.parkave-winterpark.com for more info.

8

Boating in central Florida

Another high point of a visit to Winter Park is the **Kraft Azalea Gardens** on Alabama Drive (off Palmer Avenue at the north end of Park Avenue), 11 acres (5ha) of shaded lakeside walkways, gardens and hundreds of magnificent azaleas. The main focal point, the mock Grecian temple, is a particularly beautiful setting for weddings. **Mead Botanical Gardens,** on Garden Drive (just off Highway 17/92) offers more trails through a sub-tropical forest, with native birds and plants from around the world. There is no admission charge for either.

To get to Winter Park, take Exit 87 from I-4, Fairbanks Avenue. Turn right on to Fairbanks and head east for 2 miles (3km) until it intersects with Park Avenue and turn left.

Midway between Winter Park and downtown Orlando is another botanical gem, **Leu Gardens**, a 50-acre (20-ha) retreat featuring formal gardens, peaceful walks and a boardwalk overlooking Lake Rowena. The **Leu House Museum** is open 10am–3.30pm (closed in July) with tours every 30 minutes (last tour at 3.30pm). The gardens are open daily from 9am–5pm (9am–8pm in summer) and cost $4 for adults and $1 for under 13s. You will find them on the corner of Forest and Nebraska Avenues, via Mills Avenue and Princeton St from Exit 85 on I-4.

Aquatic Wonders boat tours

To go further into the real world of Florida nature and its wildlife, **Aquatic Wonders** operates a delightful break from the theme park business on Lake Tohopekaliga in Kissimmee (the bigger of the two lakes; NOT East Lake Toho). Operated by Captain Ray Robida and limited to a maximum of 6 per trip, the choice of eight cruises offers a series of gentle adventures that are entertaining, educational and relaxing. Every cruise on the 30-ft (9-metre) covered pontoon boat is different depending on local conditions and Captain Ray's truly individual style, which is wonderfully laid back yet informative. His knowledge of the waterways and wildlife is outstanding and children with enquiring minds will benefit. His boat is fully wheelchair accessible and there is an onboard loo!

The 3-hour **Aquatic Wonders cruise** studies the local lakes and rivers, water ecology and the fish, insects and other animals of the area ($35 for adults and children). The **Eagle Watch Tour** is an ornithologist's delight as it goes out for 2 hours to look at the nesting bald eagles on the lake (and this is an area renowned for bald eagles), rare ospreys and many other birds ($21 for adults, $14 for 3–12s). The rather romantic **Sunset Sounds** is another 2-hour trip aboard *Eagle Ray* to enjoy the sights and sounds of dusk over the lake as the birds come home to roost ($18.95 and $12.95). **Starlight Wonders** is a 2-hour tour for a spot of star-gazing, gentle music and Native American stories surrounding the origins of the constellations ($25 and $16). **Rivers in Time** is a 2-hour journey back in time to the days of the river boat and the Seminole Indian War, a fascinating live history lesson with all the sights and sounds of the lake for good measure ($21 and $14).

BRIT TIP: Amazingly, the waterways feeding Lake Toho stretch all the way to Miami in the south. Captain Ray is a mine of fascinating geographical and historical information.

The **Gator Watch Tour** is a 2-hour night-time journey to view some of the locals hunting, nesting and just hanging out (and there are plenty of them out there! $25 and $16). **Family Fishing Adventures** offers 4–5 hours of fishing fun with all bait and tackle (but not fishing licence) provided, especially for beginners ($200, takes up to 6). A new 2-hour tour of unspoilt **Makinson Island** is also available, providing an interpretive guided tour of this 132-acre (54-ha) nature preserve ($21 and $14).

Games and videos are provided for the kids in case their attention wanders! All tours supply non-alcoholic drinks and snacks (but you can also take your own) and Captain Ray is fully licensed by the US Coast Guard, so you are guaranteed a high level of safety as well as entertainment. The *Eagle Ray* departs daily from 101 Lakeshore Boulevard in downtown Kissimmee (via Main Street and Broadway, turn left into Ruby and right at the end, Lakeshore Boulevard). Call 407 846 2814 for more details and to make reservations (recommended), or visit www.florida-nature.com. There is even a **Maritime Wedding Chapel** cruise, with the ceremony performed by the Captain himself, starting at $175 for a party of six.

Makinson Island is worth highlighting here as it has quickly become a valuable place for boating, kayaking and hiking, after it was opened to the public in spring 2002. It offers a series of marked hiking trails through a variety of pristine and secluded ecosystems, including cypress domes, citrus groves and beautiful pastures, with a picnic area and barbecue grill set up under a covered pavilion. Local wildlife includes armadillos, squirrels, racoons and great numbers of birds. **Big Toho Marina** (on Lakeshore Boulevard) provides small fishing boat rentals here ($55 all day, $35

half-day), while **Richardson's Fish Camp** (1550 Scotty's Road) offers scheduled airboat rides to and from the island (call 407 846 6540).

WayFun Kayak Adventures

This wonderfully fun operation is based at Richardson's Fish Camp (see above), with 4- to 5-hour guided kayak and hiking trips (including snacks and refreshments at $49/person) or a 2-hour sunset trip around Makinson Island ($25/person). It is suitable for beginners and more serious kayakers alike and, while it requires a bit of effort, it is a seriously satisfying way to get a close-up of Lake Toho and its wildlife. It is also quite gorgeous in the evening, although it can be fiendishly hot in summer months (remember plenty of sunscreen). Your tour guide provides bottled water, an energy snack and plenty of enjoyable and quite fascinating local insight, and there is no need even to get your feet wet unless you want to. Wayfun Kayaks run at weekends only (12 and over only), and you need to book in advance on 407 957 0071 or email wayfun@kua.net.

Airboat rides

The thrill of airboat rides can be experienced on many of Florida's lakes, rivers and marshes. An airboat is a totally different experience to any boat ride you will have had before, as it is more like flying at ground level. As much a thrill as a scenic adventure, it has the advantage of exploring areas otherwise inaccessible to boats.

BRIT TIP: Watch out for discount coupons in tourist literature offering up to $3 off airboat rides.

BRIT TIP: Best time for an airboat ride is first thing on a weekday morning when the wildlife is not hiding from the weekend boaters.

Family boating in Florida

Airboats simply skim over and through the marshes, to give you an alternative, close-up and very personal view. Travelling at up to 50mph (80kph) means it can be loud (hence you will be provided with headphones) and sunglasses are also a good idea to keep stray flies out of your eyes. However, it is NOT the trip for you if you are spooked by crickets, dragonflies and similar insects that occasionally land in the boat! In summer months, a good insect repellant is also advisable.

Several operations offer airboat rides in the area, from you-drive boats that do barely 5mph (8kph) to much bigger ones, but for the most quality-conscious operation my tip goes to **Boggy Creek Airboat Rides**. Their airboats can be found on Lake Toho at Southport Park (all the way down Poinciana Boulevard, off Highway 192 between Markers 10 and 11, and across into Southport Road – about a 30-minute drive) or on East Lake Toho (their main site). For the latter, you either take Exit 17 off the Central Florida Greeneway (417) and go south on Boggy Creek Road, then right into East Lake Fish Camp; better still,

WayFun Kayaks, Lake Toho

take Osceola Parkway all the way east until it hits Boggy Creek Road. Go left and then turn right at the Boggy Creek T-junction, then right into East Lake Fish Camp after 2 miles (3km).

BRIT TIP: Want to sample the Florida Everglades but don't fancy the 3-hour trip south? Boggy Creek Airboats are the perfect substitute, and at a fraction of the cost.

The **East Lake Fish Camp** is itself a little gem, offering a variety of boating and angling opportunities (call 407 348 2040 for details) as well as the wonderfully authentic rural Florida charm of the **restaurant and gift shop** (open 8am–9pm every day). If you are heading for a morning airboat ride, consider arriving early for a huge all-day breakfast at the fish camp first, where the more adventurous will want to try the local delicacies – catfish, frogs' legs and gator tail. For another great slice of local eating, try the Friday and Saturday night buffets. They are fabulous value at $9.95 and $12.95 each on an all-you-can-eat basis. Boggy Creek's **half-hour ride** features the most modern 18-passenger airboats in Florida, skimming over the local wetlands for a close-up view of the majestic cypress trees and wildlife that can

Airboat ride

include eagles, ospreys, snakes and turtles, as well as the ever-present gators. The Southport Park site tends to be the quieter of the two, with more wildlife – especially in the spring – but involves a longer drive than East Lake Fish Camp.

You do not need to book in advance, just turn up and go (9am–5.30pm daily), and rides cost $17.95 for adults and $12.95 for children 3–12 (don't forget the sunscreen as you can really burn out on the water). They also do a 1-hour **Night Tour** ($29.95, March–October only) for a completely different, and quite exhilarating, experience (gator eyes glow red in the dark!), but you do need to book at least 3 days in advance on 407 344 9550. Finally, they offer 45-minute **private tours** in their 6-passenger boat ($45/person), which provide an even more personal view of this amazing area. Visit www.bcairboats.com for more info.

Boggy Creek Parasail

Complementary to the airboat rides, this is an opportunity to float over East Lake Toho for one of the most breathtaking views of the area. You float up with the greatest of ease from the back of their 16-passenger boat at heights of up to 400ft (122 metres), 600ft (183 metres) or 800ft (244 metres) depending on how much you pay, descending again after about 15 relaxing minutes to

BRIT TIP: If you are staying in or visiting Seminole County, visit *Black Hammock Fish Camp* for their version of the wonderful airboat adventure (see page 220).

land gently, standing up – and completely dry. The sit-down harness they use requires no skill or effort on your part and makes it accessible to everyone (even me – see below!). The system is also deft enough to allow the operators to dip you in the water – upon request! Single flyers cost $45 (up to 400ft/122 metres), $55 (600ft/183 metres) and $65 (800ft/244 metres), while double flyers are $75, $85 and $95. They also offer a romantic Sunset Cruise package for couples, with drinks and hors d'oeuvres at $180 per couple. Observers may ride free if there is space in the boat. Reservations are not usually required but it is often wise to check by calling 407 348 2700 (open 10am–5.30pm daily).

The author parasailing

Cypress Glades Adventure Tours

Brand new and in conjunction with Gatorland, this is an adventurous series of offerings into the Florida countryside and waterways.

Operated by Gatorland's enthusiastic head trainer Mike Hileman, there are four basic experiences, all of which can be customised to include other activities (such as airboat rides, kayaking or hiking). Based either in Gatorland itself or out on some of the many unspoiled lakes of the area, the genuine feel of real Florida nature here is all encompassing.

The local wildlife includes whitetail deer, Osceola turkeys, bald eagles and wild hogs, as well as the inevitable gators, and birdlife, such as ospreys, cranes, white pelicans, owls, Coopers hawks, cardinals, storks and ivies.

Their four main options are a fully-guided **half-day airboat excursion**, including picnic lunch and some real local insight ($55 and $45); a **night-time airboat ride** on its own ($38 and $28), with the chance to see how amazing Florida's oldest inhabitants are by torchlight (but don't forget the bug repellant here!); the **gator egg collection** out in the 10-acre (4-ha) breeding marsh at Gatorland itself, a fairly labour-intensive tour for the true adventure seeker (12 and up only, $49); and the exclusive **Trainer for a Day** programme, also at Gatorland, with the opportunity to work behind the scenes at the park, finding out what it takes to handle such dangerous animals, behavioural training and a go at gator wrangling ($100, 2 hours long, ages 12 and up). You can also visit Bass Pro Shops Outdoor World at Festival Bay (see page 280) for their Adventure Center.

For more details, call 407 855 5496 or visit www.gatorland.com.

Balloon trips

Florida is one of the most popular areas for ballooning and, if you are up early enough in the morning, you will often see several. The experience is a majestic one. If Orlando represents the holiday of a lifetime, then a balloon flight is the ride of a lifetime. The utterly smooth way in which you lift off into the early morning sky is breathtaking in itself, but the peace and quiet of the ride, not to mention the stunning views from 2,000ft (600 metres) above ground, are quite awesome. It is not a cheap experience, but it is equally appealing to all but the youngest children or those who have vertigo or a fear of heights. It is a highly personalised ride, taking up to 6 people. Some baskets take up to 10, but it's a squeeze!

> BRIT TIP: Dresses are not advisable for balloon trips and wearing sensible shoes is essential.

Orange Blossom Balloons is one of the premier companies in central Florida, with more than 18 years' experience and a wonderfully laid-back style that stems from their British-owned operation. You meet at the Days Inn Hotel Maingate West on Highway 192, half a mile (1km) past Splendid China, at 6am (the best winds for flying are always first thing in the morning) and then transfer to the take-off site, where you help the crew set up and inflate one of their three balloons. Owner-operator Richard Ornstein and his team are a real hoot, and you are soon up, up and away in awe-inspiring style, floating serenely up into the sky or sinking down to skim the surface of one of the many lakes (disturbing the occasional gator or deer). After about an hour you come back to earth for a traditional champagne landing ceremony and return to Days Inn for a full breakfast and your special balloonist's certificate. The full experience lasts 3–4 hours and costs $165 per adult (inclusive of tax) and $95 for 10–15s (under 10s go free with their parents). Hotel pick-up is also available at $10 per person round trip, or you can pay $20 to be part of the chase crew and just enjoy the champagne landing and breakfast. Call 407 239 7677 for reservations (they do book up well in advance, even though they fly every day, weather permitting) or go to www.orangeblossomballoons.com.

Alternatively, check out **Blue Water Balloons** for a more small-scale experience, finishing with a breakfast and champagne picnic out in the peaceful wilds of Florida where you land. Owner-operator Don Edwards and his team are also a pleasure to fly with and have thousands of hours' flying time, plus a wealth of experience and stories which they are happy to pass on (they have flown in more than 30 US states and piloted the Energizer Bunny – the largest shaped balloon in America!). The picnic includes fresh fruit, cheeses and crackers, pastries, and nachos and salsa, plus champagne and fresh orange juice. Don says: 'We have asked our passengers over the years if they would prefer a restaurant breakfast or our traditional picnic, and the answer is usually "We can eat in a restaurant anytime, this is much more personal and intimate".' Each passenger receives a Flight of Ascension certificate and a souvenir balloon-etched champagne glass. Again, the price is $165/person, while you can also book a private flight for two for $400 and buy gift certificates at $150. Visit www.bluewaterballoons.com where you can download a $10 discount voucher. Call 407 894 5040 or 1-800 586 1884 to book.

Everglades and the Bahamas

Day trips are increasingly common from Orlando to the Everglades, Miami, the Florida Keys and the Bahamas and, if you are prepared to put up with a long day out (up to 16 hours) you can see a lot of the state this way. However, it's a long journey for kids for a half-hour airboat ride, in the case of the Everglades.

Real Florida Excursions and **International Divers** are two companies worth recommending.

Real Florida has a variety of tours, from an Orlando Shop Til You Drop excursion to a Miami-Bahamas 2-day getaway. For the latter, you travel down to Miami (3½ hours) by coach, shop at the smart Bayside Marketplace or take the popular Miami waterways cruise, before the 22-minute flight to the Bahamas for an overnight stay.

The following day can be spent on the beautiful beaches or at your hotel in Freeport, before a 5-hour cruise back to Fort Lauderdale with an excellent dinner buffet and then the (long) coach ride back to Orlando. This good-value package costs just $169 for adults and $99 for children aged 2–12 (plus another $76.30 in local taxes).

Another 2-day trip is the **Fort Lauderdale-Everglades** tour, which includes an overnight stay by the beaches of lovely Fort Lauderdale (plus a chance to shop at the world's biggest outlet mall, Sawgrass Mills) as well as a visit to the Everglades for an airboat ride, all for $99 for adults and $69 for children. Alternatively, their **Naples-Everglades Adventure** trip provides a taste of Florida in just a day (although a greater proportion of time is spent on the coach this way), with a 30-minute airboat ride through the Everglades, lunch in

8

beautiful Naples and an afternoon cruise along the coastal waterways. This is $99 (adults) and $49 (3–12s), with an optional swamp buggy ride in the Everglades at $14 per adult (under 6s free).

A relatively new offering is their limo evening out to Universal's CityWalk, with dinner and a pass for the clubs. Called **Be A Star in a Great Big Car**, it involves a round trip from your hotel to CityWalk in a stretch limo, and is proving highly popular at $74 for adults and $49 for 3–12s. A **Kennedy Space Center** day trip costs $59 and $48 (including admission,) and the **Shop 'til You Drop** (including buffet breakfast at Golden Corral and visits to World of Denim, Reebok Outlet Center, Belz Mall and Mall at Millenia) will set you back $31 and $19. Call Real Florida Excursions on 407 345 4996, ext. 3012 or visit www.werusa.com.

International Divers offers several other contrasting and memorable tours, chief among which is their **Florida Adventure Tour**, a personal, all-day experience in the real Florida. It includes a breakfast buffet stop, a 2-hour boat trip and snorkel on the picturesque Crystal River (where you often encounter the harmless manatees!), a relaxing lunch at King's Bay, 45-minute airboat tour on the

Manatees with International Divers

Withlacochee River and a jeep safari through a wildlife refuge that includes tigers, lions, kangaroos and raccoons. It costs $99 for adults and $79 for children 3–9 (under 3s not permitted). Alternatively, their 2-day Miami and Florida Keys tour **Swim with the Dolphins** is an excellent proposition, visiting the Everglades en route, seeing an alligator wrestling and snake-handling show and taking an airboat ride before arriving at Key Largo for a beach barbecue. Part two of the adventure, after an overnight stay and breakfast at your beach resort, is the **dolphin encounter**, a 2-hour programme of instruction, observation and interaction with the Key's tame resident dolphins (including one-on-one swims, dorsal tows and foot pushes). Prior to April 2004, prices are £199 for adults and $179 for children (3–9), with a $100 supplement for the dolphin swim. After April, it becomes $169 for adults, $149 for children (7–12) and $99 for under 7s, and $135 for the dolphin swim (not for under 7s).

Two excellent additions in 2003 were **Sun, Sand and Scales** (an all-day trip to Cocoa Beach, with time to enjoy the beach, pier, Ron Jon's Surf Shop and then head off to the Airboat Outpost for a Florida barbecue with unlimited food and drink before taking a fascinating night-time airboat ride in search of

Orange Blossom Balloons

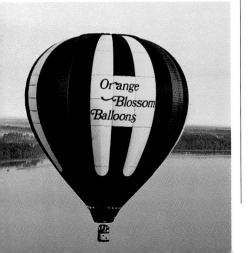

gators; $69 for adults, $49 for 3-12s) and **The Fast & The Furious** (an all-day adventure to Daytona, to visit the interactive race museum and tour the famous speedway, with lunch at a sports restaurant, then a narrated tour of Daytona Beach by amphibious trolley before a trip to see the dragsters and go-karts at the Speed Track; $95 and $75). Call International Divers on 407 352 4646 or visit their website at www.swimdolphins.com.

Flying Tigers Warbird Air Museum

Vintage aeroplane and nostalgia buffs will want to make a note of this offbeat museum adjacent to Kissimmee Airport, which builds and restores World War Two fighters and bombers. Kids who like building Airfix kits will especially enjoy the 1-hour tour of the facilities, which basically represent a couple of large hangars with aircraft in various stages of restoration and repair. It is one of the most amazing programmes of its kind, with the exhibits ranging from a fully restored B-25 Mitchell bomber and a P-51 Mustang to scraps of fuselages and engines that will gradually be incorporated into the latest rebuilding project. It's a place where you see, smell and touch the history of the 1940s' newsreels, and the guides have a detailed knowledge of everything they show you.

You could be forgiven for thinking you have walked into a scrap yard, but the main hangars reveal the full scale of the operation, with the wholesale restoration of a B-17 Flying Fortress being their pride and joy. In fact, owner Tom Reilly insists: 'All those clean, tidy sterile museums you have seen in the past, well, this isn't one of them. We have oil on the floor we refer to as bomber blood and, if you are lucky, you might get

some on you to take home as a souvenir.' Restoration projects include a Vought Corsair and a Lockheed Lightning, while a Lockheed Starfighter and MIG 21 are among about 13 planes on static display. Another 18 or so are flyable, including a Focke-Wolf 190 and a B-25 bomber. The site includes a charming gift shop that houses some more museum pieces, uniforms and memorabilia from World War Two. It is open 9am–5pm every day, and there's always some reconstruction work in progress. Charges are $9 for adults, $8 for 60+ and under 12s (under 8s free). This 'living museum' can be found off Highway 192, half a mile (1km) down Hoagland Boulevard on the left.

Anyone captivated by the sights, sounds and stories of this magnificent exhibit (also known as Bombertown) can also join in. **Warbird Restoration School** is an intensive 5-day course covering the whole rebuilding process, from sheet metal fabrication to welding and fuel systems. It culminates with a flight in a restored B-25J Mitchell bomber, but at $995, is definitely for enthusiasts only. Call 407 933 1942 or visit www.warbirdmuseum.com.

Warbird Adventures

8

Warbird Adventures

Once you have seen the displays, you should consider neighbouring Warbird Adventures. *This is the best ride in town, bar none, guaranteed.* Not only do you get to fly in one of their three 1945 T-6 Harvard fighter-trainers, but also, after a period of getting used to the front seat of this vintage 2-seater... you get to fly it! And you don't just handle the controls, your instructor will get you doing loops, barrel rolls and all manner of aerobatics. This is simply the most exhilarating ride I have ever done, enhanced by in-flight video and wingtip camera to record every moment. It is the only place where you can walk in off the street and, 20 minutes later, be flying a plane with no previous experience.

My instructor was the excellent Thom Richard and, despite my initial reluctance, he had me doing the full aerobatic business before long. Roller-coasters? They're for wimps! Mind you, this is not cheap – a 15-minute flight costs $160, while a 30-minute trip is $270 and an hour $490. Aerobatics (on 30- or 60-minute flights only) cost $30, while the PAL video is $40 and the stills $20 (or all three 'extras' for $80). Nevertheless, this is truly a memory to last a lifetime, and the thought of it still thrills me to bits. They also operate a 1966 Bell 47-G M*A*S*H helicopter for flights and instruction, call 407 870 7366 for details or visit www.warbirdadventures.com.

Green Meadows Petting Farm

From one extreme to another, here is guaranteed fun for kids of 2 up to about 11, and their parents (don't forget your cameras). It's the ultimate hands-on experience as, on the 2-hour guided tour, kids get to milk a cow, pet a pig, cuddle a chick or duckling, feed goats and sheep, meet a buffalo, chickens, peacocks and donkeys and learn what makes a farm tick. There are pony rides for the young ones and tractor-drawn hay rides for all, plus the Green Meadows Express steam train for a scenic ride through the farm and a play area of slides and swings. The shaded areas, free-roaming animals and peaceful aspect all contribute to another pleasant change of pace, especially as Green Meadows is barely 10 minutes from the tourist hurly-burly of Highway 192 (south on Poinciana Boulevard). It is open 9.30am–5.30pm daily (last admission at 4pm) and costs $17 per person ($13 for seniors, under 2s free); allow 3–4 hours for your visit. Drinks, snacks and gifts are available, but it is also the ideal place to bring a picnic. Call 407 846 0770 or visit www.greenmeadowsfarm.com.

Disney and cruising

Taking a cruise is fast becoming a regular option with your Orlando stay and, with the advent of *Disney Cruise Line* in 1998, you will now see a lot of publicity for these competitively priced 2-, 3-, 4- and 7-day sailings out of fast-developing Port Canaveral.

Although a newcomer to cruising, Disney has a couple of breathtaking ships, the 83,000-ton *Disney Magic* (1998) and *Disney Wonder* (1999), with their own dedicated cruise terminal. Classic design plus the usual Disney imagineering have produced these two huge vessels, incorporating special features for kids, teenagers AND couples without children. Both ships are a destination experience in their own right, each with four restaurants, a 1,040-seat theatre, cinema, nightclub complex, sports club and a full health spa, while they sail to the Bahamas, Caribbean and Disney's stunning private island. It is not a cheap option and the 3- and 4-night cruises can feel a little frenzied, but the 7-night Caribbean Cruises – either to St Maarten and St Thomas or Key West, Grand Cayman and Cozumel in Mexico – offer a genuinely relaxing style that is hard to beat anywhere in the world. They boast some novel touches with superb on-board entertainment, Disney character interaction and wonderful features like the adults-only champagne brunch. Many tour operators offer *Disney Cruise Line* packages but you can also book cruise-only at great rates with Dreams Unlimited Travel at www.dreamsunlimitedtravel.com (see page 27).

The ships are identical in practical terms, and the week-long cruises allow you to enjoy fully the wide range of facilities. The impact of the four-restaurant set-up (where you dine in a different one each night, including the amazing black-and-white *Animator's Palate* which comes to life all around you), the fabulous entertainment 'district', the vast array of kids' facilities (including Buzz Lightyear's Cyberspace Command Post) and the picturesque beaches of Disney's Castaway Cay island is just superb.

Other Port Canaveral options (www.portcanaveral.org) include the glitzy **Carnival Cruise Lines** (all-modern hardware, party atmosphere; call 1-888 2276 4825 in the US or 020 7940 4466 in the UK) with 3- and 4-day Bahamas voyages on the *Fantasy*, and alternating 7-day cruises to the east and west Caribbean on one of their newest and biggest ships, the *Carnival Glory*; **Royal Caribbean International** (more modern, glamorous ships, call 1-800 327 6700 in the US or 01932 834231 in the UK) with similar trips to Nassau and RCI's private island of Coco Cay, plus new 1-week Caribbean cruises on their amazing

new mega-ship *Mariner of the Seas*; **Holland America Line** (more traditional cruise elegance, call 1-877 932 4259 in the US, 020 7940 4477 in the UK) offering 1-week cruises (October–April) to the Eastern Caribbean and their private Bahamian island of Half Moon Cay; and, from May 2003, a unique 1-week cruise with **NCL**, one of the brightest and most quality-conscious brands, (call 1-800 327 7030 in the US or 08705 906060 in the UK), who takes their magnificent new *Norwegian Dawn* on a round trip from Port Canaveral to Miami, the Bahamas and New York (yes, the Big Apple itself). For more advice, consult my book *Choosing A Cruise* (Foulsham) or specialist UK travel agent, The Cruise Line Ltd, on 0870 112 1102.

For a smaller and more low-key approach, the **Rivership Romance** (daily out of downtown Sanford) is a great choice, especially for the lunch cruises on the wildlife-rich St John's River. The old-fashioned steamer can take up to 200 in comfort and adds a fine meal, live entertainment and a river commentary, as well as providing a relaxing alternative to the usual tourist scenario. Choose from the 3-hour lunch cruise (11am–2pm Wed, Sat and Sun) at $35 a head, the 4-hour cruise (11am–3pm Mon, Tue, Thur and Fri) at $45 or an evening dinner-dance voyage (7.30–11pm Fri and Sat) at $50. For reservations and info call 407 321 5091 (or visit www.rivershipromance.com). Their dock can be found off Exit 101A of I-4, east into Sanford, then left on Palmetto Avenue.

Seminole County

Having arrived in the historic town of Sanford, the heart of Seminole County, it is worth pointing out the possible diversions of a day or two in

8

this area that will get you well off the beaten track. The **Central Florida Zoological Park** is a private, non-profit-making organisation that puts a pleasant, natural accent on the zoo theme and is set in 116 wooded acres (47 ha) of unspoilt Florida countryside with boardwalks and trails around all the attractions. These include more than 100 species of animals, weekend feeding demonstrations, educational programmes, a picnic area, pony rides and a butterfly garden, plus the Zoofari Outpost gift shop. It's good value, too, at $8 for adults, $5 for seniors (60+) and $4 for kids 3–12 (half-price admission 9–10am Thur), and the park (off Exit 104 of I-4) is open every day (except Thanksgiving Day and Christmas Day) 9am–5pm. They are also in the process of adding new attractions and enlarging several of their exhibits in 2004 – notably their vulture, cougar and siamang habitats – making it even better value in future. Visit at the weekends and you will find a series of personal Animal Encounters (from gators and snakes to hedgehogs) that help to educate visitors about them. For more info, go to www.centralfloridazoo.org.

St John's River Cruise, at Blue Spring State Park, features a 2-hour nature tour of this historic waterway, with interactive narration of the history, flora and fauna (which includes manatees in winter months). This immensely personable, family-run tour costs $16 for adults, $14 for seniors (60+) and $10 for children (3–12) and leaves from Orange City marina several times a day (take Highway

Amur Leopard at Central Florida Zoo

17/92 north from Sanford to French Avenue and head west for 1 mile/ 1.6km). Call 407 330 1612 to check times and book.

One of the most fun and entertaining of the area's airboat rides is to be found at the **Black Hammock Fish Camp and Restaurant** (off Exit 44 of the Central Florida Greeneway, take SR 434 east, turn left on Deleon St and left on to Black Hammock Road). This peaceful backwater on beautiful Lake Jesup is home to Captain Joel Martin, a Frenchman who enjoys his Florida boating, and his **one-hour tours** will take you into every nook and cranny of either the east or west lake (and this really is a great lake to explore), which is positively crammed with gators (including some of the biggest I've seen in the wilds!). It is an eye-opening adventure, and Capt Martin even keeps his own gators, large and small, back at the Fish Camp (great photo opportunity). Rides are $30 for adults and $25 for children, and you should book in advance on 407 365 1244.

Afterwards you can grab lunch or dinner at the **Black Hammock restaurant** (fine local delicacies, especially the catfish and gator tail, plus other dishes and a kids' menu; 11am–10pm Sun and Tue–Thur, 11am–midnight Fri and Sat, with Happy Hour 4–6.30pm; call 407 365 2201) or visit the **Lazy Gator Bar** for karaoke (Sat) and live music

Rivership Romance in Seminole County

(Sun), with Happy Hour all night on Wed! You can even rent canoes or fishing boats and enjoy another view of this unspoilt corner. Look up www.theblackhammock.com for all the latest info.

Alternatively, **Bill's Airboat Adventures**, on the St John's River east of Sanford, offers 90-minute tours in the company of conservationist and river historian Captain Bill Daniel for $35 ($20 for under 14s) on his 6-person boat, subject to a $90 minimum. Visit www.airboating.com or call 407 977 3214 for more info.

Dana's Fishing & Scenic Tours can take you out on to Seminole County's lakes and waterways for some brilliant bass fishing or guided scenic tours (by appointment only, call 407 645 5462 or visit www.fishingincentralflorida.com).

Of course, you can just head for one of the splendid **State Parks** in this area and take your own tour of the well-marked trails. **Wekiva Springs State Park** offers hiking, canoeing and swimming, plus picnic areas and shelters and most recently started offering bike rentals, while **Little Big Econ** state forest has 5,048 acres (2045 ha) of scenic woodlands and wetlands.

Sanford itself is a fascinating city (more of a town by UK standards) on the south shore of Lake Monroe and a designated historic centre, full of brick-paved streets and rather faded antique shops. It is very much small-town America, having lost the growth battle with Orlando many years ago, but it makes a peaceful diversion with some lovely walks, notably the new Riverwalk project and First Street renovations.

Head for the **Sanford Museum** (520 East First Street) to get the full historic overview of the city's growth from its incorporation in 1877 under the patronage of pioneering lawyer and diplomat Henry Sanford as a hub destination on the St John's

River, the 'Nile of America'. The museum (open 11am–4pm Tue–Fri, 1–4pm Sat; admission free) beautifully illustrates the life and times of the city's founder, its growth into the 'celery capital of the world' and its modern history as a US Naval Air Force base.

From there, head on to **First Street** and check out the turn-of-the-19th century buildings, stop for a bite at Morgan's Gourmet Café and finish up by wandering down to the river. And, if you are in the area in September 2004, look out for the **Sanford Heritage Festival** for a weekend of well-organised local fun and festivities.

Sanford also harbours the **Rose Cottage Inn**, a wonderful tea room, restaurant and a quaint B&B, too. It is one of the prettiest settings for lunch, tea or dinner in Florida, serving a mouth-watering array of soups, sandwiches, pastas, salads and quiches, as well as fabulous fruit teas. Their Sunday brunch (noon-4pm; $25 a head) is well worth trying, too. This little treasure (open 11am–3pm and 5–9pm Wed–Sat) can be found on Park Avenue, 13 blocks out of Sanford city centre (call 407 323 9448 for a dining reservation, which is usually necessary). Their B&B operation features a full English breakfast and five completely individual rooms, all with a real turn-of-the-last-century country cottage style. Or you could try out the equally stylish and Victorian **Higgins House** (on South Oak Avenue and 5th Street; 407 324 9238; www.higginshouse.com).

Higgins House

BRIT TIP: Need a hotel in Seminole County for a night or several? Look up www.NorthOrlandoHotels.com for a great selection of short-term accommodations at good prices.

For more info on all the above, go to www.visitseminole.com or call in at one of their **Visitor Centers**, at Orlando Sanford Airport (in the Welcome Center as you exit the main building) and at 1230 Douglas Avenue in Longwood (one block west of Exit 94 of I-4; 407 665 2900).

Out on the Gulf Coast, just north of Homossasa Springs, the **Crystal River** offers another wildlife fiesta as it is home, seasonally, to the endangered manatee, and it is possible to go swimming with these wonderful creatures here. **Orlando Dive & Snorkel Tours** (call 407 239 3573 or visit www.diveorlando.com) offers organised excursions and it truly is a magical opportunity (Manatee Dive is $65, Manatee Snorkel Encounter $40).

Finally, if you enjoy hiking, biking or in-line skating – literally getting off the beaten track – then Seminole County boasts miles of trails and other recreational pursuits. **Spring Hammock Preserve** offers 1,500 acres (607ha) of wilderness to explore, while the Lake Proctor wilderness area is home to 6 miles (10km) of hiking, biking and equestrian adventures. There are more trails in the **Econ River Wilderness Area**, along the Econlockhatchee River, while Chuluota boasts 625 acres (253ha) and the **Geneva Wilderness Area** 180 acres (73ha) including the **Ed Yarborough Nature Center**. For more info, call 407 665 7352 or visit www.co.seminole.fl.us/trails.

Eco-tourism

Genuine eco-tourism is still in its infancy, in general terms, in central Florida, but there are two major exceptions worth knowing about.

Florida Eco-Safaris at Forever Florida is, for my money, one of the most outstanding, non-theme park attractions. It is both a 4,700-acre (1,900ha) wilderness preserve and a working ranch. As well as a close-up of Florida's flora and fauna and its conservation issues, you get a taste of the original cowboy life, Cracker style (Crackers were the 'real' cowboys, pre-dating their Western counterparts by 50 years), which is a fascinating slice of history. Eco-safaris, covered wagon tours, horse rides, bike trails, nature walks and, for the kids, pony rides and a free petting zoo, are the highlights, as well as the magnificent **Cypress Restaurant** and Visitor Center, which offers an essential 30-minute orientation programme into the conservancy's creation.

Beginning as a dream of gifted young biologist and ecologist Allen Broussard, Forever Florida was completed after his death (from complications of Hodgkin's disease) by his parents, Dr William and Margaret Broussard, who own the neighbouring Crescent J Ranch and continue to give their time and energy to building the wilderness as a non-profit-making memorial to their son. The education element alone is awesome, and tours feature a strong conservation message in this tranquil, untouched corner of Florida. The **Swamp Buggy Tours** (2 hours, including lunch, at $28/person) are their stock-in-trade, a tranquil trundle around much of the woods, swamp and prairie that make up the ranch and conservancy in a large-wheeled, open-sided buggy. An education coordinator provides the low-down on the history and environmental issues of the ecosystems. You are likely to encounter alligators (at a safe distance), whitetail deer, armadillos and a host of bird life – including bald eagles – and leave with a good understanding of the real Florida. They also have a new **Swamp Buggy Heritage Safari** (at $35) that includes taking part in a cattle round-up, while the **Rawhide Roundtrip** is a full half-day ranch experience, again including lunch ($89.50). Their 1-, 2- and 3-hour **Horseback Trailrides** ($35, $55 and $69.50) require a minimum of 2 people per ride, and the **City Slickers Round-up** is the full Florida ranch experience ($150). You need to call (1-866 854 3837) at least a day in advance for availability as each tour requires a minimum number to go out. Look up www.floridaeco-safaris.com for more information. In addition, there are **trail bike** rentals at $8 an hour and **pony rides** $5 for the first ride, $3 for a second.

Forever Florida is a good 80-minute drive out of Orlando, some 40 miles (64km) east on Highway 192, through St Cloud as far as Holopaw, then 7½ miles (12km) south on Highway 441, but it is well worth the journey.

On an equally authentic scale is **Disney's Wilderness Preserve**, run by the Nature Conservancy (the world's leading private international conservancy group) in Poinciana, south of Kissimmee. This restoration of a 12,000-acre (4,860-ha) preserve is a work in progress and allows visitors in for various (well-marked) hiking trails, a 1-hour guided tour on Saturdays (at 9.30am) and 2-hour buggy tours on Sundays (1.30pm).

The Preserve's pine and scrubby flatwoods, dry and wet prairies, freshwater marshes and forested wetlands are home to more than 300 wildlife species, including bald eagles, Florida scrub-jays and sandhill cranes, Sherman's fox squirrels, eastern indigo snakes and gopher tortoises, plus more than 50 butterfly species. Visit here for a chance to unwind and enjoy the peace and quiet of the real Florida countryside – just a few miles from all the tourist hubbub. Entry fee is $2 for adults and $1 for children, while the buggy tours are an additional $7 and $5. The preserve is located at the end of Pleasant Hill Road (follow Hoagland Boulevard south off Highway 192). Call 407 935 0002 for more information or visit www.tncflorida.org.

The **Kissimmee Convention and Visitors' Bureau** publishes an excellent eco-guide, if you drop by on Highway 192.

Beach escapes

When it comes to beaches – another key component of a Florida holiday – you are again spoiled for choice. The sea, sand and surf of **Cocoa Beach** is only an hour's drive from Orlando (east on the Beeline Expressway – 528 – then south on Highway A1A) and offers some good shopping (including the unmissable **Ron Jon's Surf Shop**, a massive neon emporium of all things water related) in addition to the two main public beaches. As it's the Atlantic, the sea can be pretty chilly from November to March, but Cocoa Beach is rapidly developing into a major coastal resort, so the facilities are excellent.

Its more famous neighbour, just to the north, is **Daytona Beach**, which is still only an hour away if you take I-4 all the way east. This is the prime site of the Atlantic coast scene, with an array of good beaches (some of which you can even drive on – for a $5 toll, speed limit 10mph/16kph), boating and fishing trips, sightseeing – including the **Ponce de Leon Inlet Lighthouse**,

8

Florida's Beach: St Pete's/Clearwater

The huge stretch of beaches and 'cities' from St Pete's Beach to Clearwater (collectively known as Florida's Beach) represent the heart of the Florida Beach experience, with a wonderful array of attractions as well as the 35 miles (56km) of lovely white sands and average 361 days of sunshine a year. **St Petersburg** (or St Pete's as it's affectionately known) itself, just across the Howard Frankland Bridge from Tampa, is a bright, attractive and happening city, with a range of developments, both recent and historical, which makes it a worthwhile visit. Take time here for the wonderful **Dali Museum** (open 9.30am–5.30pm Mon–Sat, 12 noon–5.30pm Sun; adults $12.50, under 11s free) and the new **Bay Walk** complex of shops, restaurants and a 20-screen cinema. An additional assortment of surprising museums, pedestrian-friendly streets and the Pier all add up to a wealth of opportunity for the interested visitor, while fan-friendly **Tropicana Field** hosts the Tampa Bay Devil Rays baseball team – April to September – for another slice of local fun (tickets from just $5).

Out in the **Beaches**, from the 800-acre (324-ha) Fort De Soto Park in the south to stunning **Caladesi Island** in the north, there is a wonderful diversity of choice, too, with the likes of Treasure Island, Sand Key and St Pete Beach all receiving the Blue Wave Award for cleanliness and safety. **Fort De Soto Park** offers free walking tours of its Spanish-American War era fort and wilderness areas, in addition to having one of the quietest and prettiest beaches. **John's Pass Village & Boardwalk** is an unusual shopping district full of art galleries and restaurants (and is also home to the fun Pirate Cruise two or three times a day – a replica sailing ship that offers a 2-hour party cruise around the waters of Treasure Island; $28 for adults and $18 for children, inclusive of beer, wine and soft drinks; call 727 423 7824), while **Dolphin Landings** in St Pete Beach is another big draw for its dolphin watch cruises, Shell Island day trips and sunset sailings (the dolphin cruise is a real highlight for its guaranteed close-up animal encounters along the calm inland waterway; the 2-hour yacht voyage costs $25 for adults and $15 for children – call 727 367 4488 or visit www.dolphinlandings.com).

Along at Indian Shores, America's largest wild bird hospital, the **Suncoast Seabird Sanctuary**, is another must-see little hideaway, usually with more than 500 injured patients. **Clearwater Beach** boasts the Marine Aquarium and Pier 60, where the daily sunset celebration, complete with craft stalls and live music, is held. Reaching **Caladesi Island** brings you to one of the most picturesque beach spots in the world and another Blue Wave award-winner.

For those wishing to take it easy, rather than drive, the **Suncoast Beach Trolley** is the perfect transport link both along the beaches and into St Petersburg ($1.50/ride or $3 for an all-day pass; call 727 530 9911 or visit www.psta.net). A new 12-seater **hovercraft service** offering trips from the Pier in downtown St Pete's to various Gulf beaches, notably the Holiday Inn Sunspree Resort in Marina Cove to the south and the isle of Egmont Key with its Spanish fort ($14 each way or $25 round trip; call 727 578 4060 or look up www.hover-usa.com). **Duck Tours** offers 80-minute trips through the heart of downtown St Pete's and into Tampa Bay for a scenic view of the waterfront in a World War Two army amphibious vehicle ($18.50 for adults, $9.95 for children, call 727 432 3825 to book).

There is a suitably wide choice of accommodation, too. A range of **Superior Small Lodgings** combine desirable beachfront locations with small-scale, personalised service (check out the Seahorse Cottages & Apartments on Treasure Island Beach as the perfect example – with weekly rates from $385 for a 1-bedroom cottage; call 727 367 2291 or go to www.beachdirectory.com). Of course, there are upmarket hotels, too, witness the superbly equipped **Tradewinds Beach Resorts** (a 1,100-room complex of three resorts that combine their wide range of facilities; call 727 562 1221 or look up www.tradewindsresort.com) on St Pete Beach and the huge (and hugely impressive) **Sheraton Sand Key Resort** at Clearwater Beach, a 10-storey edifice with 10 acres (4ha) of private beach and facilities ranging from floodlit tennis courts to a fitness centre, children's pool and playground (with supervised programmes in summer). Rates from $135–480, call 727 595 1611 or check out www.beachsand.com. The area also boasts more than 2,000 restaurants. Check out www.floridasbeach.com for all the info.

Florida beach sunset

a formidable 203 spiralling steps to the top of this magnificently preserved monument, but well worth it for the view (10am–5pm daily, $5 for adults, $1.50 for children) and surprisingly smart shopping and dining at the redeveloped **Ocean Walk Village**, next door to the main beach, pier and boardwalk area. New in 2003 were **RC Theatres' Ocean Walk** 10 cineplex, the serious film-themed fun of **Bubba Gump's Shrimp Company**, the **Mai Tai** bar and **Adobe Gila's Margarita Fajita Cantina** (check out their near-lethal range of cocktails!). Then there is the lively **Riverfront Marketplace** along historic Beach Street (see below).

New in 2002 was the **Marine Science Center** (just around the corner from the lighthouse at Ponce Inlet), which showcases whale, mangrove, mosquito and sea turtle exhibits, along with turtle rehabilitation facilities and a 5,000-gallon (22,750-litre) artificial reef aquarium, as well as static and interactive educational displays. A boardwalk and nature trail system extends throughout the park, which naturally has a gift shop. It is open 10am–4pm Tue–Sat and noon–4pm Sun (closed Mon) and costs $1 for 5–12s and $3 for 13 and older under 5s free. (www.echotourism.com/msc).

The **beaches** themselves are a lively affair around Spring Break (the big American pre-Easter college holiday) but fairly down to earth otherwise. Other highlights include

the chance to cruise the intra-coastal waterway to see the local dolphins at play – check out **A tiny Cruise Line** (call 386 226 2343 or visit www.visitdaytona.com/tinycruise/) for details of their four cruises, which vary from $11.03–18.85, with tax and include a lovely Sunset/City Lights tour from April to October.

The **Riverfront Marketplace** is the heart of downtown Daytona Beach, with a museum of local history, restaurants, nightclubs, coffee bars and a performing arts theatre, all in a quaint riverside setting. Dining out opportunities are many and inviting along the beaches, with **Inlet Harbor** and **Lighthouse Landing** among the best. The tide can retreat by up to 500ft (150 metres) and the beaches are all open to the public year-round.

Lighthouse Point Park is especially worthy of note, a 52-acre (21-ha) stretch of nature trails, fishing, observation deck, swimming and picnicking (open 8am–9pm, $3.50 per vehicle). Check out the **Lighthouse Landing** here for lunch or dinner, a truly eclectic piece of Floridian restaurant life. For the latest on all Daytona Beach has to offer, call 020 7935 7756 in the UK or look up www.daytonabeach.com. Of course, one of the biggest attractions is the Daytona USA racetrack (see page 235).

To the West you have the **Gulf Coast**, which is a good 90 minutes' drive down I-4 and through Tampa on I-275 south to **St Petersburg**

Riverfront Marketplace, Daytona Beach

Beach (105 miles/169km) or **Clearwater Beach** (110 miles/177km) or 2 hours-plus down I-4 and then I-75 to **Bradenton** (130 miles/209km), **Sarasota** (140 miles/225km) and **Venice** (160 miles/257km), plus the beautiful islands of **Captiva** and **Sanibel** (175 miles/282km) and **Fort Myers Beach**, part of the fabulous Lee Island Coast scene, a mini faraway tropical paradise, without the faraway part (look up www.leeislandcoast.com). The beaches are less 'hip', but more relaxed and refined, and the sea a touch warmer and much calmer, so it is better for families with small children. You will find it easier to get away from the crowds here, too.

Naples is further south still on I-75 but is rated one of the most welcoming beach destinations in Florida.

BRIT TIP: Be warned, during the summer months the locals all get the same urge to head for the beach at weekends, so unless you head out EARLY (i.e. before 9am) and come back late (i.e. after 8pm) you will encounter serious traffic.

SPORT

In addition to virtually every form of entertainment known to man, central Florida is one of the world's biggest sporting playgrounds, with a huge range of opportunities either to watch or play your favourite sport.

Golf

Without doubt, the number one activity in Florida is golf, with almost 150 courses within an hour's drive of Orlando. The weather, of course, makes it such a popular pastime, but some spectacular courses – many of them designed by world-famous names like Greg Norman, Tom Watson, Arnold Palmer and Jack Nicklaus – add to the attraction, and there are numerous holiday packages geared towards keen golfers of all abilities. With an 18-hole round, including cart hire and taxes, from as little as $40 on some courses (and they average around $75), it is an attractive proposition and quite different for those used to British courses. If you go in for 36-hole days, it is possible to save up to $30 by replaying the same course, while it is cheaper to play Monday to Thursday than Friday to Sunday.

Sculpted landscapes, manicured fairways and abundant use of spectacular water features and white-sand bunkers add up to some memorable golfing. The winter months are the high season, hence the most expensive, but many courses are busy year-round. Be aware also that some courses pair up golfers with little thought for age, handicap, etc. So, if two of you turn up, the chances are that you will play with two complete strangers ('A little frustrating when you get paired with two middle-aged ladies from Switzerland who have only just taken up golf,' says reader John Cartlidge).

Virtually every course will offer a driving range to get you started, plus lockers, changing rooms and showers, while the use of golf carts is universal (and many include the amazing GPS positioning system which gives the yardage for every shot, plus the ability to order drinks or even lunch while you're on the course!). They all feature creature comforts like ice water stations and drinks carts that circulate the course (please don't forget to tip the trolley girls who drive them). A handful have swimming pools, while all can offer a decent bar and restaurant for that all-important 19th-hole.

BRIT TIP: An early-morning tee-off in the summer can provide some of the most peaceful and scenic golf you will find.

Your best starting point is to visit one of the five **Edwin Watts** golf shops around Orlando to pick up a free copy of the *Golfer's Guide* or the *Guide To Golf* for a handy introduction to most of the courses available (and even pick up a new set of clubs at the Watts National Clearance Center just south of Wet 'n Wild on I-Drive; call 407 352 2535 or visit www.edwinwatts.com). Alternatively, **Tee-Times USA** (1-888 465 3356) offers an excellent advice and reservation service. The **Visit Florida** organisation publishes an *Official Golf Guide* (call 850 488 8374 or look up www.flasports.com, as does Daytona Beach (1-800 881 7065, www.golfdaytonabeach.com).

For a unique and personable touch, you can't beat the all-in-one golf instruction service of **Professional Golf Guides of Orlando**, led by owner/operator and PGA member Phillip Jaffe, who is a mine of golfing lore and knowledge, as well as great company. They take up to three golfers at a time around some of the area's finest courses, and can supply transport and high-tech (graphite and titanium) clubs if required. The playing lesson is of the highest quality and includes full on-course instruction, course management strategies, full game analysis, game improvement suggestions, shot-making demos and a wrap-up lesson that will leave you with the knowledge and skills to take your game to the next level. It is an eye-opening experience to play alongside Phillip and his staff of PGA professionals (hey, he even managed to get me hitting the green

from some way off, which is no mean feat!) and well worth it for the keen golfer who wishes to improve their game in one round. Call 407 227 9869 for rates or visit www.progolfguides.com.

Alternatively, the **Nick Faldo Golf Institute** on the lower portion of I-Drive (1-888 463 2536) is a great place to visit if you just want to hit a few golf balls.

Walt Disney World Resort in Florida has been quick to attract the golf fanatic, with five championship-quality courses, including the 7,000-yd (6,400-metre) **Palm**, rated as one of *Golf Digest's* top 25 (and reputedly with one of the toughest holes in America – the 18th), plus a nine-hole par-36 course, Oak Trail. Fees vary from $109–144 for Disney resort guests and $114–149 for visitors, with half-price reductions after 3pm. Call 407 939 4653 for tee-times. There are also private and group lessons under PGA professional guidance, video analysis and a great range of club rentals. The rolling **Osprey Ridge** (up to 7,101yd/6,493 metres) and the visually intimidating **Eagle Pines** (up to 6,772yd/6,192 metres) are the two newest – introduced in 1992 – designed by master architects Tom Fazio and Pete Dye respectively. Watch out for the **FUNAI Classic** PGA event over the Magnolia and Palm courses every October. NB: Some of the best tee times are reserved for guests at Disney resort hotels.

Another luxury experience is afforded by the nearby **Hyatt Grand Cypress** on Vineland Road (407 239 1904, rates from $130–170 depending on season). It has three elegant 9-hole courses and a superb 18-hole links-style offering (all designed by the legendary Jack Nicklaus), which presents a truly magnificent challenge.

MetroWest Country Club, on South Hiawassee Road to the north

8

of Universal Studios (407 299 1099; $79–115), is a 7,051-yd (6,447-metre) masterpiece designed by Robert Trent Jones Snr and features elevated tees and greens, with pleasant rolling fairways and expansive bunkers.

The superb **Keene's Pointe** in Windermere to the north of *Walt Disney World Resort in Florida* is Nicklaus's newest and most exciting course, measuring 7,173yd (6,559 metres) if played off the pro Bear tees (there are always five tees for the various handicaps, ladies and seniors). Surrounded by lakes, it has a truly impeccable look, not to mention outstanding facilities, including a pool (407 876 1461; $65–115).

The **Legacy Club at Alaqua**

BRIT TIP: Reader John Cartlidge, a keen Florida golfer, advises: 'Take your waterproofs with you. I was looking to buy some in Florida but could only find lightweight slipovers – no use in the UK.'

Lakes is a masterpiece of conservation and tranquillity (it is part of the Audubon preservation and restoration scheme) as well as a tour de force of lush fairways and weird and wonderful greens (a signature feature of Tom Fazio). Winding through some spectacular

Golf at sunset

forest in the suburb of Longwood in Seminole County, it is a serious challenge for serious golfers (407 444 9995; $54–64).

Also in Seminole, **Magnolia Plantation** is another wonderful contrast, a heavily wooded and peaceful haven that feels miles from the theme park world and yet is less than half an hour away up I-4. Woven among the lakes and ponds of the Wekiva River basin, Phillip Jaffe rates it a 'must play' course (407 833 0818; $55–85).

Falcon's Fire in Kissimmee is another outstanding course, featuring the 'ProShot' digital caddy system and water coolers on all golf carts. Plenty of water around the course assures a testing 18 holes, but it is wonderfully picturesque (407 239 5445; $75–150).

The **Orange Lake Country Club** is a huge vacation resort in Orlando (just 4 miles/6km from Disney) with two 18-hole courses, a 9-hole course and a par-3, floodlit 9 holes. The new Legends at Orange Lake course (designed by Arnold Palmer) is their top-of-the-range offering (407 239 1050; $70–90). **Kissimmee Oaks** features some majestic moss-draped oaks and local wildlife as well as 18 holes of memorable golf that wind around some pretty lakes, all just 3½ miles (6km) south of Highway 192 in Kissimmee in the Oaks Community off John Young Parkway (407 933 4055; $50–80).

No less than four new courses were built in 2003, with pride of place going to **Grande Lakes Orlando**, the amazing hotel/resort complex just off John Young Parkway. This Greg Norman-designed masterpiece offers 18 holes of genuine Florida nature with the added benefit of a Caddie-Concierge service for every twosome and foursome (call for rates, 407 206 2400). The monstrous **Harmony Golf Preserve** in the town of

Harmony in Osceola County (out on the east stretch of Highway 192, past St Cloud) is an incredible 7,428yd (6,792 metres) at its longest, designed by Johnny Miller and with terrific club and associated recreation facilities (407 891 8525; $40–100).

The rolling and aptly named **Victoria Hills** in DeLand (mid-way between Orlando and Daytona Beach, Exit 116 off I-4) gets a big thumbs up from Phillip Jaffe ('A great track – very challenging!'), with a par 72 course designed by Ron Garl and a superb practice facility (386 738 6000; $39–75).

Finally, the extravagant **Reunion Resort & Club** (in Davenport, just to the south of Disney, Exit 54 off I-4) is a Tom Watson, Arnold Palmer, Jack Nicklaus collaboration, with 18 holes designed by each (the latter due to open in late 2003/04). Watson's 7,257-yd (6,636-metre) Independence Course is possibly the most challenging, with a style not dissimilar to famous Augusta National (888 300 2434; $50–85).

Seminole County itself is another golf haven, with 18 public or semi-private courses, and offers golf-and-hotel packages from $65. Call 1-800 555 9589 for details or look up www.visitseminole.com.

Check when you book about each club's dress code, as there are a few differences from course to course. There are dozens of other choices, this is only a small (if representative) sample.

Mini-golf

Not exactly a sport, but definitely for holiday fun, are the many quite extravagant opportunities for mini-golf around Orlando. They are a big hit with kids and good fun for all the family (if you have the legs left for it after a day at a theme park!). Several attractions and parks offer mini-golf

as an extra, but for the best, try out the self-contained centres, of which there are six main ones.

Predictably, Disney has come up with some terrific ones of their own. **Disney's Fantasia Gardens Miniature Golf Courses**, next to the Swan Hotel just off Buena Vista Drive, is a 2-course challenge over 36 of the most varied holes of mini-golf you will find. Hippos dance, fountains leap and broomsticks march on the 18-hole crazy, golf-themed **Fantasia Gardens** – its style is taken from the Disney animated classic *Fantasia*, meaning lots of cartoon fun along the way as the park's Imagineers challenge you with a riot of visual gags as well as some diabolically difficult mini-golf. Watch out for *Toccata and Fugue in D Minor* where good shots are rewarded with musical tones, and *The Nutcracker Suite*, where obstacles include dancing mushrooms!

Fantasia Fairways is a cunning putting course, complete with fairways, rough, water hazards and bunkers to test even the best golfers. The 18 holes range in length from 40ft (12 metres) to 75ft (23 metres), and it can take more than an hour to play a full round. Each course costs $9.76 (adult) and $7.78 (child), and they are open 10am–11pm every day.

Disney's latest offering is the 36-hole **Winter-Summerland Miniature Golf Courses** at the entrance to *Disney's Blizzard Beach* water park. Divided into two18-hole courses, these mini works of art feature a 'Summer' setting of surf and beach tests (watch out for

Deep sea fishing

8

squirting fish), and a 'Winter' variety of snow and ice-crafted holes, all with a welter of visual puns as befitting the vacation resort of Santa's elves (yes, that's the theme, and kids will love it – you can even see the skid marks where Santa landed his sleigh!). An adult round is $9.76 (3–9s $7.78), a double round is half price and it is open 10am–11pm.

Elsewhere, **Pirate's Cove** has a twin-course set-up at Lake Buena Vista (by the Crossroads shopping plaza) and I-Drive (just south of The Mercado), with mountain caves, waterfalls and rope bridges to test your skill and please the eye. **River Adventure Golf** (on Highway 192, almost opposite Medieval Times) offers a Mississippi River adventure with rolling rapids, waterfalls and an authentic water wheel. **Bonanza Miniature Golf and Gifts** (next door to the Magic Mining Co restaurant on west Highway 192) has an imaginative – and tricky – 36 holes with a gold mining theme. **Pirate's Island** (further along Highway 192 to the east) is another spectacular 36-hole spread, while arguably the most impressive of the lot is the **Congo River Golf and Exploration Co**, which has courses on Highway 192, I-Drive and Highway 436 in Altamonte Springs. They could almost be Disney-inspired, they are so artificially scenic. The Kissimmee location also has paddle boats to try, while I-Drive has the option of go-karts, and all three have games and video arcades. Charges are $6–8 per round, but look out for coupons which all have a couple of dollars off each one. They open 9am–10pm or 11pm daily.

Million Dollar Mulligan is worthy of mention here, although it is neither mini-golf nor the real McCoy. Instead, Million Dollar Mulligan, just off Highway 192 on Florida Plaza Boulevard (next to Old Town – look for the giant golf ball),

is a 9-hole, floodlit pitch-and-putt course that looks spectacular at night when its lake and fountains are illuminated. It costs $11.75 for adults and $7.50 for children and seniors and is open daily from 10am–midnight (407 396 8180).

Fishing

Fishing attracts a lot of specialist holiday-makers and is fast catching on as a highly enjoyable day out with theme park visitors as well. The abundance of lakes and rivers give plenty of choice, with bass (often of record-breaking size) the prime catch. A 7-day licence costs $17 (available from all tackle shops, fish camps, sports stores and Wal-Mart and Kmart supermarkets), and there are dozens of boats for hire on the St John's River, Lake Toho in Kissimmee, Lake Kissimmee, and both coasts for some serious sea fishing. Expect to pay $160–195 for half a day and $200–295 for a full day bass fishing.

For the most complete angling service try **Cutting Loose Expeditions**, a highly experienced, personalised operator who can organise fresh or sea-water expeditions and arrange hotel pick-up if necessary. All your bait and licence requirements are included. It is run by A Neville Cutting, one of America's leading fishing adventurers, who maintains high standards with his guides and other staff. Rates start at $200 for a half day's bass fishing (2 fishermen per boat with a licensed guide), and other trips, including offshore fishing for marlin, can be arranged with him. Call 407 629 4700, or write to Cutting Loose Expeditions, PO Box 447, Winter Park, Florida 32790-0447.

Alternatively, **AJ's Freelance Bass Guide Services**, the oldest continuously operating service in central Florida, specialises in trophy bass fishing on Lake Toho in Kissimmee with professional guides (all US Coastguard-licensed captains). Day trips (8 hours from first light) are $300 for 1–2 people, a half day (4 hrs) is $250 and it is $50 extra per person, plus your licence and bait (sodas and ice provided, but you need to bring your own snacks and other drinks). Owner/operator Captain A James Jackson is renowned as one of the best bass guides in the country and provides a highly personable and insightful service. Hotel pick-ups ($35) can also be arranged, call 407 348 8764 (at least 2 weeks in advance) or visit their excellent website at www.orlandobass.com. Those in the know really do rate this as one of the greatest fishing experiences anywhere. NB: cash and cheques only, no credit cards.

Seminole County has its share of fishing action, too. Check out **Spotted Tail** for a range of angling adventures with fly and light tackle, visit www.spottedtail.com or call 407 977 5207.

Water sports

Florida is mad keen on water sports of all persuasions. So, on any area of water bigger than your average pond, don't be surprised to find the locals water-skiing, jetskiing, knee-boarding, canoeing, paddling, wind-surfing, boating or otherwise indulging in watery pursuits. *Walt Disney World Resort in Florida* offers all manner of boats, from catamarans to canoes and pedaloes, and activities, from water-skiing to parasailing, on the main **Bay Lake**, as well as the smaller **Seven Seas Lagoon Crescent Lake** and **Lake Buena Vista**. Parasailing (from *Disney's Contemporary Resort* – see page 59) costs $75 solo or $115 tandem, while boat rentals (from a

range of resorts) vary from $8/hour (14-ft/4-metre sailboats and catamarans) to $57/hour (21-ft/6-metre pontoon boats). For reservations and information, call 407 939 7529.

Several operators serve the lakes around Orlando and Kissimmee, but some leave much to be desired safety-wise. **Dave's Ski School** on Lake Bryan at Lake Buena Vista (right next to the Holiday Inn Sunspree Resort on SR 535) gets our recommendation for their safety-conscious approach and virtual guarantee to get beginners up and water-skiing. Their **Watersports Adventure** includes an hour's water-ski lesson and ride, a tube ride and a wave-runner ride ($55 adult, $48 child), and lasts up to 3 hours; an hour's water-ski school costs $40 and $36. You can also rent wave-runners at $35 for half an hour. Many tour operators endorse this ski school. For more details call 407 239 6939 (or look them up at www.bvwatersports.com).

Horse riding

Orlando is home to one of the foremost equestrian centres in America – the **Grand Cypress Equestrian Center**, which is part of the 1,500-acre (608-ha) Grand Cypress Resort, and all its rides and facilities are open to non-residents. This stunningly equipped equine haven offers a dazzling array of opportunities for horse enthusiasts of all abilities.

A full range of clinics, lessons and other instructional programmes are available, from half-hour kids' sessions to all-summer academies, plus a variety of trail rides. Serious horse riders will note this was the first American equestrian centre to be approved by the British Horse Society, and it operates the BHS test programme. Inevitably, this 5-star facility does not come cheap but it is a worthwhile experience, especially for children. Private lessons are $55 per half hour or $100 per hour, while a week's package of 8 group 1-hour lessons is $280. Young Junior Lessons (15-minute supervised rides for under 12s) are $25, while the Western Trail Ride (an hour's excursion for novice riders) is $35 per person and the Advanced Trail Ride $100. The centre is open 8.30am–6pm Mon–Fri and 8.30am–5pm Sat and Sun, and it can be found by taking Exit 68 on I-4 on to Route 535 north, turning left after half a mile (1km) at the traffic lights and then following the road north for a mile (1.6km) past the entrance to the Grand Cypress Hotel, until you reach the centre on the right (407 239 1938 or www.grandcypress.com/equestrian/).

On a smaller scale and none the less charming is the **Horse World Riding Stables** on Poinciana Boulevard, just 12 miles (19km) south of Highway 192. This gets you more out into the wilds and you can spend anything from an hour to a full day enjoying the rides and lessons on offer. The three main rides are the Nature Trail ($34), a walking-only tour of 45–50 minutes, for beginners aged 6 and up, through 750 acres (304ha) of untouched Florida countryside, the Intermediate Trail (ages 10 and up) for nearly 1 hour ($39), and the Advanced Private Trail, a 75- to 90-minute trip for advanced riders with private guide ($49). There is also a picnic area with fishing pond, playing fields, pony rides for under 7s ($6) and farm animals to pet.

Rodeo

Jetskiing at Tampa Bay

Riding lessons are $25/hour with up to 4 in a group and $45/hour privately. There is also a 3-hour Children's Horse Camp (for 8–14-year-olds every Sat at 9am – call for prices). There is no charge for just looking, and the stables are open 9am–5pm daily. Call 407 847 4343 or visit www.horseworldstables.com.

Similarly out in the wilds (in the Rock Springs Run Wildlife Preserve in Seminole County, to be precise) are **Rock Springs Riding Stables**, another slice of native Florida, with rides varying from a 1-hour Turkey Trail to a full day's Wildlife Wander, all led by trained guides. The park's 6,000 acres (2,430ha) guarantee plenty of wildlife, from otters and coyotes to the occasional wild boar and even bears, and the rides go out every day 9am–6pm, costing $25–100, with $10 pony rides for under 8s. To find Rock Springs, take I-4 to Exit 101C (Sanford–SR46) and go west 8 miles (13km) before turning left into the preserve. Take the dirt road first left and follow all the way to the horse barn, or call 407 314 1000 for more info.

Spectator events

When it comes to spectator events, Orlando is not quite so well furnished as other big American cities, but there is always something on offer for the discerning sports fan who would like to sample the local version of the big match. There are no top-flight American football or baseball teams, but there is an

Cleveland Indians pre-season baseball

indoor version of gridiron (American football), called Arena Football, plus Spring Training (pre-season) for several baseball teams (notably Cleveland in Winter Haven).

The main sport is **basketball** and the Orlando Magic of the National Basketball Association (NBA). The season runs from November to May (with exhibition games in October), and the only drawback is the 16,000-seat **TD Waterhouse Center** where they play (on Amelia Street, Exit 83B off I-4, turn left, then left again) is occasionally fully booked. Contact the Center's box office (407 649 3245) to see if there are any tickets left, although you will need to call in person to buy them (from $16 up in the gods to $60 courtside), or you can call TicketMaster on 407 839 3900 for credit card bookings.

The Orlando Predators, one of America's top **Arena Football** teams, is also popular at the same venue (from February to June, $8–40) and you would need to call several days in advance to avoid missing one of their lively home games that feature some great entertainment as well as their fast, hard-hitting version of indoor gridiron in the magnificent Center.

For the Real Thing in gridiron terms, the nearest teams in the **National Football League** are the Tampa Bay Buccaneers, 75 miles (120km) to the west, the Miami Dolphins, some 3–4 hours' drive to the south, down the Florida Turnpike, or the Jacksonville Jaguars way up the east coast past Daytona, a

3-hour drive up I-4 and I-95. Again, TicketMaster can give you ticket prices ($30–60) and availability (September to December).

Another Spring Training **baseball** opportunity can be found at Osceola County Stadium in Kissimmee, where the Houston Astros take up home for the month of March. Being part of the audience here is to experience a genuine slice of Americana. Call 321 697 3201 for more details, or TicketMaster to book tickets on 407 839 3900.

Disney's Wide World of Sports Complex™

The newest sports facility in the area is inevitably a Disney project to bring in some world-class events and competitors. *Disney's Wide World of Sports Complex*™ is a 200-acre (81-ha), state-of-the-art complex, featuring 30 sports and is quite awesome to wander round even when no one is playing. The complex's main features are a 7,500-seater baseball stadium, a softball quadraplex, an 11-court tennis complex, sports field and the **Official All Star Café**® with a massive array of sports memorabilia and even themed food. The Cracker Jack Stadium is home for spring training of baseball's mighty **Atlanta Braves**, and the crowds flock in for pre-season games in March (highly recommended).

Sadly, there is no longer a Minor League team based here, and you would need to head to Tampa for the nearest Major League team (the **Tampa Bay Devil Rays**; highly

Parasailing near Kissimmee

recommended, see Florida's Beach section on page 224). The complex is also home from mid July for a month to the NFL's **Tampa Bay Buccaneers** as they begin their pre-season training, and it is quite an entertaining and eye-opening experience to watch these amazing athletes in action, even if it is only in practice.

Other high-class events here include athletics, soccer, lacrosse, in-line hockey and even cricket. The facilities alone should inspire world-class performances in any athlete. Standard admission is $9.76 for adults and $7.78 for 3–9s, but it is also one of your optional extras with a Park Hopper PLUS Ticket (excluding special events). *Disney's Wide World of Sports Complex™* can be found off Osceola Parkway, on Victory Way. Call 407 939 4263 for events and prices.

The **Walt Disney World Marathon** is another major annual sporting event and its 11th running will be on January 11, 2004. Some 13,500 runners take part – including some of the world's leading athletes – but it also draws some huge crowds as the 26.2-mile route takes in all four theme parks. Be aware the parks face some serious disruption but, as with the London Marathon, the Disney version also serves up a great spectacle. The annual **Half-Marathon** takes place on the same day. For more details visit www.disneyworldsports.com.

Rodeo

An all-American pursuit straight out of the Old West, the **Silver Spurs Rodeo** is staged twice a year at the brand new, 8,300-seat Silver Spurs Arena. This is the biggest event of its kind in the south-east and is held in the first week in October and the last week in February. However, it sells out fast so you need to book at least a month in advance on www.silverspursrodeo.com or phone

407 677 6336. The event features classic bronco and bull riding and attracts top competitors from as far away as Canada. The new arena is part of the $84 million **Osceola Heritage Park**, which includes Osceola County Stadium (for baseball) and the Kissimmee Valley Livestock Show & Fair Pavilion.

On a slightly smaller scale, the **Kissimmee Rodeo** is held every Friday at 8pm (except when the Silver Spurs is on) at the Kissimmee Sports Arena, on Hoagland Boulevard 2 miles (3km) south of Highway 192. Events include calf roping, steer wrestling and bull riding, and admission is $10 for adults and $5 for children 12 and under. Kids love the live action, which can be surprisingly rugged (if not dangerous), and there is even a kids' contest – grab the ribbon from the calf's tail! The Catch Pen Saloon lounge is open 8pm–2am Fri and Sat, and 6pm–2am Sun, with line dancing 6pm–8pm and $1 drinks. Call 407 933 0020 for more details or look at www.ksarodeo.com.

Motor sport

For the guaranteed ultimate in high-speed thrills, *Walt Disney World Resort in Florida* has its own speedway oval where **Richard Petty Driving Experience** is based. Here you can experience one of their 650bhp stock cars as either driver or passenger at up to 145mph (233kph). The programmes have been devised by top NASCAR driver Richard Petty and offer the 3-lap **Ride-Along Experience**; a 3-hour **Rookie Experience** (with tuition and eight laps of the speedway); the **Kings Experience** (tuition plus 18 laps in two sessions); and the **Experience of a Lifetime** (an intense 30-lap programme).

The Ride-Along Experience will probably appeal to most – three laps of the 1.1-mile (1.8-km) circuit with an experienced, race-proven driver lasting just 37 seconds a lap but an unbelievable blast all the way. Your initial take-off from the pit-lane takes you 0–60mph (97kph) in a couple of seconds and you are straight into Turn One with your brain some distance behind. It is a bit like flying at ground level, it is hot and noisy and you must wear sensible clothes (you have to climb in through the window), but it is definitely the Real Thing in ride terms and a huge thrill.

You don't need to book for the Ride-Along Experience, which is available from mid-February to the end of September and there is no admission fee, so you can come along just to watch. The three driving programmes all require reservations, while the track is occasionally closed for race testing from October to February. However, before you get carried away, wait for the prices: $89 for the Ride-Along Experience, $349 for the Rookie Experience, $699.99 for the Kings and $1,199.99 for the Lifetime Experience. For more details, or to book, call 407 939 0130 or visit www.1800bepetty.com.

Race fans will also want to check out **Daytona International Speedway** just up the road in Daytona (take I-4 east, then I-95 and Highway 92) for more big-league car and motorcycle thrills. It hosts more than a dozen race weekends a year, including stock cars, sports cars, motorcycles, go-karts and trucks, and highlights are the Daytona 500 (February 15, 2004), and Pepsi 400 (first Sunday in July). The big events attract more than 200,000 devotees and provide some of the most colourful sport anywhere in the world. Call 386 253 7223 or www.daytonainternationalspeedway. com).

Daytona USA, an interactive motor sport-themed attraction, is here as well, offering a series of

BRIT TIP: Race fan Alan Rogers, of Chester, rates Daytona USA highly: 'Try the hands-on Pit Stop Live, the excellent *Daytona 500* movie and the 30-minute tour of the track. It's a real thrill.'

hands-on exhibits, rides and films to give you a taste of all the high-speed action. Change tyres in a timed pit stop, design and video test a racing car, commentate on a race and experience the *Daytona 500* film. Other elements include Acceleration Alley (for an additional fee), with full-size NASCAR simulators combining motion, video and sound to capture the thrills of head-to-head racing at more than 200mph (322kph), and Daytona Dream Laps, another elaborate motion simulator to put riders inside the Daytona 500 itself. The history and great moments of speedway are well detailed and there is a good gift shop. A half-hour, open-sided tram tour of the speedway stops in Pit Road, giving a real close-up of this amazing arena.

Hours are 9am–7pm daily (not Christmas) and adult admission is $16, seniors (60+) $13 and children 6–12 $8(under 6s free with a paying adult). The Combo ticket with the Speedway tour is $20, $14 and $17, while the tour on its own is $7 per person. Call 386 947 6800 or visit www.daytonausa.com. Finally, you can ride the Richard Petty Driving Experience here too, with the $134 fee for three laps of the world-famous, steeply banked 2½-mile (4-km) tri-oval also including entrance to Daytona USA.

Okay, that's the full daytime scene, now let's check out all the night-time entertainment…

8

Orlando by Night
(or, Burning the Candle at Both Ends)

Hands up those who still have plenty of energy left! Right, this chapter is especially for you. If we can't wear you out at the theme parks and other attractions, we'll have to resort to a full-frontal assault on your sleep time – and take most of it away.

For, when it comes to night-time fun and frolics, Orlando again has a dazzling collection of possibilities, from its purpose-built entertainment complexes, through its range of evening dinner shows and on to a full array of bars and nightclubs. The choice is suitably widespread and almost always high in quality.

Unfortunately, the development that started the evening entertainment ball rolling has now closed down. **Church Street Station**, in the heart of the downtown area, shut in 2001 and there is still no firm news of what will take its place. The site formerly occupied by Rosie O'Grady's, the Cheyenne Saloon, the Orchid Room, Apple Annie's Courtyard, Phineas Fogg's and Lili Marlene's is now home to a comedy club – **Orlando Improv**, a mini theatre with a separate bar/dining area – and **GameTime** sports bar and grill (open Wed–Sun, 4pm until midnight; 321 281 8181). Orlando Improv features stand-up comedians from various American TV shows (DEF JAM, BET and Comic Review) but plays to a largely adult audience, i.e. 21 and over only, except for Friday nights, when it's 18 and up. (Shows run Wed–Sun at 8pm – smoke-free on Thur and Sat – with a 10.30 performance on Fri and Sat. Admission varies but is usually $22. Call 321 281 8000 or visit www.orlandoimprov.com for more details.) What used to be Crackers restaurant is now **Louis'**, an equally upscale fine dining experience.

Disney joined the big evening entertainment concept in 1987 with **Pleasure Island**, an imaginative range of clubs, discos and

Downtown Disney by night

restaurants, and they continue to refine the formula all the time to keep it fresh and appealing. **Disney's BoardWalk Resort**, which opened in 1996, added more to their night-time amusement options.

International Drive (I-Drive) caught up with this process in 1997 when **Pointe*Orlando** opened. Although its prime focus is shopping and restaurants, it has a strong evening entertainment component with the big Muvico 21-screen cinema centre, its lively bars and two recent nightclubs. Finally, Universal Orlando got with the beat in late 1998 with the opening of **CityWalk**, possibly the most elaborate and sophisticated centre of the lot. They all represent yet another slick opportunity to be dazzled and relieved of your cash in the name of holiday fun. However, you should try to visit at least one if your wallet can take the strain.

CityWalk

DOWNTOWN DISNEY

The large-scale development of what is now *Downtown Disney* (the old Village Marketplace and *Pleasure Island*) has evolved into a 3-part complex (*Downtown Disney* Marketplace, *Pleasure Island* and West Side) doubling the size of the old site and providing two key evening entertainment sources.

Pleasure Island

This is the traditional nightclub zone which packs in the locals as well as the tourists and where every night is New Year's Eve. You must be 18 or over to enter (unless accompanied by a parent), while you must be at least 21 to enter two of the clubs (see below). *Pleasure Island* (which forms the centrepiece, or linking part, of *Downtown Disney*) consists of eight original club venues and just about every music type you

can think of, plus several novel twists. The **Rock 'n Roll Beach Club** is a multi-level live music venue featuring 40 years of classic rock (mainly the 1980s and 1990s) with a resident cover band and DJs. It also boasts pool tables, arcade games and several bars. The **Pleasure Island Jazz Company** offers some excellent modern jazz and blues in a 1930s-style 'warehouse' nightspot. You can grab a snack here and listen to some of the coolest sounds in town. Serious clubbers head for **Mannequins Dance Palace** (21 and over only), a huge, popular disco, with a revolving dance floor, mirrored walls, dry ice and lasers, plus a pounding sound system and superb lighting. At the **Comedy Warehouse**, the highly talented and quick-witted Improv Co gives periodical shows with guest 'volunteers' (beware sitting near a phone – you WILL end up in the show!). Queuing can begin up to half an hour before a performance, which lasts for around 45 minutes and is guaranteed to be different every time. For a touch of retro groovin', **8Trax** is a homage to 1970s' music, dance and styles (right down to the lava lamps) and usually draws a lively crowd of all ages. The unmissable **Adventurers' Club** is a personal favourite, a 2-storey live

9

entertainment lounge, in 1920s' Gentleman's Club style, which comes to life around you (watch the animal heads and masks!) and the stars of the shows mix with the guests. Once again an element of comedy improvisation is mixed in with the scripted action and, if the cast happens to pick on you, don't try to win any battle of comedic wits – they have the microphone, remember!

The **BET Soundstage Club**™ is a totally modern offering, with an interactive VJ/DJ and featuring the best of R&B, soul and hip-hop sounds (21 and over only). Finally, the newest venue **Motion** (formerly the Wildhorse Saloon) is a cavernous dance club, featuring Top 40 to Alternative music, animated DJs and a giant TV screen. This is another happening club, and is especially popular with the locals at weekends. Additionally, the outdoor **West End Stage**, which hosts *Pleasure Island*'s resident band and occasional big-name acts, is the focus for the street party and fireworks at midnight, because every night is New Year's Eve, so get ready to party!

As well as the clubs, *Pleasure Island* has a range of six shops, including **Reel Finds** for film memorabilia, **DTV**, an up-scale Disney fashion store and **Changing Attitudes**, offering some stylish men's and women's clothing. You can grab a snack at the **Missing Link Sausage Co** (hot dogs, burgers, sandwiches and fries) and stop for coffee, ice cream or frozen yoghurt at the splendid **D-Zertz**.

For a full-scale meal, the neighbouring **Portobello Yacht Club** offers excellent northern Italian cuisine in smart, lively surroundings. Of course, you can also visit the many eating outlets elsewhere around *Downtown Disney*, including **Planet Hollywood**® (the largest of this world-wide movie-themed chain, and the busiest

restaurant of the lot), **Cap'n Jack's Restaurant** (for great chowder, crabcakes, shrimp or the trademark 'fishbowl' margaritas), and **Fulton's Crab House** (for some of the best seafood in Orlando – see page 267). Lunch is served from 11am–4pm and dinner from 5–11pm.

As ever, to make a **Priority Seating** booking for a Disney restaurant, call 407 939 3463 (see page 58). *Pleasure Island*'s shops and cafés used to be open free of charge during the day, but now the hours are purely 7pm–2am each night, with the entry charge $19.95 and strict age restrictions. Admission is also one of the options on a Park Hopper Plus Ticket.

> BRIT TIP: Taking a form of photo ID is highly advisable for *Pleasure Island*, even if you are the 'wrong' side of 30. No ID equals no alcohol, and there are no exceptions.

Downtown Disney West Side is the newest element of the Downtown Disney expansion and incorporates the **AMC**® **Pleasure Island 24 Theaters Complex**, which has been increased to 24 screens, with some 6,000 seats in state-of-the-art surroundings.

Cirque du Soleil®

The most eye-catching part of West Side, however, is home to the greatest show on earth (or at least, the greatest I've seen anywhere in the world), the Cirque du Soleil® production *La Nouba*™. Twice a day, five times a week, the company's purpose-built, 1,671-seater theatre stages the most stupendous combination of dance, circus, acrobatics, comedy and live music in a 90-minute show that includes more than 60 performers. Anyone familiar with the unique styling, outrageous costumes and captivating sounds of the world-famous Cirque company will know what to expect, but even they will be left in awe by this multi-dimensional assault on the senses. It features trampolines, trapezes, balancing acts and even mountain bikes, interspersed with innovative dance routines, comedy (watch out for the inspired clowns) and spell-binding music, all with the most magnificent staging. Words alone do not do it justice – go and see it. Even at $67 a ticket ($39 for children 3–9), it is worth every cent. Booking is necessary and can be done up to 6 months beforehand on 407 939 7600. Performances are at 6pm and 9pm Thur–Mon (no performances Tue and Wed), but try to arrive 30 minutes early for some excellent pre-show fun.

More venues

The other *Downtown Disney* elements are a fantastic mix of live music, fine dining, unique shopping and *DisneyQuest*, the ultimate in interactive game arcades.

The cavernous **House of Blues®**, a combination live music venue and restaurant in backwoods Mississippi style, is a must for anyone even vaguely interested in blues, rock 'n roll, R&B, gospel and jazz (call 407 934 2583 for info). Some top-name bands play here (check out www.hob.com for events), while their trademark **Gospel Brunch** on Sundays serves up some fabulous food with a full gospel show (10.30am and 1pm; $30 for adults, $15 for children 3–9). 'Praise the Lord and pass the biscuits', is their slogan, and it is a lot of fun. The 500-seat restaurant next door to the stunning main hall also offers some fine fare, including catfish, jambalaya and a host of other delicious Cajun

dishes, with more live music, free, in the **Blues Kitchen** (Thur–Sat). The inevitable gift shop also stocks some quality merchandise.

Bongos Cuban Café™ (co-owned by Gloria and Emilio Estefan) brings the sights, sounds and tastes of Old Havana to another imaginative setting (check out the bongo-drum bar stools), with red-hot Latin music and some excellent Cuban fare. **The Wolfgang Puck® Café** offers a rich experience from the renowned Californian chef, with no less than four dining options: the Café, gourmet food in a casual setting; Wolfgang Puck Express, the fast-food version; B's Bar for sushi, seafood, pizzas and micro-brew beers; and the Dining Room, an upscale restaurant featuring the best of the Wolfgang Puck international cuisine (call 407 938 9653).

The West Side shopping is also original and engaging, from the basic sweet shop **Candy Cauldron** that resembles a fairytale dungeon, through the one-off outlets like **Sosa Family Cigars, Celebrity Eyeworks** and the wonderfully stylish glass and ceramics of **Hoypoloi Gallery**, to the predictable souvenir stores and the truly mega **Virgin**™ **Megastore**, the largest music store in Florida, with more than 100 listening stations, a full-service café, hydraulic outdoor stage and a mean sound system!

DisneyQuest

The most unusual element to *Downtown Disney*, *DisneyQuest* opened in June 1998 and brought yet another novel idea to life. It is described variously as 'an immersive, interactive entertainment environment', the latest in arcade games, a series of state-of-the-art adventure rides or, as one Cast Member told me, 'a theme park in a box'. It houses 11 major adventures,

9

like CyberSpace Mountain (design and ride your own roller-coaster), Invasion – An Alien Encounter (a fun VR rescue mission), Virtual Jungle Cruise (shooting the rapids, prehistoric style) and Aladdin's Magic Carpet (more virtual reality, riding in best cartoon fashion), a host of old-fashioned video games in the Replay Zone, the latest sports games, a test of your imagination in Animation Academy and two futuristic cafés, one with computers and internet tables, the other, Food Quest, straight out of a space-age comic book.

> BRIT TIP: You can buy a combined annual pass for *DisneyQuest* and Disney's water parks at $129 for adults and $99 for 3–9s that can work out better value for multiple visits.

Two additional highlights are Radio Disney SongMaker (a computer-generated professional audio system that creates a CD with you as the star!) and Pirates of the Caribbean: Battle for Buccaneer Gold (an amazing 3-D immersion into a swashbuckling, cannon-shooting adventure for pirate treasure).

Cirque du Soleil® at Downtown Disney

© Disney

DisneyQuest is open 11.30am–midnight daily, but, if you want to avoid the queues (the building admits only 1,500), go during the day. A 1-day ticket costs $31 ($25 for 3–9s, although it is a bit too elaborate for most youngsters) and teenagers love it.

Finally, the whole of *Downtown Disney* West Side is characterised at night by outstanding lighting and special effects and a vibrant, thrilling atmosphere that is almost intoxicating.

Disney's BoardWalk

Disney's other big evening entertainment offering is part of their impressive **Disney's BoardWalk Resort**, where the waterfront entertainment district contains several notable venues (not counting the excellent micro-brewery and restaurant of the Big River Grille and Brewing Works, the thrilling ESPN Club for sports fans and the 5-star Flying Fish Café). **Jellyrolls** is a variation on the duelling piano bar, with the lively pianists conjuring up a humorous and often raucous evening of audience participation songs ($7 cover charge; 21 and over only; 7pm–2am). The **Atlantic Dance** club features mainly modern dance music (it started life as a classic 1930s' dance club and also moved through a Latin phase) with both house and guest DJs, plus occasional live music, all with a huge dance floor and a great bar service and ambience. It is especially popular on Friday and Saturday nights (perhaps because there is no cover charge any more; 9pm–2am; closed Sun and Mon). It is strictly 21 and over, so remember your ID (no ID, no entry here). *Disney's Boardwalk Resort* also features some amusing stalls and live entertainers, which add to the carnival atmosphere.

Universal's CityWalk

As part of the big Universal Orlando development – and in direct competition with *Downtown Disney* – this 30-acre (12-ha) spread has just about everything in the world of entertainment. The resort's hub is a busy, bustling expanse of shops, restaurants, snack bars, open-air events and nightclubs. It offers a huge variety of cuisines, from fast food to fine dining, an unusual mix of speciality shops and a truly eclectic nightclub mix, from reggae to rock 'n roll to salsa to jazz and high-energy disco. Unlike *Pleasure Island*, there is no overall entry fee, but you do pay a cover charge ($5–7) at the seven clubs. You can also buy a **CityWalk Party Pass** ($8.95) or Party Pass with Movie (one free film at the 20-screen Universal Cineplex; $12) for entry to all seven (except one-off concerts at Hard Rock Live), while the Orlando FlexTicket includes a Party Pass.

The area splits into three, with the main plaza featuring shopping and restaurants. Among the most original (and amusing) of the 13 shops are **Endangered Species**, with merchandise designed to raise eco-awareness; **Quiet Flight**, a radical surf and beachwear store; the retro-American decor of **Fossil** for leather goods, watches and sunglasses; the inevitable **Universal Studios Store** for park merchandise; and **All Star Collectibles** for (American) sports fans.

When it comes to eating, you have the **NASCAR Café** (a must for motor-racing fans, 10am–late) with full-size stock cars and racing memorabilia, videos and interactive games while you dine on burgers, ribs, steaks and popcorn shrimp. **Pastamore** is a delightful indoor/outdoor Italian diner, with the choice of full-service dining (5pm–midnight) for pizza, pasta, grilled chicken and steaks or the

Pastamore Café (8am–2am) for sandwiches, pastries and ice cream. **Emeril's** restaurant is at the 5-star end of the range, a sophisticated and vibrant journey into the cuisine of New Orleans master chef Emeril Lagasse. Fine wines and a cigar bar both add to Emeril's Creole-based gourmet creations, and if you don't try the Louisiana oyster stew here, you have missed a real treat (lunch 11.30am–2.30pm; dinner 5.30–10pm Sun–Thur, 5.30–11pm Fri and Sat). It also books up well in advance at weekends, so try weekdays to avoid missing out (or call 407 224 2424 to book). **Jimmy Buffet's Margaritaville** (11am–2am) is an island homage to Florida's laid-back musical hero, with 'Floribbean' cuisine (a mixture of Key West and Caribbean), live music and three bars, including the Volcano Bar which 'erupts' margarita mix (!) when the blender needs filling. There is a cover charge ($5) after 10pm when their live band hits the stage.

Across the CityWalk waterway is the **Lagoon Front** location of another huge dining experience, the 2-storey **NBA City** which is sure to thrill basketball fans with its Cage dining room, interactive Playground area and Club lounge where you can watch live and classic games (all 11am–2am). Right next door is the massive mock-Coliseum architecture of **Hard Rock Live**, a 2,500-seat concert venue with state-of-the-art staging and sound. Big-name bands and performers are on stage several times a week (and they do book British acts from time to time –

Hard Rock Café

9

Robbie Williams and Oasis have both played here) in this slightly retro rock 'n roll theatre; call 407 839 3900 for the latest information or check out www.hardrock.com. Of course, you can't miss dining at the **Hard Rock Café** here, the world's largest example of this international chain, with its collection of rock 'n roll memorabilia (including a pink 1959 Cadillac). It remains hugely popular, so try to get in early for lunch or dinner (11am–2am) to sample their classic diner fare (notably the Pig Sandwich). Collectors of Hard Rock souvenirs will also find prices a little friendlier here than the UK in the excellent gift shop.

Finally, you come to the **Promenade** area, which offers a choice of nightclubs and some more fine dining (notably in the case of Latin Quarter), plus the ubiquitous Starbucks coffee house. **Motown Café** is the one disappointment here as it has been downgraded from a performance venue to just a Motown memorabilia restaurant and bar, with a big video arcade downstairs. It is worth perusing for its homage to the performers of the renowned record label, from the Four Tops and Jackson Five to modern artists, but there is better food elsewhere (11.30am–11pm Sun–Thu, 11am–1am Fri and Sat).

Bob Marley – A Tribute to Freedom is a clever re-creation of Marley's Jamaica home, turned into a courtyard live music venue, restaurant and bars. The bands are excellent, the atmosphere authentic and the place really comes alive at night (4pm–2am, 21 and over after 10pm; cover charge $5 after 8pm).

Next up is **Pat O'Brien's**, a faithful reproduction of the famous New Orleans bar and restaurant (4pm–1am), with its Flaming Fountain courtyard, main bar and special duelling piano bar (6pm–2am, cover charge $5 after

9pm, 21 and over, so remember your passport ID). Excellent Cajun food and world-famous Hurricane cocktails are the order of the day, but don't drink too many and expect to walk home! **CityJazz** is a real contrast, a hip, upmarket centre combining history, education and live music from a series of local and international musicians, with tapas-style food. Visually it is stunning, with good sound quality and, if you're keen on the live music, which varies from swing and R&B to pure jazz, (8pm–1am, Sun–Thur, 7pm–2am Fri and Sat, cover charge $5), you can easily spend all night here. For younger, club-minded visitors, **the groove** is the next generation in disco entertainment, a vivid, pounding, high-energy dance venue designed like a Victorian theatre but with the latest in club music, lighting and special effects (9pm–2am, cover charge $7 and 21 and over only).

BRIT TIP: Park in Universal's multi-storey car park where there is no charge after 6pm for all the CityWalk venues. For more info on the complex, call 407 363 8000 or visit www.citywalkorlando.com.

Finally, completing the Promenade tour is the **Latin Quarter**, a wonderful venue/restaurant that serves up a genuine slice of Latin American style in its atmosphere, music, dance, decor and cuisine. The food is outstanding – a combination of beef, fresh fish and poultry with tangy fruit sauces, spicy salsas and mouth-watering marinades (don't miss their version of rack of lamb) – the ambience is mesmerising and the sounds are so wonderfully vibrant and alive, you can't help dancing, even in your seat. From Cuba to Chile, here is a great experience, with the live bands whipping up a samba and salsa storm. Drop in for dinner (5pm–2am) or just check out the music on Fri and Sat (cover charge $6 after 10pm).

Breathless yet? Well, there's still the **Universal Cineplex**, a 20-screen cinema complex with a 5,000 capacity and the latest in stadium seating, curved-screen visuals and high-tech sound systems.

The Pointe*Orlando

This eye-catching development on I-Drive, almost opposite the Convention Center, is a mix of unique shops, cinemas, restaurants, the WonderWorks science centre (with its magic-themed dinner show), an arcade-style entertainment centre and two nightclubs. It is open all day but has plenty of evening appeal, too.

The big-name stores (open 10am–11pm) are all upscale and include some imaginative touches that make them stand out from the crowd (see page 279). The collection of bars and restaurants strive to be different too. On the main ground level you have **Johnny Rockets**, a highly entertaining 1950s-style diner with an indulgent burger-and-milkshake menu (and waiters and waitresses who perform dance routines if the right song comes on the jukebox!). **Dan Marino's Town Tavern** is a surprisingly elegant sports-themed diner (check out the football-shaped bar), with a mix of lively and intimate areas and a well-balanced menu from this former American football star. Head upstairs to the second level and you find **Lulu's Bait Shack** leading the way for New Orleans-style cuisine and entertainment (it looks like an old shack blown in from Bourbon Street). Then there is **Adobe Gila's**, a fine Mexican *cantina* featuring more than 70 tequilas (!) and some south-of-the-border dining delicacies (try the Gila Wraps), and the 'soon to be relatively famous' wings, burgers and seafood of **Hooters** (with its equally famous 'Hooter Girl' waitresses). Lulu's and Adobe Gila's are especially popular with locals and are often packed at weekends, as they stay open until 2am, while they feature live outdoor music and DJs several days a week. On a Friday or Saturday, the atmosphere should be kicking from 6.30pm, while on weekdays it is more likely to be from 8.30pm.

The 21-screen **Muvico** cinema, with its wonderfully vast and cleverly themed entrance foyer, boasts state-of-the-art stadium seating and sound systems, and you can often see a newly released film here several months before it gets to the UK.

Newest entertainment venue **XS Orlando** (motto: Too much is not enough!) offers three floors of fun and games where you can 'dine, dance and defend the world'. An appealing restaurant (try their excellent steaks, salads or brick oven pizzas) occupies the ground floor, and you then ride the escalator up to the entertainment levels. Here, you will find more than 110 interactive games and attractions (including a virtual reality roller-coaster, rock-climbing challenge, several state-of-the-art shoot 'em up games, a new role-playing horse-race game, some arcade-style prize games and high-speed internet access), fully stocked bars, live music with resident DJs and two roof terraces that enjoy views over I-Drive. For the games, you can get Time cards for 1 or 2 hours ($20 or $25) or buy a Cash card for any amount. XS Orlando is open noon–midnight Sun–Thur, and noon–2am Fri and Sat, and is also an ideal venue for lunch (visit www.xsorlando.com for more info).

9

'La Nouba' at Cirque du Soleil®

The Pointe also boasts two popular recent additions to the nightclub scene: **Matrix** (open 9pm–2am, Tue and Thur–Sun), a high-tech, high-energy, high-volume club, pulses to the techno beat for much of the time and has a kind of future-surreal decor that appeals to the younger (18–25) crowd. Age restrictions are strictly 18 and up (apart from Tue, over 21 all night). The dance floor is huge and is ringed by two 10-ft (3-metre) video walls, sixteen 27-in (69-cm) TV screens and a multi-million dollar light show, while the lounge area features art deco loungers, chairs and loveseats. Thursday is College Night (with $2 beers, and no cover until 11pm), Saturday is Inferno (top DJs, BreakBeats and Hip-Hop) and Sunday is Latin Night.

Metropolis (open 9pm–2am nightly, from 8pm on Thur) offers a more sophisticated atmosphere, with retro Top 40 music in a plush disco environment. It has seven Victorian billiards tables in the lounge area, various TV and video screens, and another large dance floor, and it tends to attract a slightly older crowd (25–35). It is 21 and over here only for men (18 and up for ladies), except for college night on Thursdays. At both clubs, the cover charge (after 10pm) varies per night (from $5–15, free for ladies over 21 on Fridays). Stylish dress is required (no jeans, baseball caps or trainers). Every Monday is also Teens Night for 14–18s during the summer, 8pm–1am. With a no-alcohol bar, it offers a great (and safe) environment

to let your teenagers have some space of their own on holiday. For info, visit www.metropolismatrix.com or call 407 370 3700.

For more on The Pointe, visit www.pointeorlando.com or call 407 248 2838.

DINNER SHOWS

Another source of evening entertainment comes in the many and varied dinner shows which are a major Orlando phenomenon. From murder mysteries to full-scale medieval battles, it's all wonderfully imaginative good fun, even if the food element is usually quite ordinary. As the name suggests, it is live entertainment coupled with dinner in a fantasy-type environment where even the waiters and waitresses are dressed in costume and act out roles, accompanied by unlimited free wine, beer and soft drinks.

They always have a strong family appeal and you are usually seated at large tables where you can get to know other folks, too, but, at $35–45 for adults, they are not cheap (especially when you add on taxes and tips). Beware, too, the regular attempts to shake an extra few dollars out of you with photos, souvenirs, flags, etc.

Disney shows

Walt Disney World Resort in Florida's offerings here are often overlooked by visitors unless they are staying at one of the hotel resorts. For an excellent night of South Seas entertainment, try **Disney's Spirit of Aloha** (at the Luau Cove at *Disney's Polynesian Resort*). It's a bit expensive at $49.01 for adults (including tax and tip), and $24.81 for under 12s, but it is still good value as the 2-hour show features some splendid entertainment, varying from the fun to the thrilling (Hawaiian sounds, singers, dancers and other Polynesian acts, including the amazing Samoan fire juggler, all with a strong family story). You need to come hungry for this show, too, as the food is plentiful, with salad, roast chicken, ribs, rice and vegetables, plus a fresh fruit dessert (or peanut butter and jam sandwiches, macaroni cheese, chicken fingers and hot dogs for the kids). Beer, wine and soft drinks are all included. For reservations (usually necessary), call 407 939 3463, and shows are 5.15pm and 8pm every Tue–Sat.

The **Hoop-Dee-Doo Musical Revue** at *Disney's Fort Wilderness Resort & Campground* is an ever-popular nightly dinner show that maintains the resort's impressive cowboy theme, and has great food (all-you-can-eat ribs, fried chicken, corn on the cob, baked beans and strawberry shortcake, plus unlimited beer, sangria and soft drinks). Especially loved by children, it features the amusing song and dance of the Pioneer Hall Players in a merry American hoedown-style show. Okay, it's corny and a tad embarrassing to find yourself singing along with the hammy action, but it is performed with great gusto, and you're on holiday, remember! The Revue plays nightly at 5pm, 7.15pm and 9.30pm at the Pioneer Hall, $49.01 for adults (inclusive of tax and tip), $24.81 for under 12s, and lasts almost 2 hours. Reservations are ALWAYS necessary but can be made up to 2 years in advance on 407 939 3463.

An alternative is the nightly (and free!) **Electrical Water Pageant** which circles Bay Lake and the Seven Seas Lagoon, passing by each of the *Magic Kingdom Park* resorts in turn from 9pm. It lasts just 10 minutes so it is easy to miss, but it is almost a waterborne version of the park's SpectroMagic parade, with thousands of twinkling lights on a 1,000-ft (305-metre) floating cavalcade of boats and mock sea creatures. The usual schedule is 9pm at *Disney's Polynesian Resort*, 9.15pm at *Disney's Grand Floridian Resort and Spa* (and you get a grandstand view in Narcoosee's restaurant), 9.35pm on the shores of *Disney's Fort Wilderness Resort & Campground*, 9.45pm at *Disney's Wilderness Lodge* and 10.05pm at *Disney's Contemporary Resort*. It can also be seen from the boat jetties outside the *Magic Kingdom Park* in high season.

Arabian Nights

This lovingly maintained, family-owned attraction is a real large-scale production and one of the most popular with locals as well as tourists. It's a treat for horse lovers, but you don't need to be an equestrian expert to appreciate the spectacular stunts, horsemanship and marvellous costumes as some 60 highly trained horses perform a 25-act show. Loosely based on the celebration of Princess Scheherezade's engagement to Prince Khalid, the show is staged in the huge indoor Moorish-themed arena at the centre of this 1,200-seater palace. The magnificent close-quarter drill of the Lipizzaner stallions, the daring riding and the thrilling chariot race all add up to a memorable show that kids, especially, adore. The recent addition of new characters (notably the comic Gaylord Maynard and his horse

Arabian Nights

9

BRIT TIP: Take a sweater or jacket with you when you go to Arabian Nights, as the arena is kept particularly cool for the benefit of the horses.

Chief Bear Paw), costumes and special effects, plus the incorporation of a bumbling genie, have given Arabian Nights a real boost and helped to keep its appeal fresh.

The food (green salad, oven-roasted prime rib with new potatoes, and a dessert; vegetarian lasagne on request) is above average, too. Located just half a mile east of I-4 on Highway 192 (on the left, just to the side of the Parkway shopping plaza, or just past Water Mania if you are coming from the eastern end of 192), Arabian Nights runs every evening at 7.30pm or 8.30pm, with occasional matinees. It lasts almost 2 hours, and tickets ($44 for adults and $27 for kids 3–11) may be purchased at the box office between 10am and 6pm or by credit card on 407 239 9223 (visit www.arabian-nights.com for a $10 saving offer or free upgrade). A 'VIP' upgrade ($15 for adults, $10 for children) adds a stable tour, reserved priority seating (in the first three rows), souvenir poster, pre-show drink and the chance to meet the riders and horses.

Pirate's Dinner Adventure

This show (which has been revamped several times since it opened in 1997) features one of the most spectacular settings, with the Spanish galleon pirate ship centrepiece being 150ft (46 metres) long, 60ft (18 metres) wide, 70ft (21 metres) tall and 'anchored' in a 300,000-gallon (1,365,000-litre) lagoon. It also delivers good value with its pre-show elements, plentiful

(if ordinary) food and drink, and the imaginative after-show Buccaneer Bash disco (until 10.30pm), plus the Pirate's Maritime Museum, which guests are free to wander around. The basic premise of the audience being 'hi-jacked' by the wicked 18th-century pirates is a clever one, even if the actual storyline is occasionally hard to follow. Chaos and mayhem ensue, with the local princess being abducted by the villainous crew of Captain Sebastian (Boo! Hiss!), and there is swashbuckling galore, sword fights, acrobatics, trapeze artists and boat races, and the goodies (inevitably) triumph over the evil captain and his men. There are plenty of stunts and special effects (plus audience participation opportunities, which the kids will enjoy) and ticket prices are $43.95 for adults and $27.50 for 3–11s (look for discount coupons. The show is located on Carrier Drive between I-Drive and Universal Boulevard, and runs daily from 6, 7.45, 8 or 8.30pm, with some pretty decent appetisers served for 45 minutes until seating begins.

BRIT TIP: When there are two shows of The Pirate's Dinner Adventure in one night, opt for the second one if you want the disco bash afterwards.

A new Pirates Preferred seating upgrade provides front row priority and guaranteed cast interaction for a small extra cost. Call 407 248 0590 for reservations or visit www.orlandopirates.com.

Medieval Times

Eleventh-century Spain is the entertaining setting for this 2-hour extravaganza of medieval pageantry, sorcery and robust horseback jousts that culminate in furious hand-to-hand combat between six knights. It is worth arriving early to appreciate the clever mock castle design and the staff's costumes as you are ushered into the pre-show hall before being taken into the arena itself. The weapons used are all quite real and used with skill, and there are some neat touches with indoor pyrotechnics and other special effects. You need to be in full audience participation mode as you cheer on your knight and boo the others, but kids (not to mention a few adults) get a huge kick out of it and they'll also love eating without cutlery – don't worry, there are handles on the soup bowls! The elaborate staging takes your mind off the unexciting chicken dinner, but there is positively heaps of it and the serfs and wenches who serve you make it a fun experience. Prices, which include the Medieval Life exhibition (see below), are $44 for adults and $28 for 3–11s (but check their website for discounts) and doors open 90 minutes prior to showtime. Times vary with the season, so call 1-800 229 8300 or visit www.medievaltimes.com for details.

For those who have been before, the **Knights of the Realm** show made its debut in January 2003, with a new storyline and characters (although much of the fast-paced action is the same), plus a musical score by the Prague Symphony Orchestra and the addition of a superb black Friesian stallion, which contrasts with the snowy Andalusian horses ridden by most of the cast.

The castle is on Highway 192, 5 miles (8km) east of the junction with I-4. If you have 45 minutes to spare pre-show, the **Medieval Life** exhibition makes an interesting diversion. This mock village portrays the life and times of 900 years ago, with artisans demonstrating pottery and tool-making, glass-blowing, spinning and weaving, plus a gruesome Chamber of Horrors that is definitely not for young children.

Sleuth's Mystery Dinner Shows

This is a real live version of Cluedo acted out before your eyes in hilarious fashion while you enjoy a substantial meal (with a main course choice of honey-glazed Cornish hen, prime rib or lasagne) and unlimited beer, wine and sodas. You can choose between three theatres and eight different plot settings, including *Roast 'Em, Toast 'Em* and *WKZY TV* (a clever skit on trash television), that all add up to some elaborate murder mysteries. The action takes place all around you and members of the audience can take part in some cameo roles. The quick-witted cast keeps things moving and you guessing during the 40-minute show, then during the main part of dinner you can think up some questions for interrogation (but be warned, the real murderer is allowed to lie!). If you solve the crime you win a prize, but that is pretty secondary to the overall enjoyment – and this is a show I enjoy a lot. Prices are $41.95 for adults and $23.95 for children (3–11) and again show times vary, so call 407 363 1985 for details or visit www.sleuths.com. Sleuth's Mystery Dinner Shows can be found in Republic Square Plaza, on Universal Boulevard (half a mile north of its Sand Lake Road junction).

Purely for children is **Sleuth's Merry Mystery Dinner Adventure**, with a special kids' dinner, dessert and unlimited soft drinks. At $28 for adults and $16 for children (3–12), it is designed primarily for 6- to 12-year-olds (mainly on Saturday afternoons), and features one of two adventures, *The Faire of the Shire* and *The Magical Journey of Juniper Junior*.

WonderWorks: The Outta Control Magic Show

On a smaller scale but no less fun, this is a new offering at WonderWorks on I-Drive (on one corner of Pointe*Orlando). A novel mixture of improvised comedy and clever, close-up magic, the show is accompanied by all-you-can-eat pizza, beer, wine and coke. Set in the intimate Shazam Theater, it features live music, special lighting effects and some slick magic tricks from illusionist Tony Brent and sidekick Danny Devaney. The tricks are all fairly routine, but the show is served up in style and involves plenty of audience participation. Performed twice nightly at 6pm and 8pm, it costs a reasonable $17.95 for adults and $14.95 for children and seniors. Or you could buy a Magic Combo ticket for the show and unlimited use of WonderWorks afterwards (which stays open till midnight) for $31.95 and $25.95. For ticket info, call 407 351 8800 or visit www.wonderworksonline.com.

The SoulFire Theatre & Dinner Experience

This novel and ambitious venture opened in 2002 and, after one change of storyline, has settled on being the wedding reception from hell! The basic 'show' is the story of

Soulfire Dinner Theatre

Tony and Tina's Wedding, with the audience as the 'invited guests' in a riotous and often chaotic series of misadventures between the bride and groom's respective ill-matched New Yorker families. The action begins from the moment you enter the venue, with cutting-edge theatre company The SoulFire Traveling Medicine Show staging a mixture of inspired lunacy and general craziness (some of which is hard to follow if you don't pay attention). With an out-of-control Best Man, a surly photographer, a loutish father (of the groom) and a former boyfriend who 'gatecrashes' the reception, plus two families who clearly don't get along, the stage is set for a wedding reception of the most memorable kind – for all the wrong reasons.

You have to be willing to take an active role in the ensuing madness (audience participation and interaction with the cast is a key part of the experience), and some of the zaniness is a bit wide of the mark (it also helps if you have a feel for New York-Italian humour), but the food is good (salad, roast chicken and chocolate cake, plus a vegetarian option) and some of the acting is truly outrageous. The venue is a 200-seat theatre at the back of Lake Buena Vista Factory Stores on Apopka Vineland Road (Route 535), with shows at 7.30pm (Tue–Sun), plus a Sunday matinee. Call 407 465 1886 or visit www.soulfire.net. Tickets are $43.95 for adults and $29.95 for children (3–12; although the show will probably baffle most youngsters). Soft drinks, a champagne toast and coffee are included, but other alcoholic drinks are extra. On Saturdays at 12.30pm ($10 for 4–12s, $9 for adults) there is also a children's version, **The Amazing Adventures of Professor Phineas T Phoolfoolfinger**, a wacky and semi-educational 'time-travel' trip.

Dolly Parton's Dixie Stampede

The biggest development in Orlando dinner shows for many a year opened in June 2003, when Country & Western queen Dolly Parton unveiled the fourth venue for her Dixieland extravaganza of music, comedy, horsemanship and ostrich races (!). The show features a high-energy cowboy competition (with lots of audience participation) between north and south, with various contests, speciality acts, song, dance and a huge southern-style feast. Indeed, the food is a major part of the experience – which has been a big hit elsewhere in America – as you chow down on vegetable soup, whole rotisserie chicken, corn on the cob, home-made biscuit (that's savoury scone to us), barbecue pork loin, jacket potato and apple pastry. This is a no-alcohol environment, though, hence your unlimited drinks are Pepsi, tea and coffee.

> BRIT TIP: You can hobnob with the stars of Dolly Parton's Dixie Stampede – the horses – for free from 10am till showtime along the horsewalk outside the venue.

The quality of the entertainment is high, however, and the $28 million development provides a spectacular venue, with an elaborate pre-show (featuring the trick riding and cowboy rope and whip tricks of Greg Anderson) in the Carriage Room before the audience moves into the 1,000-seat, 35,000-sq ft (3,255-sq metre) main arena. This showcases the headlining abilities of the 32 horses and 30 riders over a series of tests and races, from Roman-style riding to trick riding

Pirate's Dinner Adventure

and fast-paced barrel racing. Then there are the spectacular costumes, ostrich races, pig races and a feature buffalo 'stampede', plus a rousing, patriotic finale, American-style, with doves, flags and Dolly's closing anthem (penned after the September 11 tragedies).

Sadly, Dolly herself does not make an appearance, apart from on video screen, but it all adds up to 5-star family fun. A separate Christmas show is staged from November 1 to January 1, featuring a live Nativity scene, snow and other seasonal festivities (the show contest pits the North Pole v South Pole instead!).

Dixie Stampede operates once or twice a night, depending on the season, at either 5.40pm or 7.40pm (with the main show at 6.30pm or 8.30pm), and lasts almost 2½ hours, including the pre-show, plus browsing time in the inevitable gift shop. They bill it as Orlando's 'Most Fun Place To Eat', and it is hard to argue. Tickets are a well-priced $43.99 for adults and $28.99 for children (3–11) and it is located right next to Orlando Premium Outlets, just off I-4 at Exit 68, or via I-Drive. Call 407 238 4455 to book or visit www.dixiestampede.com.

Gator Safari by night

Brand new in 2003, this is a joint venture by Boggy Creek Airboats and Gator Tours excursions, serving up an evening of Floridian food, fun and Native American activities out

9

in beautiful Southport Park, Kissimmee, with a night-time airboat ride thrown in for good measure (tues and Sun, May–Oct only). The basic idea is to host a family barbecue under the moss-covered grandfather oaks of the park, with plenty of food and drink and the transport laid on, too. Torchlight and Native American dancers provide a wonderfully rustic yet authentic ambience, and the whole thing is enhanced with organised games for the children, with face painting, treasure hunts (with metal detectors!) and native stories in the specially built tepee. You also get to roast marshmallows on the bonfire and meet a live alligator, while the 45-minute night-time airboat ride is a real highlight and there is a Country Store for souvenirs. With the coach transport (round-trip from your hotel) and airboat ride, however, this is a pricey evening at $75 for adults and $55 for children (3–12), but it is one of the most unusual dinner 'show' offerings, and it is an extremely enjoyable experience (prices without transport are $54 and $34). To book, call 1-800 537 0917 (in Florida) or 407 522 5911 (outside) or look up www.gatortours.com.

Theatre

If the dinner shows are only playing at theatrical entertainment, there is still some genuine theatre to be enjoyed in Orlando. The **Bob Carr Performing Arts Center** is the premier venue, hosting a variety of acts from ballet to opera (it is home to the Orlando Opera and Southern Ballet companies) as well as the Broadway in Orlando series which, in 2004, features *Phantom of the Opera* (Jan), *Lord of the Dance* (Feb), *Mamma Mia* (Apr–May) and *The Producers* (June) plus productions by local theatre groups.

The Center is located in the heart of the Orlando Centroplex downtown, for info, visit www.orlandocentroplex.com or call 407 849 2001.

The **Orlando-UCF Shakespeare Festival** is a purely classical offering, year-round at the John & Rita Lowndes Shakespeare Center in Loch Haven just off Princeton Street (Exit 85 off I-4) downtown. As well as Shakespeare and other works, they stage summer workshops for children 6–9 and 10–13.

The more eclectic (as the name suggests) **Mad Cow Theatre** has grown from very humble roots to mainstream theatre in a new downtown location, with educational shows, workshops and cabaret performances (Fri and Sat). Recent productions have included *Candida*, *Loot* and *The Life Of Galileo*, and performances are usually Thur–Sun (with matinees Sun). Tickets vary from $10–20, call 407 297 8788 or visit www.madcowtheatre.com.

The **Theatre Downtown** company has an individual style as its non-profit ethos gives rise to some challenging theatre, bordering on the experimental. The venue, an old citrus-packing plant on the corner of Orange and Princeton Avenues, provides a wonderfully intimate setting for their stagecraft, and tickets are $15 ($12 for students and seniors). Call 407 841 0083 for tickets or visit www.theatre downtown.net.

THE NIGHTCLUB SCENE

Orlando is blessed with a huge variety of nightlife, from regular discos to elaborate live music clubs and no less then three 'duelling piano' bars. The majority are situated in the downtown area, away from the main tourist centres. The local *Orlando Sentinel* has a regular Friday section called *Calendar* (www.calendar.orlandosentinel.com), which details the local nightspots as well as individual events, and it is worth checking out the free *Orlando Weekly* (available in most supermarkets and tourist centres, or look up www.orlandoweekly.com).

Bars and discos come and go at an amazing rate, so don't be surprised if you go to a nightclub you have visited before to find it has had a complete change of name and personality. The basic distinctions tend to be **Live Music Clubs, Mainstream Nightclubs**, which also have the occasional live band, and **Bars** with evening entertainment.

Live music clubs

The following should give you a representative taste of the most popular venues (for those aged 21 and over only in most cases).

The rock 'n roll piano bar idea was pioneered here in Orlando by the wonderfully named **Howl at the Moon Saloon** on West Church Street and is still going strong (6pm–2am Sun–Thur and 5pm–2am Fri and Sat). Classic rock 'n roll, show tunes, current hits, the saloon's duelling pianists play them all, with full audience involvement and non-stop banter. No cover charge Sun–Tues, while Wed–Thur it is $5 after 7.30pm, on Fri it's $7 after 6pm and Sat $7 after 5.30pm. The live piano action begins at 8pm (it gets rowdy and even bawdy later, so remember your sense of humour).

Then, of course, you have **Jellyrolls** at *Disney's BoardWalk Resort* and **Pat O'Brien's** (the original New Orleans version) at Universal's CityWalk, which are both popular with locals and tourists alike.

Country music fans (and others in search of the 'in' crowd) will definitely need to check out **:08 Seconds**, a huge, multi-level entertainment centre. It earns its 'unique' tag by hosting live bull riding (!) and monster truck wars as well as having a huge dance hall with live bands, line dancing lessons, 12 bars (and bottled beer at $2, a real bargain), a pool hall, games room and classic country barbecue. The atmosphere is both authentic and infectious, right down to the well-priced gift shop. This is one of my favourite clubs in town. On West Livingston Street in the heart of downtown, it has bags of style, but call 407 839 4800 for the latest details (usually, ladies' night Wed – ladies get in free all night and drink free until 11pm – monster trucks Fri, and bull riding Sat; $7 ages 18–20, $5 for 21 and up). By the way, the :08 Seconds refers to the average time a bull-rider stays on his bull!

Blues, rock and jazz are the staples of **The Social** (formerly Sapphire) at 54 North Orange Avenue (407 246 1419), where resident DJs, a wide range of bands and special guest acts vary from week to week. With San Francisco-inspired decor, this has the reputation for being one of the 'hippest' places to be seen in.

For pure, relaxed jazz, check out the Bosendorfer Lounge at the **Westin Grand Bohemian** hotel (see page 78), also on South Orange Avenue. Usually from 6–10pm every evening (and with a Saturday Jazz Brunch from 10.30am–2.30pm), there is no cover charge and the sounds of their $250,000 Bosendorfer piano are well worth travelling to hear.

As a complete alternative to the music scene, **Sak Comedy Lab** (on West Amelia Avenue in the Theater Garage) is like a live version of the TV show *Whose Line Is It Anyway?* Fast-paced and funny (and with a 'no obscenity' rule for worried parents), the Sak performers do a mix of competitive ad lib comedy, with every show offering something different and the young performers living on their wits. On stage

Tue–Sat (with two different shows Fri and Sat), admission varies from $5–13. Their Lab Rats show (Tue) features Sak's 'students' and costs just $5. Call 407 648 0001 (or www.sak.com) for reservations (advisable on Fri and Sat) and find out why Sak's has been consistently voted Florida's best live comedy.

Mainstream nightclubs

In addition to the mainstream DJ dance centres at *Downtown Disney's Pleasure Island* and Universal's CityWalk, **Tabu** (formerly the Zuma Beach Club on North Orange Avenue, just up from Church Street) appeals widely to the young, disco crowd with regular nightly line-ups, guest DJs and special events, usually of a fairly raucous nature! Call 407 648 8363 for the latest details, and admission varies from $7–12 (21 and over only) from Wed–Sun.

Bar Orlando, on South Orange Avenue, is another high-energy offering, with modern techno styles jostling with retro sounds from the 1980s and 1990s. **Cairo** has quickly become a haunt of the younger set on South Magnolia Avenue featuring dance music, reggae and out-and-out disco – house music on Wed, and ladies' night on Fri (no cover charge and free drink until 11.30pm for ladies). Call 407 422 595.

The **Independent** (formerly Barbarella) on Orange Avenue on the corner of Washington Street,

offers alternative and new wave music 9pm–3am most nights. Again, it is more of a techno-dance sound, but features various retro-progressive, old wave and Video Go-Go nights. Friday is ladies' night, and the club has three contrasting levels, including an area with pool tables. Cover charge varies from $5–10, call 407 839 0457 for details.

The Club at Firestone is also hard to categorise but scores well with the alternative/progressive crowd. It occasionally hosts rock and pop acts too big for The Social but otherwise ranges from mainstream disco to acid jazz lounge, with something different each night Wed–Sat (gay night on Wed). Two venues – the Den and the Glass Chamber – feature dance, house, jungle and hip-hop, with their Latin night, El Club Caliente, usually on Fri. About half a mile north of Church Street on the corner of Orange Avenue and Concord Street, The Club is open 9pm–3am with cover charge ranging from $6–12. Call 407 872 0066 for nightly info or visit www.theclub-online.com.

The **Blue Room** (West Pine Street) is another lively offering, although more intimate, drawing a more diverse crowd with its mixture of art, music and style. With DJs Thur–Sat (closed Sun–Wed) and live music (occasionally) on Thur, it successfully mixes hip-hop, dance and R&B in highly successful style. The club runs from 10pm until late with a $7–10 cover charge. Call 407 423 2588 or visit www.blueroomorlando.com.

For the gay scene, **Parliament House** (on North Orange Avenue) and **Southern Nights** (Bumby Avenue) remain the most happening venues, while the **Cactus Club** (on North Mills Avenue), **Faces** and **Studz Orlando** (both on Edgewater Drive) and **Wylde's** (out at 3535 South Orange Blossom Trail) are also popular.

Sunset on the Gulf of Mexico

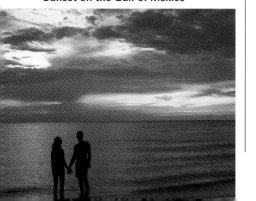

Bars

Live entertainment, extrovert barmen, sports-themed bars and raw bars (offering seafood, often by the bucket!), the choice is, as ever, wide-ranging. Bars of all types simply abound in Orlando.

The area around Church Street is the core of this development (even since much of Church Street Station closed), with a terrific range of restaurants and bars. Look out in particular for **Pebbles** (above-average food, good bar), the raucous **Mako's** and **Hogs & Honeys** (featuring a mechanical bull and bar dances, and a wonderfully sleazy style). Upstairs to the raucous **Antigua** (DJ house music) is **Ybor's Martini Bar**, an upscale cigar and cocktail emporium. Also on this floor (and easy to overlook next to Antigua) is the highly recommended **Big Belly Brewery** with a micro-brewery and an impressive range of other beers (as well as an outrageous collection of wall art), and above that is roof-top bar **Latitudes**.

Travel out past Church Street into Orange Avenue and Pine Street and you are into real locals' territory with the likes of **One-Eyed Jack's**, which has a party pop atmosphere and live music singalongs, and is connected to the **Loaded Hog** and **Wall Street Cantina**, which are packed at weekends (there is often a queue to get in, but, once in, you can roam between all three). Turn left on to West Central Boulevard and you find **Kate O'Brien's Irish Pub** for more lively bar entertainment (and a neat beer garden), the similarly Irish-themed **Scruffy Murphy's** is a block further north on Washington Street. Again, there is no cover charge and it has a real good-time atmosphere. South on Orange **Tanqueray's Bar and Grille** offers live music on Fri and Sat.

On Pine Street you have the **Pine Street Bar & Grill** (Mon–Fri,

The Latin Quarter at CityWalk

11am–2am, Sat and Sun 8pm–2am) for one of the best bar-restaurants in the area, ideal for a late-night snack, with pool and billiards, and the fun Hawaiian style of **Maui Jack's Draft House & Raw Bar**.

The eclectic duo of **Slingapour's** and **The Globe** (the latter an off-the-wall 24-hour diner) are also worth seeking out for a lively drink or three on Wall Street, just off Orange, boasting a range of bars, a pool hall and live music, as well as The Globe's fun eating style.

Sports bars

Finally, with the multitude of sports bars that are another particularly American pastime, **Friday's Front Row Sports Grill** on I-Drive (just south of the Sand Lake Road junction) really sticks out as a major tourist trap which even the locals enjoy. Here you can catch ALL the action (and, yes, they do show soccer) on 84 TV screens, plus enjoy some

American radio

American radio stations come in a vast number of types and styles that conform to fairly narrow musical tastes. Here is a quick guide to finding the main ones in your car:

CONTEMPORARY
98.9 FM (WMMO)
99.3 FM (WLRQ)
105.1 FM (WOMX)
107.7 FM (WMGF)
POP
99.9 FM (WFKS)
106.7 FM (WXXL)
OLDIES
100.3 FM (WSHE)
790 AM (WLBE)
NEWS/TALK
90.7 FM (WMFE)
104.1 FM (WTKS)
SPORT
540 AM (WQTM)
740 AM (THE TEAM)

CLASSICAL
90.7 FM (WMFE)
91.5 FM (WPRK)
JAZZ
89.9 FM (WUCF)
103.1 FM (WLOQ)
COUNTRY
92.3 FM (WWKA
97.5 FM (WPCV)
98.1 FM (WGNE)
102.7 FM (WHKR)
ROCK
91.5 FM (WPRK)
93.1 FM (WKRO)
96.5 FM (WHTQ)
101.1 FM (WJRR)
105.9 FM (O-ROCK)

(I recommend WJRR and O-ROCK as the best rock radio anywhere!)

100 beers from around the world – the bar features $1 domestic 12oz drafts! – as well as try out their basketball nets, pool tables and shuffleboard, and rub shoulders with the local sports stars from time to time. The food is standard American diner fare and there is plenty to keep the kids amused, too (paper tablecloths to colour and video games). The atmosphere varies according to the time of day and the sports event (pretty rowdy for Orlando Magic basketball games), so call 407 363 1414 for up-to-the-minute info. No cover charge or reservations and it is open 11am–2am Mon–Sat, 11am–midnight Sun.

Other choices for the sports bar experience include the massive **Players Sports Pub** on Curry Ford Road; 87 TV screens, with 12 big-screens, open 11am–2am every day (407 273 7363) and **Headlightz Sports Bar** on East Colonial Drive, which also offers live music (407 273

9600). My favourite is the **Orlando Ale House** on Kirkman Road, just opposite Universal Studios (407 248 0000). With more than 30 TVs, a raw bar and great seafood, it also has an above-average range of beers.

Walt Disney World Resort in Florida can boast the excellent **ESPN Club** at *Disney's BoardWalk Resort*, a full-service restaurant with sports broadcast facilities, video games, more than 70 TV monitors, giant scoreboards and even a Little League menu for kids. No sports fan should miss it. Equally, **NBA City** (for basketball fans) at Universal's CityWalk, and the **Cricketers' Arms** (for British sport) in The Mercado should not be overlooked as great venues, especially for TV/video addicts.

Now, you will also want to know a lot more about where, when and how to tackle that other holiday essential – FOOD. So, read on…

Dining Out

(or, Man, these portions are HUGE!)

Eating is a big deal in America. Consequently, dining out is a vital component of their entertainment business. Whether it be breakfast, lunch or dinner, the experience needs to be well-organised, filling and good value. To say Americans take mealtimes seriously would be the understatement of the year.

It is sometimes hard to dispel the notion that food is the 'be all and end all' of some Americans' holiday experience, as the options for dining are seemingly omnipresent and large scale. However, this is all good news for us Joe Tourists.

Variety

The variety, quantity and quality of restaurants, cafés, fast-food chains and hot-dog stalls is in keeping with the American tradition of eating as much as possible, as often as possible.

At first glance, the full selection of food is rather overwhelming. Cruising along either I-Drive or Highway 192 will quickly reveal a dazzling array of eateries, the choice of which can be quite bewildering.

As a general rule, food is plentiful, relatively cheap, available 24 hours a day and nearly always appetising and filling. You will even encounter an increasing number of fine-dining possibilities, but the basic premise remains that you will get good value for money and are unlikely to need more than two full meals a day. Put simply, portions tend to be large, and of a heavily steak, chicken or pizza-based variety, with service of

an efficient, friendly character. It is actually hard to come by a BAD meal. The one real exception (as pointed out by several readers) is if you like fresh veg. The US diet often overlooks this staple, but if you look up the vegetarian options lower down or check out one of the outlets of **Chamberlin's**, notably at the Market Place on Dr Phillips Boulevard and in the new Winter Park Village shops, you will find a healthy, balanced choice.

Exceptional deals

In keeping with the climate, most restaurants tend towards the informal (T-shirts and shorts are usually acceptable) and cater readily for families. This also leads to two exceptional deals for budget-conscious tourists, especially those with a large tribe. Many hotels and restaurants offer 'kids eat free' deals, provided they eat with their parents. The age restrictions can vary from under 10s to under 14s, but it obviously represents good value for money and they are worth looking for. The second item of interest is the

BRIT TIP: As portions are so large, you can save money by sharing an entrée, or main course, between two. Your waiter or waitress will be happy to oblige (provided you keep their tip up to the full rate).

'all-you-can-eat' buffet, another common feature of many of the large chain restaurants. This means you can have a hearty meal for not too much and probably eat enough at, say, breakfast, to keep you going until dinner! A few establishments also offer 'early bird' specials, a dinner discount if you dine before 6pm.

Don't be afraid to ask for a doggy bag if you have leftovers (even if you haven't brought the dog!). It is common practice to take away the half of that pizza you couldn't finish, or those chicken legs or salad. The locals do it all the time and, again, it is highly wallet-friendly. Just ask for the leftovers 'to go'.

Don't hesitate to tell your waiter or waitress if something isn't right with your meal. Americans will readily complain if they feel aggrieved, so restaurants are keen to make sure everything is to your satisfaction.

And, please, don't forget to tip. The basic wage for waiters and waitresses is low, so they rely heavily on tips to supplement their income. Unless service really is shoddy, in which case you should mention it, the usual rate for tips is 10% of your bill at buffet-style restaurants and 15% at full-service restaurants. It is worth checking to see if service is added to your bill, although this is less common in the US.

With Orlando being the world's favourite holiday destination, and with the city springing up from such eclectic roots, you will encounter a monumental array of food types. Florida is renowned for its seafood, which comes at a much more reasonable price than in the Mediterranean. Crab, lobster, shrimp (what we call king prawns), clams and oysters can all be had without fear of breaking the bank, as well as several dozen varieties of fish, many of which you won't have come across before (by the way don't worry about eating 'dolphin', it's not a mammal related to Flipper but a totally different species called dolphin fish or mahi-mahi).

Cuban, Cajun/Creole and Mexican are other more local types of cooking which are well represented here, and there is plenty of Oriental fare from Chinese and Indian to Japanese, Thai and Vietnamese.

The big shopping complexes and malls offer a good choice of eateries in their food courts, which are often particularly good value. Cracker (cowboy) cooking is original Floridian fare, and the more adventurous will want to try the local speciality – alligator meat. This can be stewed, barbecued, smoked, sautéed or braised. Fried gator tail 'nuggets' are an Orlando favourite. Of course, you have to try the great traditional Key Lime Pie, a truly decadent dessert. Look for the stall in *Pleasure Island* selling it at $1 a slice – true heaven!

How to order

Ordering your food can also be an adventure in itself. The choice for each item is often the cue for an inquisition of exam-type proportions from your waiter or waitress. You can never order just 'toast' – it has to be white, brown, wholegrain, rye, muffin or bagel; eggs and bacon come in a baffling variety of ways; an order for tea or coffee usually

The fabulous Planet Hollywood®

> **BRIT TIP:** American bacon is always streaky and crisp-fried and sausages are chipolata-like.

provokes the response 'Regular or decaf? Iced, lemon or English?' and salads have more dressings than the National Health Service. Whenever I've finished ordering, I'm tempted to ask 'Have I passed?' Ask to see a restaurant's menu if it isn't displayed. It is no big deal to Americans and they won't feel insulted if you decide to look elsewhere.

Vegetarian options

In a country where beef is culinary king, vegetarians often find themselves hard done by, and Orlando is little different to the general rule. However, there are a couple of bright spots, plus a handy hint when all seems lost.

Firstly, there are two speciality vegetarian restaurants in Orlando, The **Lower East Side** at 3401 LB McLeod Road (407 648 4830) and the Chinese Garden Café on West Colonial Drive downtown (407 999 9799), while the tapas-style **Café Tu-Tu Tango** on I-Drive serves a good variety of veggie dishes.

Most of the upscale restaurants should be able to offer a vegetarian option and will be happy for you to ask in advance. *Walt Disney World Resort in Florida* is slightly more enlightened in that the **California Grill** (in *Disney's Contemporary Resort*), **Citricos** (*Disney's Grand Floridian Resort and Spa*), **Le Cellier** (Canada pavilion in *Epcot* park) and **Spoodles** (*Disney's BoardWalk*) feature vegetarian dishes, while all the full-service restaurants (notably **Bongos Cuban Café**™ and **Wolfgang Puck's**® **Café** in *Downtown Disney*), plus some of the counter-service ones are usually keen

to try to cater for non-menu requests. It is always worth asking.

Sweet Tomatoes is a salad buffet restaurant (distinctly vegetarian-friendly) with possibly the best meal deals in central Florida. On I-Drive (by Kirkman Road junction), it offers an astonishing all-you-can-eat choice for just $6.99 at lunch ($7.99 at dinner, after 4pm) that includes a vast salad spread, a choice of soups, pizza, pasta, bread and pastries, plus fruit and frozen yoghurt. Drinks are $1.59 (with free refills) and kids meals are $1.59 for under 6s and $4.99 for 6–12s. Open from 11am–10pm, it should be sought out by all value- and health-conscious eaters. **Chamberlin's Market & Café** (with eight Orlando locations) is another more enlightened choice, with homemade soups, vegetarian chilli, sandwiches, salads and blissful fresh fruit smoothies (www.chamberlins.com).

An excellent section of the *Unofficial Walt Disney World Information Guide* also lists special dietary requests, including veggie, on www.wdwig.com/special.htm.

Eating 24-7

It is not unusual to find restaurants that never close – you can eat around the clock, or 24-7 as the Americans say. So especially for those who can't sleep on their first few nights in the USA (plus those who just like to eat!), here is a guide to where you can go for a snack or even a full-scale meal at 4 in the morning:

10

Inside Planet Hollywood®

Chain restaurants: Denny's, Waffle House, Steak & Shake.
Individuals: B-Line Diner (Peabody Hotel, I-Drive), Mickey D's (world's largest McDonald's, Sand Lake Road; high season only), The Globe (downtown Orlando), Planet Java (Gaylord Palms Resort), Baskervilles (Grosvenor Resort), Tubbi's Buffeteria (Disney's Dolphin Hotel), and the Village Inn (in St Cloud).

Drinking

The biggest complaint of Brits on holiday in the USA is about the beer. With the exception of a handful of English-style pubs (see pages 261–2), American beer is always lager, either bottled or on draught, and ice cold. It goes down great when it's hot, but it is generally weaker and fizzier than we're used to.

> **BRIT TIP:** If there are several of you, ordering a pitcher of beer will work out cheaper than buying it by the glass.

Of course, there are exceptions and they are worth seeking out (try Killian's Red, Michelob, Amber, Bock or Dos Equis for a fuller flavour), but if you are expecting a good, old-fashioned British pint, forget it. Spirits (always called 'liquor' by Americans) come in a typically huge variety, but beware ordering just 'whisky' as you'll get bourbon. Specify if you want Scotch or Irish whiskey and demand it 'straight up' if you don't want it with a mountain of ice! If you fancy a cocktail, there is a massive choice and most bars and restaurants have lengthy happy hours where prices are very consumer-friendly (hic!). Good-quality Californian wines also work out better value than imported European ones. If you are sticking to

> **BRIT TIP:** Tourist brochures often include money-off coupons for many restaurants so you can make useful savings. See www.floridacoupon.com.

soft drinks ('sodas') or coffee, most bars and restaurants give free refills. You can also run a tab in most bars and pay when you leave.

Another few words of warning. Florida licensing laws are stricter than ours and you need to be **21 or over** to enjoy an alcoholic drink in a bar or lounge. You will often be asked for proof of your age before you are served (or allowed into entertainment complexes like *Downtown Disney Pleasure Island*), and this means your passport or new-style driving licence with a photo. It's no good arguing with a reluctant barman. Licensing laws are strict and they take no chances. No photo ID, no beer! Anyone under the age of 21 may not sit or stand near a bar either.

Right, that gives you the inside track on HOW to eat and drink like the locals, now you want to know WHERE to do it, so here's a handy guide to that veritable profusion of culinary variety. At the last count there were almost 4,000 restaurants in the metro Orlando area, with new ones being added and some biting the dust all the time and, while it would be a tall order to list every one, the following section covers the main tourist areas and chain groups.

Fast food

If you are a **McDonald's** fan you are coming to the right place as there are no less than 64 outlets in the greater Orlando area, varying from small drive-in types to the mega, 24-hour-a-day establishment on

Sand Lake Road, Mickey D's (near the junction with I-Drive), that also has the biggest play area for kids of any McDonald's in the world and a number of differently themed eating areas. **Burger King** is also well represented, with 40 outlets, as is another familiar American franchise, **Wendy's**, which has 22 restaurants. If you're a burger freak and want to sample a variation on the theme, give **Checkers** (eight outlets) or **Hardees** (four) a try.

KFC has 22 restaurants around the area, but for something different on the chicken theme, try **Popeye's Famous Fried Chicken & Biscuits** (11). If it's pizza you're after, **Pizza Hut** has 38 restaurants and **Domino's** has 18, and both offer local delivery, even to your hotel room.

A particularly American form of takeaway is the 'sub', or torpedo-roll sandwich. This is what you will find at any one of the 44 local branches of **Subway**, or the 12 of **Sobik's** or eight of **Miami Subs**. They're a rather healthier option than yet another burger, and offer some imaginative fillings. Two other variations on the fast-food theme are **Arby's** (with eight outlets), which offers a particularly appetising roast beef sandwich and other beefy delicacies, and **Taco Bell** (26 outlets), which does for Mexican food what McDonald's does for the hamburger. If you've never had Mexican food, this is probably not the place to start but, for anyone familiar with their tacos, nachos and tortillas, it's a quick and cheap meal.

Most of these establishments will have a drive-through part, which will be fun to try at least once on your visit. Simply drive around the side of the building where indicated and you will find their take-away menu with a voice box to take your order. Please, don't wait for the food to be produced from the voice box! Carry on around the building and your food will be served from a side window where the cashier also takes your money. You will probably find your car has a slide-out tray from the central dashboard area that will take your coffee or soda cup.

Family restaurants

This section may, at first, seem similar to the American Diner type (on page 262), but there are two major differences. First, these are restaurants *only*. You usually won't find a bar here as with a diner. And second, they make a big effort for family groups in terms of kids' menus, activities (in many cases the kids' menu doubles up as a colouring and puzzle book) and budget-conscious prices. They also all serve breakfasts and you will find the best of the all-you-can-eat buffet deals here. Nearly all are chain groups in the same way that you find Little Chef all over Britain, but there are one or two worthy individuals, too.

The most popular are the **Ponderosa Steakhouse** restaurants (I used to include the **Sizzler** chain, too, but I have had recent reports of poor quality). Whether it's breakfast, lunch or dinner, you will find great value and good, reliable food. You order and pay for your meal as you enter and are then seated, before being unleashed on some of the biggest buffet and salad bars you will have seen. Ponderosa has the rather flashier style, but you'd be hard pushed to tell whose food was whose. Expect to pay about $4–5 for their breakfast buffets and $6–9 for lunch and dinner (there IS a difference in price depending on

10

BRIT TIP: A buffet breakfast at Ponderosa or a similar establishment should keep you going until tea-time and is a good way to start a theme-park day.

location, with the I-Drive area tending to be a dollar or two dearer than elsewhere). Standard fare includes chicken wings, meatballs, chilli, ribs, steaks and fresh seafood, while their immense salad bars in particular represent major value for money. Both are open from 7am until late evening and are handily located in all the main tourist spots.

> BRIT TIP: Reader Alastair Gillies says: 'We took your advice with Ponderosa (good value buffet breakfasts and dinners), but we also liked Shoney's for a slightly dearer but definitely superior buffet.'

A more homely touch can be found at the following selection, with equally good if not better value for money. For a hearty breakfast at any time of day, **International House of Pancakes** (otherwise known as IHOP) or the **Waffle House** will both appeal to you. You will struggle to spend more than $6 on a full meal, whether it be one of their huge breakfast platters or a hot sandwich with fries. The Waffle Houses are also open 24 hours a day, while IHOPs open 6am–midnight. Another traditional American 24-hour family restaurant is **Denny's Diner**, the nearest thing to our Little Chefs. Again, they make a traditional bacon and egg breakfast seem ordinary with their wide selection, and they do an excellent range of hot, toasted sandwiches and

Fulton's Crab House

> BRIT TIP: Reader John Cartlidge says: 'While we agree with the recommendation for Ponderosa, one morning we found a huge line for their breakfast buffet, so we drove 200yd (180 metres) down the road to the Black Angus – and the biggest buffet we saw all the time we were there. And no queue!'

imaginative dinner meals, like grilled catfish, as well as a Senior Selections menu, featuring smaller portions at reduced prices for the over 55s.

Similarly, **Perkins Family Restaurant** has a lookalike menu (with some open around the clock). For a really hearty breakfast try Perkins Eggs Benedict (two eggs and bacon on a toasted muffin with hash browns and fresh fruit), while their bread-bowl salads are equally satisfying. Another that impresses for its clean, fresh style is **Golden Corral**, which has already chalked up a number of reader recommendations, and offers a delicious Carver's Choice of hand-carved meats plus the usual buffet deals and a terrific dessert bar.

If you are travelling on the major highways of Florida, one of the 44 branches of **Cracker Barrel** may catch your attention, in which case you should check out their delightful Old Country Store style, with mountainous breakfasts, well-balanced lunch and dinner menus, Kid's Stuff choices and a real old-fashioned charm that is a nice change from the usual tourist frenzy.

Two new alternatives worthy of note for any time, but especially breakfast, are the mushrooming chains of **Panera Bread** (wonderful pastries, salads and sandwiches) and

First Watch (all manner of egg dishes, plus great coffee and pastries, and all served double-quick!).

One of the most popular one-off restaurants for wide family appeal is **Captain Nemo's** on Highway 192 opposite Fort Liberty. It serves breakfast 8am–noon, lunch until 3pm and dinner until 11pm, and its seafood and steak menu means Mum and Dad can try oysters, lobster, salmon, swordfish or grouper while the kids are still able to get their burger fix. Prices are budget-orientated, with daily specials, and Happy Hour 3–7pm.

For a real fun family treat (and the biggest crossover into the diner-type restaurant), take the clan to **Jungle Jim's** at Crossroads of Lake Buena Vista. From the parrots that welcome you to the restaurant, you know you are in for an unusual dining experience, and sure enough you will find an entertaining 'jungle' setting. There are 63 (!) choices of burger, including the World Famous Headhunter, a 1lb (450g) burger with ham, bacon and cheese and the same weight in fries – polish off the lot and your next one is free! The alternatives are ribs, steak or chicken, but it would be a shame not to try at least one of the 63 varieties. The kids' menu is suitably varied, and a huge cocktail range is served by Dr S'Tiph Shotta Likker (ouch!). Open 11am–1.30am Sun–Thur, 11am–2am Fri–Sat.

Another one-off establishment worthy of high praise is **Everett's Old Tymes Eatery** at 2754 Orange Blossom Trail (just south of Osceola Parkway on the right heading south). This typical Florida family diner (open 6am–8pm Mon–Sat and 7am–2pm Sun) offers some of the best value fare in Kissimmee in best down-home style (all drinks are served in jam jars!). Portions are huge (the family breakfast, supposedly for six, includes a dozen scrambled eggs, 1lb (450g) of bacon, 1lb (450g) of sausage, fries and grits, biscuits and toast for just $18.99), while the daily breakfast special is $1.59. It's a bluff, no-nonsense kind of place, well used by the locals (and you'll often find the police here having breakfast), but don't be put off by appearances. Recommended by reader Liz Storey and her family, it more than passes the *Brit's Guide* test for a genuine, good-value establishment that will add to your holiday experience.

Home from home

To complete this section it is appropriate to mention the handful of British pubs and diners which seek to attract the UK visitor. All offer a fairly predictable array of pub grub and a few imported British beers. You'll find the odd Brit or two working behind the bars, and you can happily take the kids into all of them, providing they don't sit at the bar. First and foremost is the **Cricketers' Arms** in The Mercado on I-Drive. This has become a favourite haunt of British visitors due to the large selection of beers, appetising food, live evening entertainment and (soccer fans take note) live Premiership matches on their giant TV screen on a Saturday morning (from 10am – remember the time difference). It gets busy in the evenings, their live music is usually pretty good, and many of the staff are Chelsea fans, but we won't hold that against them! NB: There is usually a cover charge for soccer matches.

10

Sunday brunch at the Renaissance Orlando Resort

Highway 192 in Kissimmee sports a number of fairly derivative pubs all keen to appeal to the home market. The best are **Harry Ramsbottom's** at Fort Liberty (between Markers 10 and 11), which also has its own fish 'n chippie, and the wonderfully kept **Stage Door**, 6 miles (10km) west of the junction with I-4 (and west of Marker 4, just past Lindfields Boulevard). This bar/restaurant gets full marks from the locals, too.

American diners

Not surprisingly, there are so many American-style restaurants, it would be a full-time job just to keep track of them all. Therefore, I will limit this particular survey to the main tourist areas, plus a couple off the beaten track that are well worth tracking down. The $ price listings are intended only as a rough guide for a 3-course meal:

$	=	$10–15
$$	=	$15–20
$$$	=	$20–25
$$$$	=	$25–30
$$$$$	=	$30 plus

Steak and Ale is a popular diner and can be found at five locations around Orlando (11.30am–10pm Mon–Thur, 11.30am–11pm Fri, noon–11.30pm Sat, noon–10pm Sun; $$). They do some great steaks and ribs, plus tempting seafood and chicken dishes, with early bird specials of a 3-course set meal 4–7pm (4–6pm Nov–Mar), and two-for-one drink specials at the same time. The nationwide chain **Bennigan's** has five outlets in Orlando and is a particular personal favourite for their friendly, efficient service, smart decor and tempting menu, especially at lunchtime. They make the ordinary seem appetising and have a bar atmosphere straight out of the TV programme Cheers! Their Irish flavour really comes into its own on St Patrick's Day (March

17), and they have happy hour(s!) 2–7pm and 11pm–midnight (11am–2am; $$).

Another enjoyable dining experience can be found at the two branches of **Darryl's** (one on I-Drive, the other at Fort Liberty on Highway 192). Their weird and wonderful decor is totally original; they also have a great bar area and a nicely varied menu with some interesting choices, like Cajun-fried shrimp. Thick, wood-fired steaks, delicious burgers and southern-style dishes are their main fare, but they also offer tasty soups and quiches (11am–1am; $$).

Hooters makes no bones about its style. 'Delightfully tacky yet unrefined' declares the menu proudly, and sure enough here is a relatively simple, lively establishment, especially popular with the younger crowd for its beach-party atmosphere – and the famous Hooter Girl waitresses (11am–midnight Mon–Thur, 11am–1am Fri–Sat, noon–11pm Sun; $). Their 10 restaurants have a truly entertaining menu featuring great value seafood, salads and burgers, plus Hooters Nearly World Famous Chicken Wings in five strengths: mild, medium, hot, 3 Mile Island or Wild Wing. You have been warned!

By contrast, **Pebbles** (three outlets) goes for the casual but sophisticated style, with a genuinely imaginative menu that will appeal to the amateur gourmet and won't cost a fortune (11am–midnight; $$$). You can eat burgers or roast duck, salad or steak and be sure of an individual touch with every meal. Their pastas are particularly appetising and they offer a kids' menu, too.

Uno Chicago Pizzeria is the place to go if Pizza Hut has become passé. Their four outlets offer great deep-dish pizzas with the addition of pastas, chicken dishes, steaks and salads (11am–midnight; $$).

The **Olive Garden** restaurants (12 of them) are one of America's big success stories as they have brought Italian food into the budget, mass-market range (11am–10pm Sun–Thur, 11am–11pm Fri–Sat; $$). Their light, airy restaurants create a relaxing environment and, while they don't offer a huge choice, what they do they do well and in generous portions. Pastas are their speciality, but they also offer chicken, veal, steak and seafood and some great salads, and unlimited refills of salad, garlic breadsticks and non-alcoholic drinks add to their good value. Their large, new property between Race Rock and Trainland on I-Drive is also a distinct cut above their other outlets for quality and style.

The two **Bahama Breeze** restaurants (one on I-Drive, the other on SR 535 at Lake Buena Vista, next to the Holiday Inn Sunspree) are a must for their striking Caribbean styling – and popularity (the I-Drive one features an hour's wait at peak periods!). As the Bahamas are not strictly in the Caribbean, their theming is a little suspect, but we'll forgive them as the food is well above average for a typical diner. Try West Indies Patties or Creole Baked Goat Cheese as a starter, while the main courses (primarily pastas, seafood, chicken, beef or pizza) feature outstanding items like Black Pepper Seared Tuna or the Cuban beef stew Ropa Vieja, with every dish coming up immaculately fresh.

Service is in keeping with their lively, personable style and there is a pleasing individual touch about all they do. The plantation-room decor, delightful outside wooden deck for a pre- or post-dinner drink and live music most nights fully endorse their own slogan: 'At Bahama Breeze there are no worries, just happy, friendly people and island hospitality!' (4pm–2am Mon–Sat, 4pm–midnight Sun; $$$).

Hard to categorise but well worth visiting is the **Cheesecake Factory** in Winter Park Village and the new Mall at Millenia. While they make a feature of their desserts, the rest of the menu (menu? More like a book!) is pretty impressive, too, not to mention the eclectic, high-tech setting. Mexican dishes jostle with pizza, pasta, seafood, burgers, steaks and salads, and they also offer a great brunch selection, as well as plenty of everything (you really need to come hungry here). If you do nothing else in this selection, visit the Cheesecake Factory for dessert (as many do) and sample one of their 30 varieties of cheesecake (11am–11pm; $$$$).

Ribs

When it comes to steaks, ribs and barbecue food, Orlando has a magnificent array of restaurants that all proudly proclaim some kind of 'world famous' variety. In many instances they are right, and here's a selection of the best.

Cattleman's Steak House (on Vineland Road, at the intersection of SR 535 and Highway 192, and on I-Drive south of The Mercado) goes for the cowboy approach once again, with a neat saloon bar, early bird specials (4–6pm) and the Little Rustlers' Round-up menu for the kids. Steaks are again the order of the day, but you can also order chicken and seafood, and their Heavenly Duck is worth trying for something different (4–11pm, saloon open until 2am; $$$).

The upmarket version of this type of establishment is **Wild Jack's** (on I-Drive, just north of Sand Lake Road) where you are greeted by the most magnificent wood-smoked barbecue aroma as you walk in the door. The huge, western-themed interior features a big, open-pit barbecue where you can watch your food being cooked (11.30am–11pm;

10

> BRIT TIP: Don't miss
> Wild Jack's jalapeño
> mashed potatoes, dynamite
> chicken wings, cowboy
> baked beans and the Jack
> Daniels chocolate cake
> for dessert!

$$$). Steaks, ribs, chicken and
turkey represent the main choices
and they are all served with bags of
panache and a big helpin' of Wild
West style. Happy Hour is 4–7pm,
kids eat free with a full-paying adult
and you can even buy a Wild Jack's
souvenir boot-shaped beer mug.

Another good choice which also
pulls in a lot of positive reader
feedback is **Key W Kool's Open Pit
Grill** on Highway 192 (just opposite
Splendid China). Choice cuts of
meat, mouth-watering steaks – check
out the eye-popping 32-oz (900-g)
porterhouse! – prime rib, daily
specials and a wonderfully succulent,
inviting aroma add up to an
outstanding dining choice, and at
good prices (4–11pm; $$$).

I can also recommend any of the
six restaurants of **Tony Roma's**,
which rightly pronounce themselves
'famous for ribs'. The airy but
relaxing decor and ambience, clever
kids' menu (the Roma Rangers
Round-up, full of puzzles and
games), junior meals, and their melt-
in-the-mouth ribs (try their Original
Baby Backs) make a winning
combination. You can still get
chicken, burgers and steaks, but why
ignore a dish when it's done this

Hard Rock Café

well? The Rib Sampler is a great
platter, with chicken-rib and shrimp-
rib combos (11am–midnight Sun–
Thur, 11am–1am Fri and Sat; $$).

Tex-Mex

What the Olive Garden does for
Italian cuisine, **Chili's** (with 10
outlets) does for Mexican. Actually,
it's an Americanised version of
Mexican cooking that originated in
Texas (hence Tex-Mex), with the
emphasis more on steak and ribs and
less on tortillas and hot spices
(11am–1am Mon–Sat, 11am–11pm
Sun; $$). Service is frighteningly
efficient and, if you are looking for a
quick meal, you'll be hard-pushed to
find a quicker turnaround. The
atmosphere is lively and bustling and
they do a good kids' menu that is
also a colouring/puzzle book.

Similarly, the rather identikit
Chevy's chain has eight restaurants
in the area and offers a healthy slice
of Mexicana, while still offering
some reassuring American selections
(4–11pm Mon–Thur, 4–midnight
Fri, 11am–midnight Sat,
11am–11pm Sun; $$).

The most elaborate Mexican
offering is the cavernous **Don
Pablo's**, next to the Visitor Center
on I-Drive. Clever theming, lively
atmosphere (especially around the
Cantina bar!) and a classic, well-
explained menu add up to a fun
experience (11.30am–10pm Sun–
Thur, 11.30am–11pm Fri–Sat; $$).

Another one-off restaurant that
has a lot of Brit appeal is **Café Tu-
Tu Tango** on I-Drive, next to Vito's.
The accent is artist-colony Spanish
(whatever that means), with a really
original menu, live entertainment
and artwork all over the walls that
changes daily. Vegetarians will find
themselves well catered for here, and
you can try some particularly
succulent pizzas, seafood, salads and
paella. Mexican and Chinese dishes

also make an appearance, and there is a thoughtful kids' menu (11.30am–midnight; $$). The style is based more on a tapas bar, so you order several different dishes rather than a starter and main course. Ultimately, it is as much an artistic experience as a meal, and the fun atmosphere complements the rich array of dishes perfectly.

Steakhouses

Serious steak-lovers will have to pay a visit to **Ruth's Chris Steak House** (with new restaurants in the Winter Park Village and on West Sand Lake Road) where prime beef in a mouth-watering variety of choices is the order of the day. It isn't cheap, but you'll be hard-pushed to get a better steak (5–11pm Mon–Sat, 5–10pm Sun; $$$$$). 'Only the best', proclaims their slogan. 'Come judge for yourself, but come hungry'.

Similarly, the **Butcher Shop** (in The Mercado on I-Drive) offers steaks, steaks and more steaks. Hugely impressive is the cold counter, where you can select your own piece of meat, and the hickory charcoal grill where you can actually cook your steak to the desired degree with, of course, the help of a chef to do it for you or offer advice (5–10pm Sun–Thur, 5–11pm Fri–Sat; $$$$).

Charley's Steak Houses (of which there are three, the biggest being on I-Drive just north of The Mercado) continue the theme of excellent steaks, cooked over a specially built pit woodfire. They are not cheap (although their Orange Blossom Trail location, 2 miles (3km) north of the Florida Mall, is noticeably less expensive than the other two), but the bar area is splendidly furnished, and if you don't fancy steak, which you can watch being grilled on a large, hardwood grill, you can have seafood (5–11pm; $$$$$). Charley's

is frequently highly rated in American steakhouse reviews.

Another imaginative choice is **Vito's Chop House** in front of the Castle Hotel on I-Drive. Their choice beef cuts – check out the Tuscan T-Bone – are aged 4–6 weeks and cooked over wood fires, while they also offer pork chops, seafood and pasta, as well as an extensive wine list (5pm–10.30pm Sun–Thur, 5pm–11pm Fri–Sat; $$$$).

For more steak-induced hedonism, **Morton's** of Chicago (on the Market Place on Dr Phillips Boulevard) is hard to beat. Its rather more upmarket (and sometimes pretty smoky) style is offset by a lively ambience that adds to the enjoyment of its trademark steaks, which you can watch being cooked on an open range. You are provided with a fully exhibited menu (they bring examples of the food to the table) and invited to enjoy some of the biggest, most succulent steaks it has been my pleasure to sample. The porterhouse is an inspired choice, as is one of the principal alternatives, Shrimp Alexander. Needless to say, this does not come cheap, especially as vegetables are extra, but it is a memorable experience (5pm–midnight Mon–Sat, 5pm–11pm Sun; $$$$$).

Similarly, **Shula's Steak House** in the Walt Disney World Dolphin Hotel is both expansive (on your waistline) and expensive. The porterhouse and prime rib are outstanding, and this restaurant (the

10

Morton's Steakhouse

latest in a chain owned by famous former American football coach Don Shula) is extremely popular with locals (5–11pm; $$$$$).

Also in expensive territory, and one that frequently gets the locals' vote for Best Steakhouse, is **Del Frisco's** at 729 Lee Road just north of Winter Park. Here in a fairly down-to-earth atmosphere (although a jacket is advisable attire), they concentrate on prime cuts of US beef, generous portions and reliable, friendly service (5–10pm Mon–Thur, 5–11pm Fri and Sat; $$$$$).

The **Outback Steakhouse** chain (in four Orlando locations) has an Australian slant with thick, juicy well-seasoned steaks, ribs and a small seafood selection. Appetizers include the 'Bloomin Onion', a large fried onion accompanied by their special dipping sauce. Queues build up in the evening, so try to arrive slightly before the usual dinner time or slightly after to avoid a wait (or visit the bar). They also feature a good kids' menu (4–10.30pm Mon–Thur, 3.30–11pm Fri and Sat, 3.30–10.30pm Sun; $$$$).

Perhaps more fun is **Logan's Roadhouse** (with five central Florida outlets, notably on Highway 192 at its junction with I-Drive South) where the funky, rustic atmosphere is enlivened with masses of peanuts in their shells, which liberally carpet the wooden floor by the end of the evening. Burgers, chicken, steaks and ribs are their stock in trade, while they also offer an Express lunch selection if you need to be quick (11am–10.30pm Sun–Thur, 11am–11.30pm Fri and Sat; $$$). **Black Angus** and **Western Steer** complete the line-up of steakhouses along more budget lines as they also serve breakfasts and aim for the family market. Black Angus (two outlets on Highway 192) offers an all-you-can-eat breakfast buffet as well as a typical range of

steaks, and has a nightly karaoke session (7am–11.30pm; $$). Western Steer (on I-Drive, opposite Wet 'n Wild) has a breakfast buffet and dinner buffet. Steaks are the main fare, and with a large tribe to feed, it's great value (7am–11.30pm; $$).

Seafood

You won't be surprised to learn that the choice of seafood eateries is equally wide. **The Crab House** (locations on Goodings Plaza on I-Drive and Palm Parkway) should be self-explanatory. Garlic crabs, steamed crabs, snow crabs, Alaskan king crabs, etc. Yes, this is THE place for crab. You can always try their prime rib, pasta or other seafood, but it would be a shame to ignore the house speciality when it's this good (11.30am–11pm Mon–Sat, noon–11pm Sun; $$$).

Red Lobster (eight restaurants) is part of the same company that has made a success of the Olive Garden chain. This is seafood for the family market, with a varied menu, lively atmosphere and one of the best kids' menu/activity books. While lobster is the speciality, their steaks, chicken, salads and other seafood are equally appetising, and they do a great variety of combination platters (11am–10pm Sun–Thur, 11am–11pm Fri–Sat; $$$).

Charlie's Lobster House (on I-Drive at The Mercado) has a similar menu, with nightly fresh fish specials and reservations recommended. The bar areas are immaculately furnished and service has that extra charm (4–10pm Sun–Thur, 4–11pm Fri–Sat; $$$$).

Completing the chain restaurants here are the three outlets of the **Boston Lobster Feast**, with elaborate nautical decor and an unlimited lobster and seafood buffet (hence the 'Feast'). They have early bird specials from 4.30–6pm

Mon–Fri, 2–4.30pm Sat–Sun which are excellent value, while their 40-item Lobster Feasts are guaranteed to stretch the stomach (4.30–10pm Mon–Fri, 2–10pm Sat–Sun; $$$$).

Of the one-off restaurants, **Ocean Grill** (on I-Drive, just north of the Sand Lake Road junction) offers great seafood at moderate prices. Daily specials, including the early bird variety from 4–6pm, jostle with the likes of fried clams, south-western swordfish, fried catfish, shrimp Creole and seafood lasagne. Their fish and chips would put most British chippies to shame and, for the really hearty appetite, their surf 'n turf is superb (lobster or shrimp and steak), although at a hearty price (4–11pm; $$$) .

The **Atlantic Bay Seafood Grill** (on Highway 192, just east of I-4) surprisingly offers a breakfast buffet on top of its well-priced seafood dishes, early bird specials (4.30–6.30pm) and steaks, ribs and pasta. It's not gourmet but it is hearty and good value, especially the all-you-can-eat seafood bar (4–11pm; $$).

Inside the new Omni Rosen hotel on I-Drive is the **Everglades Restaurant**, an upmarket seafood and steak choice which again combines unusual decor (an environmental look at the Everglades, complete with manatee, swamp scenery, tropical music and a 12-ft/3.5-metre aquarium) with fine cuisine. Daily seafood specials jostle with wild boar, venison and buffalo steak, while the Gator Chowder is a must-try starter. There is a relaxing adjacent bar area in this cavernous hotel, and diners at the Everglades also enjoy complimentary valet parking (5.30–11pm daily; $$$$).

My vote for the most memorable seafood dining experience in town is a split decision, however. **Fulton's Crab House** in *Downtown Disney*'s Marketplace is a wonderful choice. This mock riverboat has six differently themed dining rooms (albeit with the same menu), plus the Stone Crab Lounge which features a complete raw bar (and always seems to be busy). Nautical props, photos and lithographs fill the interior, giving it a wonderfully eclectic, period atmosphere, but the real attraction is the food – some of the freshest and most tempting fish, crab and lobster dishes in Florida. The Alaskan king crab is a rare treat, as is tuna filet mignon, but there are fresh specials every day (the air shipping bills for which are posted in the main hall), as well as a children's menu. Fulton's features an extensive wine list, micro-brewed beers and its own specialities, but the dining rooms often have a queue as early as 6pm, so it is advisable to book (407 394 2628). The Stone Crab Lounge serves lunch and dinner 11.30am–midnight, while the restaurant is open for dinner (5–11pm; $$$$).

The **Flying Fish**, at *Disney's Boardwalk Resort*, is, if anything, even better at what it does. The menu is not overburdened with choice, but what they do they do with great panache and wonderful presentation. Their 'Peeky Toe' Crab Cake starter is melt-in-the-mouth territory, while the Oak-Grilled Wahoo and Coriander Rubbed Yellowfin Tuna are both outstanding. They also offer steak and pork, plus a vegetarian option, but it's really the seafood you want to try here (4–11pm Mon–Sat, 4–10pm Sun).

The newest contender for this crown is **McCormick and Schmick's Seafood Restaurant** at Mall at Millenia, where the ambience, decor and service are all suitably upscale. This is the latest in a quality-conscious US chain, but there is nothing mass-produced or identikit about their style. The chef creates a daily menu based on product, price and availability from local waters, as well as the Pacific

10

BRIT TIP: Want great quality snacks at bargain prices? Visit McCormick and Schmick's during daily Happy Hour (5–7pm) and all their appetisers are $1.95 if served as bar snacks.

Northwest and the Atlantic (with a prominent listing of what's fresh). Oysters are a speciality, along with their soups and salads (not to mention their stellar wine list), and it is hard to believe anyone offers better shrimp, scallops and Atlantic salmon. However, there is little choice, apart from a couple of steaks, outside their seafood specialities (11am–11pm Mon–Thur, 11am–midnight Fri and Sat, 11am–10pm Sun; $$$$$).

All under one roof

Arguably the greatest restaurant selection in one place is in the new Mall at Millenia, just off Exit 78 of I-4. Here you will find the aforementioned Cheesecake Factory and McCormick and Schmick's, plus **Brio Tuscan Grill** (signature wood-grilled and oven-roasted steaks, cops and fresh fish, all with a highly pleasing American-Italian ambience), **PF Chang's** (see page 270), **California Pizza Kitchen** (for a more notably health-conscious selection, such as Vegetarian with Japanese Eggplant and Caramelised Pear & Gorgonzola, plus great salads and pastas), **Panera Bread**

Race Rock

(sandwiches will never be the same again!) and **Johnny Rockets** (the latest outlet of the popular 1950s-style diner chain). The Food Court takes the choice still further (and maintains the sophisticated style) with 12 outlets, including several new to Orlando such as **Bistro Sensations** (salads, fresh pastas, pittas and wraps), **Cajun Grill** (a real taste of exquisite New Orleans), **Chinatown** (fast food Mandarin-style) and **Nori Sushi & Grill** (authentic Japanese chicken and beef Teriyaki). Not keen on shopping? The Mall at Millenia (see page 285) will convert you!

Novel dining

There are four other restaurants that could be categorised as diners but are really delightful, one-off restaurants. All four provide an exciting dining experience in novel settings that will linger long in the memory, and without costing a fortune.

Planet Hollywood®, the largest restaurant in the recently troubled worldwide chain of this glitzy, showbiz-style venture, is next door to *Downtown Disney Pleasure Island* and is a pure fun entertainment venue. The food is fairly predictable diner fare, although everything is served with pizzazz, but the cavernous interior lends itself to a party atmosphere, complete with film clips and a stunning array of movie memorabilia. Some memorable house cocktails, too, but visit either mid-morning or mid-afternoon to avoid the serious queues (11am–2am; $$$).

B-Line Diner, inside the Peabody Hotel on I-Drive, is an amazing art deco homage to the traditional 1950s-style diner, faithful in every detail, including the outfits of the staff. You sit at a magnificent long counter or in one of several booths, with a good view of the chefs at work and with a rolling menu that changes four times a day (which isn't bad when it is open around the clock). The food is way above usual diner standards, but the prices aren't, so you can munch away on catfish in a papaya-tartare sauce or pork chops with apple-sage chutney, as well as the traditional favourites of burgers, steaks and ribs, happy in the knowledge you won't break the bank. Their desserts are displayed in a huge glass counter and I defy you to ignore them (open 24 hours; $$).

The two versions of **Rainforest Café**, an eco-aware, jungle-themed restaurant chain, are adjacent to *Disney's Animal Kingdom Theme Park* and in the heart of *Downtown Disney* Marketplace, one with a huge waterfall exterior and the other topped by an active, smoking volcano, and they have to be seen to be believed. You don't dine, you go on a 'safari adventure' in a rainforest setting amid audio-animatronic animals (including elephants and gorillas), thunderstorms, tropical birds, waterfalls, aquariums and some of the cleverest lighting effects I have seen. It is an amazing experience, especially for children, and the food is well above average. Try the Rasta Pasta or Mojo Bones ribs, but the menu alone will take a while to negotiate. Unless you arrive before midday, you'll have to wait for a table, but that's no hardship

given their locations. Beware the huge gift shop! (11am–11pm; $$$).

Another unmistakable landmark on I-Drive is the super-charged, super-large restaurant of **Race Rock**, packed with rare motor-racing memorabilia and eye-catching machines of all kinds. This does for motor sport what the Hard Rock does for music, and how! Two giant car transporters line the entrance, which also boasts a giant-wheeled buggy, two dragsters and a hydroplane speedboat, welcoming you into the circular, 20,000-sq ft (1,860-sq metre) restaurant itself. Giant TV screens and a host of regular TVs, video games, virtual-reality racing machines and loud, loud music, plus chequered flag tables complete the atmosphere, while the central bar sports an upside-down racing car circulating as the world's biggest ceiling fan!

The food is traditional diner fare given a few tweaks like Start Your Engines (the starter selections), Circle Tracks (pizza), Stock and Modified (burgers and sandwiches), Pole Position Pastas and The Main Event (ribs, chops, chicken and salmon). I rate the Road Runner chicken, marinated in lime juice, olive oil and garlic and char-grilled, very highly. A Quarter Midget menu costs $4.99 for children 12 and under (11.30am– midnight; $$).

Chinese

Chinese food is well established in America and well represented in Orlando, although many outlets are

Inside Race Rock

10

pretty uninspired, not to mention downright insipid.

Ming Court on I-Drive, just south of King Henry's Feast, is the Rolls-Royce of local Chinese restaurants. With such a magnificent setting and live entertainment you can easily convince yourself you have been transported to China itself. The menu is extensive and many dishes can be had as a side order rather than a full main course (they specialise in dim sum) to give you the chance to try more (11am–2.30pm and 4.30pm–midnight; $$$).

Bill Wong's Famous Super Buffet (yes, they really do call it that) on I-Drive offers a cross between Chinese and diner-type fare. Their all-you-can-eat buffet features jumbo shrimp (and they mean Jumbo!), as well as crabs, prime rib, fresh fruit and salad (11am–10pm; $$).

A rather classier version of this style is the **China Garden Buffet** at The Mercado. The elegant surroundings are the perfect complement to the extraordinary buffet choice, with more than 50 items – from spring rolls to chilled crab claws – on offer at any time. There is also a full à la carte selection, but the buffet price of $15.95 for adults and $6.95 for 3–10s ($8.59 and $4.95 at lunch) make this one of the best deals going (10am–11pm; $$).

Similarly, the **Sizzling Wok**, on Sand Lake Road, just across from the Florida Mall, offers an opportunity to get stuck into a massive Chinese buffet at a very reasonable price (11am–10pm Sun–Thur, 11am–10.30pm Fri–Sat; $$).

The **China Café** on I-Drive (at the corner of Kirkman Road) is also above average, with a lunch buffet from 11am–3pm and a well presented array of dishes (the crispy duck is outstanding). Daily specials also feature (11am–11pm; $$).

Arguably the best of the bunch, though, is the latest 'chain' offering, **PF Chang's China Bistro** (at Winter Park's Village Shops and Mall at Millenia), which mixes classic Chinese fare with an American bistro style that makes fans of virtually all who sample it. Seek out their Spicy Ground Chicken and Eggplant, the Cantonese Roasted Duck or Oolong Marinated Sea Bass for dishes with real distinction. There is also a good vegetarian selection (5–11pm; $$$).

Japanese

The more adventurous (and those already familiar with their cuisine) will want to try one of the fine Japanese restaurants that Orlando is blessed with. **Shogun Steakhouse**, on I-Drive under the Rodeway Inn, is ideal for those who can't quite go the whole hog and get stuck into sushi (basically, raw fish). If you decide to 'chicken' out, you can still order a no-nonsense steak or chicken, but their full Japanese menu is well explained and vividly demonstrated by their chefs in front of you at long, bench-like tables (6–10pm Mon–Thur, 6–10.30pm Fri–Sun; $$).

Kobe brings a touch of Americana to its dining content. With four locations around the area, Kobe goes for the mass market but still achieves individual style with the chef preparing your food at your table in a style that is as much showmanship as culinary expertise (11.30am–11pm; $$).

Ran-Getsu, on I-Drive opposite The Mercado, does for Japanese cuisine what the Ming Court does for Chinese – it's stylish, authentic and as much an experience as a meal, and still reasonably priced. The setting is simple and efficient, and you can choose to sit at conventional tables or at the long, S-shaped sushi bar (5pm–midnight; $$$).

Benihana completes a formidable quartet of outlets, situated in the Hilton Hotel at Lake Buena Vista. Again, it's a memorable experience, with everything cooked in front of you by expert chefs, and their steaks are among the most tender you will ever experience (5–10.30pm; $$$).

Indian

If you have come all this way and still fancy a curry, believe it or not you will be able to get one as good as any you have enjoyed back home. There are already more than a dozen Indian restaurants around the Orlando area and they all maintain a pretty fair standard, from the upmarket **Far Pavilion**, at the intersection of I-Drive and Kirkman Road, to the budget-price **New Punjab** at the upper end of I-Drive and on West Vine Street, Kissimmee, which has excellent lunch and dinner specials.

For a medium-range restaurant, **Passage to India** (also on I-Drive) gets the locals' top vote and is a cut above the average, with unusual and exotic chicken dishes and vegetarian Sabzi Dal Bahar. It is a particular personal favourite for its attentive service and relaxed atmosphere, and you'll probably find yourself dining with a few fellow Brits. (11.30am–midnight; $$$).

The newest Indian game in town is **Flavours of India** in South Kirkman Road, not far from Universal Studios. Their style again aims to be traditional rather than avante garde (you won't find that curious Indian-English hybrid the Balti dish here) and they have already impressed the *Orlando Sentinel* restaurant critic – no mean feat (11.30am–2.30pm; 5.30–10.30pm Sun–Thur, 5.30–11pm Fri and Sat; $$$).

Thai and more

For other types of Oriental cooking, the **Siam Orchid** (on Universal Boulevard, round the corner from Wet 'n Wild) offers exceptional Thai food in a picturesque setting overlooking Sandy Lake (5–11pm; $$). **Little Saigon** (on East Colonial Drive) will introduce you to Vietnamese cuisine and a whole new array of soups, barbecue dishes, fried rice variations and other interesting treats that take up where Chinese food leaves off (10am–9pm; $).

The new **Thai Passion** (on Sand Lake Road, west of its I-4 junction) is simply a must for anyone who enjoys a meal in suitably bona fide surroundings. The menu is authentic and features some fabulous curries (order the Massaman Curry if you like your food seriously spicy!), but it is as much the sumptuous setting and low-rise tables which make this such an enjoyable dining experience (11.30am–2.30pm, Mon–Fri, 5–10.30pm all week; $$$$), not to mention their 2-for-1 Happy Hour from 5–7pm!

Cuban

Cuban food is a Floridian speciality and you'll find some of the best examples at **Rolando's** (on Semoran Boulevard, in the suburb of Casselberry; head east from I-4 Exit 92). Try the red snapper or pork chunks and find out why the *Orlando Sentinel* rates this the best Cuban food north of Havana (11am–9pm Tue–Thur, 11am–10pm Fri–Sat, 1–8pm Sun; $).

However, the new **Samba Room** on West Sand Lake Road is the 5-star experience hereabouts, an elegant lakefront restaurant full of Latin verve and ambience. The menu exhibits a wonderfully exotic touch, with the likes of Mango-barbecued Ribs, Cachaca-smoked Boneless Chicken and Sugar Cane

10

Beef Tenderloin (with Chipotle Mashed Potatoes and Mushroom Sofrito), and their range of cocktails is suitably Cuban-laced (with lots of rum and martini). Definitely worthy of investigation, but also extremely popular, so reservations are advised (407 266 0550; 11am–midnight Mon–Sat, noon–10pm Sun; $$$$$).

Italian

No survey of Orlando's restaurants would be complete without mention of its fine tradition of Italian cooking. **Pacino's** on Highway 192, opposite Old Town, goes for the family market and scores a big hit with value, a friendly atmosphere and Sicilian style, plus clever animated puppet operettas, a fountain that occasionally spouts flame and a relaxing open-air feel that is enhanced by the clever use of the differently arranged seating areas (4pm–midnight; $$$).

Bergamo's, in The Mercado, is actually German-owned but nonetheless authentic for all that. Don't be surprised if your waiter suddenly bursts into song – it's all part of the unique charm of this extremely tempting and highly entertaining restaurant (5–10pm Sun–Thur, 5–11pm Fri–Sat; $$$$).

Italianni's (on I-Drive just south of its Sand Lake Road junction) won't hurt your wallet quite so much and does a great pizza among a typical selection of Italian fare. Don't miss their homemade cheesecake (11am–11pm; $$$).

The 5-star version of Italian cuisine here belongs to three contrasting restaurants, Christini's on Dr Phillips Boulevard, Antonio's on Sand Lake Road and Michaelangelo on Kirkman Road. Strolling musicians, elegant surroundings and a 40-year history of award-winning cuisine characterise **Christini's**, where their homemade pasta and filet mignon are as good as anything you will find in Italy. (5–11pm; $$$$$). The new **Antonio's**, up on the second floor in the Fountains Plaza on West Sand Lake Road, is another haven of quality (albeit at a price) in an area fast becoming synonymous with fine dining. This is the biggest and fanciest of three local outlets and has an exclusive style as well as outstanding cuisine – sensational risottos are a signature dish while veal or New York strip steak are an equally wise choice – (5–10pm Mon–Sat; $$$$$).

Michaelangelo, just north of Universal Studios in Turkey Lake Village, promotes a candlelit atmosphere with live music in the cocktail lounge, formal, dinner-jacketed staff and a northern Italian cuisine that features delicious veal, snapper and pasta delicacies. The pasta, bread and desserts are homemade, and it is all presented in an old-world style that is a million miles from the tourist hurly-burly of the parks (meals 6–11pm, 6pm–2am in the bar; $$$$$).

Continental

A somewhat unlikely but highly worthwhile discovery is **Gain's German Restaurant**, on the South Orange Blossom Trail (just past Oakridge Road going north), both for food and an excellent selection of bottled and draught beers. The friendly welcome, authentic Bavarian decor and tempting menu come as a real surprise in the heart of tourist Orlando, but owners Hans

The Palm Restaurant

and Kessy Gain have lavished much care and attention on building up their trade here. A tasty ragout is an ideal appetiser, while there are sausage specialities (naturally), wiener schnitzel (of course), and rotisserie chicken and pan-fried rainbow trout (for something different). Apple strudel and Black Forest cake are the ideal desserts, while the Diebels amber ale is a fine choice for beer connoisseurs (407 438 8997 for reservations; 11.30am–2.30pm and 4.30–10pm Tue–Thur, 4.30–11pm Fri and Sat, 4.30–10pm Sun; $$–$$$).

Another surprise but welcome choice is **The Melting Pot** (a national chain that now has three outlets in central Florida, including their newest in the Fountains Plaza on West Sand Lake Road). As the name suggests, this is fondue territory and an extremely quality-conscious version of the genre. Their Fondues for Two feature a cheese fondue, salad course and entrée course (a main fondue with one of three meat selections in a choice of four cooking styles). You can still order from a standard entrée list (including chicken, shrimp and steak), but that would be to miss the point (5.30–9.45pm Sun–Fri, 5.30–10.45pm Sat; $$$$).

Splashing out – the Ultimate Nine

Finally, if you fancy really splashing out, here are some notable suggestions where both the food and ambience are way above average (albeit with a price tag to match). This fine dining aspect has become a real growth area in Orlando's culinary panorama, and long may it continue! Most notably, the area of Sand Lake Road immediately to the west of I-4 (the Fountains Plaza area and the opposite side of the street) has become a gourmet's delight. Its

popularity also requires that you book well in advance for each one.

One of the newest on the scene is the wonderfully trendy **Seasons 52**, the most upmarket offering of the Darden group (Bahama Breeze, Olive Garden, Red Lobster). The restaurant's name refers to the fact every week, all year long, different products come into season, hence the menu is designed to feature new items weekly, with some seriously creative choices from their culinary team. It is also designed to be more healthy than the average restaurant, with a balanced approach to carbohydrate/fat content. All appetisers, side salads and soups range from 100–250 calories, the vast majority being either grilled or oven-roasted, and all entrées are in the 300–475 calorie range, Your server will be able to offer bags of advice – not least with an extensive wine list – and the whole contemporary, bustly atmosphere makes for a thoroughly refreshing experience (407 354 5212; 4.30–11pm; $$$$).

The **Park Plaza Gardens** is part of the Park Plaza Hotel on Park Avenue, Winter Park, and this beautiful courtyard restaurant gives you the feel of outdoor dining with the air-conditioned comfort of being indoors. Attentive service is coupled with an elegant, versatile menu that offers the choice of a relatively inexpensive lunch or a 3-course adventure featuring escargots, pasta

Jiko at Disney's Animal Kingdom Lodge

10

with salmon, medallions of beef or one of several tempting fish dishes. Cuisine is distinctly 'nouvelle' rather than American, but nonetheless satisfying for all that. Its setting becomes even more intimate and charming in the evening with lights scattered among the foliage. Enjoy Happy Hour in the lounge (5–7pm, with complimentary buffet Thur and Fri), while their popular 3-course Sunday brunch features unlimited champagne and live jazz (407 645 2475; 11.30am–3pm Mon–Sat and 11am–3pm for Sunday brunch, 6–10pm Mon–Thur, 6–11pm Fri–Sat, 6–9pm Sun; $$$$$).

A highlight of the Renaissance Orlando Resort is the **Atlantis** seafood signature restaurant. This wonderfully elegant and quite intimate corner of an equally smart hotel not only offers fine dining in the normal course of events, but also a scintillating range of daily fresh Floridian seafood specials that just demand to be sampled. A fine wine list complements the full à la carte dinner menu (5–10.30pm; $$$$$).

For another meal with a difference check out the **Renaissance's Sunday Brunch**, which is something of an Orlando tradition. Not so much a buffet as a 100-item banquet, it costs $30.95 for adults, $15.95 for children 4–12. Try this and brunch will never be the same again (407 351 5555; 10.30am–2.30pm).

Another standout in seafood territory (and another in the West Sand Lake Road group) is the splashy **Moonfish**, a true individual in both decor and menu terms. You could make a feast of their appetisers alone, while their inspired sushi range is just to die for. Many restaurants that go for the avant garde look fail to deliver in cuisine terms, but Moonfish certainly does not fall into that trap, and it also makes a good romantic excursion for two (but not at the tables nearest the

bar). Dare to be different could be their motto here – and they do (407 363 7262; 11.30am–10pm; $$$$$).

A recent arrival in The Mercado and a pleasant addition to the upscale style in this largely mass-market location is **DiVino's**, a rural-themed Italian restaurant with the full essence of Tuscany. Relatively simple pastas jostle with wood-grilled swordfish, braised chicken and the trademark Osso Buco (roast veal shank), plus some excellent daily specials (seafood especially). It is not a cheap exercise (main courses run from $20–30) but the deep flavours, allied with excellent service, create a memorable meal. Reservations are not always necessary but it does get busy around 8pm most evenings (407 345 0883; 5–11pm daily; $$$$$).

The opening of Universal's Hard Rock Hotel brought with it the **Palm Restaurant**, the latest in an upscale nationwide chain which has a big celebrity following. Founded in New York in 1926, it is famous for prime-aged steaks and jumbo lobsters, served in spacious, elegant surroundings and with personable, knowledgeable service. The house speciality Jumbo Nova Scotia Lobster is spectacular. Their steaks are a bit special, too (check out the Double Steak, a 36-oz/1kg+ New York strip for 2 at $60), plus there's swordfish, crab, salmon, pork, veal and pasta. All this decadence is, reflected in the prices, and the vegetable dishes are extra, but the lunch menu shows a more modest touch while maintaining the quality (407 503 7256; 11am–11pm Mon–Sat; noon–10pm Sun; $$$$$).

Sticking with the hotel theme, **Jiko** in *Disney's Animal Kingdom Lodge* is possibly their most imaginative and impressive culinary offering to date. Maintaining the hotel's African theming with its decor and lighting, Jiko ('The Cooking Place') features twin wood-burning ovens, a masterful menu and an exclusive selection of South African wines sure to please any connoisseur. The menu reflects influences from India and Asia as well as Africa and offers dishes like Banana-leaf Steamed Sea Bass, Whole Roast Papaya Stuffed with Spicy Minced Beef and Oven-baked Garlic Chicken Tagine with Grapefruit, Olives and Herbs. The personal level of service and ethnic ambience underline the adventure of any meal here and make it a real highlight of this amazing hotel (407 939 3463; 5–11pm; $$$$$).

Old Hickory Steakhouse is another hotel-based offering in the new Gaylord Palms on I-Drive South. Its elaborate Everglades theming gives it an extra dimension, but the steak needs few gimmicks as the house speciality certified Black Angus beef is aged for 21–35 days and cooked to perfection. Side dishes are extra, hence it is an expensive option, but the attentive service and alternatives like oven-roasted swordfish and Maine lobster provide a memorable experience. Watch out, too, for their signature artisanal cheese course, imported by trendy New York chef Terrance Brennan. If you are fortunate enough to be staying at this amazing hotel, Old Hickory should definitely be on your to-do list. Otherwise, it is a great excuse to pay the Gaylord Palms a visit (5–10.30pm Mon–Fri, 5–11pm Sat, 5–10pm Sun; $$$$$).

Finally, I have saved the very best until last with what I consider to be the most amazing and enjoyable restaurant experience currently in central Florida. **Tchoup Chop** (pronounced Chop Chop) at Universal's Royal Pacific Resort is the latest offering from the gourmet stable of New Orleans master chef Emeril Lagasse, and it goes for a grand exercise in Asian-Pacific fusion cuisine with the most eye-catching decor imaginable. The huge central pond is a study in feng shui, and you can easily sit and study the interior for much of the meal and still be noticing new things at the end. Service is a team effort at every table (which can be a touch off-putting), but the superb menu is well presented and explained.

And oh, that menu! Taking some of the most aromatic and flavoursome elements of Thai, Chinese, Japanese, South Seas and other Pacific Rim cultures, Lagasse has conjured up a mouth-watering array of dishes, all immensely tempting and tasting as good as their promise. Start off with Home-made Dumpling Box (with a fresh port and ginger filling, hand-rolled, steamed and served with sake soy dipping sauce) or the Polynesian Crabcake (with ginger scallion aioli and papaya-serrano salsa), then graduate to superb entrées like Macadamia-nut Crusted Atlantic Salmon (served with ginger soy butter sauce, steamed rice and stir-fried vegetables), Tchoup Chop's clay pot of the day (served with steamed rice and seasonal vegetables) or the Hawaiian-style dinner plate including kiawe-smoked ribs, kahlua pork, teriyaki-grilled chicken, chorizo potato hash and baked macaroni. If that little lot doesn't set your tastebuds trembling, nothing will! The only drawback is that no sooner have you settled on one option than the menu immediately tempts you to another!

Dinner here is exceptionally busy, so try lunch if they cannot squeeze you in (407 503 2467; 11.30am–2pm; 5.30–10pm Sun–Thur, 5.30–11pm Fri and Sat; $$$$).

Now on to another of my favourite topics. The other main way in which Orlando will seek to separate you from your hard-earned money is shopping…

10

11 Shopping

(or, How to Send Your Credit Card into Meltdown)

As well as being a theme park wonderland, the vast area that constitutes metropolitan Orlando is also a shopper's paradise, with a dazzling array of specialist outlets, malls, flea markets and discount retailers. It is also a vigorous growth market, with new centres springing up seemingly all the time, from the smartest of malls to the cheapest of gift shop plazas – and you can hardly go a few yards in the main tourist areas without a shop insisting it has the best tourist bargains of one sort or another.

In fact, in many ways the shopping centres have become as much of a tourist trap as the theme parks, and you will be bombarded by opportunities every way you turn. The only hard part is avoiding the temptation to fill an extra suitcase or two with the sort of goods that cost twice as much back home. As a general rule, you can expect to pay in dollars what you would pay in pounds for items like clothes, books and CDs, and there are real bargains to be had in jeans, trainers, shoes, sports equipment and cosmetics.

But beware! Your duty-free allowance in the catch-all duty category of 'gifts and souvenirs' is still only £145 per person, and it is easy to exceed that sum by a distance. Paying the duty and VAT is still often cheaper than buying the same items at home, however, so it is worth splashing out, but remember to keep all your receipts and go back through the red 'goods to declare' channel on your return. You will pay duty (which varies depending on the item) on the total purchase price (i.e. inclusive of Florida sales tax) once you have exceeded your £145 allowance, plus VAT at 17.5%. Unfortunately, you cannot pool your allowances to cover one item that exceeds a single allowance. Hence, if you buy a camera, say, that costs £200, you have to pay the duty on the full £200, taking the total to £213.20, and then the VAT on that figure. However, if you have a number of items that add up to £145, and then another which exceeds that, you pay the duty and VAT only on the excess (and the customs officers will usually give you the benefit of the lowest rate on what you pay for). Duty rates are updated regularly and vary from 2.7% (golf clubs) to 15% (mountain bikes). If you have any queries, contact the Customs and Excise

BRIT TIP: If you are tempted to use 'doctored' receipts to show a lesser value – don't, it is illegal. Your goods will be confiscated and there are heavy fines. Also, you can't escape the duty by saying the items have been used (in the case of golf clubs, for example) or that they are gifts for someone else.

ORLANDO'S SHOPPING CENTRES

A Downtown Disney Marketplace
B The Mercado
C The Pointe*Orlando
D Old Town
E Festival Bay
F Belz Factory Outlet World
G Quality Outlet Center
H Belz Designer Outlet Center
I Kissimmee Manufacturers' Outlet Mall
J Lake Buena Vista Factory Stores
K Orlando Premium Outlets
L Flea World
M Osceola Flea And Farmers' Market

N Florida Mall
O Colonial Plaza Mall
P Altamonte Mall
Q Seminole Towne Center
R Osceola Square Mall
S Orlando Fashion Square Mall
T Mall At Millenia
U Park Avenue
V Winter Park Village
W Kissimmee Historic District
X Goodings International Plaza
Y Crossroads Plaza
Z Fountains Plaza

11

National Advice Service on 0845 010 9000 or visit www.hmce.gov.uk.

Your ordinary duty-free allowances from America include 200 cigarettes and 1 litre of spirits or 2 litres of sparkling wine and 2 litres of still wine. Alligator products, which constitute an endangered species, require a special import licence, and you should consult the Department of the Environment first.

Be aware, also, of the hidden 'extras' of shopping costs. Unlike our VAT, the local version in Orlando, the Florida State sales tax, is NOT added to the displayed purchase price, so you must add 6 or 7% (depending on which county you are in) to arrive at the 'real' price. This frequently catches visitors out. The sales tax is added to everything you buy in Orlando, from theme park tickets to a beer at the hotel you are staying in and all meals (but not groceries).

If those are the mechanics of shopping, here is a rundown of the main attractions and the sort of fun and bargains to be had, divided into four categories. First, the purpose-built shopping complexes, specifically out to catch the visitor's eye; second, Orlando's speciality flea markets and discount outlets; third, the large shopping malls; and finally a few shops for the bargain-hunter. The best examples of the first category are all in the main tourist areas, starting, of course, with Disney.

Downtown Disney

The heart of *Walt Disney World Resort in Florida* in many ways is their *Downtown Disney* development. And the **Downtown Disney Marketplace** is typical Disney, a beautiful location, imaginative building and landscaping and a host of one-off elements that make shopping here a pleasure, along with 24 standout shops and dining opportunities. Don't miss the awesome **World of Disney** store, the largest of its kind in the world, the **Lego Imagination Center** (an interactive playground and shop), the amazing **Art of Disney** and **Team Mickey's Athletic Club**. New in 2002 was **Once Upon A Toy**, a gigantic toy emporium complete with a host of classic games, many with a novel Disney theme, for kids to try out. Other recent additions are the wonderfully scented **Basin** (for hand-carved soaps, bubble baths and shampoo bars) and **Disney's Wonderful World of Memories** (for all scrapbook fans, plus the only place to get a Disney postmark for your postcards home!). Dancing fountains and squirt pools (where kids tend to get seriously wet), the lakeside setting and boating opportunities all add to the appeal here. Restaurants include the superbly themed **Rainforest Café** and a **McDonald's**, plus the excellent **Cap'n Jack's Restaurant**, while ice cream and chocolate fans should check out **Ghirardelli's** for some cool sundaes and super shakes. Those keen on the Disney hobby of pin trading should definitely check out **Pin Traders**, while **Summer Sands** offers an excellent range of swimwear and casual clothing. For a typically British touch, you can opt for a bite (speciality hot sandwiches) at the **Earl of Sandwich**, a new restaurant which is a joint venture between Planet Hollywood and Lord John Montagu, the 11th Earl of Sandwich himself.

Then you can stroll over to **Downtown Disney West Side**, see a film at the superb **AMC 24** cinema complex, visit the world's largest **Virgin Megastore** or another of the 17 retail and dining outlets. The **Hoypoloi Gallery** is one of my favourites for a wonderfully eclectic range of artwork, from metal to glass, while **Magic Masters** (all kinds of magic tricks and souvenirs, with demonstrations) and **Wetzel's Pretzel's** are both new. In all, there are 32 shops to browse, including several more in *Pleasure Island*, which are open during the day and don't require an entry ticket (before 7pm). And, when it all gets too much, you can visit the **Zen Zone** in *Pleasure Island* for a soothing aqua-massage! The whole *Downtown Disney* complex is open 9.30am– 11pm every day (7pm–2am in *Pleasure Island*, separate admission required). It is off Exits 67 and 68 of I-4 and is well signposted (Exit 68 can be congested at peak periods).

I-Drive

This core tourist area has three cleverly built developments which offer some unique shopping attractions, starting with **The Mercado**, the original speciality complex, in the heart of the I-Drive corridor just south of Sand Lake Road. Although it is looking a bit tired compared to the newer developments, this Mediterranean-style 'village' includes 25 speciality shops, five high-quality restaurants (Italian duo **Bergamo's** and **Divino's, Charlie's Lobster House**, the **China Garden Buffet** and the **Butcher Shop**), the **Cricketers' Arms** pub (essential for Brit banter, proper beer and footy on the TV!), evening entertainment (in the courtyard) and an impressive food court (especially for the budget-conscious – check out the All American Grill for great breakfasts).

BRIT TIP: Coffee shop Café Grande in The Mercado is the place to go if you need to log on to the internet and check your email while in town.

The Mercado is open 10am–10pm daily (from 8am in the food court and to 11pm at the restaurants), and will amuse you and your wallet for an hour or two.

Shops like **The Looking Glass, Andean Manna, One For The Road, Del Sol** and **Crystal Nature** are all good for a variety of unusual gifts, while hand-carts and artists also enliven the scene. Visit www.themercado.com for more info.

The second shopping complex to stand out on I-Drive is the 17-acre (3-ha) **Pointe*Orlando** (see also Orlando by Night, page 243), which is as much an evening adventure as mere shopping. The 60-plus stores here are all more upmarket than usual tourist fare, and you can indulge your passion for fashion at

BRIT TIP: The Pointe is the only centre where there is a charge for its (multi-storey) car park. However, if you visit any of Muvico, XS Orlando, Dan Marino's Town Tavern, Adobe Gila's, Hooters or LuLu's Bait Shack, you can get your parking ticket paid for, while Chico's women's clothing store offers parking validation for up to 2 hours.

places like **Gap** and **Gap Kids, Victoria's Secret, Armani Exchange, Image Leather, Tommy Hilfiger, Abercrombie & Fitch** and the **Everything But Water** swimwear store, or stock up on gifts and souvenirs at **Disney Worldport, Bath & Body Works, Yankee Candle** (highly recommended), **Glow** and **Sunglass Hut**.

If nothing else, you should let the kids loose in the huge interactive toy shop **FAO Schwarz**, go to the state-

11

of-the-art, 21-screen **Muvico** cinema complex, and finish up with a meal at lively **Johnny Rockets** American diner, where the staff all join in with various jukebox favourites. The landscaping and two-level design are also extremely eye-catching, and the new **XS Orlando** arcade-and-restaurant offers the chance to let the kids play for a while on a vast array of video games and simulators while Mum and Dad do the shops. **Dan Marino's Town Tavern** is another personal dining favourite here for its varied menu, and then there is a **Hooters, Adobe Gila**'s (casual cantina-style dining – and drinking!) and **LuLu's Baitshack** (Cajun and Creole specialities). Visit www.pointeorlando.com for the full details.

The newest centre is **Festival Bay**, right at the top of I-Drive and with a lot to recommend it. It has been under construction for three years, and the second phase finally opened in 2003, with more in store. The mix of shops and entertainment is quite unusual, and many of the stores will be unfamiliar to British visitors – but don't let that put you off as there is much to discover here. The main entrance sees **Ron Jon's Surf Shop** battling for prominence with **Fuddrucker's** diner (superb burgers), while inside the covered mall area is a huge water feature and another 38 stores and restaurants, plus **Vans Skate Park** and the superb **Cinemark 20-screen Movie Complex**, arguably the fanciest cinema in Orlando. The massive **Bass Pro Shops Outdoor World** is

worth checking out for its range of outdoor clothing and equipment (fishing, boating, hunting, hiking) as well as the amazing themed decor, while **Shepler's Western Wear** also has to be seen to be believed for their range of apparel, boots and other footwear (and all at great prices, too). **Steve & Barry's University Sportswear** is another unusual clothing store (especially for the value-conscious), while **Hilo Hattie's** is a wonderful emporium of all things Hawaiian. Other standouts include **Candle Time, Charlotte Russe** and **Swim Smart**, plus a

> BRIT TIP: Fans of ice cream should make a beeline to Festival Bay and the Cold Stone Creamery for some truly magnificent concoctions.

unique, glow-in-the-dark mini-golf course, the **Putting Edge**, which is a great place to occupy the kids for a while. Of course, Vans Skate Park is the perfect opportunity to unleash anyone with a skateboard obsession (look up www.vans.com/skateparkorg/orlando.htm) and offers six 2-hour sessions a day (10am–11pm) as well as a full range of safety equipment and board rentals, plus a chill-out lounge. The whole emphasis of Festival Bay, though, is on entertainment as much as shopping, and the relaxing, village street style of the mall is aimed squarely at (and rewards) the casual wanderer. There is no food court as such, but there are small dining outlets dotted around, notably **Long John Silver's, Auntie Annie's, Villa Pizza Cuccina** and **Mrs Fields**, as well as the full-service **Fuddrucker's**. See www.belz.com/realestate/ retail/festival for more info.

Kissimmee's version of the purpose-built tourist shopping

FAO Schwarz

centre is **Old Town**, an antique-style offering in the heart of Highway 192, with a tourist-friendly mix of shops, restaurants, bars and fairground attractions, all set out along brick-built streets. The shops – some 75 of them – range from standard souvenirs, novel T-shirt outlets and Disney merchandise to sportswear, motorbike fashions and other collectables (check out the **General Store** for a step back in time, too, or the **Old Town Portrait Gallery** for period style).

The **International Space Station** is new, with a host of NASA-inspired gifts and games, as is the fascinating **Petrified Rock Forest**. In addition, you will find 12 restaurants or snack bars, the 5-storey **Haunted Grimm House** ($7 for adults, $5 for children), and a host of rides, including the 60ft- (18 metre) tall Century Wheel, the Windstorm roller-coaster, go-karts, a **Kids' Town** area of junior rides and the 365 ft (111 metre) **Slingshot** mega-ride (0–100mph/60kph in 2 stunning seconds!). Tickets are sold separately for most rides (at $1 each), but if you plan to do several, go for the Valuepak at $20 for 22 tickets or $30 for 35. Allow up to 4 hours here and try at all costs to take in the weekly **Saturday Nite Cruise** at 8.30pm, a drive-past of 300-plus vintage and collector cars (the biggest in America) which has become a real trademark here and celebrates its 14th anniversary in June 2004. A **Friday Nite Cruise** features cars built from 1973–85, plus live music and prizes. The second Thursday of each month is also **Motorcycle Mania** evening from 6pm. Parking is free and Old Town is open 10am–11pm daily (rides open from 5pm Mon–Fri, from noon Sat–Sun).

Damon's Clubhouse restaurant is the stand-out dining choice, with great ribs, burgers and salads (and the chance to play various Trivia games and watch every kind of sport on their big screens) but the **Blue Max Tavern** is a fun alternative. **Del Boy's English Restaurant** offers repeats of *Only Fools And Horses*, as well as typical fare like shepherd's pie, a Sunday roast, and a fried breakfast with proper black pudding. Classic American diner fare is also provided by **A&W**, while Old Town as a whole really comes alive in the evening.

Discount outlets

Belz Factory Outlet World is easily the biggest in this category of shops, the 'factory' or discount outlet, and is a big draw for British shoppers on I-Drive. It is a combination of mall and outlet centre spread over a huge area at the top of I-Drive at its junction with West Oak Ridge Road. It consists of more than 170 shops arranged in two indoor malls (both with lively food courts and one with a vintage carousel to amuse the kids), plus four separate annexes that all require a separate journey by car (unless you want to wear out a lot of shoe leather). Avoid Belz at weekends as the locals come here in force then. The aim is to sell name brands at factory-direct prices and, while you may have to wade through a fair amount of worthless stuff, you will

The Mercado

11

find shoes, clothes, books, jewellery, electronics, sporting goods, crockery and more at bargain rates. Check out the Nike superstore (Annex 1), Calvin Klein outlet (Annex 2), Reebok footwear (Annex 4), the Van Heusen factory store (Malls 1 & 2), OshKosh B'Gosh kidswear, the Levis/Docker store, adidas and Guess Jeans (all Mall 2). Belz Factory Outlet World is open 10am–9pm Mon–Sat and 10am–6pm Sun.

> BRIT TIP: For the best value genuine Disney merchandise, try the Character Warehouse in Belz Mall 2 and Character Premiere in Mall 1.

Quality Outlet Center further down I-Drive offers much of the same, although not in the same quantity, but Disney Gifts for heavily discounted Disney items is worth a look (9.30am–9pm Mon–Sat, 11am–6pm Sun).

For a classier version, the **Belz Designer Outlet Center**, just south of Belz on I-Drive has a more upmarket range of 45 shops, including DKNY, Bose, Fossil, Fila, Liz Claiborne Shoes and Polo Ralph Lauren (10am–9pm Mon–Sat, 11am–6pm Sun).

Kissimmee's version of the discount outlet is the **Kissimmee Manufacturers' Outlet Mall** on Old Vineland Road (just off the central drag of Highway 192, between Markers 13 and 14). With 30 shops again featuring brands like Nike, Levis and Van Heusen, plus Publishers Outlet for a wide range of discounted books, it is open 10am–9pm Mon–Sat, 11am–5pm Sun.

The newly expanded **Lake Buena Vista Factory Stores** offer another range of big-name products at discount prices, from Fossil, Sony, Reebok and Calvin Klein to a budget-priced Disney Character Corner, OshKosh B'Gosh Superstore and (the better-priced) Carter's Childrenswear, plus a lively food court and a kids' playground. A 1999 expansion added Gap and Liz Claiborne stores and, in 2002, shops for Old Navy, Perfume Outlet, SAS Shoes, Welcome Home, Rack Room Shoes and Danskin. And it all has the bonus of being one of the closest outlet centres to Disney's attractions. The new SoulFire Dinner & Theater Experience and welcome centres for both Travel City Direct and Virgin Holidays are also here. The Factory Stores can be found on SR 535 (2 miles/3km south off Exit 68 on I-4) and are open 9.30am–9.30pm Mon–Sat, 10am–6pm Sun. They also have a daily shuttle service that picks up at various hotels and timeshare units in a 10-mile (16-km) radius (call 407 238 9301 for info or visit www.lbvfs.com).

Possibly the best of the lot, though, are the **Orlando Premium Outlets**, which were an instant hit with UK shopping devotees when they opened in 2000. Offering a fresh look and style, and with a legion of big-name designers (from Burberry and Ralph Lauren to Hugo Boss, Versace and Ermenegildo Zegna) they can be found on Vineland Avenue between I-Drive and I-4 (just south of SeaWorld; Exit 68 on I-4). In all, they offer 110 stores of well-known brand names (like Timberland, adidas, Reebok, Banana Republic, Nike and Calvin Klein) over four Mediterranean-themed areas (Plaza de las Flores, Plaza del Sol, Plaza de las Fuentes and Plaza de las Luces), with easy parking and the convenience of being at the southern end of the I-Ride Trolley (Main Line). New in 2003 were Travel 2000 (luggage and travel accessories), Ecko Unltd (upscale T-shirts, jeans and sportswear), Fendi (stylish women's clothing and signature handbags), Little Me (baby/toddler clothes), Rack Room Shoes (a mini-warehouse of footwear fashion) and KB Toys (a huge discount choice for kids of all ages). Watch out also for big Disney bargains at the Character Premiere store and Universal items at Universal Studios Outlet Store. Even the food court is above average, with a choice of six eateries (including Japanese, Chinese, Subway and Villa Pizza), plus a Starbucks, the mouth-watering Rocky Mountain Chocolate Factory and the A&W Diner. Opening hours are 10am–10pm (Mon–Sat) and 10am–9pm (Sun). Call 407 238 7787 or see www.premiumoutlets.com. Highly recommended (especially if you can get hold of their Discount Voucher booklet). For those without a car, there is a daily shuttle bus service at $6/person round trip from hotels in the Lake Buena Vista area and $9/person from Highway 192/Kissimmee. Call 407 390 0000 for schedule and reservations. The Lynx bus service also calls here (407 841 2279) or you can try Star Taxi (407 857 9999).

Flea markets

Flea World is America's largest covered market, with 1,700 stalls spread out over 104 acres (42ha), including three massive, themed buildings, plus a 7-acre (2.8ha) amusement park, Fun World, to keep the kids amused (rides cost about $2 each). It is open Fri, Sat and Sun only, 9am–6pm, and can be found a 20 to 30-minute drive away on Highway 17/92 (best picked up from Exit 90 on I-4) between Orlando and Sanford (to the north). The stalls include all manner of market goods (nearly all new or slight seconds), from fresh produce to antiques and jewellery (leather lingerie, anyone?) and a whole range of arts and crafts (try Rag Shoppe USA for some real bargains in materials and lace), while there is a full-scale food court and a 300-seat pizza and burger eatery, the **Carousel Restaurant**, plus free entertainment on the Fun World Pavilion stage. Call 407 330 1792 for more details.

On a slightly smaller scale is the **Osceola Flea and Farmers' Market** at the eastern end of the tourist area of Highway 192 in Kissimmee (Fri–Sun, 8am–5pm), offering food, clothing, household and kitchen supplies, electronics, sporting goods, collectables and handicrafts (call 407 846 2811 for more details). Similarly, the **192 Flea Market**, on the central Vine Street stretch of Highway 192, has some 400 booths, plus a food court, in four bright-blue buildings under big oak trees, selling everything from Nintendo games to Florida souvenirs (open 7 days a week, call 407 396 4555).

> BRIT TIP: Need a good book? Make a beeline for Barnes & Noble on West Sand Lake Road by the Florida Mall or opposite Colonial Plaza (on Route 50) for a magnificent array of titles (especially travel) and a great coffee shop.

11

Malls

The area's big indoor malls tend to run a touch more expensive than the outlets already mentioned, but they do have a huge range of pretty stylish shops and their periodic sales usually make things great value. The outstanding **Florida Mall** features 264 shops, with seven large department stores and an excellent food court offering a choice of

BRIT TIP: For great deals on CDs, DVDs and video games, head to Best Buys on the Orange Blossom Trail in front of the Florida Mall.

17 outlets, plus the lively bar-restaurant **Ruby Tuesday** and the excellent **California Café Bar & Grill**. It is located on the South Orange Blossom Trail, on the corner of Sand Lake Road, and is open 10am–9.30pm Mon–Sat, 11am–6pm Sun. Highlights of this spacious and extremely smart mall are the range of six department stores, led by the upmarket (but expensive) Saks Fifth Avenue and Burdine's (Florida's oldest – and biggest – department store), plus JC Penney, Sears and Dillard's. New in October 2002 were Nordstrom, another upscale department store, and Lord & Taylor, renowned in the US for high-quality clothing (men's, women's and children's). You can also benefit here from a discount coupon packet (from Guest Services) and the regular sales at many stores, which can make the Florida Mall as competitive price-wise as the discount outlets. Additional services include free wheelchair use, pushchair rental and video arcade (for the kids) in the food court. There are even spa and beauty treatments available in the Lancôme Institut de Beaute in Dillard's, the

Saks Fifth Avenue at Florida Mall

JC Penney styling salon and day spa, and the Elizabeth Arden salon at Saks Fifth Avenue. It is also worth knowing you can visit the smart Adam's Mark hotel here for their **Le Jardin** restaurant and bar. For more info, visit www.shopsimon.com.

The huge 2-storey **Altamonte Mall**, on Altamonte Avenue in the suburb of Altamonte Springs (take Exit 92 on I-4 and head east for half a mile on Route 436 and it is on the left), is also above average and slightly off the beaten tourist track. It is one of the largest in Florida, featuring 175 speciality shops, four major department stores – Burdines, Dillard's, JC Penney and Sears – 15 outlets in the food court, plus four more restaurants, including Ruby Tuesday and the **Orlando Ale House**, and an elegant design with marble floors that makes shopping a pleasure. A major refurbishment was completed in 2003, adding an 18-screen cinema, a remodelled food court and children's soft-play area. You can also get away from the usual tourist frenzy here to do some serious shopping from 10am–9pm Mon–Sat and from 11am–6pm Sun (weekdays are best, though), and they offer a VIP savings book for foreign visitors (go to the Customer Service Center). Visit www.altamontemall.com for more details.

One of the most extensive mall developments is **Seminole Towne Center** just off I-4 to the north of Orlando on the outskirts of Sanford. This vast complex (opened in 1997) offers another 2-storey wonderland of 100 designer shops and boutiques and five department stores (like Burdines and JC Penney) as well as craft stalls, a wide-ranging food court and six full-service restaurants (including Orlando Ale House, **Olive Garden** and **Red Lobster**). Turn right off Exit 101C on I-4 and you are there, and it makes a handy place to while away your last few hours if you have an afternoon flight from the nearby Orlando Sanford Airport. The Towne Center is open 10am–9pm Mon–Sat, and noon–6pm Sun.

The spacious **Osceola Square Mall** (where Highway 192 mysteriously becomes Vine Street along its central stretch) is the only enclosed mall in Kissimmee, with 54 shops and a 12-screen cinema complex (open 10am–9pm Mon–Sat, noon–6pm Sun), including the local outlet of the retail store Ross, which deals in end-of-line items from big-names like Calvin Klein, Gap and Tommy Hilfiger. If you are prepared for a good rummage through their packed racks, you can collect some real bargains. 'Ross should be on every Brit's shopping list,' advises reader Mrs B Mair of Stockport.

Orlando Fashion Square Mall, just out of the city centre, has undergone a major redevelopment and now offers a 165-shop spread, four restaurants, a 14-counter food court and an eight-screen cinema complex. Four department stores – JC Penney, Dillard's, Sears and Burdines – anchor a typically broad range of outlets, including Gap, Everything But Water, Bath & Body Works, Zales and The Disney Store. Open from 10am–9pm Mon–Sat and noon–6pm Sun, Orlando Fashion Square Mall is on East Colonial Drive (Route 50), take Exit 83B off I-4 and head east 3 miles (5km) to Maguire Boulevard.

The big mall news, though, was the opening in October 2002 of the **Mall at Millenia**, just off I-4 to the north of Universal Orlando (Exit 78). It features the most upmarket, dramatic and technologically advanced shopping complex in Florida, with New York's most famous department stores, Bloomingdale's, Neiman Marcus and Macy's, leading the way among a select number of other top-name boutiques such as Tiffany and Louis Vuitton. You need only walk in the main entrance to realise that this is a modern marvel of the retail world and worth investigating whether you enjoy shopping or not (in fact, it may well convert you if you are not normally a mall fan). The principal entrance (of six) features a 60-ft (18-metre) glass rotunda with a flowing water garden theme and a helpful concierge desk (valet parking is also available). Then you can head out in one of four directions over the marble and terrazzo floors or go upstairs to the refreshing high-quality 12-outlet food court, the Orangerie Cafés, where the only difficulty is deciding which of the tempting (and decidedly health-conscious) eateries to choose. Look out in particular for **Bistro Sensations** (wonderful salads, pastas, pittas and wraps), the authentic Mandarin-style cuisine of **Chinatown**, the fresh taste of **Nori Sushi** (beef and chicken teriyaki and excellent sushi, all prepared on the spot) and the **Southwest Grill** (succulent chicken, barbecue beef and salads), not to mention the **Tango Grill**, an Argentinean-style café (steaks, chicken and signature crepes) where they deliver the food to your table.

The grand architecture is also focused on five separate courts along a flattened, serpentine 'S' shape, which is topped with a flowing, arched glass roof like some gigantic conservatory. On two airy levels (three in Macy's and Bloomingdale's)

11

The Mall at Millenia

and with eight 'Juliet' balconies connecting the two sides, the mall consists of a colossal amount of glass, plus a stunning central Grand Court, featuring a dozen 20-ft (6-metre) columns capped by curved plasma screens showing various images to support the theme of Man, Time and the Environment.

And, while around 20% of the 150 outlets are upscale and exclusive (Cartier, Chanel, Lacoste, Jimmy Choo, Bang & Olufsen, etc, plus the ultimate luxury of Neiman Marcus, for brands like Gucci and Prada), the other 80% offer more mainstream outlets like Gap, Banana Republic and Victoria's Secret. Several outlets offer a truly distinctive shopping experience – Metropolitan Museum of Art, Blunauta and Rocks Fine Jewelery – without necessarily the price tag to go with it.

Other stores that should appeal to Brits are Burberry, Crabtree & Evelyn, L'Occitane, Guess and Lladro. For those in need of a little on-the-spot pampering, check out the Aveda Salon Cieda, Blooming Beauty and Signature Salon hairdressers. There is even a mall gift-wrap service.

The four main restaurants are also an attraction in themselves as they are the heavenly **Cheesecake Factory**, gourmet seafood offering **McCormick & Schmick, PF Chang's China Bistro** and **Brio Tuscan Grille** (see also Dining Out, Chapter 10). On top of that little lot (AND the Orangerie Cafes), you also have the excellent fresh bread and sandwich style of **Panera Bread**, the **California Pizza Kitchen** and a **Johnny Rockets** 1950s-style diner. All in all, it takes the shopping experience to a new level in Florida (check out www.mallatmillenia.com for more details) and is open from 10am–9.30pm Mon–Sat, 11am–7pm Sun.

Traditional shopping

The attractions and possibilities of Winter Park's **Park Avenue** have already been detailed in Chapter 8 (see page 209), but the area also has the new **Winter Park Village**, a small, upscale, open-plan development of boutique shops, larger speciality stores like Borders Books, and some fine restaurants. The Village replaced the old Winter Park Mall and is on North Orlando Avenue (Exit 87 on I-4, head east on Fairbanks Avenue and then north on Highway 17/92, North Orange Avenue, for 2 miles (3km), and it is on the right; their website can be found at www.shopwinterparkvillage.com). It has proved immensely popular with the locals and offers a nice change from the usual malls and plazas – as well as some excellent dining. Check out **PF Chang's China Bistro** (their spicy Szechuan chicken is delicious), **Brio Tuscan Grille** (fine Italian fare) and the amazing (not to mention cavernous) **Cheesecake Factory**.

> BRIT TIP: You can take advantage of the FREE internet services – ideal to check your email – at all main public libraries (www.ocls.lib.fl.us/).

More traditional shopping can also be found in the revamped **Historic District of Kissimmee** on Broadway, two blocks south of Highway 192 on Route 17/92, along Main Street and Broadway. These are a number of restored turn-of-the-century buildings featuring craft and gift shops, a children's boutique, country store and seven restaurants (including **Azteca's** for fine Mexican fare), plus antiques, western and sports wear. Every Thursday, the Downtown Farmers' Market displays its wares here, too. The Historic District shops are open 10am–5pm (10am–3pm on Sat). Look up www.kissimmee.org for more.

Another recent development (and off the beaten tourist path) is the shops and restaurants of Disney's town of **Celebration**, a unique collection of speciality stores, an ice cream and candy shop, restaurants, cinemas, lakeside dining and a Saturday Farmers' Market, plus boat and bike rentals and the superb Celebration Hotel. Follow the signs to downtown Celebration along Celebration Avenue, just off Highway 192, a quarter of a mile east of its junction with I-4. The shops are open 10am–9pm Mon–Sat, noon–6pm Sun. This is a re-creation of the 'ideal' 1950s-style town, complete with white picket fences, while there are some lovely walks around the main lake. The dining opportunities – notably the stylish Spanish-Cuban ambiance of the **Columbia Restaurant**, the Italian offering of **Café D'Antonio** and the New England seafood accent of the **Celebration Town Tavern** all on Market Street – are quite superb.

Supermarkets

Apart from the big chemist chain stores, **Eckerd** and **Walgreens**, there are a few more typical large-group stores. The main supermarkets you will find are **Publix** and **Goodings**, which are comparable with Asda, Safeway or (in the case of Goodings) Marks and Spencer. **Albertson's** supermarket on Dr Phillips Boulevard, is another well-priced choice.

For clothes, DIY, home furnishings, souvenirs, toys, electrical goods and other household items as well as groceries, the big discount stores are **Kmart, Wal-Mart** (owners of Asda – see page 39 – and open 24 hours for serious

shopaholics!) or **Target** (like a big version of Tesco's, but without the food). If there is anything you've forgotten, the chances are you can get it at one of the seven **Wal-Mart Supercenters** (notably on Highway 192 next to Medieval Times, another at the junction of Sand Lake Road and John Young Parkway, on Kirkman Road north of Universal, and a new one towards the east end of Osceola Parkway in the Buenaventura Lakes area).

For photographic supplies and film processing, try one of the many branches of **Eckerd Express Photo** (although they are dearer in the main tourist areas).

Specialist shops

Finally, a few shops worth making a note of for specific items are the various outlets of **World of Denim** (no explanation necessary), **The Sports Authority** and **Sports Dominator**, the former on Sand Lake Road and the latter north of Sand Lake Road, on I-Drive, which both offer all manner of sporting goods and apparel, while serious sportsmen and women will also want to visit the magnificent range of the five **Edwin Watts Golf** shops, including their national clearance centre on I-Drive, or any of the five **Special Tee Golf & Tennis** shops. On golf clubs in particular you can pick up some great deals and save a lot on the same equipment back home. By the same token, keen anglers can stock up on the latest fishing gear at bargain prices at **Bass Pro Shops Outdoor World** (Festival Bay). Last but by no means least, **Greg's Western Wear** (on Highway 192 opposite Medieval Times) offers the chance to get yourself fully kitted out in the latest cowboy gear. However, with the shopping all done, it is now time to think about the journey home…

11

Going Home

(or, Where Did The Last Two Weeks Go?)

And so, dog-tired, financially crippled but (hopefully) blissfully happy and with enough memories to last a lifetime, it is time to deal with that bane of all holidays – the journey home.

If you have come through the last week or two relatively unscathed in terms of the calamities that can befall the uninformed or the plain unlucky, here's how to avoid any last-minute pitfalls.

The car

The hire car has to be returned and that can take a little time if you had to use an off-airport car depot. It is wise to allow half an hour, just in case. The process tends to be slicker with the firms who operate directly from the airports.

Now you probably have some time to kill, so here is a detailed guide to the two main airports.

Orlando International Airport

Orlando International is 46 miles (74km) from Cocoa Beach and 54 (87) from Daytona Beach on the east coast, 84 miles (135km) from Tampa and 110 (177km) from Clearwater and St Petersburg to the west, 25 (40km) from *Walt Disney World* and 10 (16km) from Universal Studios; so always allow plenty of time for the journey, and for check-in – 2 hours for a US domestic flight, 3 for an international one.

This modern airport is the twenty-fourth largest in the world, one of the fastest-growing and one of the most widely acclaimed for its overall passenger satisfaction values (regularly No 1 in America). It topped 30 million passengers in 2000 for the first time (some 80,000 a day on average), putting it level with Gatwick and Hong Kong, and with half the traffic of Heathrow (which has four terminals to Orlando's one). It can, therefore, get busy at peak times, but its 854-acre (345-ha) terminal complex usually handles the crowds with ease, and this is one of the most comfortable airports you will find. It boasts a great range of facilities, and its wide, airy concourses feel more like an elegant hotel (not surprising when one end of the terminal is taken up by the airport-run Hyatt Regency Hotel).

Ramps, restrooms, wide lifts and large open areas ensure easy access for wheelchairs, and there are special features like TDD and amplified telephones, wheelchair-height drinking fountains, Braille lift controls and companion-care restrooms to assist travellers with disabilities.

You will also find plenty to do here and, should you have more than a couple of hours to spare, it is worth leaving your hand luggage at the Baggage Checkroom and taking the 15-minute taxi ride to the Florida Mall, or checking in early, keeping the car and going to somewhere like Gatorland (about 20 minutes' drive away).

In keeping with the Orlando area,

ORLANDO INTERNATIONAL AIRPORT

20m

ORLANDO SANFORD AIRPORT

21m

12

the International Airport is always engaged in staying a step ahead, and a major renovation completed in 2003 added a host of new elements, including a major food court (with a feature McDonald's outlet) and more shops. A fourth (and ultra-smart) satellite arm to the main terminal was opened in 2000, and a multi-billion dollar project to add a second terminal, a fourth runway and a new taxiway is under way (although the second terminal is currently on hold).

Landside

As with all international airports, you have a division between **LANDSIDE** (for all visitors to the airport) and **AIRSIDE** (beyond which you need to have a ticket). Orlando's Landside is divided into three levels: **One** is the enhanced area for ground transportation, tour operator desks, parking, buses and the car rental agencies; **Two** is for Baggage Claim (which you negotiated on the way in) and for any private vehicles meeting passengers; **Three** is where you should enter the airport on your return journey as it holds all the check-in desks, plus shops, restaurants, lockers, bank and information desks. Level Three is effectively sub-divided into four sections: **Landside 'A'** is the check-in section for **Gates 1–29** and **100–129**. Here you will find American Airlines, ATA (American TransAir), Continental, Southwest, JetBlue and AirTran. Landside 'B' has check-in desks for **Gates 30–99** and other main airlines, including Northwest, United, USAirways, BA, Delta and Virgin.

Once you have checked in, you can choose to explore the **East** and **West** sections of the main concourse, which occupies the centre of Level Three. The West end houses the **Great Hall**, with some more

shopping and eating areas, plus a currency exchange and ATM machine (cash dispenser). Inevitably, Disney & Co makes one last attempt to part you from what's left of your money, so you will find some more impressive gift shops for *Walt Disney World* (The Magic of Disney), SeaWorld and Universal (with no airport mark-up). Other outlets include Sunglass International, Orlando Harley Davidson, the eclectic pet shop Bow Wow Meow, jewellers Erwin Pearl, the clothing and gifts of Spirit of the Red Horse, Keys Gift Shop and Global Cellular & Electronics. Then there are two newsagents and a secondary food court, including Burger King, TCBY Yogurt, Mrs Field's Cookies, Pizza Hut and Nathan's Famous Hot Dogs, plus Stinger Ray's table service restaurant, Big Apple Bagels and Seattle's Best Coffee. Up the escalators in the centre of the hall is Chili's, a Tex-Mex diner and bar.

Travelling (along moving walkways) between the two ends of the terminal, you pass through the newest and smartest area of the airport, with more shops on the **North Walk** and **South Walk** (Borders Books, The Body Shop, Swatch, The Discovery Channel Store, Perfumania, Gem Collection, GNC Nutrition, Flag World, music store Altitunes and the Power Play Arcade). The grand new (October 2003) **Food Court** here is one of the most upscale you will find, with plenty of seating and different cuisines, including that eye-catching McDonald's, plus Sbarro pizza, Zyng's noodlery, Chick-Fil-A, Krispy Kreme Donuts and Carvel ice cream. In spring 2004 there will be Fox Sports Bar and the Macaroni Grill. Then there is a SunTrust Bank, a new massage spa and hair salon (called D-parture), a post office and ATM machine.

The **East** end of Level Three is quieter and more picturesque as it is dominated by the 8-storey Hyatt Hotel atrium, featuring palm trees and a large fountain. There are fewer shops but they include: Universal Orlando, Anheuser-Busch, Disney's The Earport (!) and the new Kennedy Space Center shop.

There's a Hudson's newsagent, a **Starbuck's** and a WH Smith's, more ATM machines, a currency exchange and two business centres. Both West and East halls also have an airport Information kiosk. Up the escalator (or lift) is the entrance to the **Hyatt Regency Airport Hotel** if you fancy seeing out your visit in style (see page 79). **McCoy's Bar and Grill** (up and turn right) is a smart bar-restaurant with a grandstand view of the airport runways (good for kids). The surroundings are stylish and a long way from the average airport lounge, and all flight timings are shown on TV monitors.

To go really upmarket, take the hotel lift to the ninth-floor **Hemisphere Restaurant**. Not only do you have an even more impressive view of the runways, its superb continental cuisine and monthly wine tasting evenings offer some of the best fare in the city. It's pricey, but the service and food are 5-star (from 5–10.30pm daily).

Airside

Once it is time to move on to your departure gate, you have to be aware of the four satellite arms that make up the airport's **AIRSIDE**. Also note that they have installed Advanced Technology Checkpoint screening here, and you can encounter some long queues.

These are divided into **Gates 1–29** and **30–59** at the West end of the terminal, and **60–99** and **100–129** (American domestic flights only) at the **East** end. ALL the departure gates are here, plus duty-free shops, more restaurants and lockers.

The airport's four satellites are

each connected to the main building by a shuttle service, so you need to be alert when it comes to finding your departure gate. There are no tannoy announcements for flights, so it's wise to check your departure gate and time when you check in. However, there are large monitors in the terminal that display all the departure information. As a rule, British Airways, Virgin and Delta use Gates 60–99. Northwest, United and USAirways usually use Gates 30–59, while ATA, American and Continental depart from Gates 1–29. Airlines using the new Gates 100–129 include low-cost carriers Southwest, JetBlue and AirTran.

In most airports, once you have moved Airside it is not possible to return to the Landside area again. However, that is not the case here, and, if you find the crowds milling around your departure gate too much to bear, you can always return to one of the terminal hostelries, for a bit of peace and quiet **(but bear in mind you will need to go through the security checkpoints again)**.

However, you should find the Airside areas just as clean and efficient as the main terminal, with the bonus of three duty-free shops.

As you pass through the ticket and baggage check at the West end of the terminal, you will find the **Alpha Retail Duty Free** on your right. This is the biggest of their four shops and is open only to departing international passengers, so you will need your boarding card. Your purchases will be delivered to the departure gate for you to collect as you board because it caters for international and domestic flights, and duty-free shopping does not apply to internal flights.

At **Gates 1–29**, you will find another duty-free shop, plus a newsagents (the Keys Group News and Gifts), two **Café Azalea** lounge bars, a kids' play area and a mini food court, featuring **Burger King,**

12

ORLANDO INTERNATIONAL

- **LIFTS**
- **RETAIL**
- **FOOD SERVICE**
- **CHECK-IN DESKS**
- **DUTY FREE**
- **ESCALATORS**
- **MOVING WALKWAY**
- **TOILETS**
- (i) **INFORMATION KIOSK**

Check-In Area for 1-29 Check-In Area for 100-129

Gates 1-29 Gates 100-129

Great Hall   Food Court   Hotel

Gates 30-59 Gates 60-99

Check-In Area for 30-59 Check-In Area for 60-99

Cafes & Restrooms are available in all areas

Gates 1-29   Gates 30-59   Gates 60-99   Gates 100-129

ORLANDO SANFORD INTERNATIONAL AIRPORT

To Gates

- **LIFTS**
- **RETAIL**
- **FOOD SERVICE**
- **OBSERVATION DECK**
- **DUTY FREE**
- **ESCALATORS**
- **TELEPHONE**
- **MAIL BOX**
- **TOILETS**
- **INFO & CURRENCY EXCHANGE**

Chadwick's Pub

Travel Pursuits

DEPARTURE LOUNGE

Main Entrance from check-in

Food Court

Altitude's Arcade

The Guest House

Cinnabon and **TCBY** (which stands for The Country's Best Yogurt). **Gates 30–59** also have their own duty-free shop, plus a **Café Azalea** lounge bar, **Pepito's Cuban Café**, the Floribbean Court (with **Miami Subs, Villa Pizza** and **Freshens**

Yogurt) and Hudson News.

Travelling from **Gates 60–99** (the main satellite terminal for return flights to the UK) gives you another duty-free shop, a currency exchange, Stellar Partners newsagents, the speciality Mindworks, The Grove gifts and WH Smith Books. A food court contains **Burger King**, **Nathan's Famous Hot Dogs**, the table service **Shipyard Brewport** and a lounge bar. A sea-themed play area is a bonus for parents with young children.

Gates 100–129 offer two **Johnny Rivers Smokehouse Express** outlets, a food court with **The Coco Oasis Bar & Lounge, McDonald's** and **Sbarro Pizza**, plus four more shops, including Bijoux Terner Fashion Jewelry and Sunglass International.

For more details on Orlando International Airport, visit www.fcn.state. fl.us/goaa, which features 'live' departure and arrival information.

Orlando Sanford Airport

Returning to what is now the main Orlando gateway for British charter flights should be a relatively simple experience, providing you retrace your route on the Central Florida Greeneway and come off at Exit 49. Go across one set of lights, turn right at the second set on to Lake Mary Boulevard and follow it all the way back to the airport, following the signs. The efficiency of the Alamo and Dollar car-rental return adds to this simplicity.

Orlando Sanford was created as a full international airport in 1996, as an initiative between the airport authorities and several of the main British tour operators. And so MyTravel (Airtours), Britannia (Thomson), Monarch, Thomas Cook Airlines and Air 2000 (First Choice) all now go for this cheaper and simpler option. With its small, uncomplicated design (straight off the plane into Immigration, one baggage carousel and then a walk across the road into the Dollar or Alamo offices) it can get you mobile much quicker. Of course, you are further north, so your journey time

is 35–40 minutes longer and you have to pay an extra $2–3 in tolls compared with the journey to and from Orlando International but, providing you follow the simple directions to the main tourist areas, you can save up to an hour overall.

And, while this charter gateway lacks many of the extra amenities of Orlando International, it boasts an extremely spacious check-in area and works hard to make the departure as painless as the arrival process, especially with their new Guest House facility.

A new terminal opened in March 2001, relieving earlier congestion. And its facilities are perfectly adequate for a comfortable stay, with **Chadwick's Pub** serving a decent range of food as well as British beers, a completely revamped (in 2003) food court, **Altitudes Arcade** (neatly located in one corner), a well-stocked duty-free shop, a **Ron Jon** gift store, **Reel Stuff** film memorabilia shop and a new entertainment shop, **Travel Pursuits**, which features travel games, electronic toys, soft toys, Lego and Knex sets, mood jewellery and novelty sweets. The excellent new **Food Court** offers American Grill (burgers and fries), Daily Specials (shepherd's pie, chicken pot pie, lasagna and more), Sweet Endings (baked goods and pastries) and Grab-N-Go (soft drinks, snacks and bottled water). There is also a large outdoor smoking deck (smoking is severely restricted inside).

The big extra here, though, is that of the **Guest House**, a premium lounge available to all passengers for a modest additional fee. The Guest House is located in a separate annexe from the main departure lounge, and is an oasis of comfort and quiet, more reminiscent of an upscale hotel. There is a lovely conservatory-style café, where you can take advantage of the unlimited tea, coffee, soft drinks and snacks (plus two alcoholic drinks per

12

person), or opt for something from their exclusive lunch menu. It also provides a home theatre set-up, with widescreen TV and surround-sound, for recently released films, and a reading lounge with newspapers and magazines. You can check your email or surf the net while the kids enjoy the youth entertainment centre, with eight Sony Playstation 2 consoles. And, for the young 'uns, there is a separate playroom with soft toys and games.

The Guest House is billed as an airport lounge with the comforts of home and, to my mind, it is well worth the $20 extra ($10 for children) to while away your last few hours here. You can have a preview of the Guest House on www.orlandosanfordairport.com.

Whether you are travelling from Orlando International or Orlando Sanford, you can expect your return flight to be about an hour shorter than the journey out thanks to the Atlantic jetstreams that provide tail-winds to high-level flights.

Nevertheless, you will land back at Heathrow, Manchester, Glasgow, etc, rather more jet-lagged than on the trip out. This is because the time difference is more noticeable on eastward flights, and it may take a good day or two to get your body clock back on to local time. It is even more important not to indulge in alcohol on the flight if you are driving when you get home.

And, much as it may seem like a good idea, the best way to beat Florida jet-lag is NOT to go straight out to the travel agency and book another holiday to Orlando!

But, believe me, the lure of this theme park wonderland is almost impossible to resist once sampled – you WILL return!

Your chance to give something back

After hopefully having the holiday of a lifetime, you might like to know about two charities helping children with serious and terminal illnesses to have a memorable time in Orlando, too. **Give Kids The World** is a unique, amazing organisation in Kissimmee which provides a week's fantasy holiday for terminally ill children who wish to visit the central Florida attractions. GKTW works with other wish-granting foundations worldwide and basically provides all the local facilities for children – and their families – to have a great holiday. It is set up as a village resort and includes all meals, accommodation, transport, attractions, tickets, use of video camera and many other thoughtful touches in a magical setting. It is a truly wonderful charity, one I am happy to support myself, and I hope you will help, too. You can make a donation through the charity's website – www.gktw.org – or send it to: Give Kids The World, 210 South Bass Road, Kissimmee, Florida 34746, USA. Equally, **Dreamflight** is a fabulous registered UK charity which takes seriously ill children (between 8 and 14) to Florida annually, usually with the assistance of British Airways. It costs around £1,400 per child and, while many people generously donate their time to help out, cash donations are essential to keep the operation going. You can contribute to their fund-raising efforts by writing to: Dreamflight, 3 Saxeway, Chartridge, Bucks, HP5 2SH (tel: 01494 792991) or by email to 72016.2631@compuserve.com. Thank you for your contributions to these two swholly worthwhile organisations.

Your Holiday Planner

Example: with 5-day Park Hopper Plus Ticket

DAY	ATTRACTION	NOTES
SUN	DAY	
	EVE	
MON	DAY	
	EVE	
TUE	DAY	
	EVE	
WED	DAY	
	EVE	
THUR	DAY Arrive 2.40pm local time Orlando Sanford Airport	*NB: 55 mins to drive to hotel*
	EVE Check out local shops and restaurants	
FRI	DAY Welcome meeting/UNIVERSAL STUDIOS	
	EVE	
SAT	DAY DISNEY'S ANIMAL KINGDOM THEME PARK	*(8am start)*
	EVE Medieval Times Dinner Show	
SUN	DAY DISNEY–MGM STUDIOS	
	EVE	
MON	DAY SEAWORLD	
	EVE	
TUE	DAY BUSCH GARDENS	
	EVE	
WED	DAY KENNEDY SPACE CENTER	
	EVE Skull Kingdom/WonderWorks/Pointe*Orlando	

Disney's 5-Day Park Hopper Plus Ticket gives 5 days at the main theme parks, plus TWO of Blizzard Beach, Typhoon Lagoon, Pleasure Island and Disney's Wide World of Sports™; there may be a separate charge for big events at Wide World of Sports.

DAY	ATTRACTION		NOTES
THUR	DAY	Blizzard Beach/EPCOT	*(Arrive late)*
	EVE		
FRI	DAY	ISLANDS OF ADVENTURE	
	EVE	Universal Orlando's CityWalk	*(until late!)*
SAT	DAY	Winter Park Lakes/shopping/museums	
	EVE		
SUN	DAY	EPCOT	*(early start – 9am)*
	EVE		
MON	DAY	Fantasy of Flight and Splendid China	
	EVE	Pleasure Island	
TUE	DAY	Aquatic Wonders Tours/Warbird Air Museum	
	EVE	Arabian Nights	
WED	DAY	THE MAGIC KINGDOM PARK	
	EVE		
THUR	DAY	Gatorland/Back to airport	
	EVE		*Flight 6pm; return car at 3pm*
FRI	DAY	Return Gatwick 7am	
	EVE		
SAT	DAY		
	EVE		
SUN	DAY		
	EVE		

Busy Day Guide

Day	Busiest	Average	Lightest
Mon	Disney's Animal Kingdom Magic Kingdom	Epcot	Disney-MGM Studios Universal Studios Islands of Adventure Busch Gardens Kennedy Space Center SeaWorld Water Parks
Tues	Epcot Disney-MGM Studios Universal Studios	Islands of Adventure Magic Kingdom	Disney's Animal Kingdom Busch Gardens Kennedy Space Center SeaWorld Water Parks
Wed	Epcot Islands of Adventure	Disney's Animal Kingdom SeaWorld Water Parks	Magic Kingdom Disney-MGM Studios Busch Gardens Kennedy Space Center Universal Studios
Thurs	Magic Kingdom Universal Studios	Busch Gardens Disney-MGM Studios SeaWorld Water Parks	Epcot Disney's Animal Kingdom Islands of Adventure Kennedy Space Center
Fri	Disney's Animal Kingdom Epcot SeaWorld Water Parks	Disney-MGM-Studios Islands of Adventure Busch Gardens Kennedy Space Center	Magic Kingdom Universal Studios
Sat	Disney-MGM Studios Busch Gardens Islands of Adventure Kennedy Space Center SeaWorld Universal Studios Water Parks	Epcot Magic Kingdom	Disney's Animal Kingdom
Sun	Magic Kingdom Islands of Adventure Kennedy Space Center SeaWorld Water Parks	Disney's Animal Kingdom Busch Gardens Universal Studios	Disney-MGM Studios Epcot

13

Index

Page numbers in *italics* refer to maps or tables. Those in **bold** refer to major references.
(A) = Animal attraction, (D) = Dinner show, (R) = Restaurant, (T) = Tour company, (W) = Water park

accommodation 15, 16, 19–20, **56–84**
  bed and breakfast 82
  budget 58, 66–67, 75
  camping 60
  family 78–80
  Highway 192; *20*, **66**, *73*
  holiday homes 21, 23, 24, 25, 26, **80–82**, **83–84**
  hotels 19–20, **56–78**
  independent organisations 67, 68, 70
  International Drive *20*, **70–72**, *76*
  Kissimmee *20*, **66**
  Lake Buena Vista 19–20, **65–66**, *69*
  looking for on arrival 57
  resorts 80
  suites (apartments) 78–80
  Universal Orlando 72, **74–75**
  Walt Disney World Resort 19, **57–65**, *69*
  see also internet sites
adults 35
Adventure Island (W) 179
adventure tours 214, 215–216, 218, 219–222
  see also eco-tourism
air conditioning 50, **56–57**
airboat rides 28, **211–213**, 214, 215–216, 221
aircraft museums 28, **192–193**, **217–218**
  see also flying
Airport Access Fee 50
airports *see* Orlando International Airport; Orlando/Sanford Airport
Airtours (T) 23
Alamo (Car hire) **45**, 46
Albin Polasek Museum and Sculpture Gardens 209
alcohol *see* drinking
alligators 28, 187, 188, **190–192**, *192*, 211, 214
  meat 191, 256
Altamonte Mall 284
American English 37, 38
American football 233
anniversary celebrations 40
Aquamania 17

Aquatic Wonders Boat Tours 210–211
Arabian Nights (D) 245–246
Arena Football 233
art museums 200, **208–209**
Astronaut Hall of Fame 184
Atlantis® 274
attractions 6, 7–10, *12*, **27–30**
  evening 29, 35, **236–254**
  new for 2004; 15–16
  for repeat visitors 37
  smaller 28, *181*
  see also individual named attractions
autographs 111

B-line Diner® 268–269
baby-swap 86
babysitting 83
baggage allowances 23
Bahama Breeze® 263
Bahamas 215, 219
balloon trips 214–215
bars 253–254
baseball 234
basketball 233
beaches 223–226
Beeline Expressway (Route 528) 51
beer 178, 258
bicycle tours 209
birthday celebrations 39–40
Blue Springs Manatee Festival 17
boat tours 209, **210–214**, 220, 221
  see also cruises
Boggy Creek Airboat Rides 28, **212–213**
Boggy Creek Parasail 213
botanical gardens 210
British Airways Holidays (T) 25
British Consulate 41
Busch Gardens (A) 10, 16, 28, **170–179**
  at-a-glance 170
  Bird Gardens 177–178
  Congo 176
  Crown Colony 174
  Egypt 178–179
  Gwazi 178
  Land of the Dragons 177
  location 171
  map 172
  Morocco 173–174
  Nairobi 174–175
  planning visit 171–173
  Serengeti Plain 174
  shops 179
  Stanleyville 176–177
  Timbuktu 175–176
  tours 171–173, **179**

Busch Shuttle Express 47, **171**
buses 46

cabarets *see* dinner shows
camping 60
canoeing 211, *212*
Captain Nemo's® 261
car hire 45–46, **49–50**
  returning to airports 288
  see also fly-drives
Carnival Cruise Lines 219
cars 48, 49
  controls 50
  crime and safety 43
  fuel 55
  see also driving; motor sports; roads
Celebration 287
Celebration Hotel 68, *72*
Cellurent 41
Central Florida Zoological Park (A) 220
Chalet Suzanne *184*, 186–187
Cheesecake Factory ® 263
chemists 32
children **33–34**, 83, 86
  resort services 19, 58
  theme park services 31
  travel company services 22, 23, 24, 25, 26
  see also headings beginning 'family' and individual attractions
Christmas time 100, 123, 134
churches 39
CineDome 199
cinemas 199, 237, 243, 280
  see also Disney-MGM Studios; Universal Studios
Cirque du Soleil 238–239, *240*
CityWalk 237, **241–243**, *253*
climate 14, **18–19**, 30–31
clothing 18, 30–31
  measurements 37
Cocoa Beach 216, **223**
comedy (live shows) 236, 237, 238, 251–252
Cornell Fine Arts Museum 208
Country Inn & Suites 78–79
Cracker Barrel® 260
credit cards **15**, 49
Cricketer's Arms® 261–262
crime 40–41
crocodiles *see* alligators
cruises 20, 21, 22, 23, 24, 25, 26, **219**
  Disney 218–219
  birthday cruises 40
  see also boat tours; split holidays

Cypress Gardens 28, **184–185**
Cypress Glades Adventure Tours 214

Daytona 17, 217, 223, *225*
  speedway 235
dehydration, avoiding 31
dentists 32
dinner shows 29, **244–250**
disabled travellers 34–35
  access to buses 47
  airport facilities 288
  driving cars 53
  travel company services 22
discos 237, 242
Discovery Cove (A) 10, 157, **167–169**
Disney Cruise Line *21*, 218–219
Disney Hotel Plaza 64–65
Disney-MGM Studios 9, 15, 28, **115–123**
  at-a-glance 115
  children's attractions 123
  location 117
  main attractions 118–122
  map 116
  parades 122
  planning your visit 117
  restaurants 122
  Rock'n Roller Coaster 118, **120**
  shops 122–123
  Twilight Zone Tower of Terror 118, **121**
Disney's All-Star Resorts *21*, **62**
Disney's Animal Kingdom Lodge 63
Disney's Animal Kingdom Theme Park (A) 9, 15–16, 28, **124–134**
  accommodation 62–63
  Africa 130–132
  Asia 132–133
  at-a-glance 126
  Camp Minnie-Mickey 128
  children's attractions 134
  DinoLand USA 129–130
  Discovery Island 127–128
  Expedition Everest 15–16
  Festival of the Lion King 128
  location 124–126
  map 125
  The Oasis 127
  parades 133
  planning your visit 126–127
Disney's Beach Club Resort 62
Disney's Blizzard Beach Water Park (W) 9, **204–205**
Disney's BoardWalk Resort 61, 237, **240**
Disney's Caribbean Beach Resort *56*, 61
Disney's Contemporary Resort 59

Disney's Coronado Springs Resort 62
Disney's Fort Wilderness Resort and Campground 60
Disney's Grand Floridian Resort & Spa 60
Disney's Old Key West Resort 64
Disney's Polynesian Resort 59
Disney's Pop Century Resort 15, *60*, **63**
Disney's Port Orleans Resort 63–64, *65*
Disney's Spirit of Aloha (D) 244–245
Disney's Typhoon Lagoon Water Park (W) 9, **202–204**
Disney's Wide World of Sports Complex 9, **233–234**
Disney's Wilderness Lodge Resort 59, *61*
Disney's Wilderness Preserve 223
Disney's Yacht Club Resort *33*, 62
DisneyQuest 28, **239–240**
DiVino's® 274
doctors 31–32
Dolly Parton's Dixie Stampede (D) 16, **249**
dolphins 158–159, 164–165, 166, 168–169, 216
Doubletree Castle Hotel 72
Downtown Arts District 200
Downtown Disney 9, 28, *236*, **237–240, 278–279**
  accommodation 63–64
Downtown Orlando 198–199
Dreams Unlimited Travel (T) **27**, 219
drinking 30, 35, 57, 258
  and dehydration 31
  and driving 50, 53–54
driving 45–55
  AA members 54
  accidents 49–50, **54**
  from airports 51
  parking and restrictions 53–54
  safety 43
  see also cars; motor sports; roads
duty-free allowance 276

e-mail services 279, 286
eco-tourism 222–223
electrical appliances 56
Electrical Water Pageant 60, 245
emergency services 31, **41**
Epcot 9, 27–28, **102–114**
  accommodation 61–63
  at-a-glance 103
  children's attractions 114
  festivals 114
  Future World 102, **103–109**
  guided tours 114

IllumiNations 113
  location 102
  map 104
  Mission Space 15, **105–106**
  parades 113
  planning your visit 113
  World Showcase 102, **109–113**
Everglades 215–216

factory stores 282
family
  accommodation 78–80
  packages 22, 23, 24, 25, 26
  restaurants 33–34, 255, **259–261**
Fantasy of Flight 10, **192–193**, *193*
FastPass rides 89–90
Festival Bay 16, **280**
festivals 16–17
First Choice (T) 24
fishing 17, 211, 212, 221, *229*, **230–231**
Florida *8*
  beaches 224
Florida Keys 215–216
Florida Mall 283–284, *284*
Florida Sales Tax 15, 276–277
fly-drives 21, 22, 23, 25
flying 17, 218
Flying Tigers Warbird Air Museum 217
food *see* restaurants
Forever Florida (A) 222
Fort Lauderdale 215
fuel 55
Fun 'n Sun 17
Fun Spot 195–196
Funway Holidays (T) 26

gas stations 55
Gatorland (A) 28, **190–192**, *192*
Gaylords Palms Resort 70
Give Kids the World 294
golf 77–78, **226–229**
  see also mini-golf
Grande Lakes Orlando 16, **75**, *80*
Green Meadows Petting Farm (A) 218
Greeneway (Route 417) 51, 52
Gulf Coast 225–226

Hard Rock Café® *241*, **242**, *264*
Hard Rock Hotel 57, 74
Hard Rock Live 241–242
Hard Rock Vault 194–195, *196*
Harry Ramsbottom's® 262
health care 31–32
Highway 192; 20, **55**, *73*
Historic Bok Sanctuary 185–186
history museums 199–200
holiday homes 80–82
  buying 83–84

Holiday Inn Family Suites
  Resort 79
Holiday Planner 295–297
holidays, American 18
Holy Land Experience 201–202
Hoop-Dee Doo Musical Revue
  (D) 245
Hopper passes 10–11, 13
horse riding 231–232
hospitals 31–32
hotels **56–78**
  air conditioning 56–57
  chains 67
  eating and drinking in 56
  independent 67, 68, 70
  mid-range 75
  prices 15, 57
  security 42–43
  telephone calls from 33, 42, 57
  see also accommodation
hovercraft see airboats
Hyatt Regency Hotel 78

I-Drive see International Drive
I-Ride Trolley 45, 46–47
Independence Day 17
information 17, 27, **44**, 57
insect repellents 31
insurance
  car 49–50
  health 31
  travel 32–33
International Drive 20, 44, 53,
  54–55, 193
  accommodation 20, **70–72**,
    76, 78–79
  attractions 16, 28, **193–197**
  shopping 279
  see also Pointe Orlando
internet sites 17, **44**
  holiday deals 27, 57
Interstate 4; 19–20, **54**
Islands of Adventure 10, 28,
  147–156
  at-a-glance 147
  children's attractions 156
  Halloween Horror Nights 156
  Jurassic Park 153–154
  the Lost Continent 154–155
  map 148
  Marvel Super Hero Island
    150–151
  planning visit 149–150
  Port of Entry 149–150
  Seuss Landing 155–156
  Toon Lagoon 151–152

jet-lag, avoiding 50, 294
Jetsave (T) 26
Jiko® 274–275
Jungle Jim's® 261
JW Marriott 77

Keith Prowse Agency (T) 13–14
Kennedy Space Center 10, 28,
  180–184
Kissimmee 55
  accommodation 20, **66**
  shopping 280–281, 282,
    286–287
Knights of the Realm (D) 247
Kraft Azalea Gardens 210
Kuoni (T) 26

Lake Buena Vista 41
  accommodation 19–20,
    65–66, 69, 79
  Factory Stores 282
Lake Wales 187
Leu Gardens 210
licensing laws 258
Lynx Bus System 46

Magic Kingdom Park 7–8, 27,
  87–101
  accommodation 59–60
  Adventureland 93–94
  at-a-glance 87
  character meals 100
  children's attractions 101
  Fantasyland 95–97
  Frontierland 94–95
  Liberty Square 95
  location 90–91
  Main Street USA 91–93
  map 88
  Mickey's PhilharMagic 15
  Mickey's Toontown Fair 97–98
  night-time 99–100
  parades 99–100
  parking 89, 91
  planning visit 89–91
  restaurants 89, 92, 94, 95, 97,
    99
  shopping 89, 92, 94, 95, 97, 99
  Tomorrowland 98–99
  tour 101
magic shows 248
Magical Midway 196
Makinson Island 211
Mall at Millenia 268, 285,
  285–286
maps 52, 54, **55**
marathon 234
Mead Botanical Gardens 210
measurements, American 37
medical treatment 31–32
Medieval Times (D) 246–247
Mercado Center 279, 281
Miami 215
mini-golf 205, **229–230**
Mission Space 15, **105–106**
mobile phones 41, 43
money 14–15, **42–43**
Moonfish® 274

Morse Museum of American Art
  208, 208–209
motor sport 234–235
museums
  aircraft 28, **192–193**, **217–218**
  art 200, **208–209**
  history 199–200, 221
  science 198–199
music (live) 237–243, **251–252**
Muvico cinema (IMAX) 237, 243

Naples 215–216, 226
newspapers 235
night-clubs 236–244, **250, 252**
night-time entertainment 29,
  236–254

Old Hickory Steakhouse® 275
Orange Blossom Balloons
  214–215, 216
Orange County History Center
  199–200
Orlando 7, 11, 12
  see also attractions
Orlando Fashion Square Mall
  285
Orlando FlexTickets 13, **135**
Orlando International Airport 7,
  45, **288–293**
  airside 291–293
  car hire at 45–46
  double baggage collection 45
  driving from 51
  driving to 288
  landside 290–291
Orlando Premium Outlets
  282–283
Orlando/Sanford Airport 292,
  293–294
  driving from 51
  driving to 293
Orlando Science Center
  198–199, 200
Osceola Parkway 52
Osceola Square Mall 285

pacing yourself 30
Pal Mickey 15, **90**
Palm Restaurant® 272, 274
parasailing 213
Park Avenue Walking Tour 209
Park Plaza Gardens ® 273–274
Peabody Orlando 70
Perkins Family Restaurant ® 260
phones 33, 42, 57
  mobile 41, 43
Pirates Dinner Adventure (D) 246
Planet Hollywood® 256, 257, **268**
planning your holiday 6, 14, 18,
  27–30, 295–297
  time of year 14, 18–19
Plant City Strawberry Festival 17

Pointe Orlando 237, **243–244**
  shopping 279–280
police 40–41
Ponderosa Steakhouse® 259–260
Port Canaveral 218–219
Portofino Bay Hotel 72, 74, 77
pregnant women 34
public transport 46–47
pubs, British 261–262
pushchairs 34

Quality Inn International 72
queuing 29, 94, 117, 135
  see also FastPass rides;
    Universal Express
Quick Transportation 47–48

Race Rock® 269
radio stations 51, **254**
Rainforest Café® 269
Renaissance Orlando Resort 71,
  261, 274
resorts 80
  see also individual resorts
restaurants 255–275
  '24/7' 257–258
  American diners 262–263
  British 261–262
  Chinese 269–270
  CityWalk 241–242
  Continental 272–273
  Cracker 256
  Cuban 271–272
  'deals' available 255–256
  dinner shows 29, **244–250**
  doggy bags 256
  Downtown Disney 238, 239, 240
  drinking in 258
  family 33–34, 255, **259–261**
  fast food 258–259
  German 272–273
  gourmet 273–275
  Indian 271
  Italian 272
  Japanese 270–271
  lack of in hotels 56
  Mall at Millenia 268
  ordering in 256–257
  Pointe Orlando 243
  ribs 263–264
  romantic 36
  seafood 256, **266–268**
  steakhouses 265–266
  Tex-Mex 264–265
  Thai 271
  tipping in 256
  variety of 255
  vegetarian options 257
  see also under individual
    attractions
rides 86
  and pregnant women 34

see also individual theme parks
Ripley's Believe It Or Not 28,
  193–194, *196*
Rivership Romance 219, *220*
roads *11*, 51–52, 54
  key routes 54
  names and signs 51–52
  toll roads 51, 52
  see also cars; driving; individual
    roads
rodeo 17, 234
Rose Cottage Tea Room® 221
Rosen Center Hotel 72
Royal Pacific Resort 74–75

safety 40–43
Sanford 221
Sanford Heritage Festival 17, 221
science museums 198–199
Sea World Adventure Park (A)
  10, 16, **157–166**
  at-a-glance 158
  children's attractions 166
  Key West at Sea World 164–165
  killer whales 161
  location 159
  map 160
  night-time 165–166
  planning visit 159
  restaurants 166
  rides 160–161, 165
  shops 166
  tours 157–159
  see also Discovery Cove
Seasons 52® 273
self-catering 26, 78–82
Seminole County 219–222
Seminole Towne Center 284–285
senior citizens 35–36
Sheraton Studio City Hotel 71–72
Sheraton World Resort 71
shoes 30
shopping 30, **276–287**
  airports 290–293
  books 283
  CityWalk 241
  discount shops 281–283
  Downtown Disney 238, 239,
    278–279
  flea markets 283
  food 287
  International Drive 279–280
  Kissimmee 280–281, 282,
    286–287
  Lake Buena Vista 282
  malls 283–286
  map 277
  Pointe Orlando 243
  Seminole County 284–285
  specialist shops 287
  sports shops 287
  supermarkets 287

traditional 286–287
  Winter Park 208, 209, 286
  see also individual attractions
shuttle launches 183–184
shuttle services (transport) 47–48
Sidewalk Arts Festival 17
Silver Springs (A) 10, 16,
  187–189
single-parent discounts 22
Skull Kingdom 28, **195**, *197*
Sleuth's Mystery Dinner Shows
  (D) 247
SoulFire Theatre & Dinner
  Experience (D) 248
Space Center *see* Kennedy Space
  Center
spectator sports 232–235
Splendid China 10, *189*,
  189–190
split holidays **20–21**, 22, 23, 24,
  25, 26
sports 226–235
  spectator 232–235
  see also individual sports and
    water parks
sports bars 253–254
Style Holidays (T) 26
suites (apartments) 78–80
sun cream 31, 33
Sunstart (T) 24
supermarkets 287
Swamp Buggy Tours 222–223

taxes 14–15, 276–277
taxis 48–49
theatre 250
theme parks 6, 7, 9–10
  attendance figures 32
  busy guide 297
  planning your visit 27–30
  rides, rating of 86
  see also individual parks
Thomas Cook Holidays (T) 25–26
Thomson (T) 22–23
Thornton Park 201
tickets **10–14**, 85–86, 135
timeshares 86
tipping 14, 15, 58, 256
Titanic 194
toll roads 51, 52
tour operators 13–14, **21–27**,
  32–33
tourist information *see*
  information; visitor centers
tours 215–216
  adventure 214, 215–216, 218,
    219–222
  bicycle 209
  boat 209, 210–213
  Everglades 215–216
  walking 209

see also cruises; eco-tourism
and individual attractions
traffic lights 53
Trailfinders (T) 26–27
Trainland Inc 198
Travel City (T) 21–22
travel companies 13–14, **21–27**,
32–33
internet services 27
travellers' cheques 14
Tchoup Chop® 275

Unijet (T) 24
Universal Express 135
Universal Orlando 9–10, 16, 29,
135–156
accommodation 72, 74–75
see also CityWalk; Islands of
Adventure; Universal
Studios
Universal Studios 10, 28,
136–146
at-a-glance 138

and children 146
Hollywood 145–146
location 137–138
map 136
New York 140–141
planning visit 137–138
Production Central 138–140
San Francisco/Amity 141–142
street entertainment 146
Woody Woodpecker's
KidZone 143–144
World Expo 142–143

VAT 276–277
villas *see* holiday homes
Virgin Holidays (T) 22
visas 15
visitor centers 44, **57**, 85–86

Walt Disney World Resort
Florida 7, 9, 15, 29
accommodation 19, **57–65**, *69*
see also individual theme parks

Warbird Adventures 218
Warbird Air Museum 217
Water Mania (W) 207
water parks 9, 10, **202–207**
water sports 231
WayFun Kayak Adventures 211,
212
wedding packages 22, 23, 25, 26,
37, **39**, 211
Wedding Pavilion 9, *36*, **37**, **39**
Wet 'n Wild (W) 10, **205–206**
Wild Waters (W) 188
Winter Park **208–210**, 286
WonderWorks 28, **196–197**, *197*
WonderWorks Magic Show 248
Wyndham Orlando Resort 70

XS Orlando 243

Zellwood Corn Festival 17

COPYRIGHT NOTICES

Acknowledgements

The author wishes to acknowledge the help of the following in the production of this book: The Orlando Tourism Bureau in London, the Orlando/Orange County Convention & Visitors' Bureau, Visit Florida, The Kissimmee/St Cloud Convention & Visitors' Bureau, Walt Disney Attractions Inc., Universal Orlando, The British-American Chamber of Commerce, The Greater Orlando Aviation Authority, Orlando-Sanford International Airport, The Busch Entertainment Corporation, The Orange County Sheriff's Office, Seminole County Convention & Visitors' Bureau, Central Florida Visitors' and Convention Bureau, Visit USA Association, St Petersburg/Clearwater Area Convention & Visitors' Bureau, Daytona Beach Area Convention & Visitors' Bureau, Winter Park Chamber of Commerce, Alamo Rent A Car, Grand Theme Hotels Group, HM Customs and Excise Office.

In person, Oonagh McCullagh and Margaret Melia (Orlando Tourism Bureau) and Zoe Ward (Icas PR), Nicole Walsh, Louisa French, Jason Lasecki (Walt Disney), Danielle Courtenay, Rick Gregory (Orlando CVB), Larry White, Geo Morales and Abby Montpellier (Kissimmee CVB), Wit Tuttell (St Petersburg/Clearwater CVB), Susan McLain (Daytona Beach CVB), Michael McLane, Camille Dudley (Universal), Kate Burgess (Visit Florida), Carolyn Fennell (Orlando Aviation Authority), Craig Dorris (Orange County Sheriff's Office), Susan Flower and Jacquelyn Wilson (SeaWorld), Honoria Nadeau (Busch Gardens), Anthea Yabsley, Sarah Bolam (Synergy PR), Suzan Bunn (Seminole County CVB), Laura Richeson (Bennett & Company), Mary Kenny (Grand Theme Hotels), Amanda Keefer (Kennedy Space Center), Al Riley (Splendid China), Steve Specht (Silver Springs), Michael Caires, Greg Dull (Orlando-Sanford Airport), Suzanne McGovern (Yesawich, Pepperdine & Brown), Joyce Couch (Travel City Direct), Allan Oakley (Alexander & Associates), Nigel Worrall (Florida Leisure), Bob Mandell (Greater Homes), Christen Svendsen and Bill Cowie (BACC), Wrenda Goodwyn, Zina Talsma (International Drive/I-Ride), Sonya Snyder (Quill Communications), Todd Hansen (Ripley's), Chris Tomasso (Hard Rock Café), Keith Salwoski (Gaylord Palms Resort), Melissa Gotlin (Orange County History Center), Jeff Stanford (Orlando Science Center), Donna Turner (Medieval Times), Michelle Harris (Gatorland), Terry Lynn Morris (Lake Buena Vista Factory Stores), Christine Hale (Historic Bok Sanctuary), John Stine (Dixie Stampede), Bruce Siegel (Grande Lakes Orlando), Michele Plant (Disney's Wide World of Sports), Phillip Jaffe (Pro Golf Guides of Orlando), Lisa Klemme (Pointe*Orlando), KT Budde Jones (Warbird Museum), Thom Richard (Warbird Adventures), Mella Jacobs (Florida Eco-Safaris), Rocell Melohn and Sally March (Mall at Millenia), Leigh Jones (Orlando Premium Outlets), Brian Wettstein (Winter Park Chamber of Commerce), Margie Long (Boggy Creek Airboats), Rod Wiltshire (Alpha Retail Services), Nick Hobbs (Thomas Cook Signature Holidays) and Naomi Lewis (Virgin Holidays), plus my research team Michele Carpenter, Marcia Harris, Michele Plant and travel writer Karen Marchbank. Very special thanks to my principal research assistant Susan Haass for her huge input to this edition.

Big thanks to Pete Werner and all at the DIS – you know who you are!

Got a red-hot Brit Tip to pass on? The latest info on how to beat the queues or the best new restaurant in town? We want to hear from YOU to keep improving the guide each year. Drop us a line at: Brit's Guide (Orlando), W. Foulsham & Co Ltd., The Publishing House, Bennetts Close, Cippenham, Slough, Berkshire SL1 5AP. Or e-mail simonveness@yahoo.co.uk.

Reader tips from: Roy Carlisle, Les Watson, Peter Crumpler, Judith Bingham, John Cartlidge, Geoff Avis, Gary Baldwin, the Tyler family, Hilary Stones, Penny Parker, Sally Jordan, Nicola Roberts, Andrew Bamford, Carole Agar, the Storey family, Ray Hoyle and Tim Smith (via e-mail), Mrs W Smith, Weston-super-Mare; the Feltham family, Sidcup, Kent.